THE COMPLETE BORDEAUX VINTAGE GUIDE

THE COMPLETE BORDEAUX

VINTAGE GUIDE

One hundred and fifty

YEARS FROM

1870 *to* 2020

NEAL MARTIN

Hardie Grant

QUADRILLE

Publishing Director Sarah Lavelle
Editor Sarah Thickett
Copy Editor Nick Funnell
Proofreader Emma Bastow
Head of Design Claire Rochford
Designer Luke Bird
Typesetter Seagull Design
Production Director Stephen Lang
Production Controller Martina Georgieva

Published in 2023 by Quadrille, an imprint of Hardie Grant Publishing

Quadrille
52–54 Southwark Street
London SE1 1UN
quadrille.com

Cataloguing in Publication Data: a catalogue record for this book
is available from the British Library.

ISBN 978 1 78713 980 0

Printed in China

MIX
Paper from
responsible sources
FSC
www.fsc.org
FSC™ C020056

For Lily & Daisy

(even though they didn't care about the last one)

CONTENTS

INTRODUCTION

A vintage is more than a slice of time. It is the unscripted act of a never-ending play. Drama and upheaval, tragedy and triumph unfold in every vineyard, every year. The growing season is the sculptor behind every bottle of wine, not least those produced in marginal climates such as Bordeaux's, where vines lie at the mercy and caprice of Mother Nature, pushed to the brink in order to bestow the highest-quality fruit. Neighbouring the Atlantic, the region's vast hinterland is exposed to maritime forces that can swing from winter storm to tropical heat, frost to drought via vicious hail and torrential downpours. On some days despairing winemakers might feel they have endured all of those in a single morning.

Flicking back through the pages of time, the heterogeneity of growing seasons forms a tapestry of meteorological thumbprints that shapes not only the reputations of individual wines but of vintages themselves; some eulogised and anointed legends at birth (or even prenatally at en primeur), others denigrated, forgotten, occasionally ridiculed. Historically, there is no logical pattern to any series of growing seasons. Look closer and you'll see cycles emerge. Yet even the most gifted clairvoyant or expert meteorologist cannot put hand on heart and accurately predict the following year's weather, maybe not even tomorrow's. It is this unknowable fate, randomness and unpredictability that has fascinated oenophiles since time immemorial.

In 2003, the "Bordeaux Vintage Guide" debuted on my website, Wine-Journal, and like much of its content, it was crude and pot-marked with grammatical errors. Nevertheless, it proved popular among readers, serving as a straightforward chronological summary of the region's growing seasons, accompanied by notes on notable bottles tasted over the years. It differed insofar as each vintage was accompanied by an event, song and film tied to that specific year. The idea was to anchor each vintage to a moment in history and make it resonate more strongly – perhaps it might conjure memories and some kind of emotional attachment, or evoke nostalgia.

This original incarnation was marched off Wine-Journal in 2006 with the intention of rewriting and republishing it at some later date, preferably without so many grammatical errors. Alas, it languished in the furthest recesses of my hard drive until 15 years later when, confined during lockdown, I swept away the dust and began to tinker. You are reading the result of that tinkering. The time frame was stretched back to 1870 and forward to 2020 to make a temporally tidy century-and-a-half with epochal 1945 its midpoint. The original selection of events, songs and films was questioned, scorned, deleted, replaced, shuffled, reintroduced and fretted over. Had I chosen wisely? Would someone more erudite chide my choices? This coerced me to add short explanatory paragraphs, background information to provide context, reasoning and justification, a task that I underestimated since it obliged hours of research into a dizzying array of subjects, a majority of which I had negligible knowledge of. But it turned out to be a worthwhile exercise and lent the hitherto rather jejune prose a certain completeness, and added flesh to the bone.

There is nothing novel about a vintage guide, not least for a region as omnipresent as Bordeaux. It has been done many times before. Hopefully, this iteration achieves a greater sense of depth and comprehensiveness, notwithstanding that to the best of my knowledge, no previous vintage guide has referenced Einstein, Eilish or Eyjafjallajökull.

Finally, taste is individual. Opinions expressed about the wines in this book are personal and might not necessarily chime with yours. My reviews and scores for wine mentioned in this book are available to subscribers at www.vinous.com. Feel free to agree or disagree, but always respectfully.

Criteria Behind the Selections

What factors underlie the selection of events, songs and films?

Events were not chosen for their significance. The most momentous events tend to be either natural disasters or wars, reminders that Mother Nature can be cruel and that humankind has never lost its penchant to take up arms. Frankly, I did not want a depressing book, quite the opposite. So I churned up the entries in order to portray the jumble of major and minor happenings that constitute our lives. I could not ignore the global impact of, say, the eruption of Krakatoa, the Second World War or Covid. But during the darkest periods of history we need relief from the *Sturm und Drang*, which is why major events are occasionally substituted for inventions, sporting achievements and trivia.

Those familiar with my writing will know that I am a nigh obsessive music lover. That made the songs often impossible to choose. The fundamental criterion was that each choice had to evoke a memory of that year. It didn't have to be the biggest seller, most influential, critically acclaimed or coolest. I put aside my personal taste to select songs that hopefully trigger memories, even if the reader is unfamiliar with the specific artist or musical genre. There had to be an element of popularity or more accurately, recognisability, contemporaneous or not. If you are aggrieved at the omissions, then trust this author is even more so. I embrace as many musical genres as possible to convey the eclecticism of listening pleasure, from opera to hip-hop, ragtime to grunge, rock 'n' roll to grime. As genres have splintered and mutated, it became more and more difficult to choose just one song to symbolise a year. Consider how many musical genres exist now compared to 1870. Before leaving this subject, if this book prompts one philosophical question, it is how did we get from *Ride of the Valkyries* to *WAP*?

With respect to films, the medium's pioneers were still a few years away from inventing moving images back in 1870. The earliest surviving film, commonly known as *Roundhay Garden Scene,* dates from 1888 and is just over one-second long. As with the song choices, I strive to embrace as many genres as possible: comedy, horror, rom-com, action, art-house, western, sci-fi, thriller, film noir, animation, musical. A majority are in the English language: that is my mother tongue and so I have watched a disproportionate number of English and American films. Conscious of this bias, I include films from France, Germany, Italy, Russia, Japan and Korea, among others, if only to reflect that a great movie is unconnected to language. The birthplace of cinema is after all France, not Hollywood.

I Am the One and Only

There are two self-imposed cardinal rules for the music and film choices, *appellation contrôlée* edicts that run through this entire book: **There is only one choice of song and film per year and a musical artist or filmmaker cannot appear more than once.**

This one-in/one-out policy engenders more diversity. If you're fulminating about the omission of your favourite artist, you have to justify why the incumbent musician or film director must be shown the exit door. I had to do this myself numerous times. Ultimately I threw over 70 fully completed entries on a bonfire of rejects as I continually shuffled the deck. It might have been easier to offer a short list for each year, but that felt like a cop-out. The final and ineluctably flawed roll-call seems to spark debate and there's nothing wrong with that. I'll probably change my mind again come a second edition.

No Stars in the Sky

One thing that perhaps makes this vintage guide anomalous is its omission of any grading system. When I began learning about Bordeaux, like many, I found Michael Broadbent's one- to five-star grading of vintages indispensable and considered doing something similar. But in the end, I decided not to dish out any stars for three reasons.

First, before 1982, I have only tasted a fraction of the wines compared to the great Broadbent and even in the case of vintages such as 1928 and 1945, where I have been lucky enough to taste many, I regard myself as unqualified. Either all vintages are graded or none and I choose the latter. Second, grading encourages readers to restrict themselves to the most esteemed vintages, whereas in my experience, less fêted and challenging seasons are often more fascinating.

What went awry?
How did winemakers react?
What were the consequences?

Any winemaker or vineyard manager must find a difficult season traumatic, yet in hindsight such years can reveal as much, if not more about a vineyard or producer's methods than a straightforward one. Tough vintages add contrast to the tapestry of growing seasons, where renowned years rub shoulders with the reviled. Yet I adopt an egalitarian approach by affording the same attention to each vintage, irrespective of calibre.

Third, and perhaps most important, over a quarter-century of tasting Bordeaux, I have learned to never prejudge any bottle based on its birth year. Sure, it gives you an idea of what to expect, but it is never guaranteed. I can recount numerous occasions when a bottle from a disparaged year has defied expectations and wowed its startled audience. In recent months I've had a bottle of 1951 Latour that rescued a lunch plagued by corked bottles and, days later, a 1984 Pichon-Lalande that left winemaker Nicolas Glumineau grinning with surprise. Conversely, there are famous names from lauded vintages that fail to pass muster. Bottles suffer off-days, fluff their lines as they enter the stage. The famous adage that there are no great wines, only great bottles, will forever ring true.

This guide provides details of the growing seasons from a meteorological and viticultural standpoint, augmented by my own experiences, but my advice is for you to keep an open mind and draw your *own* conclusions based upon your *own* experiences. There are always turn-ups for the books that can represent better value for money than a big name from a lauded vintage.

Missing Reels

In the earliest years in this book, winemakers could be termed what the French call *paysans* – men or women who worked the land, absorbing and memorising its minutiae. They had no incentive to diarise the weather or what might be occurring in the vineyard. Consequently, there is a dearth of first-hand observations and if anyone did maintain a diary of some kind, then in all likelihood it has been long lost. However, some accounts have survived and these precious insights are interwoven into the text.

I explored multiple sources of information to assemble a picture of each growing season and tried to fill in those missing reels as best I could. The 19th century was challenging and only basic summaries are possible, though I embellish these with some first-hand encounters with ancient bottles. Chronicling events from 1899 onwards, the invaluable Tastet-Lawton archives break down growing seasons into diary form, providing a fascinating journey back through time and a treasure trove of detail, even if one must remain aware that there is a bias towards the Left Bank. From the fifties there are detailed vintage summaries courtesy of the Sichel family. I am also indebted to Bill Blatch, who lent me his hand-typed vintage reports from 1988 onwards that break down the seasons into incredible detail. Then I interweave my own first-hand reports from around 1998 along with information gleaned from numerous articles and interviews conducted over the years.

Everything Is Connected to Everything

Although this book is logically compartmentalised into vintages, in real life, to quote Leonardo da Vinci, "everything is connected to everything". At first glance each growing season begins with a blank canvas whose size and texture is determined by land and vine. As the months roll by, changing weather patterns add brushstrokes, some resulting in broad, deep and indelible colours, others more nuanced, perhaps imperceptible. The vineyard manager and winemaker respond during the season and winemaking process by contributing from their own palette, which is determined by their tenets, practices, talent and means. Then barrel maturation or *élevage* places that picture in a frame that hopefully complements the artistry. Finally, you step back to admire the completed portrait, entitled "the finished wine".

But is the canvas really blank?

While natural to view each growing season as a separate entity, truth is that the previous growing season influences the next. It lays the groundwork. To take one example germane to recent vintages, a dry summer followed by average winter rainfall means that vines will have access to smaller reserves of water to fuel their growth cycle over the next growing season. A frost-affected vintage that threatens vines' survival encourages them to compensate the next year by bearing more fruit in case of a repeat. Think of vintages like a *solera* insofar as preceding seasons influence the current one by exponentially lesser degrees, so hypothetically, every vintage in this book has a bearing on the most recent. You could argue that the manner in which 1870 "flapped its butterfly wings" has a causal effect on 2020, if only to an infinitesimally small degree.

In geographical terms, we can stand in a vineyard and gaze up at the sky to gauge the weather. Is it raining, cloudy or sunny? Does it feel warm or cold? In the 19th century, forecasting was rudimentary and communications were absent. Winemakers perspicaciously observed their surroundings, noted cloud formations, became attuned to changes in air temperature or humidity, keenly observant of Mother Nature's behaviour. Without recourse to long-term forecasts, they could only react to situations and try to remedy them. As meteorological forecasting became more sophisticated, predicting the path of an Atlantic-borne ridge of high pressure or a tongue of Arctic air threatening a late spring frost, winemakers looked beyond the horizon to see what might lie ahead. Nowadays, we look even further afield. The temperature of the Pacific's waters can shift the jet stream, warmer waters creating the El Niño effect that nudges the jet stream south; colder waters creating the La Niña effect that pushes it north. Of course, these phenomena were little understood in this guide's earliest vintages, whereas winemakers today can pre-empt them by spraying vines before forecasted rainfall, turning on wind-fans to mitigate against a pernicious morning frost, or examining weather conditions down to the smallest detail during harvest to dispatch pickers into the vines not only on the optimal day, but at the optimal hour.

The Centre of Calm

Upon finishing the first draft of the book, I couldn't help but notice an unavoidable juxtaposition between the rhythmic, cyclical nature of the growing season and the chaotic churn of life beyond vineyards' boundaries. Trawling through the growing seasons one by one renewed my appreciation for the inexorable power of Mother Nature. Come spring, vines reawaken from winter's dormancy, shoots grow, vines flower and eventually fruit needs to be picked. Repeat until…?

Remarkably, this cycle has passed without interruption over the span of this book in times of war and peace, prosperity and poverty. Vines are oblivious to whatever transpires elsewhere. That said, two events threatened the cycle and brought the wine industry close to the precipice: phylloxera in the 1880s and, to a lesser extent, the winter freeze of 1956. The difference between the two is that phylloxera threatened the entire existence of viticulture until a viable solution was found, whereas the freeze obliged winemakers to roll up their sleeves and replant. It is worth remembering that despite their magnitude, both events were followed by esteemed vintages such as 1899 and 1900 (with a caveat that I shall broach in the relevant decade summary) and 1959 and 1961. These vintages prove how vines have a preternatural capacity to recover from the most perilous circumstances. The same can be said for the people who have worked the land. Men and women succeeded in the gargantuan task of re-grafting all their vines onto American rootstock after the devastation of phylloxera and continued to pick fruit during the bleakest days of war.

As new and unforeseeable obstacles get thrown in their path – most recently the Covid-19 pandemic – winemakers not just in Bordeaux but around the world continue to work out ways to jump over them. Could climate change be the phenomenon that endangers Bordeaux winemaking for perpetuity or, at the least, alters it completely? What will Bordeaux's landscape look like in another 150 years? Whatever transpires in the future, despite being contained by rules and regulations that govern the region, its winemakers have always been willing to adapt and evolve.

How Permanent Is Change?

One takeaway from writing this book is understanding how perceptions and assumptions are determined by the limitations of collective memory. First-hand experience only goes as far back as infancy and so – unless you are an avid historian – you tend to give less consideration to events that predate your lifetime because they derive from second-hand sources – from textbooks, say, or a grandfather who worked the same patch of land. During my relatively short time as a wine professional I've witnessed warmer winters and hotter summers becoming increasingly frequent, a rising number of erratic and extreme weather events, harvests creeping ever earlier and stylistic shifts in terms of richness and alcohol. All these have all been laid at the door of climate change caused by human-made carbon-dioxide emissions and pollution.

During my research, I reconsidered how different things had been in the past, over the 150-year span of this book. Trawling through the minutiae of growing seasons did not change my notions, but it did challenge them. I am unequivocally not denying that climate change is detrimental and possibly catastrophic, yet it modified my idea that we are witnessing novel meteorological phenomena. I was surprised to read about multitudinous incidences of drought, tropical heat and erratic weather that beset winemakers before any of us were born. Vintage summaries in the 19th century are sometimes eerily similar to those of today. Should we deduce that there have always been meteorological cycles that we are now only beginning to understand? Perhaps climate change skews them, distorts long-term patterns and the randomness of events, loads the dice in a different way.

Writing this in June 2022, the morning after hail the size of golf balls has (yet again) devastated enclaves of Bordeaux, I feel both disquieting fear about what the future holds and an opposing sense of cold-hearted statistical objectivity that this is not the first or last time such things have happened. Winemakers must take Nature's malice on the chin. It's part of the job. As the song goes, you might get knocked down, but you get up again. For every act of malevolence it has inflicted, Nature has time and again rescued vintages. Several Bordeaux winemakers have privately admitted that climate change has made life easier, rendering under-ripe vintages a thing of the past, which is good news for wine lovers, if maybe less good for the future of mankind. Climate change has altered what you might term the ledger between winemaker and Nature: bigger deposits of fortune yet heftier withdrawals. It is a complicated and emotive picture that will only be comprehended in hindsight – by which time, the vagaries of the growing season might be shifting once again.

Time Is on Your Side

When is the right time to open a bottle of Bordeaux, for which you can read, any fine wine? There is the old axiom that a Grand Cru Classé requires a decade in bottle, though changes in technique have rendered young claret far more approachable than it was just 20 years ago. While there is no definitive answer on the optimal moment to open any wine, two factors that determine a wine's drinking window are its longevity and the predilection of the person drinking it.

Let's tackle the first. Not everyone will agree, but a prerequisite for a bone fide great Bordeaux wine is an innate ability to mature over many years, a virtue that distinguishes it from most other wine regions, though less than my friends in Bordeaux might believe. If a self-proclaimed "fine wine" falls apart after several years, then frankly, your hard-earned pennies are better spent on the vast number of delicious wines from around the world with no pretensions towards longevity.

Great Bordeaux is a marathon runner, not a sprinter. It has no fear of age, but welcomes it, exploits it and uses it to its advantage.

Inherent longevity is necessary in order to allow time to sculpt primary aromas and flavours into a wine of alluring complexity, nuance and intellect. Like a simple major chord gradually augmented by diminished sevenths or an unexpected root note, aromatics should be allowed to evolve as primary fruit transforms into a cornucopia of tertiary, spicy, floral, herbal or meaty scents. It's a long list. Mature Bordeaux can often be mercurial in the glass, changing with each sip as it responds to oxygen, as if celebrating its freedom after imprisonment in bottle. Generally, the aromas of a young wine tend to show the hand of the winemaker and these gradually ebb away to reveal its terroir. Likewise, tannins might initially be obdurate and unappealing. But they will polymerise, becoming mellow and pliant, thereby lending a more pleasurable texture or umami. Time may allow an initially disjointed wine to cohere and reveal its personality in terms of human traits. (Deliberating over the choice of words for a mature Saint-Julien on one occasion, I simply wrote one word: grumpy. It encapsulated exactly what I wished to communicate.)

What factors determine the longevity of wine? Opinions diverge. After I posed that question to Robert Parker and Michel Rolland, both answered "fruit", as evinced by renowned vintages such as 1947, 1982 and 2009. Though correct, it infers that wine without fruit cannot age, when empirical evidence gallantly undertaken by this writer (i.e. a lot of wine-drinking) has proven time and again that there is no positive correlation between fruit and longevity, though it helps.

Other factors are just as important. Ask the same question to some English writers seeking "traditional claret" and they often point to acidity – after all, it is a known preservative. Wine born without acidity will never have tension, the live-wire sense of electricity that enlivens the senses, keeps wine fresh and vital throughout its life and occasionally into its afterlife.

How about structure, which is governed by tannins? These can be excessive in some vintages, such as 1975, when the fruit dried out before their hard tannins could soften. There is a famous quote from Burgundy winemaker Henri Jayer, oft-repeated by Robert Parker, that if a wine tastes too tannic, it is too tannic. Partially correct. After all, how did vintages such as 1928, 1945 and 1961 taste in their youth? Clue: six letters beginning with "t". By all accounts, just as Jayer described, they were unapproachable and demanded years to evolve into legends, with the 1928 Latour infamously taking half a century before it even entertained the thought of drinkability. At the other end of the spectrum, there are vintages such as 1959 and 1982 that were so approachable upon release that experts were convinced they would never last, but are now likewise bejewelled with fabulous wines. The latter even lit the torch-paper for Robert Parker's career.

There is no definitive answer to which aspect of a wine determines how many years it should be cellared or will give drinking pleasure. It is a combination of factors. One must also consider the humidity and temperature of storage and, as anyone who has drunk bottles from the same case will attest, bottle-to-bottle variations caused by microscopic discrepancies in the pores of natural cork that allow different rates of oxygen ingress. No two bottles of wine are anatomically identical.

Now let us broach the second factor: the predilection of each wine lover. Fact is, we all prefer to drink wines at different stages of their evolutions. Some relish precocious fruit, power and the seductive sheen of new oak. That is probably anathema to somebody searching for secondary aromas and flavours. Others might look for a liminal point between the two in order to savour the best of both worlds. There are also people who take pleasure in drinking history, seeking the thrill of time-defying acrobatics in their wine glass; ergo, the older the better. In recent years, Bordeaux has tweaked winemaking techniques to fashion wines that appeal to wine lovers unwilling to wait for maturity, especially clarets with much finer, malleable tannins. The ritual of cellaring claret across decades – creating a stash for the next generation to inherit – is regrettably fading. We cross our fingers and hope that contemporary Bordeaux and fine wine in general will mature as gracefully as it has in bygone eras. There are naysayers, but I suspect many will.

Foraging for Bordeaux

As the availability of mature Bordeaux dwindles, prices have become exorbitant and access has withered. Commencing my Bordeaux odyssey in the late nineties, it was pretty easy foraging for mature bottles, often at affordable prices. Merchants' lists were once festooned with off-vintages they were only too happy to get rid of. I filled my boots, partly out of curiosity, mostly because they were all I could afford. Nowadays, those same derided vintages are only affordable to the wealthy. That is a great pity because it has closed what was mine and countless others' conduit into Bordeaux wine. On the other hand, the emergence of the internet and the ability it has given like-minded wine lovers of whatever denomination to organise and share bottles, coupled with the generosity of enthusiasts and collectors, have opened a new means of gaining first-hand experience without having to remortgage the house.

But wherever and from whoever you buy bottles of Bordeaux or any fine wine, provenance is key. The most eminent merchants are successful because they have built up a reputation for service and the quality of their wines, so always check their track record. I would rather buy a less-reputed producer or vintage with sound provenance than a famous one with an unknown or dubious background. I am also not a fan of reconditioned bottles, even those produced at châteaux. Wines are fragile things. Suddenly exposing them to oxygen, even for a briefest moment, seems to discombobulate them. Suffice to say that I have had more pleasure drinking bottles with low ullage, even down to mid-shoulder level, than those topped up and re-corked. Always hold the bottle up to the light and check its clarity. If there is no turbidity, it usually bodes well, though nothing can ever be guaranteed.

Bigger is better, isn't it? Received wisdom is that larger formats, from magnums to nebuchadnezzars, allow wines to age more slowly and develop more complexity. But it is not black and white. First, if the large-format centrepiece of your swanky dinner is hideously corked, it can ruin an evening. Again, provenance reduces risk, but never to zero. Second, I don't buy the idea that half-bottles always age wine more rapidly. That hasn't been borne out by experience. If micro-oxygenation ingress through pores in the cork dictates the rate of evolution, why would the smaller cork width accelerate maturity? I am not disparaging larger formats, rather I suggest not dismissing half-bottles out of hand, especially if you chance upon a particular wine that you are looking for.

The Rudiments of Bordeaux

How do weather conditions impact short-term and long-term work carried out in the vineyard, the timing of the harvest and how grapes are transformed into wine? This section provides basic information on those subjects, alongside synopses of the major Bordeaux appellations that appear most frequently in the book.

Work in the Vineyard

Though new practices have been introduced or become popular, and others have fallen out of fashion or made unexpected comebacks, fundamental vineyard practices in Bordeaux have remained more or less the same. Somebody working the vines in the 19th century would be startled by the prevalent use of technology today, yet the basic aim in terms of ploughing, pruning, spraying and so forth is unchanged. Every winemaker is motivated by quantity and quality, but without doubt, the sea change among top estates is the shift in priority from the former to the latter. The rhetoric is "quality at any cost", even if that entails depleted volume because the most famous estates can afford to do so. Consequently, their vineyard husbandry might be different from that of a modest estate charging just a few euros for its wine or that of previous generations whose vines supported their family.

Instead of following the calendar year, the growing season is more akin to an academic year insofar as it starts and finishes from the moment the last bunch is picked in autumn.

September/October The final bunch is snipped and loaded into the plastic bucket strapped to the harvester's back or placed into a small 10 kg (22 lb) or 15 kg (33 lb) crate known as a *cagette*. The vines' job is done for another year. Their energy expended, leaves turn from green to golden-reddish hues and fall to the earth, if they have not done so already. The focus of the winemaking process has shifted from the vineyard to the winery.

November/December These are quiet months for the vines. Many producers use this time to clean up the vineyard, remove any weeds and perhaps plough the soil around the base of the vines, a process known as *buttage*, in order to protect them from severe frost. Hopefully, falling temperatures will encourage the vines to enter a period of dormancy, which is vital for preserving energy for the following year. We all know how lousy we feel after a sleepless night – and we don't have to bear fruit in the morning! Pruning may take place if it is cold enough (see January, opposite).

January With luck, cold temperatures mean that the sap has retreated, allowing pruning to take place. Many vineyard managers prefer to do this later in the winter to allow the vine to rest and to delay budding. Pruning is an arduous task that must be done by hand. A skilled pruner armed with electric secateurs can tackle around 1,500 vines per day, or around half that number with regular secateurs. Once the vine is pruned any remaining canes will be attached to the wire trellis. There are various cane-pruning methods around the world, but the most common in Bordeaux are the single and double Guyot. Single Guyot leaves one cane from the trunk, while double Guyot leaves two canes directed left and right to form a T-shape. The important decision is how many buds to leave on each cane as this will determine the yield for the following year, with each bud producing two or three bunches. Most Bordeaux vineyards use double Guyot.

February The period of dormancy is hopefully continuing. Cold weather is preferable not only to allow pruning, but also to kill off viruses and bugs that might plague the vineyard once the weather warms up. In 1908 and 1909, for example, mild winters predicated later infestations of creepy-crawlies such as grape moths and red spiders. However, you do not want temperatures too low. Vines are hardy, but a long period of freezing sub-zero temperatures can kill them off, as it did to devastating effect in February 1956. Some ploughing may also be done to aerate the soil and allow rain to penetrate. Given the dry, virtually drought-like conditions that have marked recent years, rainfall throughout winter is essential to ensure that vines have sufficient underground water reserves to keep their energy levels up and photosynthesise. In fact, this has been one of the key things that has allowed Bordeaux to produce excellent vintages in extremely dry seasons.

March Warmer temperatures are like a parent gently nudging their sleepy child awake. Winter buds will begin to swell, auguring bud burst, the start of the vines' vegetative or growth cycle. Timing is critical. An early start to the cycle means the vines will probably be more advanced come April or May, and so a late spring frost could lead to widespread damage, potentially writing off that year's harvest. This is what happened in 1991 and 2017. Therefore, an unseasonal early bud break will leave winemakers on tenterhooks until the end of May when the risk of frost is finally over.

April Hopefully the mercury continues to rise and this will encourage shoot growth, turning the landscape from winter brown to springtime green. Leaves will start unfurling. Some vineyard managers will begin spraying to keep a check on insects or diseases. This is also the time to control cover crops – plants cultivated between the rows that force the vines to compete for nutrients and limit yields. April is often rainy and so teams have to be vigilant for any outbreaks of mildew and spray copper sulphate, known as "Bordeaux mixture", according to their own regime.

May Increasingly warmer temperatures will encourage buds to continue developing. Any incursion of coldness at this late stage poses significant risk. A forecast for frost will result in vineyard teams lighting wax candles across the vineyard in order to manipulate temperatures upwards, or switching on exterior fans to push the cold air away. A damaging spring frost is not a complete disaster. Depending upon timing, vines can produce secondary buds, like a reserve parachute, that might enable a harvest later in the year. However, this poses its own challenges in terms of quality and bifurcated growth cycles.

June A crucial month. Vines will begin to flower either at the end of May or early June. Flowering, or *fleuraison*, is where embryonic grape clusters pollinate and fertilise. No flowering, no grapes. The better the flowering, the larger the potential harvest. Winemakers pray for an even flowering so that all bunches are on approximately the same ripening schedule. Hopefully, that means come picking, all of the fruit is at the same level of phenolic maturity and obviates the need for sorting. For an even flowering, you need clement and settled weather conditions, not too quick and not too slow, with little or no wind. Of course, this is not a given and some growing seasons have been nixed by changeable weather.

July With flowering now over, vines will bear "baby" bunches consisting of hard green berries. Vineyard managers can roughly estimate the potential yield and some châteaux might snip a few off – a "green harvest" – in order to keep a cap on yields as this improves quality. Green harvesting became popular during the nineties, to the disdain of the previous generation who saw the practice as tantamount to throwing money down the drain. It means the vine can share its energy between fewer bunches and therefore achieve ripeness more easily. Towards the end of July or sometimes the beginning of August, the bunches for red varieties will change pigment from green to red and those for white varieties will develop a golden tinge. This is known as *véraison* and will preferably occur uniformly across as many bunches as possible so that the entire vineyard is evenly ripe. The process can be assisted by snipping away a few shading leaves, known as de-leafing or *effeuillage*, which enhances air circulation and therefore inhibits rot. July and August are usually the hottest months and in recent years have been terribly dry with prolonged heat waves. If these are severe, they sap vines' energy levels – just as they do with humans. But while we lie and rest, vines simply shut down and stop photosynthesising or start shedding leaves. This tends to happen above 35°C (95°F). The stomata close and you risk divergence between physiological and actual ripeness, so that an excessively hot summer paradoxically yields what tastes like high-sugar but under-ripe fruit. The French often refer to a long heat wave – when temperatures remain above 33°C (91°F) during the day and above 20°C (68°F) at night, giving the vines little respite from the heat – as a *canicule*, which literally translates as "dog-days".

August There is a French saying: "*août fait le moût*", in other words, August determines the quality of the must. Basically, August is the hottest and sunniest month and so has the most bearing on final quality. Climate change has meant Bordeaux has suffered heat spikes, with temperatures touching 40°C (100°F), most notoriously in 2003. If winemakers had cut away some of the leaves in July, the bunches may now be exposed to direct sunlight and will shrivel and burn (*grillure*). Consequently, vineyard managers have become less dogmatic about *effeuillage*, or limit plucking leaves to just the sun-exposed side of the vine. The dry white varieties – Sauvignon Blanc, Sémillon and Muscadelle – are usually picked mid to late-August.

September Once upon a not so long ago, I would have written that September is when the vineyard is a hive of activity as harvest, or *vendange*, gets underway. However, harvests have become earlier in recent years due to climate change, to the extent that in 2020 some estates had finished by the end of August. Vineyard teams will be out in the vines measuring sugar levels with their glucometers or taking them to laboratories for analysis. Some stick by the old method of eating the berries and chewing the pips to decide when to pick. They will also be watching the weather forecast carefully and hoping for sunny and warm weather. Rain and humidity can dilute the fruit at the last moment, and create the perfect conditions for grey rot. Rain during harvest is not necessarily a bad thing – it might already be too late for the vines to suck up moisture and dilute the berries, and it could even be welcome if the vines lack energy and need rejuvenating, kick-starting photosynthesis. But sunny weather is what winemakers want at this time of year, not least to lift harvesters' spirits – after all, you are depending on them to pick as efficiently and meticulously as possible and happy pickers tend to make good pickers (and vice versa).

Earlier-ripening Merlot will be picked before later-ripening Cabernet Franc and Cabernet Sauvignon. There is usually a gap of a few days between them. So, the Cabernets are usually picked from around the last week of September. If the weather forecast predicts inclement weather, picking might be expedited, perhaps by forgoing a gap and moving straight onto the Cabernets after the Merlot, by recruiting a bigger team, or by working longer hours. A long period of clement weather means you have more time and can pick at leisure. Whereas historically pickers worked in one mass through the entire vineyard, nowadays vineyards are picked parcel by parcel according to ripeness, or even by sub-plot, since technology allows such accurate readings.

October The month will probably begin with the Cabernets being picked. Of course, if the weather turns sour after a clement September, winemakers could have a season in which the Merlot has thrived but the Cabernets are compromised, precisely what happened in 1964 and 1998. Conversely, a lousy September followed by an unseasonally warm October can bestow a "Cabernet" vintage such as 1986 or 1996. Of course, the later the picking, the higher the risk of the weather turning poorer. Once the final bunch is snipped, the cycle starts again.

The Harvest

The purpose of the grape harvest will never change, but the biggest revolution to have occurred during the time span of this book is the introduction of mechanical harvesters that replaced teams of manual labour. These must have seemed like a panacea to all the problems that picking by hand entails, though winemakers soon realised that mechanisation compromised quality. Too much MOG (material other than grapes) – in other words leaves and small branches – and too many damaged berries that can rapidly oxidise meant that the quality-driven estates either reverted back to manual picking or simply never entertained the idea in the first place. Recruiting pickers is more costly and entails more risk since you depend upon teams being trained and ready when the winemaker fires the starting gun. But nothing matches a well-trained, experienced crew of harvesters and their presence is the life and soul at this crucial juncture, fomenting an infectious team spirit with all the end-of-harvest parties (known as *Gerbaude* in the Gironde and *Acabailles* in Sauternes).

There has been little change in terms of where harvesters come from. Flick back through the pages of history and more often than not it was the owner's family, friends and locals who brandished the secateurs. The same hands picking the same vines year after year meant little instruction was necessary. They knew what was expected and went about their job. The team worked en masse through the vines, commencing with the white varieties if planted, then early-ripening Merlot, followed by later-ripening Cabernet Franc and Cabernet Sauvignon, also Malbec when it was more widely planted. It was roughly the same, almost ritualistic route through the vineyard.

Nowadays, proprietors still lend a hand in picking. I have witnessed members of the most aristocratic families roll up the sleeves of their tailored shirts and get their hands stained with purple juice. Experienced pickers are more in demand than ever, with producers preferring the same team, those already familiar with their vines, to return year after year. For example, Climens always employs a team from Portugal, while d'Issan recruits one from Holland. But with more and more legislation and rules, some châteaux outsource recruitment to companies that can handle the complicated paperwork and are more reliable. While top châteaux have little problem recruiting pickers, partly because of their prestige and partly because they can afford to pay better, less-renowned estates, not least those off the beaten track, face a bigger challenge. Even in September 2021, I spotted posters in Pauillac put up by a fairly well-known estate ostensibly begging for people to pick its imminent harvest. According to latest figures presented in Jane Anson's *Inside Bordeaux* tome, 69% of estates now pick by machine and 31% by hand, a figure I suspect might be lower than many assume.

The other major change in recent years is that the harvest has become more complex. Whereas before teams would just work their way from one side to the other where instructed, now vineyard managers are armed with technology that can measure ripeness levels down to individual vines. Consequently, in the last two decades there has been a move to pick parcel by parcel according to the ripeness of fruit, with the most meticulous managers sub-dividing parcels to achieve optimal ripeness and even out potential differences in the vineyard. Of course, this has long been mandatory in Sauternes, where winemakers need specific bunches/berries to be affected by noble rot, but now the approach is almost *passim* across the top Bordeaux estates. I say "almost" because there are those who believe a bit of under-ripe fruit or the odd twig not only does no harm but can add a bit of seasoning to the blend, lending more complexity in the long term. I concur with that view. You can take things too far and effectively airbrush out the nuances and quirks that make wine interesting and lend it personality.

Finally, do not discount mechanical harvesters making a return. They are still widely used across the Bordeaux region, especially at estates that can ill-afford to pay a team of pickers. Moreover, advances in technology mean they are now far more precise and efficient, and often more reliable. No more stressing about your recalcitrant pickers turning up at the crack of dawn; just switch on your latest state-of-the-art harvest machine. They will not usurp the men and women dotted around vineyards every late summer and autumn, but I believe their use will become more widespread. For example, imagine how an AI robot could analyse berries to decide in a nanosecond whether to pick or wait.

Winemaking

The adage that great wine is made in the vineyard ricochets from one winemaker to another, circling around and around. It's untrue. Grapes are made in the vineyard. They turn into wine in a winery. That's why it's called a winery.

In recent years, it has become fashionable to downplay the importance of decisions made during the vinification process. The reality is that they underlie quality and from the second that berries enter the reception area to the moment bottles rattle off the bottling line, every choice counts. A wrong one can undo everything achieved in the vineyard. As bunches enter the winery, they are inspected as they pass along the sorting table, a process known as *triage*. These days this is either done on a moving conveyer manned either side by sharp-eyed workers or by an optical sorting machine, sometimes both. Bunches are crushed and de-stemmed, apart from at Les Carmes Haut-Brion in Pessac-Léognan, which is successfully incorporating partial stem addition. Personally, I am surprised more estates haven't dabbled.

These are then transferred into vats, which were traditionally made of wood or concrete; since the sixties, stainless steel has also been used. Many modern wineries are designed vertically so only gravity is required for bunches to fall into the vat, obviating the need for pumps, which can have a negative impact on quality. But not all properties can excavate deep into the earth to create gravity-fed wineries. One alternative is to use what are ostensibly large stainless steel buckets on wheels, known as *cuvons*, which gently hoist grapes into the vat – l'Église-Clinet, Lynch-Bages and many others opt for these. Châteaux often use cultured yeasts to start the alcoholic fermentation, and some practise a pre-fermentation skin maceration to extract colour and tannins, though my feeling is that this is less popular than a decade ago as the trend is towards less deeply coloured, full-bodied wines.

With a bit of luck, natural yeasts indigenous to the winery then get to work on the fermenting must and convert sugar into alcohol. Fermentation releases heat and so it is important to control temperatures. Yeast will keep working up to around 35°C (95°F) but most winemakers maintain a level around 28–30°C (82–86°F). Must is pumped from the bottom to the top of the vat to distribute the heat and prevent the cap of solid matter from drying out, a process known as *remontage*, or winemakers break and push the cap down using a metal grill, *pigeage*, which helps extract colour and tannins.

Sometimes the alcoholic fermentation doesn't get going – known as a stuck fermentation – a common problem in bygone times when winemakers had little scientific knowledge and only rudimentary means to control temperatures. Check out Jean-Michel Cazes's travails during the 1981 vintage (page 350). You might have one vat that sprints out of the block and begins fermenting, so one remedy is to siphon that off and blend it with recalcitrant vats to kick-start the process. Winemakers need to control temperatures throughout fermentation, otherwise they risk destabilising the wine with bacterial spoilage and volatile compounds. Nowadays, temperatures are managed by computer

to the nearest tenth of a degree. Previously, winemakers used heated/
cooling coils inserted into the vat or simply dunked in blocks of ice to
keep temperatures down. (See my decade summary for the 1940s for
more.) There are always exceptions – Alfred Tesseron reviving manual
control of the vats, day and night, for example.

The fermented wine is left in contact with skins to extract colour,
tannins and aromas for perhaps a few days. Usually, the wine is
transferred into vats for blending, then run off into barrels for ageing,
or *élevage*. Traditionally, châteaux have used 225-litre (49-gallon) barrels
(*barriques*) that are manufactured at different cooperages. These char
the inside of the barrels according to the winemaker's request, a high
toasting imparting more flavour than a medium or light one. The
trend has been towards light toasting in recent years as more producers
seek to dial down the influence of oak, especially new oak, which is
more impactful than used barrels. Traditionally, elite producers used
100% new oak almost as a badge of honour, aware that their wines
possessed sufficient fruit concentration and were likely to be cellared
over enough years for the oak to be assimilated into the wine. The
imprint of oak on a wine depends on winemaker preference. While
a seductive trait for some, others find it a turn-off. In my mind the
optimal level of oak influence is such that it never impedes terroir
expression, nor is used to mask a wine's deficiencies. Therefore, a more
difficult season that yielded a less concentrated wine might encourage
more limited use of new oak in order to maintain balance.

During *élevage*, the wine is racked in order to separate it from the dead
yeast cells, the gross lees, though contact with the fine lees can enhance
complexity. Standard practice in Bordeaux has been to rack every three
months. Nowadays, many rack less often as reductive winemaking
becomes more popular, driven by a growing number of winemakers
seeking to minimise the use of sulphur, a vital tool that acts as an
antioxidant and anti-microbial agent, stabilises wine, and prevents it
from spoilage. Less protection means that it is better to open barrels
less frequently and decrease maturing wines' exposure to oxygen.

In the past, cellar-masters bottled directly from barrel, so there could
be differences between bottles depending on how long that took.
Historically, the timing was governed by demands and merchants'
requests. In times of economic malaise, such as during the thirties or
during the war, some wines were left too long in barrel, sometimes
five or six years. These days, most Bordeaux is bottled at 18–24 months
after fining and filtering. These final processes have become much
more refined in recent years and many top estates eschew filtering,
hence the need to decant as you will find sediment swimming around
inside a shaken bottle.

Making Sauternes

Sauternes is quite a different and eternally fascinating, alchemical winemaking process. Come late August, winemakers cross their fingers and pray for cool misty mornings generated by the Ciron river that weaves its way through the appellation. Mist, preferably followed by a sunny afternoon, gives rise to humidity and then warmth – optimal conditions for the development of *pourriture noble*, or "noble rot", a kind of fungus (*Botrytis cinerea*) whose filaments penetrate the skins of white berries: Sémillon, Sauvignon Blanc and, to a much lesser degree, Muscadelle. It first mottles the berries – known as *pourri plein* – then, as the juice inside concentrates, acting as a catalyst for biochemical reactions that impart complexity, they shrivel and darken – the *pourri rôti* stage. The berries end up looking like raisins covered in fine grey powder. Not all vines, bunches or even berries are botrytised uniformly and, depending on atmospheric conditions, pickers are obliged to make two, three or more treks through the vineyard, known as *tries* or passes, in order to painstakingly pick the affected bunches or berries. These berries possess a much higher potential alcohol than red wine grapes, around 20%, so that residual sugar remains after fermentation. This level has risen in recent years due to the growing seasons and a vogue for sweeter Sauternes. Hey presto, your aforementioned mush has now transformed into a refulgent golden elixir. Then begins the hardest job of all – selling it.

The Major Appellations

There are 57 appellations in Bordeaux. I will ration summaries to those populated by châteaux whose wines crop up frequently in this book. That does not infer that you cannot find wines from other appellations with the ability to age wonderfully in bottle. But the reality is that they are fewer in number compared with the most reputed appellations on the Left and Right Banks. Unfortunately, terroir is not evenly spread. In these summaries I reference the types of gravel terrace formed during the geological Quaternary period that spans approximately the last 2.5 million years. A series of ice ages covered the landscape with glaciers that deposited gravel as they melted, creating the undulating topography we recognise today. The oldest is Terrace 1, found in the Haut-Médoc and Listrac, while the youngest, Terrace 6, is close to the estuary and rarely planted with vines. Of course, gravel is not the only contributing geological factor. Limestone also plays a key role, especially in Saint-Émilion.

Saint-Estèphe (1,250 hectares) The most northerly of the major appellations has a different ambiance to others on the Left Bank. It just seems... quieter. There is a sense of solitude and remoteness not found elsewhere in the Médoc. Saint-Estèphe feels exposed to the elements – the sky always seems bigger. In a way that is true because it lies closer to the Atlantic, and the yawning estuary exerts greater sway over the climate here than further downstream. Gravel deposits in Saint-Estèphe are Terrace 3, 4 and 5. The appellation is home to a wide array of soil types, though generally it is known for having a higher proportion of clayey soils compared to Pauillac or Saint-Julien and therefore it can sometimes act more like a Pomerol, even though the wines are very different. Clay retains more water, which benefits this appellation in dry growing seasons, most notably in the torrid heat of 2003. There are areas of limestone towards its western flank as well as sandier areas. In terms of grape plantings, the higher proportion of clay encourages more Merlot, so here you find around 43% Merlot, 50% Cabernet Sauvignon, with the remainder a mixture of Cabernet Franc and Petit Verdot. The appellation hierarchy is crowned by two Second Growths; Cos d'Estournel, directly over the border from Pauillac, and Montrose, near to the waters of the Gironde Estuary. This duopoly is now strongly challenged by Calon Ségur with Lafon-Rochet fast-improving. All four have been purchased by non-Bordeaux investors in recent years and seen an influx of investment. Montrose is organic with more of the vines being turned over to biodynamic, though not certified at the time of writing.

In the past, Saint-Estèphe's wines tended to be structured, tannic and intermittently rustic. They were notorious for taking many years to soften and entertain the thought of drinkability. The upside is that this stood them in good stead for long-term ageing, through in recent years, thanks mainly to better tannin management, even the most long-lived wines have become more approachable in their youth. That said, my own rule of thumb is not to broach the top wines for a decade.

Pauillac (1,213 hectares) Inarguably the most famous Bordeaux appellation, not least because since 1973 it has boasted not one but three First Growths. It lends Pauillac an aristocratic allure that has attracted oenophiles since Bordeaux took its career officer's advice and began making wine. Underpinning the quality of Pauillac wines are its deep gravel beds: Terrace 3 in the north of the appellation and Terrace 4 towards the south, which can be up to 12 m (39 ft) deep. These gravel deposits lie over limestone and marl bedrock with clay subsoils scattered here and there, particularly close to Latour. Cabernet Sauvignon is the perfect match for the well-drained gravel soils and represents around 63% of vine plantings, with Merlot comprising around 31%, according to the latest figures to hand. Pauillac is home to many famous Grands Crus Classés, famous names with global renown, though beyond this hegemony lie numerous smaller estates occupying less propitious terroir, many on sandier soils. Pauillac is where you find Pontet-Canet, the font of everything biodynamic. Claire Villars Lurton is another winemaker who has dedicated her vines to Steiner's tenets at Haut-Bages Libéral, while Latour is certified organic. Pichon-Lalande is also organic but without certification.

The bedrock of Pauillac is Cabernet Sauvignon. Eméline Borie, co-owner of Grand-Puy-Lacoste, describes Pauillac as "a good mix between Saint-Julien and Saint-Estèphe, because you have the elegance and finesse of Saint-Julien combined with the tannins and the structure of Saint-Estèphe." Black fruits dominate, often crème de cassis, alongside signature scents of tobacco, graphite and mint; the latter often something that draws me to Pauillac whenever tasting blind. The best examples are among the most expensive wines in Bordeaux, but while consumers pay a premium for the privilege, the pedigree of a great bottle from this appellation can represent the apotheosis of wine.

Saint-Julien (910 hectares) Many Bordeaux aficionados regard this as the most reliable appellation, with a large number of estates ranked within the Second, Third and Fourth Growths tiers of the 1855 classification and none classed as a Fifth. (As pointed out by Bernard Ginestet in his *Saint-Julien* book, had the classification followed medieval parish boundaries, the First Growth of Latour would be a Saint-Julien since the commune of Saint-Lambert was originally a subsidiary of the appellation. That said, despite lying adjacent to each other and being separated by a mere tributary, Latour is quintessential Pauillac and Léoville-Las Cases is quintessential Saint-Julien.)

If there *were* any reclassification, Léoville-Las Cases and Ducru-Beaucaillou would be two estates with claims to First Growth status. Sure, there is rivalry like anywhere else and proprietors do not meet up to go clubbing every weekend (at least not to my knowledge), yet Saint-Julien has a strong team of quality châteaux. Smaller in size than Margaux, its terroir is more uniform, its gravel deposits derived from two geological eras: Terrace 3, located more centrally in the appellation, and Terrace 4, which lies nearer the estuary. These gravel deposits lie predominantly over clay subsoil with localised limestone. Just under two-thirds of the appellation is planted with Cabernet Sauvignon, which, surprisingly, is a slightly higher proportion than in Pauillac. Several estates, including Gruaud Larose, Branaire-Ducru and Léoville-Las Cases, practise organic viticulture, though my feeling is that Margaux's proprietors have embraced it more enthusiastically.

The cornerstone of Saint-Julien is also Cabernet Sauvignon, yet it offers a different take on the grape variety: less mint on the nose, slightly more savoury, less emphasis on floral and graphite traits, yet with endearing tobacco and occasionally peppery notes. I often find there is greater pliancy compared to Pauillac. The wines can be extraordinarily long-lived, as testified by a number of century and even older bottles of Gruaud Larose tasted.

Margaux (1,500 hectares) As you drive northwards along the D2 on the Left Bank, with the Gironde Estuary on your right, you pass one or two notable Haut-Médoc estates such as La Lagune and Cantemerle, before reaching the region's largest appellation: Margaux. Home to five communes, it encompasses six different gravel deposits from different geological eras transported from the Pyrenees and the Massif Central. The gravel tends to be slightly finer here than further north. All the wines labelled Margaux AOC are red, though there are several white wines, notably Pavillon Blanc from Château Margaux, as well as others by Brane-Cantenac and Cantenac Brown. Personally, I have a penchant for an elusive Palmer Blanc. Of course, the most famous estate is the First Growth, Château Margaux, which is also one of the most aesthetically pleasing with its tree-lined driveway leading to its Doric pillars – one of Bordeaux's iconic images. In terms of renown, it is closely followed by Château Palmer, which has occasionally had the audacity to surpass it, while Rauzan-Ségla and Brane-Cantenac can certainly deliver. The heterogeneity of terroirs predicates less consistency vis-à-vis other appellations, though this has been addressed over the last decade as more châteaux have upped their game. Its wines tend to be distinguished by floral aromatics, often violet, and are less structured and elegant than Pauillac or Saint-Julien, leading some to misconstrue that Margaux cannot age. It has also embraced organic and biodynamic viticulture quicker than others, partly due to Gonzague Lurton's advocating at Durfort-Vivens and more recently, Thomas Duroux's at Palmer. A biodiversity charter in 2013 resulted in 70% of its vineyard adopting more eco-friendly practices.

Margaux's wines are more tender than its northerly appellations and more sensitive to the vagaries of the growing season. The aromatics can be the purest and certainly the most floral with disarming violet, sometimes iris-flower aromas. Margaux wines can be silky in texture, which belies their structure.

Pessac-Léognan (1,791 hectares) This might be described as an ambidextrous appellation insofar as it is a dab hand at producing red and white wines, the latter constituting approximately 20% of plantings. This is because the soils are varied with younger gravel deposits (Terraces 5 and 6) compared with the Médoc, and in places these can reach 8–9 m (26–29 ft) deep. Vineyards are dispersed scattershot across the city suburb of Pessac, oases of serried vines suddenly rearing into view out of nowhere. Over decades, many estates have been swallowed by urban sprawl, the number of hectares under vine withering from

5,000 in the mid-18th century to 500 by the seventies. Jean-Philippe Delmas remarked that Haut-Brion and La Mission Haut-Brion's urban locations made no difference to the microclimate, though I aver that being surrounded by concrete and busy roads must surely have an effect. The appellation extends beyond the city ring road to communes such as Gradignan, Martillac, Talence and Villenave-d'Ornon where you find Smith Haut Lafitte, Haut-Bailly and Domaine de Chevalier, among others. What differentiates Pessac-Léognan from the Médoc is the higher percentage of Merlot in blend. Plantings comprise around 52% Merlot compared with 42% Cabernet Sauvignon, imparting a fleshier, slightly more fruit-driven style that might be described as a hybrid of the Médoc and Saint-Émilion. So Pessac-Léognan goes more its own way compared with the Left Bank. There are a cluster of organic and biodynamic estates such as Smith Haut Lafitte, Haut-Bergey, Les Carmes Haut-Brion and Domaine de Chevalier.

Stylistically, the reds of Pessac-Léognan can offer the best of the Left Bank and the Right Bank in one irresistible cocktail. It's interesting that over the years, while the likes of Latour and Lafite Rothschild command the highest prices and most demand, ask what people enjoy drinking and they frequently reply Haut-Brion. The Pessac-Léognan reds have the same approachability and pliancy as Margaux, though the higher Merlot content lends them fleshiness and more roundness. The dry whites are often drunk young, which is a pity because they can age magnificently and offer an alternative to the Chardonnays of Burgundy and elsewhere. Often, it is the texture imparted by Sémillon that distinguishes the best dry whites, slightly waxy and pithy in style that marries well with the sharpness brought by the Sauvignon Blanc. One should briefly mention premature oxidation, which beleaguered the whites of Burgundy. Sadly, in my experience, Bordeaux is not immune, yet few of its dry whites are allowed to mature and so it doesn't attract so many negative headlines here.

Pomerol (785 hectares) Pomerol has always marched to a slightly different tune to other Bordeaux appellations. It is certainly not visually spectacular: the Pomerol plateau, where its most famous names congregate, is considered vineyard land above 30 m (100 ft) in altitude and "peaks" at 40 m (130 ft) in Gazin. The plateau is formed by up to 3-m (10-ft) deep gravel deposits that combine with clay soils to provide exceptional terroir, including pockets of clay rich in iron oxide known locally as *crasse de fer*. There is a singular "buttonhole" of blue clay or smectite, which possesses remarkable geological properties that enable it to regulate water to vines' roots. The only estate whose vines exclusively occupy this buttonhole is Pétrus, though its neighbours such as L'Évangile, Gazin, La Conseillante and Vieux Château Certan, all have sections located on blue clay. As the land falls away from the plateau, it becomes flatter and sandier, and these lower reaches are occupied by less familiar names whose wines often represent easy-drinking fare. Merlot is king in Pomerol, comprising around 85% of vines; the rest is Cabernet Franc, though plantings have increased over the last decade as clonal quality has improved and estates' own massal selection programmes – propagating cuttings from the best-performing vines – have begun feeding into their own supply. What was once deemed a variety tricky to ripen is now a saviour in hotter summers. A visitor to Pomerol might spy a few rows of Cabernet Sauvignon too and some notable names have planted a few more rows since 2016. In terms of biodynamics, only Gombaude-Guillot and Mazeyres could be considered full-time practitioners, though many estates, particularly the top names, have been organic for several years.

Pomerol wines have a distinctive bouquet. Often complex on the nose with black cherries and wild strawberries, many also have black truffle aromas, and are occasionally a little ferrous, especially with age. They can be powerful on the palate, driven along by the Merlot that revels in its deep clayey soils and has made them so approachable that for many years connoisseurs doubted their longevity. But Pomerol wines have a trick up their sleeve – their innate ability to mature over decades – though you cannot ignore the gap in quality between its most celebrated names and its minnows on lower, sandier soils.

Saint-Émilion (5,311 hectares) This sprawling appellation covers such a vast array of terroirs that some rightfully argue that it should be whittled down in size, though that will never happen. The most revered sectors are the limestone plateau, Astéries limestone to be exact, that predominantly lies to the east of Saint-Émilion town; the gravel *croupes*, which are ostensibly an extension from the Pomerol plateau where you find, most notably, Cheval Blanc and Figeac; and thirdly, the côteaux de Saint-Émilion, the slopes that descend from the plateau down to the plain and enjoy the best exposure. Some vineyards, such as Pavie and Ausone, occupy both the plateau *and* these slopes. The expanse of lower reaches consists of a hotch-potch of more sandy soils.

Merlot is the bedrock grape variety with around 80% of vine plantings, augmented by 15% Cabernet Franc and 5% Cabernet Sauvignon, though as in Pomerol, Cabernet Franc plantings have increased in recent years. Just under 700 producers call Saint-Émilion home, many of them known only locally. The Saint-Émilion classification was introduced in 1955 and bestowed its top Premier Grand Cru Classé "A" designation on just two estates, Ausone and Cheval Blanc, until the promotion of Angélus and Pavie in 2012. The next rank is Premier Grand Cru Classé "B" followed by a seemingly endless list of Grands Crus Classés. Unlike with the 1855 Classification, châteaux can gain promotion or (more rarely) demotion in reviews that have been undertaken in 1959, 1969, 1986, 1996, 2006 and 2012, though 2022 hangs in the balance at time of writing, the classification reeling from the withdrawal of Ausone, Cheval Blanc, Angélus and La Gaffelière. We await the repercussions and damage to its credibility. There are a number of organic and biodynamic estates, too many to mention here.

Given the wide variety of exposures, soil types and techniques, it is difficult to specify a precise style for Saint-Émilion. Underpinned by Merlot, its wines always have a sense of hedonism about them and how much that dominates overall style can depend on the winemaker's approach. Drier and hotter summers in recent years have shepherded wines in that opulent direction, with winemakers' only other alternative being to harvest unripe fruit. Those blessed with limestone soils tend to possess more natural freshness, *mineralité* and bite that counterbalances their decadence. Aromatics play a crucial part in Saint-Émilion, the bait that draws so many to its charms.

Sauternes/Barsac (3,111 hectares) The sweet wines of Bordeaux are a whole different ball game to the dry red and dry whites. I use "Sauternes" as a catch-all name for the appellations of Sauternes and Barsac, though other sources of sweet wine also exist, such as Cérons and Loupiac. Sauternes shares the gravel soils of the Médoc, though Barsac tends to contain more limestone, either *Astéries* or molasse, which lends their vines a slightly different growth cycle and slightly more natural acidity. "Sauternes tends to be more ripe, with more roundness and candied fruit," Bérénice Lurton at Climens explains, "whereas Barsac, in principle, has more minerality, more freshness in terms of structure but also aromas with fresher fruits and white flowers."

The undisputed king, Yquem, was the solitary estate anointed Premier Cru Supérieur in 1855 and boasts unparalleled history and *réclame*. But its eminence should not divert attention away from other outstanding estates, such as Climens, Coutet, Doisy Daëne and Suduiraut, to name but four that occasionally challenge Yquem's supremacy.

As you will read from the decade summaries, Sauternes was once Bordeaux's must coveted and expensive wine, but fashions and taste change. Nowadays, not only do Sauternes' winemakers take a huge gamble every year in producing their wine, but the rewards are not proportionate to what they ought to be. Consequently, many have whittled down production of their botrytis-affected wine and diversified, producing dry whites that under current legislation must be ignominiously labelled Bordeaux Blanc. Opinions are divided over whether this is their only option to remain economically viable or whether it risks diluting the association between Sauternes and sweet wines. There are strong views on either side, though I firmly believe that the presence of dry whites takes nothing away and if it means châteaux can stay afloat, then there ends the debate.

Pre–1870 Bottles

The mid-19th century were halcyon days for Bordeaux. After 1789, Napoleonic laws resulted in estates being split between the heirs with all the internecine family disputes and inheritance tax levies that ensued. These immutable laws continue to be imposed to this day, too often to the detriment of the estates and regions themselves. Many on the Left Bank circumvented the rules by transferring ownership from single wealthy proprietors, often those of noble birth, to groups of shareholders or merchants, such as the Barton and Guestier families, who could exploit free trade. These comparatively large estates benefited from economies of scale, with their sheer volume of production allowing them to maintain market presence overseas, not least within the important English market. From the early 18th century, the aristocracy and landed gentry had begun demanding better drinking fare than *vin ordinaire*. Now they wanted proper claret. During the Second Empire, between 1851 and 1870, the profitability of Bordeaux attracted financiers, most notably the Rothschild family.

The size of Bordeaux estates, larger than those of many classic regions such as Burgundy or the Rhône, remains unchanged, so although sometimes threatened, the region has never relinquished a global presence. As the Left Bank turned over almost every square foot of suitable land to vines, the Right Bank was ostensibly an unknown backwater comprising a polyculture of vines alongside strips of cereals and pasture. Farming's primary aim was to sustain families' livelihoods, to put food on the table, with wine often just a hobby or intended for private libation. It was only as the decades rolled by that the Right Bank incrementally turned into a monoculture of vines.

Winemakers were completely at the mercy of weather conditions, crossing their fingers and praying at church every Sunday for a benevolent growing season. Based on their experience and that of their forebears, they anticipated two, maybe three decent crops each decade, muddling through the rest the best they could. There was little technical know-how on how to remedy a poor growing season and more often than not, a bad season was written off – a mindset that only really changed in the last half-century.

Harvests were undertaken by local hands in a single sweep through the vineyards, often north to south. The priority was to get the fruit picked efficiently and avoid inclement conditions that could ruin a crop at the last gasp. Picking was far from today's bespoke harvests, which are organised with military precision. Bunches were loaded into wooden carts and driven by horse or oxen to the winery or maybe the nearby co-operative. The bunches would be manually rubbed over an iron griddle in order to detach stems. I speculate what percentage were actually de-stemmed and how many were just heaved into ancient wooden vats when time was pressing. Fermentations were uncontrolled and could be rapid, apparently as short as two days at Bélair during the 1860s. The wines were then transferred into used barrels for ageing, usually with regular racking, where they matured until a merchant came and chose which barrels they wanted to buy. If no one came, the wine just stayed there and would have to be sold off as best as possible.

Of course, the châteaux were not averse to promoting their standing both at home and overseas. Coinciding with the Exposition Universelle de Paris of 1855, the Gironde Chamber of Commerce requested courtiers to tally the most expensive wines to formulate a five-tier ranking of Médoc chateaux, including those in Sauternes, and giving a special pass to the historically important Haut-Brion. The clarity and moreover immutability of the 1855 Classification of what became Bordeaux's Grands Crus Classés was, in hindsight, an ingenious piece of marketing, making the region's elite names even better known and renowned across Europe. The classification was concurrent with a succession of fecund growing seasons that meant Bordeaux lovers had a surfeit of excellent wines to stock in their cellar. English writer Edmund Penning-Rowsell described the period between 1858 and 1878 as an "unequalled series of fine and plentiful vintages".

It was not all plain sailing. Mildew and oidium were constant threats and a remedy using copper sulphate lay some years ahead. Proprietors were unaware that good times never last.

In the 19th century, alcohol levels tended to be lower than today with higher levels of acidity. The late Jacques Boissenot analysed some of the ancient bottles at Gruaud Larose from the 1830s to the 1970s and alcohol hovered just under 11%, under 9% for the 1883, though my hunch is it would have been higher when the wine was made. Wines tended to contain more volatile acidity, part of the character of old claret, and I vividly remember Anthony Barton remarking how a bit of volatility lent something to his wines.

In the salad days of my career I read vicariously about the ancient wines imbibed by the likes of Michael Broadbent and David Peppercorn. Their writings evoked images of cool dark cellars in some remote Highland castle: caches of forgotten bottles under a thick dust, surely long past their drinking windows and silently turning into vinegar – the final fate of all undrunk wine.

Some bottles from this era have tasted exactly like something you might sprinkle onto your fish and chips and were grievously poured straight down the sink. But many have been quite the opposite. They were like meeting a grandiloquent dame in her twilight years who has lost none of her wit or guile. They revel in their antiquity, tasting mature rather than old, blessed with time-folding alchemy, merging past with present. I am not romanticising ancient claret by dint of venerability. My egregious principle is that there is no age barrier, no point after which a bottle is old enough to be spared scrutiny. Some centenarians continue to sparkle having lost none of their preternatural ability to give sensory pleasure, while sating those who enjoy drinking "bottled time".

Although this guide commences in 1870, over the years I have been fortunate to drink even older claret.

The oldest? Step forward, carefully mind you, 1831 Gruaud Larose, gently prized open at one of a quartet of memorable verticals at the château organised on the eve of en primeur. These deep-dives into Gruaud Larose's extensive library explain why a disproportionate number of the 19th-century antiquities mentioned here come from this Saint-Julien estate. For the record, that 180-year-old wine, born the same year that Charles Darwin was aboard the *Beagle* and six years before Queen Victoria took the throne, was fragile and ephemeral, yet perfectly drinkable. The best bottles pre-dating 1870 that I have encountered include an ethereal 1842 Gruaud Larose and, even if it seemed propped up by residual sugar, 1852 Gruaud Larose. Other notable encounters include a briny 1858 Latour and a crystalline 1865 Latour that exhausted superlatives, both tasted in Hong Kong little more than an hour after stepping off the plane. Also, there was an elegant and ethereal 1868 Lafite Rothschild prized from the Rothschild family's cellar to celebrate 150 years of family ownership in May 2018 that dazzled actor Dominic West, who turned and asked quite rightly: "How can wine be this old and taste so fine?" Well, I guess not all wines are Lafite Rothschild... Finally, there was the bottle of 1869 Yquem served in Beaune that had an almost flor-like, syrup-scented nose and was quite exotic on the palate, with fig and dates mixed with elderflower. It was magical. That is about the extent of my experience. The likes of André Simon and Michael Broadbent are our first-hand experts and commentators on ancient Bordeaux, their writings having lost none of their value.

THE
1870s

The 1870s was the beginning of the Belle Époque, a period of political stability in Europe that lasted from the Franco-Prussian War to the First World War and fomented a sense of optimism and artistic creativity. That did not necessarily apply to Bordeaux, however, which was beset by all manner of woes during this period. Nevertheless, the first few years of the decade were trouble-free. Land under vine continued to expand and production increased from an average of 2,558,000 hl between 1860 and 1869 to 2,967,100 hl between 1870 and 1879. Prosperity attracted outside investors and a number of estates changed hands: Lafite Rothschild in 1868, Giscours in 1875, Carbonnieux in 1878 and Château Margaux in 1879.

In terms of grape varieties, surveys in the 18th century such as those by Abbé Bellet in 1736 and Nicolas Dupre de Saint-Maur (1783-1784) show that vineyards were a mish-mash and as time passed, those deemed the best quality and easiest to grow, ergo the most profitable, began to usurp inferior varieties. This would be done through massal selection, taking cuttings from the best vines and propagating them to plant fledglings. By 1878, publisher and researcher Édouard Féret estimated that around three-quarters of the Haut-Medoc was planted with Cabernets, disputing the idea that Cabernet Sauvignon's dominance came about after phylloxera. It was already kingpin of the Médoc and probably found favour after the oidium crisis. Malbec comprised one-third of Saint-Émilion and Pomerol, popular due to its resistance to oidium and vigour on less rich soils. For the whites, Sémillon comprised 75% of vines.

In hindsight, it could be seen as an inopportune moment to invest in a Bordeaux château as the 1870s marked the end of an era. It was the final decade when every vine in Bordeaux was "French", from the top of its canopy to the tip of its roots. The destructive phylloxera aphid was allegedly brought to France in the 1830s, when winemakers in Hérault imported American vines via steamship. First observed in the Bordeaux region in 1866, mainly around the palus – the alluvial soils bordering rivers in Floirac and Bouliac – it perniciously spread from Entre-Deux-Mers into Saint-Émilion and Pomerol. Doubtlessly, proprietors of historic châteaux on the Left Bank assumed their vineyards would be immune, aristocracy providing some kind of shield.

In 1870, the alarmed authorities offered a reward of 20,000 francs, upped to 300,000 four years later, for anyone who could find a cure for what they termed "this horrible plague". In 1874, reputed Bordeaux historian Théophile Malvezin published a 56-page pamphlet that offered alternatives to whole-scale re-planting onto phylloxera-resistant American rootstock, the solution advocated by a collective of growers led by a Bouliac winemaker, Léo Laliman, who was, in fact, accused of importing the insect. These included several radical measures, such as flooding the entire vineyard, though in the end the most employed solutions were carbon bisulphide and potassium sulpho-carbonate. They were expensive to use but eventually adopted by many châteaux that could not countenance re-planting and re-grafting.

By 1878, phylloxera had already made inroads into the Right Bank. In Pomerol, La Conseillante proprietor Louis Nicolas had already authorised the planting of 24 rows of American rootstock. The aphid had its eye on the vines over in the Médoc and it marched through the region with the same dire consequences as everywhere else. Baron James de Rothschild had purchased Lafite Rothschild just ten years earlier and now a pernicious enemy threatened its entire existence. It dawned on everyone that the aphid was indifferent to reputation and so began the complete re-planting with phylloxera-resistant American rootstocks that I shall detail in the following decade's summary.

Discussing pre-phylloxera claret with Michael Broadbent at his pied-à-terre in London back in 2005, he contentiously opined that Bordeaux wine lost a certain "*je ne sais quoi*" after it sacrificed its original rootstock in order to survive. I have a mere fraction of his experience, though on the rare occasion I have encountered a Bordeaux of such antiquity, I understand Broadbent's grounds for argument. Alas, it can never be proven. Even if it is true, it is moot because so few wines of this era exist – apart from perhaps those from vines at Bel Air-Marquis d'Aligre in Margaux that the recalcitrant Jean-Pierre Boyer reckoned to be planted as far back as 1870. This is despite the concerted efforts of the equally recalcitrant Loïs Pasquet, who traduced post-phylloxera Bordeaux wines as "soup" at one tasting event and cultivates his vines in the Graves on their own roots, convinced the region needlessly ripped up its sacred vines. I disagree with many of Pasquet's views, but I admit that the handful of pre-phylloxera clarets I have tasted contained an ineffable bit of magic. Like a glimmer from a distant star, they sparkled that tiny bit brighter.

Nowadays we talk of the Left Bank, which is to say the appellations that comprise the Médoc bordering the Gironde Estuary, and the Right Bank, most famously Saint-Emilion and Pomerol. In the 1870s Bordeaux was defined by its Left Bank estates, some of whose histories stretched back centuries. Names of famous vineyards were already known across France and overseas, cellared and consumed by the wealthy upper class and given further renown thanks to the 1855 Classification. Oenophiles became transfixed by the hierarchy

of Grands Crus Classés, from the pinnacle of its four First Growths (Lafite Rothschild, Latour, Château Margaux and Haut-Brion) down to the Fifth Growths, and it remained unchanged but for Mouton Rothschild's promotion to the top tier in 1973.

By contrast, the unclassified Right Bank was a relatively unknown, its often Malbec-based wines enjoying a fraction of the kudos given to the Left Bank. In particular, Pomerol was regarded as just a rather bucolic neighbour of Saint-Émilion, off the radar of every wine-lover apart from a few appreciative palates in Holland and Belgium. In the 1868 edition of the *Féret* Bordeaux guide, Pomerol is afforded only a couple of pages and while the book doesn't disparage its wines, it remarks they are more easy-drinking than Saint-Émilion. Conversely, Sauternes was revered as the apotheosis of Bordeaux. Sauternes maven Bill Blatch argues that there were two golden eras for this region in the 19th century: 1828 to 1851, after which the vineyards had to fight off oïdium, and from 1858 to the arrival of phylloxera in 1878. Sauternes in this era was highly coveted and cellared, often the most expensive wine on merchants' and restaurants' lists.

The main export market for Bordeaux wine was the UK, chiefly thanks to the Anglo-French accord of 1860 that opened up this lucrative market. Whereas in 1859 around 18,500 hl of Bordeaux wine was exported to the UK, that figure leapt to 56,000 hl the following year and then to 274,000 hl by 1874.

Growing seasons in this decade varied in quality, though 1870 and 1875 were both highly esteemed. During this period, more and more Bordeaux merchants were leaving châteaux to undertake the ageing of their wines in barrel, obliging many to expand their buildings to accommodate vintages. The role of the cellar-master also became more important and skilled. Of course, vineyard practices and wineries were rudimentary, using basic tools and lacking temperature regulation measures, save for dunking blocks of ice into vats to keep the alcoholic fermentation on track. Nevertheless, there were some innovations, as there always are in Bordeaux. One technique that became popular was *fonçage*, sealing the top of the vat to reduce the must's exposure to oxygen during fermentation, a practice that has become more popular in recent years. Topping up the casks was becoming a more refined art, with a report by Marquis de Flers in 1872 recommending that "the topping up should always be done with the Premier Vin", and the first mention of glass bungs used to seal *barriques* appearing in 1876.

1870

The 1870 vintage is one of the most renowned of the 19th century. As they would in 1961, spring frosts – on 30 April and 4 May – reduced the potential crop. Warm conditions quickly returned and were even excessive as early as 20 May. The prolonged hot summer bestowed rich fruit, although vineyard managers had to deal with shrivelled and grilled berries. Fortunately, by August temperatures had moderated, though sugar levels were already high. The harvest began around 7 September. The wines were always renowned for their longevity and sold for high prices at the time. Ian Maxwell Campbell described them as "pachydermatous", an adjective used for the first and I suspect only time in relation to wine. "Scalded grapes, rich, full-bodied, complete wines!" raves Émile Goudal, Lafite Rothschild's estate manager, in the browning pages of the château archives. Not everyone was smitten. "Those unsatisfactory '70s", writes a somewhat grumpy Professor George Saintsbury. The great chronicler of 19th-century Bordeaux was unimpressed by their obduracy and rued the fact that he could have bought triple the amount of "sound bourgeois wine" for the same amount of shillings splashed out on Classed Growths. Even by 1910, Saintsbury finds the 1870s "dumb" and they apparently did not begin to open until the following decade.

Bottles with sound provenance can dazzle, though let's face it, you are not going to find them on supermarket shelves. Unsurprisingly given their antiquity they are exceptionally rare and in my career I have been privileged to try three bottles and a magnum. First and foremost was the monumental 1870 Lafite Rothschild served blind at the culmination of Jordi Oriols-Gil's milestone birthday at La Trompette in London. Without exaggeration, it stands imperiously above every other Bordeaux I have ever encountered – even the mighty 1945 Mouton Rothschild and 1961 Latour must kowtow in its presence. It was so intense and ineffably complex on the nose, astounding in terms of precision and grandeur, a multi-dimensional behemoth undimmed by time. Almost as spellbinding is the 1870 Gruaud Larose, first poured at a vertical organised by Linden Wilkie that left an entire room awestruck. Curiously, this outclassed a magnum opened at the property a couple of years later. Both surpass a 1870 Mouton Rothschild that was a little fatigued when served blind with the 1970, though I remember Michael Broadbent being smitten by the bottle and eulogising accordingly.

Event
Start of the Franco-Prussian War

The Franco-Prussian War broke out when Prussian chancellor Otto van Bismarck persuaded Prince Leopold of Hohenzollern-Sigmaringen to accept the vacant Spanish throne and threaten France's domination of Europe. Bismarck acceded to France's demand to withdraw Leopold's candidacy, though his rhetoric infuriated the French government so much that war was declared on 19 July. The German army's crushing victory the following year established their empire and instilled a sense of militarism and animosity against the French that lasted until 1945. According to English writer Edmund Penning-Rowsell, the Franco-Prussian War was partly responsible for winemakers neglecting to deal with the spread of the phylloxera louse. It was not the first nor the last time that war directly affected winemaking.

Music
Ride of the Valkyries
– Richard Wagner

Richard Wagner's *Die Walküre* is an appropriately epic way to commence our journey through 150 years of music. Though it was completed in 1857, Wagner worked on other operas before its maiden performance in Munich on 26 June 1870 in front of an audience who included Liszt and Brahms. Wagner was apparently irked by constant requests to perform the rousing *Ride of the Valkyries* separate from his magnum opus. These days, it is inextricably linked with the movie *Apocalypse Now*, which shows napalm raining down on a Viet Cong-held village as Wagner's masterpiece blares from helicopter-mounted speakers.

1871

This growing season followed the coldest winter since 1829–1830. The *Féret* guide reported that between 1 and 4 January, temperatures fell to a bone-chilling -14°C (6.8°F), enough for the Garonne to ice over bank-to-bank through Bordeaux city. An estimated one-third of the vines completely froze, prefiguring the catastrophic winter of 1956. An uneven season followed with light hail on 6 June and drought impeded *véraison*. Storms plagued the harvest that commenced on 17 September and the result was a small crop of irregular wines. "A veritable Cinderella", remarked Ian Campbell Maxwell before praising the wines' diaphanous outward appearance. He was certainly smitten by the vintage – his wine merchant company bought the entire crop of Latour, which had "a perfume of summer flowers and a delicate flavour not unlike ripe nectarines". Charles Walter Berry felt that the 1871s were pretty in their flush of youth but advised not keeping them because, "They may soon go beyond."

I have tasted two bottles of 1871 Gruaud Larose from the château cellars. They revealed one respectable example that insinuated a proportion of Malbec in the vineyard, commonplace at that time; the other had fallen by the wayside.

Event
Queen Victoria opens the Royal Albert Hall in London

London's most iconic venue was officially opened by HRH Prince of Wales on 29 March 1871 in lieu of Queen Victoria, who was present but too overwhelmed by the occasion, even though her husband, after whom it was named, had passed away a full decade earlier. The inaugural First Night of the Proms was held 14 years later and in recent years has attracted an increasingly eclectic array of musicians.

Music
Onward, Christian Soldiers
– Rev. Sabine Baring-Gould

In 1871, Arthur Sullivan put words to this rousing English hymn written six years earlier by Rev. Sabine Baring-Gould. He had composed it for his children to sing on their walk to Horbury St. Peter's Church, where he was curate, from Horbury Bridge.

Eighteen seventy-two was shaping up to be a good vintage thanks to clement weather from 13 June onwards. Mid-harvest downpours began on 15 September and did not finish until exactly one month later, though the archives at La Conseillante report a dry and exceptionally warm September, save for rain on 3 and 4 September that evened out what hitherto had been an irregular ripening crop. The Nicolas family, who had purchased the château the previous year, commenced the harvest with 42 pickers relatively late on 2 October. The picking finished on 15 October at Lafite Rothschild. The result for Bordeaux overall was a "fair to middling" batch of wines, according to André Simon, in all likelihood, catching the great wine connoisseur in euphemistic mood.

I have had one solitary encounter with an 1872 Gruaud Larose opened at the estate, though it was rather fatigued and eclipsed by the 1873 tasted one year later.

Event
First FA Cup final

Music
Symphony No. 2 in C Minor
– Anton Bruckner

Wanderers beat the Royal Engineers 1-0 at the maiden FA Cup Final held at the Kennington Oval on 16 March. Two-thousand spectators watched Morton Peto Betts score the winning goal after 15 minutes, though for some unknown reason Betts played under the pseudonym A.H. Chequer. The crowd had also seen the Engineers' Lieutenant Creswell break his collar-bone five minutes earlier. No record of any Gary Lineker post-match punditry exists.

The first version of Bruckner's Symphony No. 2 was composed in 1872, a second version five years later. It was, in fact, his fourth symphony and is known as the *Symphony of Pauses*. The Vienna Philharmonic was due to premiere the piece under conductor Otto Dessoff, but in rehearsals, Dessoff and several members of the orchestra felt it was impossible to play.

1873

The 1873 growing season was poleaxed by a late spring frost. The winter was quite mild and a warm early spring encouraged rapid vine growth. But from 5 April, the mercury began to fall and from 25 to 28 April, particularly on the morning of the latter, temperatures plummeted to around -4°C (25°F). Hail on 25 and 26 April decimated around three-quarters of the nascent buds among more inland vineyards and one-quarter of those closer to the estuary. Grey rot finished off whatever survived. "The harvest [beginning on 2 October] is completely destroyed," lamented Louis Nicolas at La Conseillante. André Simon talks of a poor crop of wines and in Sauternes, an estimated 90% of crops were damaged.

The only Bordeaux that I have tasted is an ex-cellar 1873 Gruaud Larose. It was so animally that it belonged in a zoo, one run by a lazy zookeeper. And yet, despite André Simon's pillorying of this vintage, I found it bizarrely delicious considering that it was a 140-year-old bottle of fermented grape juice. I doubt I will be in similar condition at that age.

――――――

Event
The first commercially successful typewriter

Designed by newspaper editor Christopher Latham Sholes with Carlos Glidden, Samuel Soulé and Mathias Schwalbach, the Sholes & Glidden typewriter began production in 1873 and was the first commercially successful machine of its type (no pun intended). It employed an inked ribbon and QWERTY keyboard that was designed to stop the metal arms from clashing by separating common letter pairings. Introduced the following year, it opened the doors for nimble-fingered women to enter the office environment.

――――――

Music
String Quartet No. 5
– Antonín Dvořák

Dvořák composed his String Quartet No. 5 between September and October 1873. Composed for a semi-professional chamber ensemble led by Josef Portheim that occasionally included Dvořák on viola, the piece left the players unimpressed, according to music critic Václav Juda Novotný. A furious Dvořák thrust the score into Novotný's hand, informing him that he never wanted to see it again. Ergo, the score was only published after the composer's death and performed for the first time in 1930 in Prague.

The 1874 vintage witnessed a large crop of wines to compensate for the annual shortfalls since 1870. A northerly wind slowed down the vines' growth cycle in May and winemakers were on tenterhooks, fearing a late frost until the wind veered in another direction at the end of the month. Picking was early, commencing on 14 September at Lafite Rothschild, for example, though over in Pomerol, La Conseillante started much later on 25 September. The wines were renowned at the time of release and sold for the highest prices on record – 5,500 francs per barrel for the First Growths and 6,000 francs per barrel for d'Yquem, attesting the premium paid for Sauternes in its halcyon days. Indeed, 1874 was fêted for its sweet wines. Ian Maxwell Campbell appreciated the vintage but warned that it lacked "the superlatively unsophisticated charm and sunniness of the 1875." Writing in *In Search of Wine*, Charles Walter Berry cuts to the chase about 1874: "Entertain it, and be entertained by it, before it is too late."

No Bordeaux wines from this vintage tasted.

Event
First Impressionist
Exhibition in Paris

In April–May 1874, the First Impressionist Exhibition took place in a gallery on Rue du Capucines in Paris. Organised by Monet, Pissarro, Degas and Renoir, it featured 165 pieces, including their own works as well as ones by Cézanne and Sisley. Was it a success? Acerbic critic Louis Leroy lambasted the exhibition and exhorted, "Wallpaper in its early stages is much more finished than that." Monet and Renoir made the princely sum of 200 francs each and Degas didn't make a single franc.

Music
Messa da Requiem
– Giuseppe Verdi

When Gioachino Rossini died in 1868, Verdi initiated a collaborative project with 12 leading composers to create a requiem in his honour. Verdi wrote the final movement, *Libera me*. Due to be premiered a year after Rossini's death, the appointed conductor, Angelo Mariani, began to lose enthusiasm for the project and it was shelved just days before its scheduled premiere. Another passing prompted Verdi to revive his work. Verdi was an acquaintance and admirer of humanist Alessandro Manzoni and after his death in May 1873, *Libera me* was taken back off the shelf and reworked as a requiem to Manzoni. It premiered the following May at the San Marco church in Milan with Verdi himself wielding the baton. Though well-received, its maiden performance at the Royal Albert Hall failed to sell out.

1875

A textbook growing season produced perfect fruit in abundant quantities thanks to a regular flowering. However, June was inclement and July changeable. Those months were compensated by a sunny August and the weather remained benign until September, which was interrupted by occasional showers. Harvest at Lafite Rothschild commenced on 24 September according to its records. Michael Broadbent noted that it was the largest crop until 1960. The wines were purportedly elegant and charming on release, so much so that they were deemed too light for the English market and consequently they sold poorly. As it turned out, many of the finest wines lasted for over a century. In Professor George Saintsbury's *Notes on a Cellar-Book*, he describes purchasing some magnums of 1875 Mouton Rothschild, "before it had established its reputation", indicating how the First Growth-in-waiting was a couple of steps behind the top rank. Saintsbury adored both this vintage and the preceding one, writing: "As long as the '74s and '75s lasted nothing quite touched them."

The only bottle encountered from this vintage was an 1875 Lafite Rothschild and sadly, it had seen better days (probably around 1878). Given the season, another bottle would surely show better.

Event
First person swims the
English Channel

Shropshire-born Captain Matthew Webb became the first person to swim the Channel on 24 August 1875. He had made an unsuccessful attempt two weeks earlier and lathered himself in porpoise oil to keep warm. He was stung by a jellyfish after eight hours and drank brandy to numb the pain, finally arriving against the tide, 21 hours and 45 minutes after entering the water. A delayed Eurotunnel crossing can be just as stressful.

Music
Toréador Song
– Georges Bizet

Carmen, Bizet's famous opera telling the downfall of Don José who is seduced by the titular gypsy, premiered on 3 March 1875 at the Opéra-Comique in Paris. The galloping *Toréador Song* is sung by the bullfighter Escamillo in the second act and became one of the more recognisable arias. Not bad for an opera that Bizet predicted would be a "definite and hopeless flop".

Wine literature has scant information about this vintage. According to the records at Lafite Rothschild, a late frost in April was followed by coulure, then an overcast and wet September predicated grey rot. Altogether, these conditions conspired to make this a tiny crop and in general, quality left something to be desired. Château proprietors no doubt had their minds on other things, not least the first sporadic and localised outbreaks of the phylloxera louse. Émile Goudal, estate manager at Lafite Rothschild, damned his own First Growth, commenting that the 1876 was "green and harsh".

No Bordeaux wines from this vintage tasted.

Event
Invention of the telephone

It was on 10 March 1876 that Scotsman Alexander Graham Bell made the first telephone call. The call was an instruction to his assistant: "Mr. Watson, come here. I want to see you." One assumes that he wanted to complain about the 1876 Bordeaux vintage.

Music
My Grandfather's Clock
– Henry Clay Work

The sheet-music for this brass band standard was published in 1876. Self-taught musician Henry Clay Work wrote the words and lyrics about the clock that seemed to chime, both literally and figuratively, with an imaginary grandfather's life. It is said to be the origin of the term "grandfather clock". There are numerous cover versions, from Johnny Cash to Sam Cooke, not to mention Kenneth Williams' parody for BBC Radio show *Round the Horne*, entitled *My Grandfather's Grunge*.

1877

The 1877 vintage was purportedly irregular, though it did produce a clutch of fine wines. The winter had dragged on and been wet, but the season rallied and saw an intense heat wave from 1 August that lasted three weeks. Picking commenced on 26 September *chez* La Conseillante, although this refers to its white grape varieties, which many Pomerol estates cultivated at a time when there were no rules dictating grape plantings. At the beginning of *élevage*, some were concerned about a lack of maturity although this was allayed when the wines were finally bottled and exceeded expectations. Ian Maxwell Campbell opined that the wines were "light and elegant with just a soupçon of a squeezed lemon in the final farewell". Maurice Healy described the 1877s as "rather of the Peter Pan order, never quite growing up." Poets both.

No Bordeaux wines from this vintage tasted. I suspect many were drunk by André Simon since this was the Bordeaux maven's birth year.

Event
Inaugural Wimbledon tennis championship

July 9 saw the first ever Wimbledon tennis champion-ship organised by the All England Croquet and Lawn Tennis Club. Dr. Henry Jones helped draw up a majority of the rules that remain in place to this day, although the prize money has since increased. Twenty-one amateurs paid the one pound and one shilling entry to compete for the 25-guinea trophy that was won by old Harrovian rackets player, Spencer Gore.

Music
Swan Lake
– Pyotr Tchaikovsky

The story of Odette, a beautiful princess turned into a swan by an evil sorcerer, became one of Tchaikovsky's most enduring ballets, despite its initial lukewarm reception. It was first performed by the Bolshoi Ballet in Moscow on 4 March 1877. It had taken Tchaikovsky just one year to compose, though the score was in fact revised and debuted in 1895. It is this version that is commonly performed today.

This is a vintage that improved as the calendar pages flipped over. It began with dry conditions – La Conseillante reporting on 25 March that not a drop of rain had fallen in seven weeks – followed by snow and hail, then an attack of oidium in a changeable August just to compound woes. Harvest was late, around the end of September, after some settled sunny periods. "Sweet and well constituted," is how Ian Maxwell Campbell described the 1878s, though notes that they were initially received as "coarse and common" and lacking the class of 1874 or 1875. Professor George Saintsbury begged to differ and was more complementary. Quantities were small, often around half the average crop.

No Bordeaux wines from this vintage tasted.

Event
Invention of the cylinder phonograph

Thomas Edison was awarded the patent for his cylinder phonograph on 19 February 1878. The invention was the result of his work on the telephone and telegram – he basically wrapped a cylinder in tin-foil into which a needle made indentations that corresponded to sound vibrations. His first recording was the nursery rhyme *Mary Had a Little Lamb* and Edison was astonished when he replayed it to hear the first recording of the human voice. Though a commercial success, the cylinder could only record several times.

Music
HMS Pinafore
– Gilbert & Sullivan

Opening on 25 May 1978, Gilbert & Sullivan's fourth two-act opera was their first major commercial success, running for 571 performances. Taking place on the titular vessel, it poked fun at the British class system, the First Lord of the Admiralty, party politics and patriotism. Such was its international success that its creators tried and failed to stop approximately 150 unauthorised performances. Today, it remains one of their most popular operas. As an aside, for many years I conflated Gilbert & Sullivan with seventies singer-songwriter Gilbert O'Sullivan, and it took me years to untangle the two.

1879

Ignominiously, the first Bordeaux vintage widely affected by the scourge of phylloxera. The 1879 growing season witnessed inclement conditions with a terrible spring and awful flowering, and coulure widespread throughout a rainy and overcast summer. (As an aside, the UK suffered its wettest summer since 1766.) The late harvest began on 9 October and continued until the end of the month. Volumes were generally low.

The only wine I have tasted from this vintage is the 1879 d'Yquem that had been re-corked in 1993, poured at the end of a dinner held by Silvio Denz, the owner of Lafaurie-Peyraguey, at his home in Zurich. It had held up well and though it came across as a bit timeworn, I remarked that it "continues to emit pleasure like a distant twinkling star."

Event
The Tay Bridge disaster

On the evening of 28 December, as a force 10 or 11 gale bore down upon Scotland, the central navigation spans of the Tay Bridge collapsed into the Firth of Tay. The bridge had not been open for two years but a subsequent investigation into its design found that it was vulnerable in high winds. A train crossing the bridge plunged into the dark waters and 72 passengers and three crewmen lost their lives.

Music
Berceuse, Op. 16
– Gabriel Fauré

The actual date of Fauré's short piece is unconfirmed, either 1878 or 1879, though for certain it premiered the following year. Instantly recognisable to this day, the choirmaster and deputy organist at the Église de la Madeleine in Paris originally wrote the score for violin and piano.

The

1880s

The infamy of this decade rests upon phylloxera's unstoppable spread throughout Bordeaux. Many hoped that a remedial application would soon be found and as a consequence there was no hasty uprooting of vineyards, not least because these were historic châteaux, the apogee of fine wine, and cornerstones of French culture. Not only was uprooting considered sacrilegious, but rumours also began circulating that American rootstocks imparted a distasteful foxiness. One outspoken critic of imported rootstocks was Alcide Bellot des Minières, who arrived at Haut-Bailly in 1872 and became one of the era's towering winemaking figures. Not one to mince words, he declared that grafting would decimate centuries of French viticulture, going on to write that "any wine produced from grafted vines is not a complete wine". Thereafter, with almost monomaniacal zeal, he set about finding alternative solutions that included planting several esoteric grape varieties, some of which remain in situ at Haut-Bailly having defied ampelographers' identification.

Though the aphid was acknowledged to be a serious threat, Bellot des Minières was not the only winemaker who sought alternative means of eradication. Some of them more successful than others. At Montrose, where half the vines had succumbed, owner Mathieu Dollfus spent a fortune installing kilometres of iron piping to make the ground more humid, as it was believed this stopped the spread. Down the road at Latour, in May 1880, 27 employees were given the day off so they could take part in a religious procession against the fast-spreading louse, which sounds like a lost scene from *The Wicker Man*.

The metastasis of phylloxera was so rampant that by 1882, 138,000 out of 141,420 hectares of vines were affected. Some winemakers reported that in some acutely devastated vineyards, vines could be pulled from the ground with a gentle single-handed tug. Re-grafting tens of thousands of vines was a time-consuming, disruptive, systematic process that lasted until the 1920s. Philippe Roudié in his book *Vignobles et Vignerons du Bordelais* provides fascinating information that details exactly how the region was re-cultivated. By the middle of the decade only around 1,400 hectares of vine had been replanted, mostly on lesser terroirs that were ostensibly testing grounds. According to Roudié, from 1885 to the turn of century, between 2,700 to 5,300 hectares were replanted per annum.

By the middle of the decade, only around 1,400 hectares of vine had been replanted, mostly on lesser terroirs, ostensibly testing grounds, with 2,700 to 5,300 hectares replanted per annum. In 1885, botanist Alexis Millardet, professor at the faculty of sciences at Bordeaux University, published his research that recommended the most phylloxera-resistant rootstocks: *Vitis riparia*, *Vitis rupestris*, *Vitis cordifolia* and *Vitis cinerea*. This well-respected expert offered a prescription for Bordeaux's ills, instead of alternatives offering limited success, thus its publication must have persuaded more winemakers to follow his sage advice. The French government offered tax concessions for estates that planted American stock until the new vines reached their fourth leaf. By 1889, Roudié noted that around 10,000 hectares had been re-planted, so the pace had picked up, though that still left around 130,000 hectares on their original French rootstocks, either treated by alternative sprays or left to their own defences. In fact, a year earlier, some Bordeaux winemakers mistakenly assumed that phylloxera was in retreat and recommenced planting French rootstock, at least until June 1889 when the louse made considerable progress in hitherto unaffected vineyards.

Millardet deserves greater recognition. His research not only helped combat phylloxera, but he also formulated "Bordeaux mixture" (page 21), which protected vines against downy mildew and black root, first discovered in Cérons in 1887. His statue stands in the Jardin Public in the city of Bordeaux. It must be emphasised that oidium was just as devastating year to year, although unlike phylloxera its eradication did not mandate whole-scale uprooting of vineyards.

Unsurprisingly, in the 1880s, average production fell to around the same level as the 1860s. Unlike the previous two decades, there was no outstanding growing season such as 1865 or 1870, in no small part due to the climactic aftereffects of the Krakatoa eruption, which lowered global temperatures for several years. As a consequence, it was a comparatively poor decade for wines. Ian Maxwell Campbell observed that the fledgling vines were constitutionally weak and more susceptible to disease, encouraging many châteaux to pasteurise their wines to retain sugar. Bordeaux lovers began to look elsewhere for their vinous pleasure. Bottles from this decade were generally not cellared and are nowadays rarely seen.

Few estates can boast a library of precious ancient bottles like Gruaud Larose; snapshots of the past dating back to a dusty bottle of 1815. This 1880 was born as phylloxera began its pernicious spread across Bordeaux.

1880

André Simon describes 1880 as a "cold and damp" season, one that saw a poor spring and uneven flowering and consequently a small crop. The growing season was in some ways a repeat of the previous one, though winemakers enjoyed a clement late summer. Harvest began around 21 September.

I have tasted two bottles of the 1880 Gruaud Larose at the property, one implicating a little *Hermitagé* in the cellar (the blending of sturdier wines to reconstitute a potentially feeble wine from the Rhône) and the other, much better and flattering in terms of its fruitiness.

Event
Australian outlaw Ned Kelly is captured and hanged

Australia's most notorious outlaw was hung on 11 November 1880 after a shootout that finally led to his capture. To some, he was a poster-boy for the anti-establishment, a man who escaped his impoverished childhood to take on corrupt British colonists. To others, he was a murderer who ruthlessly killed three police officers. Maybe one or two think he is the lead singer of the Rolling Stones.

Music
Roses from the South, Op. 388 – Johann Strauss

Roses from the South is a waltz that premiered in Vienna, which comes as no surprise considering Strauss was the king of Viennese waltzes. It was first performed at a series of Sunday concerts at the Musikverein, conducted by the composer's younger brother. Inspired by the operetta *The Queen's Lace Handkerchief*, it went on to become one Strauss's most famous compositions and was used in a number of films.

The summer began very cool but the mercury rose as the season progressed and finished with what André Simon describes as "fair quality" wines harvested from around 12 September for the Merlot. Apparently, many of the wines were born with green and unripe tannins, though estate manager at Lafite Rothschild, Émile Goudal, opined that "They lack the mellowness that would make them exceptional". For some reason a handful of Bordeaux cellars seem to be stocked with more of this particular vintage than others of this era. Ian Maxwell Campbell found the 1881s "inky and dry".

I have tasted two wines from this vintage. First, a superb 1881 Gruaud Larose that was still drinking well in 2011, neither inky nor dry after more than a century. Then there was the 1881 Batailley, the oldest vintage of a spectacular dinner served to hundreds of invitees who could scarcely believe that an ancient vintage was poured with such profligacy. Proprietor Philippe Castéja later told me he had opened 15 bottles that evening. It was still drinking well with a cigar box nose and a palate that I likened to a mature Chambolle-Musigny. Both these bottles of 1881 suggest that this growing season was not a total write-off.

Event
Gunfight at the O.K. Corral

Music
My Bonnie Lies Over the Ocean
– Charles E. Pratt

On 26 October in Tombstone, Arizona, the most legendary shootout of them all took place. Wyatt Earp, his two brothers and Doc Holliday were on one side, defenders of law and order. On the other, outlaws Billy and Ike Clanton, Tom and Frank McLaury and Billy Claibourne. It was not a fight between good and bad since there were dubious characters on both sides. The actual gunfight lasted 30 seconds, sufficient for subsequent press reports to turn Earp into a hero.

Nobody really knows the origin of this Scottish folk song. Does it refer to Bonnie Prince Charlie? Possible, though "Bonnie" is not gender specific, so it could be a lament for a lover who lives far away. For certain, in 1881, Charles E. Pratt, under the pseudonym "H.J. Fuller and J.T. Wood" published the sheet music, so you can imagine this standard being sung in smoke-filled public houses at the time. Perhaps the most famous version was recorded in Hamburg in October 1961 by Toni Sheridan, a rather ordinary recording that did modestly in the charts. He was backed by an upcoming Liverpudlian band called The Beatles.

1882

This was another poor growing season as a result of widespread mildew and phylloxera's pernicious march through the vineyards. Châteaux began applying potassium sulpho-carbonate to combat its progress. There was widespread downy mildew in the Médoc caused by a humid spring and summer, and harvest commenced around 28 September. Little more can be found about this vintage.

A bottle of 1882 Gruaud Larose was fungal but passable after 13 decades. No other wines tasted and the chances of tasting an '82 from the "wrong century" remain small.

Event
First Ashes cricket match

On 29 August 1882, the English cricket team lost to Australia for the first time on home soil. Such was the scale of the upset that the following day, *The Sporting Times* printed a mock obituary that jibed: "The body will be cremated and the ashes taken to Australia". Upon returning Down Under, the English captain, the Honorable Ivo Bligh, vowed to return with the "ashes". At one of the cricket matches, he was presented with a tiny terracotta urn and it remained on his mantelpiece for over 40 years until his widow donated it to the MCC. The rivalry persists to this day, though at time of writing, it appears to have become a rather one-sided contest.

Music
The Snow Maiden
– Nikolai Rimsky-Korsakov

Rimsky-Korsakov premiered his opera *Snegurochka*, or *The Snow Maiden*, on 10 February 1882 at the Mariinsky Theatre in St. Petersburg. The four acts had taken two years to compose and soon became Rimsky-Korsakov's favourite piece.

This is a growing season written off by incessant rain – André Simon lamented the poor quality of the wines, which were reportedly rather anaemic. Pickers went out into the vines around 27 September and the resulting wines were said to be pale and very light. But Professor George Saintsbury has kind words for the estate-bottled 1883 Château Margaux that he bought for "an absurdly moderate price" at auction. Simon is more scathing in his assessment and wrote: "The '83s and '85s are the only two [vintages] which I cannot remember having ever drunk with pleasure."

My sole encounter was with an ex-château bottle of 1883 Gruaud Larose that, despite having never moved from the cellar, was barely drinkable. Interestingly, analysis conducted by Jacques Boissenot at the time showed the wine had less than 9% alcohol, though of course that would have decreased over the decades through evaporation. Even so, the level must have been low from the outset.

Event
Krakatoa erupts

Music
The Jolly Dude – Sam Lucas

Since May, seafarers had spotted plumes of ash rising from the uninhabited island of Krakatoa, enticing sightseers to the area. In the early afternoon of 26 August 1883, a tremendous explosion obliterated two-thirds of the island, followed by four gigantic blasts the next day. One of the loudest events in history, the eruption could be heard 2,800 miles (4,500 km) away in Perth in Western Australia. Over 36,000 people lost their lives as the volcano collapsed into the caldera below sea level and shorelines were pulverised by 30-m (100-ft) tsunamis, sweeping away some 165 coastal villages in Java and Sumatra. The volcanic activity induced climate changes around the world so that average global temperatures were 1.2°C (34°F) cooler for the next five years, including, of course, in Bordeaux.

Ohio-born Sam Lucas was one of the first African-American entertainers. Initially working for minstrel troupes, he successfully branched out into serious acting work, becoming the first black actor to play Uncle Tom in *Uncle Tom's Cabin*. *The Jolly Dude* is taken from a musical play created by Lucas to showcase his talents as the show toured the Midwest. "Dude" had just entered parlance around New York to refer to a stylish and well-mannered gentleman, and was later repopularised after the success of my film choice for 1998 (page 413).

1883

1870

2020

1884

André Simon provided a geographic analysis of this season, reporting that despite the fine summer, mildew was endemic north of Saint-Julien. South of that dividing line, quality was good, though Ian Maxwell-Campbell observed that the mildew-affected wines, in a poetic turn of phrase, "collapsed hopelessly". Harvest began around 25 September. Maxwell-Campbell, a French Robert Parker of his day, declared this vintage would surpass the revered 1875s and bet a silk hat on it. He lost his silk hat.

No Bordeaux wines from this vintage tasted.

_____

Event
First roller coaster opens on Coney Island

Russia and France had developed their own slides for entertainment, but the first roller coaster is generally considered to have been made by LaMarcus Thompson at a park in Coney Island in New York. Built of steel and wood, the 137-m (450-ft) tracks supported cars that ran at a not-so-stomach-churning 6 mph (10 km/h). Thompson applied for the first of numerous patents for his invention the following year.

Music
Oh My Darling, Clementine
– Percy Montrose

This earworm of a folk-ballad was adapted from Henry S. Thompson's *Down by the River Liv'd a Maiden* by American songwriter Percy Montrose. It tells the tale of how Clementine, the daughter of a "miner forty-niner" and singer's paramour, hits her foot while driving ducklings and falls into a torrent of "foaming brine". Her lover, unable to swim, can only stand by and watch her drown. After what one assumes is a very short period of grieving, he then kisses her little sister and forgets about poor Clementine. That's men for you.

1885

The 1885 vintage was another vintage that succumbed to mildew. According to the Lafite Rothschild almanac: "Everywhere, we have seen grapevines with varying degrees of leaf loss that appear dark in hue when seen from a distance, analogous to that which indicates the first autumn frosts." Harvest commenced around 29 September. André Simon reported "poor quality" wine. Bottles are rarely seen, not least because at just over 1 million hl, this is the smallest harvest on record in the Gironde, around half the normal volume.

No Bordeaux wines from this vintage tasted.

Event
Mark Twain publishes The Adventures of Huckleberry Finn

Samuel Langhorne Clemens, who wrote under the pen name of Mark Twain, published his most famous and controversial book on 18 February 1885 in the US. Narrating the journey of Finn and Jim, a runaway slave, down the Mississippi River, it satirised race and religion, painting white characters in an unappealing light. Ernest Hemingway claimed that it marked the beginning of American literature.

Music
Symphony No. 4
– Johannes Brahms

Brahms conducted the maiden performance of Symphony No. 4 in Meiningen on 25 October. An apocryphal story exists that a page-turner working at the premiere opined: "For this whole [First] movement I had the feeling that I was being given a beating by two incredibly intelligent people." Being surrounded by wine bores is known to induce a similar feeling.

1886

This vintage was beset by problems, commencing with a spring frost and mildew that reduced the potential size of the crop, then a clement summer spoiled by localised hailstorms. The harvest kicked off around 25 September although there was just two-thirds of a normal crop and despite heavy chaptalisation, it was irregular in quality.

No Bordeaux wines from this vintage tasted.

Event
The Statue of Liberty is dedicated

The iconic 46-m (150-ft) tall statue of Libertas, the Roman goddess of liberty with her torch held aloft in her right hand and tabula in the left, was dedicated by President Grover Cleveland on 28 October 1886. As the country began receiving thousands of migrants in the early 20th century, the Statue of Liberty became a symbol welcoming them to their new home. Originally, it was a dull copper hue, gaining a green patina as the copper began to oxidise.

Music
The Swan
– Camille Saint-Saëns

The penultimate movement of *The Carnival of Animals* scored for a solo cello has become one of the most recognisable pieces of late 19th-century classical music. The composer dismissed his masterpiece as frivolous and banned any public performance until after his death, fearing it might damage his reputation as a serious composer. As a result, *The Carnival of Animals* was not played publicly until 1922, whereafter it became immensely popular.

The 1887 growing season saw a cool and wet spring that delayed flowering until 15 June, after which summer was extremely hot. Louis Mortier, estate manager at Lafite Rothschild, reported that the measures against downy mildew were effective and picking started around 28 September, the wines said to be healthy, rounded and sumptuous. André Simon pours scorn on them and waspishly comments that they "lacked charm" although Michael Broadbent describes it as the best vintage between 1878 and 1893. David Peppercorn concurs to an extent, suggesting that it offered the first "rays of hope" following the onslaught of phylloxera.

The only Bordeaux that I have tasted from this vintage is a bottle of 1887 Latour that completed a vertical tasting at Trinity in London in 2018. This 131-year-old antiquity did not come from the château cellars and I found it rather fungal and musty, not dissimilar to how Michael Broadbent had found it. When Latour struggles in a vintage, you assume the rest of Bordeaux struggled even more.

Event
The Yellow River floods in China

Some 900,000 people lost their lives when the Yellow River flooded in September 1887, one of the deadliest natural disasters ever. The swollen river broke through dikes in Henan province and an estimated 50,000 square miles (130,000 km²) of surrounding flat farmland was deluged. Soon after, the two million displaced men, women and children suffered a pandemic that took as many lives as the flood.

Music
Violin Sonata No. 3 – Edvard Grieg

Norwegian composer Edvard Grieg began composing his third sonata in autumn 1886, though this took longer to finish than his first two. The effort was worthwhile as it became Grieg's most popular and the composer's own favourite.

1888

The 1888 vintage was essentially the inverse of the following season: a cool summer followed by an Indian summer in September that saw some mildew pressure. "The 1888s made a brave effort to return to type," remarks Ian Maxwell Campbell, "and very nearly succeeded, but alas, the reconditioned vines lacked strength to resist the second-front attacks of mildew." Louis Nicolas at La Conseillante reported a litany of woes that included phylloxera, oidium, anthracnose, brown rot and black rot. Harvest commenced on 2 October and according to Maxwell Campbell the wines were initially attractive, potential successors to the 1875s. But it was a false dawn and they faded rapidly.

No Bordeaux wines from this vintage tasted.

Music
Where Did You Get That Hat? – Joseph J. Sullivan

Surely one of the catchiest melodies ever written, *Where Did You Get That Hat?* was a popular comic music hall song. It was originally written by American Joseph Sullivan. Finding his late father's top hat, Sullivan wore it down the street, upon which a young lad, presumably in a mocking tone, exclaimed the title of the song.

Event
Van Gogh cuts off his ear

On 23 December 1888, Vincent Van Gogh cut off his ear after a blazing row with his friend, Paul Gauguin, while they cohabited in the Yellow House in the town of Arles. The following morning, he wrapped it in newspaper and presented it to a prostitute working in a brothel. Van Gogh could not recall the incident and claimed it was a "simple artist's bout of craziness". However, he was suffering an undiagnosed mental illness, his act of self-mutilation triggered by his feelings of inferiority against the more experienced Gauguin and exacerbated by his alcoholism.

Film
Roundhay Garden Scene
– Louis Le Prince

While films might predate *Roundhay Garden Scene*, it is the oldest celluloid film in existence. Shot on a single-lens camera at Oakwood Grange in Roundhay in Leeds on 14 October 1888, this 1.66-second-long scene features Le Prince's son Adolphe walking in circles around the garden with his parents-in-law and his wife's friend, Annie Hartley. It might be short but there is something remarkable about watching real people just enjoying themselves so many decades ago.

The 1889 vintage was all geared up to be a classic. After a cold spring that delayed flowering, there followed a hot summer and a blissfully scorching September. Then, rainclouds gathered towards the end of the season and put paid to the harvest, which had began on 6 October. The wines initially had a little more body than the previous vintage. Though it was a large crop, quality was mixed and the wines purportedly did not age well in bottle.

No Bordeaux wines from this vintage tasted.

1889

Event
The Eiffel Tower opens in Paris

Completed in March 1889, France's most iconic landmark was opened on the last day that month, officials having to ascend on foot because the lifts were not yet operational. Built for the Exposition Universelle, held to mark 100 years since the Revolution, the 312-m (1,024-ft) wrought-iron tower was named after Gustave Eiffel, whose company had been charged with its construction. It requires 61 tonnes (60 tons) of paint every year to stop it rusting. Changes to the flagpole and antenna mean that its total height is now 12 m (39 ft) higher than when it was built.

Music
Symphony No. 1
– Gustav Mahler

Composed from 1887 through to 1888 while Mahler was second conductor for the Leipzig Opera, the four-movement Symphony No. 1 premiered at the Vigadó Concert Hall in Budapest on 20 November. It was poorly received. Part of the reason is that the music was supposed to illustrate literary ideas and pictorial scenes, yet the audience did not receive any notes on what Mahler's music intended to portray or what it represented, leaving them confused, not least after the funeral march. Mahler rearranged his original score over subsequent years and conducted many of the premieres around the world himself.

The

1890s

The 1890s witnessed the inexorable gut-wrenching march of phylloxera across Bordeaux and the realisation that applications of carbon bisulphide and potassium sulpho-carbonate were not only prohibitively expensive, but did not constitute long-term remedies. To remain viable the wine industry had to accept there was only one radical solution: the whole-scale re-planting of the region.

Philippe Roudie's research shows how plantings of American rootstock accelerated at the beginning of this decade, in particular around 1893–94 (the first of the "First Growths" Lafite-Rothschild instigated what they termed the "Americanist" method in 1893), though it still left around 40,000 hectares of vine completely unprotected. Replanting led to a shortfall in volume, though figures indicate that it was 14% above the 1870s average, partly due to the bumper yield of 1893. So what explains these bountiful crops?

Without legislation, unscrupulous winemakers began blending wines from outside Bordeaux with their own in order to deepen the colour and add more alcohol and fruit-driven flavour. These were sourced from warmer wine regions, not just the south of France but also from Algeria, where the number of hectares under vine expanded from 96,000 to 145,000 between 1890 and 1900, with the country exporting some 3.5 million hl into France in 1897. Chateau Latour's *régisseur* Daniel Jouet, an erudite and redoubtable agronomist, termed these concoctions as "*pistrouillage*" (a pejorative old term to describe doctored claret, unscrupulously blended with wines from outside the region). Some added dried grapes or colouring additives to bolster their blends, despite the French government having outlawed their use in 1889, stipulating that wine must come from fermented fresh grapes. Three years later, in order to combat fraud and discourage the import of overseas wines for adulteration, the French government levied import taxes according to alcoholic degree, which provoked retaliatory protectionist measures from European countries and a loss of market.

This adulteration undermined confidence in Bordeaux's wine and coupled with a bit of *fin de siècle* "Bordeaux bashing", some English commentators scurrilously pronounced that phylloxera had permanently ruined vineyards. This esteemed region was endangering its reputation. Demand and prices crashed, particularly during the latter half of the decade – for example, the price of Gruaud Larose (from the Bethmann part of the then-divided vineyard) tumbled 48% compared with the previous decade. Edmund Penning-Rowsell points out that Bordeaux prices fell 40% between 1873 and 1896. Inevitably, real estate suffered deflating prices: Louis Victor Charmolüe purchased Montrose in December 1897 for 800,000 francs, almost half the 1.5 million francs that the Holstein brothers had paid just eight years earlier.

The 1890s is not a decade with a standout vintage, even if the 1899 became revered. One interesting observation made by Penning-Rowsell is that the quality of wines in 1899 and 1900 allayed fears that American rootstocks were detrimental to quality. However, at that time, vast swathes of Bordeaux remained on French rootstock. At least they gave some incentive to replant over the following years. The other vintage of note is the precocious 1893, prefiguring the hot summers of 2003 and 2018. One style of Bordeaux continued to flourish – Sauternes. The sweet wines of Bordeaux remained highly coveted and continued to fetch some of the region's highest prices.

Workers posing outside the vat room of Château Lafite-Rothschild in the late 19th century, reproduced in Les Vins du Médoc in 1900. Notice the horse's elaborate bridle.

1890

The 1890 vintage saw a cool spring, with temperatures plummeting to -14°C (6.8°F) in Pomerol on 3 March. This was followed by intense attacks of cochylis during *véraison*. Despite the hot summer, the vintage produced mostly average wines. At La Conseillante, the Nicolas family felt that their vines were fatigued by the onslaught of diseases such as phylloxera and oidium. Harvest began around 29 September and the wines were supposed to have good colour, but were rather delicate. Charles Walter Berry lamented their hardness and dryness in their youth, a view shared by David Peppercorn in his *Bordeaux* tome.

I have two tasting notes for the vintage: an 1890 Gruaud Larose opened at the first of the annual numerically-themed verticals. It was perfectly drinkable but, to be honest, not earth-shattering. Second was an ancient 1890 Coutet served at one of the evening dinners at the annual Southwold blind tasting. This Barsac sported a lot of chlorine on the musty nose, the palate was decayed and decades past its best.

Event
Ulm Minster is completed

At 161.5 m (528 ft), Ulm Minster, the tallest church in the world, was completed in 1890. Like a lot of building work, it had run seriously over schedule, though I suspect your patio or loft conversion did not take 513 years to finish, even if at times it felt like it had. Work on the minster commenced in 1377 but was halted in 1543, only for tools to be picked up again in 1817. The original plans were for the steeples to be a couple of metres (a few feet) shorter, but they could not resist beating Cologne Cathedral and being that bit closer to God. Mozart is said to have played its organ, once the largest in the world. The town was bombed heavily during the Second World War, but the minster thankfully remained undamaged.

Music
Prince Igor
– Alexander Borodin

Borodin's opera *Prince Igor* premiered in his birthplace of St. Petersburg on 4 November 1890. Unfortunately, the composer himself was unable to attend since he had passed away three years earlier. Borodin was a polymath who had pursued a successful career in chemistry and medicine, making important discoveries in the study of aldehydes, before turning to music. *Prince Igor* was completed posthumously by Nikolai Rimsky-Korsakov and Alexander Glazunov.

By all accounts the 1891 vintage was a rerun of the previous year, albeit flowering was tardy and the summer even more inclement. Not only did vineyard managers have to cope with phylloxera but also cochylis. The season was rescued by a benevolent September. The harvest was later, commencing around 2 October.

Despite its poor reputation, my one encounter with an 1891 Gruaud Larose was surprisingly pleasant, even if I suspect it was propped up by a soupçon of *Hermitagé* or Algeria's 'finest' (page 73).

Event
Basketball played for the first time

Wanting an indoor game to play between baseball and football seasons, Canadian-American physical education teacher Dr James Naismith wrote down 13 rules for what he named "basketball". Working for the International YMCA Training School in Springfield, Massachusetts, he designed a game to keep young people active in winter and so one prerequisite was that it had to be playable indoors. According to an article in *National Geographic*, he asked the school janitor to search for goals and he returned with two peach baskets that were then nailed to the 3-m (10-ft) high gym balcony. Unfortunately, the first basketball game ended up in a free-for-all brawl between the boys – nevertheless, they badgered him to play it again. Naismith used the YMCA network to spread the word so it rapidly became a popular recreation. In 1936, he flew to Berlin to witness basketball becoming an Olympic sport.

Music
Wot Cher! Knocked 'em in the Old Kent Road – Albert Chevalier

Try uttering the title of this song without a cockney accent. This music hall comedy ditty was sung by actor and singer Albert Chevalier, otherwise known as "The Singing Costermonger". Chevalier himself was not born within the sound of Bow Bells, but in Hammersmith and as his Gallic-sounding name implies, his family were of French descent.

Film
Dickson Greeting – William K.L. Dickson

This short silent film consists of a gentleman passing a hat to himself. It was filmed at the Photographic Building in New Jersey with Thomas Edison and was made for the Kinetoscope, an exhibition device that displayed a series of sequential images that gave the illusion of motion to a viewer looking through a peephole. One was installed at the National Federation of Women's Clubs, thus this could claim to be one of the first publicly shown films.

1892

Next time you hear a Bordeaux winemaker lament a late spring frost, spare a thought for their forebears who in 1892 endured two of them. These were followed by a very hot summer, which sounds like a recipe for 1961, but temperatures were too high and a sirocco wind scorched vines as the mercury reached a blistering, grape-shrivelling 43°C (109°F). Apart from that, everything was hunky dory. Harvest began around 22 September and yields were half their normal volume.

The only encounter with this vintage came courtesy of a bottle of 1892 Latour in Hong Kong that defied the appalling growing season and delivered a gentle, elegiac Burgundy-like First Growth that rapidly faded in the glass.

Event
The Adventures of Sherlock Holmes
is published

Arthur Conan Doyle had published his first Sherlock Holmes story, *A Study in Scarlet*, in 1887, but it was when his publisher collected together 12 short stories, printed in *The Strand Magazine* between July 1891 and June 1892, that the pipe-smoking detective became a phenomenon. Over countless adaptations, Holmes has been played by more than 70 actors, with this writer's favourite the incomparable Jeremy Brett.

Music
After the Ball
– Charles K. Harris

Written the previous year but published in 1892, Charles K. Harris's *After the Ball* was one of the biggest hits of the time. It was apparently inspired when Harris saw a couple at a dance in Chicago argue and depart separately. He tweaked the narrative to that of an aged man lamenting about the loss of his young love to his niece. Footage exists of Harris singing the song shortly before he passed away.

1892

(Continued)

Film
Le Clown et Ses Chiens
– Émile Reynaud

Released on 28 October 1892,
Reynaud's *Le Clown et Ses Chiens*
comprises 300 individually
painted images. The 10-minute
clip of dogs jumping through
hoops in a circus ring formed
part of Reynaud's *Pantomimes
Lumineuses* show at the Musée
Grévin. His patented Théâtre
Optique film system was the
first to utilise film perforations,
predating Auguste and Louis
Lumière's cinematograph by
three years. Want to see it?
Unfortunately, that is not possible
because in a fit of depression,
Reynaud threw all but two of
his films into the Seine before
passing away in 1918.

1893

This vintage demonstrated there was life after phylloxera – the first to boast a clutch of wines worth talking about after the string of fallow years. It is remarkable from a meteorological standpoint. The season galloped ahead so that flowering was finished by 20 May, some three weeks earlier than usual. Then came a summer so hot that it put 2003 in the shade. In fact, it was the hottest since 1822. According to André Simon and confirmed by records at Gruaud Larose, the harvest began on 15 August, the earliest on record (though 2020 must come close to challenging it). At Lafite Rothschild, the harvest began on the same day and for the first time ever finished before the end of the month, while Château Margaux commenced on 17 August. On the Right Bank at La Conseillante, the Nicolas family began on 31 August but with "a minute harvest" wrapped up by 7 September. By all accounts it sounds as if the heat was excessive for the reds, notwithstanding the lack of means for regulating fermentation temperatures, except for dunking blocks of ice. "These are very rich, tannic wines, at times displaying too much oxidation," sniffed Louis Mortier, estate manager at Lafite Rothschild, though Professor George Saintsbury was smitten by this year's Latour and Rauzan-Ségla. The statistics from Yquem's records are astonishing: flowering on 5 May and *véraison* on 28 August. Picking commenced on 15 September as the berries had attained high levels of sugar and they soon reached maximum capacity in terms of pressing (75 barrels). It was a huge crop, 300 barrels at Gruaud Larose, the largest for many years. October showers botrytised the remaining crop in Sauternes with some reaching 30% potential alcohol. The wines were warmly received, perhaps in no small part because of the dearth of decent vintages in recent years, to the extent that, according to David Peppercorn, the 1893s were completely sold out by Christmas and had doubled in price within three years.

I have tasted three wines from this vintage; two reds and one sweet white. First, the very last bottle of 1893 Gruaud Larose, which proprietor Jean Merlaut graciously opened after finding not one but two out of condition. (I did not have the tenacity to cajole him into opening the bottle and left that to my French colleagues.) It was exquisite. Likewise was a dusty bottle of 1893 Montrose poured blind over dinner at the château. I was forced to drink parsimoniously since I was driving yet it was still so vivid and detailed. Served in 2019 at Hide restaurant in London following a memorable Pétrus dinner, the 1893 Yquem was extraordinarily vigorous and decadent, a Sauternes that defied the passing decades. I nailed the vintage blind. Don't ask me how.

Event
Peter Rabbit makes his debut

In September 1893, Beatrix Potter was writing a letter to Noel Carter Moore, the little son of her former governess. Running short of things to say, she made up a story involving "four little rabbits whose names were Flopsy, Mopsy, Cottontail and Peter". It was not until 1900 that she adapted the tale and another two years before *The Tale of Peter Rabbit* was published. It has sold over 45 million copies to date.

Music
The Liberty Bell
– John Philip Sousa

Sousa dominated popular music in the 1890s and released a series of marching band standards. *The Liberty Bell* was composed for his unfinished operetta *The Devil's Deputy* and became one of the most popular and recognisable marching songs. The Columbia Phonograph Company used Sousa's Marine Band in some of their first recordings, thereby making them among the world's first recorded celebrities. It is played at presidential inaugurations, though many will recognise it from the opening to *Monty Python's Flying Circus*. Sousa's marching songs are the fount of popular music with the likes of Scott Joplin adding syncopation to the composition to create ragtime.

Film
Blacksmithing Scene
– William K.L. Dickson

This 27-second, 35 mm print depicts three blacksmiths, in actual fact, staff at Thomas Edison's laboratory in New Jersey, bashing away around an anvil. It was shot using a Kinetograph in what might be considered the first purpose-built film studio, constructed so that natural sunlight could enter by adjusting panels in the roof. The studio was used up until 1918.

1893 *(Continued)*

2020

1894

This was a poor vintage. Vines had not really recovered from the previous year's torrid heat and were stunted in growth. A rain-plagued summer caused endemic coulure and there followed a late harvest that only began on 5 October. The season bestowed a small crop of irregular wines that were apparently thin and under-nourished. Louis Mortier, estate manager at Lafite-Rothschild, trashed the vintage as "green, thin wines with no defining characteristics". Down in Sauternes, vines also suffered some coulure and the harvest was delayed due to a lack of rainfall in September. The appellation produced a large crop that lacked botrytised fruit.

No Bordeaux wines from this vintage tasted.

Event
Coca-Cola bottled for the first time

Coca-Cola was bottled for the first time on 12 March 1894. For several years, the so-called "temperance drink", a non-addictive morphine substitute invented by pharmacist John Pemberton, had only been available from a soda fountain. Pemberton had sold the rights to Asa Griggs Candler for the princely sum of $2,300, but Candler doubted that bottling the beverage would be profitable, allowing storeowner Joseph A. Biedenharn of Vicksburg, Mississippi to become the first to capitalise. It was not until 1915 that the familiar contoured bottle was adopted and though I rarely drink it myself, in my mind, it *does* taste best from bottle.

Music
The Cat Came Back
– Charles Marsh

Tin Pan Alley songwriter Harry S. Miller wrote this children's song as a minstrel number in 1893 and Charles Marsh recorded the first version the following year for the Columbia Phonograph Company. The kitty manages to evade death despite its owners increasingly extravagant attempts. He finally drops dead when he meets an organ grinder, only to return in ghostly form.

Film
Falling Cat
– Étienne-Jules Marey

Having succeeded in creating
a camera that could take
12 shots per second, Marey set
about recording the movements
of different animals. The most
famous was a cat being dropped
in the Bois de Boulogne in Paris,
in order to see if it landed on its
feet. It did. It's a shame the film
was silent as it could have used
The Cat Came Back (opposite) on
its soundtrack.

1895

The 1895 vintage has parallels with the 2016 vintage insofar as it rained continuously before the weather turned on its heel. July and August were extremely hot with drought conditions between 18 August and 20 September. Harvest commenced on 19 September. Maurice Healy wrote that temperatures was so high that "the must lacked oxygen and refused to ferment," though Michael Broadbent posited that 1895 marked the first vintage in which winemakers learned how to handle sensitive fruit in a hot vintage and curtail volatile acidity. There is an interesting story about how Professor Ulysse Gayon, a friend of Louis Pasteur and director of the Bordeaux Station Agronomique et Oenologique, was residing at Lafite Rothschild at the time. Noticing that the temperature of some of the vats was getting too high, he urged Baron de Rothschild to cool them with ice ordered from Bordeaux city without putting it in bags. The technique was also employed at Mouton Rothschild and apparently saved both wines. Others, including Pontet-Canet, adopted the same remedial measures, according to Edmund Penning-Rowsell. But not all estates had the wherewithal to follow suit and Penning-Rowsell consequently found many 1895s "pricked" – turning vinegary in bottle. In Sauternes, winemakers were hampered by a lack of botrytis formation.

The only bottle I have drunk from this vintage is an 1895 Montrose that culminated a vertical in London. It was medicinal yet compelling, never oxidising one iota in the glass.

Event
The trial of Oscar Wilde

The flamboyant Anglo-Irish playwright had become a celebrity after the publication of *The Picture of Dorian Gray* and the premiere of *The Importance of Being Earnest*, renowned for his dapper attire and razor-sharp wit. When the Marquess of Queensbury denounced Oscar Wilde as a homosexual in response to his relationship with his son, Lord Alfred "Bosie" Douglas, Wilde sued for libel and the scandal rocked society. A verdict of not guilty was given. However, it triggered a second trial in which Wilde was accused of sodomy and gross indecency. The jury was unable to return a verdict, but a third trial found him guilty. Diminished and bankrupted by prison, he died five years later in a fleapit hotel, allegedly with the famous last words: "My wallpaper and I are fighting a duel to the death. One or the other of us has to go." Wilde might have been on his deathbed, but his wit was clearly not.

Music
Waltzing Matilda – Banjo Patterson and Christina Macpherson

It was while staying at a sheep and cattle station in Queensland that Australian poet Banjo Patterson penned the lyrics to Australia's most famous bush song, about a jolly swagman camping under a coolibah tree. Playing on a zither, Macpherson, one of the family members at the station, put Patterson's words to music based on *The Craigielee March. Waltzing Matilda* had its first public outing on April 1895 when it was played at the North Gregory Hotel during a banquet for the premier of Queensland.

Film
La Sortie de l'Usine de Lumière à Lyon – Louis Lumière

On 22 March 1895, around 200 people gathered in Paris for a screening of *La Sortie de l'Usine de Lumière à Lyon* (Workers Leaving the Lumière Factory in Lyon). Directed and produced by Louis Lumière, this 46-second, 800-frame, 35-mm film is considered to mark the birth of cinema and was shot on Louis and his brother Auguste's cinematograph device, which could record, process and project images all in one. Louis and Auguste patented the device, though some dispute their claim as inventors.

1896

Eighteen ninety-six was shaping up to be a fine vintage. Winter was fairly mild up until the end of March. There was a bit of frost, too early to do real any real damage, and flowering took place around 1 June. A warm spell from 15 June to 15 July followed by hot weather prompted Albert Fourcaud-Laussac at Cheval Blanc to compare it to the 1893 season in his diary records. He reported cold and wet conditions on the Right Bank on 7 and 8 August that provoked widespread oidium, then a violent thunderstorm on 8 September when large hailstones devastated parts of Saint-Émilion. Harvest began on 20 September, yet rain had ruined a potentially great vintage, André Simon remarking that it just never stopped. Picking at Cheval Blanc began on 23 September. "Terrible weather during the harvest," rues Fourcaud-Laussac. "The preceding week was so wet that the grapes were already rotten in the first days." His team picked through until 15 October. In Sauternes, the first passes through the vineyard in late September/early October provided some botrytised fruit but subsequent pickings were less consistent. Despite all this, the 1896s were seen as elegant wines on release and Édouard Féret notes some melioration in bottle.

The only bottle I have encountered was a rather decrepit 1896 Latour in London at Linden Wilkie's Fine Wine Experience vertical.

Event
The Olympics is reborn after 1,500 years

One-thousand five-hundred years after they were banned by Roman Emperor Theodosius I, the Olympic Games were reborn in Athens on 6 April 1896. Thirteen nations and 280 athletes competed in 43 events, with American James Connolly becoming the first Olympic champion in the modern era after winning the triple jump. No women were allowed to compete, though that oversight was addressed four years later. Despite 60,000 spectators watching the opening ceremony, the games struggled to gain support in their early years. It was not until the 1924 Paris Games that they found a sure footing.

Film
The Kiss
– William Heise

Audiences were titillated when William Heise filmed an 18-second re-enactment of the kiss between May Irwin and John Rice, two actors from the stage musical *Widow Jones*. The first on-screen kiss didn't go down well. "The life-size view, bestial enough in itself, was nothing compared to this," spat the reaction in literary magazine *The Chap-Book*. "Their unbridled kissing, magnified to gargantuan proportions and repeated thrice, is absolutely loathsome." Good job that writer is not around to see what is available on the Internet today.

Music
Sunrise (Also sprach Zarathustra)
– Richard Strauss

Inspired by Nietzsche's novel *Thus Spoke Zarathustra*, the composer premiered his most famous work in Frankfurt on 27 November 1896. The opening fanfare, *Sunrise*, is instantly recognisable for its use in the movie entry for 1968 (page 298), as well as during the television transmission of the Apollo space missions. Even Elvis Presley used it to open his concerts during the seventies.

1897

This was an extremely poor and "topsy-turvy" growing season. According to Féret, the winter was very mild and so the vines sprinted out of the blocks as soon as spring began. Strong maritime breezes badly affected the young shoots on 30 April, especially in the Bas-Médoc. Lafite Rothschild was hit by hailstones the size of chicken eggs on 27 April, according to château archives. Flowering from 6 to 15 June was prolonged and uneven with widespread coulure that particularly affected the Malbec and Merlot, then incessant downpours plagued July through to September. Black rot devastated much of the Médoc. Fourcaud-Laussac at Cheval Blanc remarks that it was more humid than wet with fog that lasted throughout the night and often into the daytime. The rot particularly affected the Malbec, which inexplicably managed to retain its freshness. It was a very early harvest from 3 September, but grapes were already rotting before they had ripened. At Cheval Blanc, picking began later on 14 September with 50 harvesters entering the vineyard under sunny conditions that Fourcaud-Laussac described as warmer than in August. Unfortunately, he also notes green, rotten and burnt berries in the same bunch, the must weight just 10.70%. Tastet-Lawton said the last vintage with such poor quality wines was 1866, while the Gilbeys at Château Loudenne spoke of "the complete failure of 1897." Unsurprisingly, much of the crop was declassified. Prices were just one-third of the previous year and one-sixth compared to seven years earlier. Sauternes' winemakers endured a challenging growing season and despite two weeks of sunny weather in October, yields were so low that at Yquem they picked just two barrels of wine per day.

I've had two experiences with this vintage. First, a magnum of 1897 Pétrus bottled by a local merchant, Georges Gerchy, prized from the cellars of a German castle. Though it had no documented provenance, after inspecting the bottle and cork and observing the wine's frailty and decrepitude, I could not find any reason to doubt its authenticity. The same year in Hong Kong, I drank an 1897 Latour with a scorched nose that was quite pliant and holding up well.

Event
The inaugural Boston marathon

Now one of the most famous marathons, Boston's maiden race took place on Patriots' Day, 19 April 1897. Crossing the line first out of 15 runners was John J. McDermott in 2:55:10, though the distance was then 24.5 miles (39.4 km) instead of the now requisite 26 miles and 385 yards (42.195 km). The first woman to complete the race was Roberta Gibb in 1966, though she hid in the bushes until the starting gun was fired since the Amateur Athletic Union did not accept women's long-distance running.

Music
Louisiana Rag
– Theodore H. Northrup

Louisiana Rag is one of the earliest ragtime compositions. It was released at the end of the year by the Thompson Music Company, which promoted Northrup as "the greatest living ragtime pianist". San Francisco-born Northrup had followed his mother's musical footsteps and even tried his hand at a couple of operas at the beginning of his career. In 1897 he released several prototype ragtime songs, including *Savannah Jubilee*, *A Night on the Levee* and *Louisiana Rag*.

Film
Leaving Jerusalem by Railway
– Alexandre Promio

This silent film, directed by Promio and released by the Lumière brothers, is a silent, 50-second reel of various ethnicities tipping their hats and waving goodbye as a train departs what looks like the outskirts of Jerusalem. It is significant as one of the first films to feature a moving camera shot.

1898

This was set up to be a promising growing season. Here was another in a succession of mild winters, though a fresh April put the brakes on those swelling buds and a cold May retarded growth, plus it became wetter, making it difficult to spray the vines according to Féret. Consequently, there was a late flowering, between 12 and 21 June, under good conditions. Soon after, vines suffered the twin evils of black rot and cochylis, but strong heat through July and August stymied their spread and pushed ripening on. According to Fourcaud-Laussac at Cheval Blanc, it was extremely dry with not a drop of rain from June and the drought-like conditions prevailed all the way to harvest to the extent that local wells began to dry up. In some ways, it mirrors recent Bordeaux growing seasons. The harvest commenced on 23 September, four days later at Cheval Blanc. Welcome rain on the first days helped gorge some of the berries that must have shrivelled. Fourcaud-Laussac notes that later-picked lots were superior to the first ones as the water began rejuvenating the vines. The wines were supposedly hard in their youth, requiring time to soften, though they appear to have been well received with many merchants placing their orders in October. Sauternes winemakers had to wait until showers between 11 and 20 October manifested botrytis and picking did not commence until 24 October, the latest ever recorded, yet it was too late to concentrate the berries.

No Bordeaux wines from this vintage tasted.

Event
The War of the Worlds is
published

Having been serialised in
magazines the previous year,
H.G. Wells's *The War of the Worlds*
was published for the first time
in 1898 and has never been
out of print. Martians invade
Earth – or more accurately, leafy
Surrey, since the author lived in
Woking. Perhaps Wells enjoyed
laying the nearby towns to waste?
War of the Worlds portends sci-fi
literature and inspired several
films, including Steven Spielberg's
commendable adaptation.

Music
When You Were Sweet Sixteen
– James Thornton

This vaudeville hit was inspired
by Thornton's wife Bonnie when
she asked whether he was still
in love with her, to which he
replied, "I love you like I did
when you were sweet sixteen".
The sheet music sold over one
million copies and went on to
be covered by Al Jolson, The Ink
Spots and Barry Manilow.

Film
Laughter and Tears
– Jan Kříženecký

Kříženecký was a Czech pioneer
of film who, upon seeing the
Lumière brothers' cinematograph
in Prague, bought his own and
began making documentary
films. This one features a
close-up of actor Josef Šváb-
Malostranský's face.

1899

The century finished with a great vintage. Winter dragged on into March with temperatures dipping to -9°C (15°F) at the end of the month, damaging vines more advanced in growth – the Graves was particularly hit hard. Heavy frost in Sauternes inflicted acute damage, with -6.3°C (20.6°F) recorded at Yquem. Flowering between 1 and 15 June was unproblematic, though there were skirmishes with mildew a few days later. Thereafter, the summer was hot according to Tastet-Lawton, peaking at 38°C (100°F) on 4 August, while dry conditions inhibited spread of disease. Fourcaud-Laussac remarks in his private notebook that he had never seen the bunches looking more beautiful or nourished. A breeze caused some hydric stress among the more particularly exposed vines, though to a lesser extent than the previous year. A splash of rain during picking from 11 September to 15 October did little harm as potential alcohol levels reached 13% to 14%. The raft of outstanding wines demonstrated finesse in their youth. Harvest in Sauternes commenced around the end of September after widespread botrytis and two passes through the vineyard at Yquem yielded a bevy of rich and concentrated berries.

I have been fascinated by this vintage since I sat in Christies' auction room to bid on an ex-château 1899 Latour on behalf of a wealthy Japanese businessman. I cannot recall the price as the gavel came down, but it was certainly more than I could ever afford. Subsequently, the only two wines I have tasted are a stunning bottle of 1899 Lynch-Bages that culminated a bibulous evening dinner at Saint-Julien restaurant in Saint-Julien; vague recollections of proprietor Jean-Charles Cazes materialising around midnight as if he were part-and-parcel of this ancient bottle. Was it real – the bottle, I mean, not Jean-Charles? I like to think so. It was the first 19th-century bottle I had ever encountered so I had little context at the time. The other was a fabulous half-bottle of 1899 Suduiraut that finished a vertical in London, evidence that quality was not the preserve of the dry reds. Needless to say, 1899s are extremely uncommon.

Event
Start of the Second Boer War

The Second Boer War between Great Britain and the South African Republic/Orange Free State broke out on 11 October, predominantly driven by Britain's desire to retain control of the lucrative gold mines. Although the Boers were outnumbered, their guerrilla tactics and the difficult terrain meant the fighting dragged on for almost three years. It was a war between two races of white people within a largely black population.

Film
L'Angélus
– Alice Guy

Nothing to do with the Saint-Émilion estate, *L'Angélus* depicts a farmer and his wife praying while bells ring out. Guy was just 26 years old. After applying for a position as director Léon Gaumont's secretary, she made her mark in the male-dominated industry by essentially talking her way into making short silent movies.

Music
Nimrod (Enigma Variations)
– Edward Elgar

Elgar's most famous work, the *Enigma Variations*, was premiered at St. James's Hall in London on 19 June 1899. Wielding the baton was renowned Hungarian conductor János Richter, then leading Manchester's Hallé Orchestra. The piece was inspired by an exchange with Elgar's wife, Alice. After returning home from teaching violin, he began to improvise on piano and charmed by the melody, Mrs. Elgar asked how some of his friends might play it. Inspired by this idea, the composer dedicated each variation to 14 people – and a bulldog called Dan. The ninth variation, *Nimrod*, is the best-known, dedicated to his friend A.J. Jaeger who had supported Elgar when his reputation was flagging.

The

1900s

Given back-to-back fêted vintages in 1899 and 1900, you might presume that *fin de siècle* winemakers were in an optimistic frame of mind as the new century dawned. With vineyards being replanted with American rootstock, albeit at a slow pace, Bordeaux was incrementally safeguarding its future, which had looked perilous a couple of decades earlier. But replanting resulted in a significant reduction of vineyard land. Between 1880 and 1900 some 15% of land under vine was lost, though this was less dramatic than in other French wine regions, with some losing two-thirds under vine. Consequently, yields dropped sharply, partly due to challenging growing seasons but also because large swathes were out of production.

A considerable amount of vines remained on un-grafted rootstock, or *franc de pied*. Albert Fourcaud-Laussac, proprietor of Cheval Blanc, kept a harvest diary during this period in which he provides insight into his re-planting of the vineyard, each vintage assessing the performance of American vis-à-vis French stock and noting how each reacted under different climactic conditions. He continued planting vines on their own roots up until 1904; from then on new plantings were exclusively regrafted onto American rootstock. At Château Latour, American rootstock was only introduced in 1901. The estate delayed the inevitable not only because it feared replanting would damage its reputation, but because Bordeaux merchants coerced it and other esteemed producers to resist the practice in order to protect their most lucrative sources. Rauzan-Ségla vineyard manager Charles Skawinski provides more clarity on the composition in 1900. That year 64% of Rauzan-Ségla's wine came from un-grafted vines on their original roots, with only 20.1% of vines re-grafted onto phylloxera-resistant American rootstock up to that point. The remaining vines were in poor condition and half were missing wooden stakes. Four years later Skawinski broke down the composition of grape varieties planted: exactly 58.6% comprised Cabernet Sauvignon and Gros Cabernet (Cabernet Franc crossed with an indigenous Basque variety to create Hondarribi Beltza, then crossed with Fer); 6.6% were Petit Verdot (a figure higher than you might presume); 1.2% were Malbec and a paltry 0.8% were Merlot. The remainder was called a *vieux mélange française*, or in other words, a gallimaufry of other French grape varieties.

Many Bordeaux châteaux were put up for sale during the decade. They were not only unprofitable but constituted a drain on money – money that proprietors did not have. A majority remained unsold until their price was discounted. For example, in 1900, Malescot Saint-Exupery in Margaux was put on the market for 400,000 francs, having been acquired for 1 million francs in 1869. The final selling price in 1901 was a derisory 155,000 francs. It was a far cry from the halcyon days of the 1860s and 1870s when châteaux had suitors at their beck and call. Concurrent was a malaise in consumption. The English market was flatlining due to stagnating wages, while demand in France also declined, partly for the same reasons as in Britain and partly because a cadre of doctors had publicly denounced wine as bad for your health. Exports to the United States were small, averaging just 11,400 hl. The bottom line was that Bordeaux was producing excess quantities of wine, which might have been less problematic if quality had been good.

As more and more consumers learned how French wines were being cut with foreign juice, prices tumbled. This hit workers' wages. Unrest in the Midi saw mass protests and violent demonstrations and these spread to Bordeaux, where in 1906, coopers laid down their hammers and went on strike. The prospect of having no vessels for ageing wine available forced the *gendarme* to intervene on 28 August in Saint-Macaire to get some barrels released. On 23 June the following year, around 4,000 workers gathered to demonstrate in Lesparre despite demonstrations being forbidden by authorities. It ultimately led to a governmental decree on 3 September 1907 specifying that wine had to come from fermented grapes in France, and nowhere else.

Mother Nature certainly gave Foureaud-Laussac and his fellow *vignerons* a succession of challenging seasons throughout the first decade of the 20th century. Apart from in 1904, winemakers must have spent numerous sleepless nights worrying about the unpredictable weather and the dire state of the market. Examining the Tastet-Lawton archives, there was tremendous meteorological turbulence. Storms swept across the region, deluging vineyards at inopportune moments, with mildew and/or oidium following in its wake. Throw in the occasional hailstorm and this decade posed numerous challenges for even the most skilled winemaker.

Many tried to meliorate their pallid wines by chaptalisation, adding sugar to the must. Its moderate use is part of winemaking and continues to this day, but back then, it became so excessive that the French government introduced a tax on sugar, one of the grievances that led to the aforementioned workers' demonstrations. More stringent rules were necessary to control what winemakers could and could not do, though these would only be administered the following decade. At least one appellation started to move in the right direction when Louis Nicolas, proprietor of La Conseillante, co-founded and became the first serving president of the Syndicat Viticole de Pomerol on 10 June 1900. Another change this decade that would have significant ramifications in the future was the migration of families from the region of Corrèze, such as the Moueix and the Janoueix. Many wines from this decade were consumed in their youth and are now as rare as hens' teeth. If they do appear, even with perfect provenance, drinking windows are likely to be in the rear-view mirror. The one bright light, virtually forgotten by the passage of time, is that this was a fine decade for Sauternes. Vintages dismissed because of the poor quality in the Médoc were actually benevolent for the sweet wines of Bordeaux. The growing seasons of 1900, 1901, 1904, 1906 and 1908 were all very respectable in Sauternes:

Bottling at Château Yquem at the turn of the century, back in those times, a time-consuming, manual task.

1900

The century kicked off with a textbook growing season and a raft of exceptional Bordeaux wines that would enter folklore. Just like in 2000, merchants must have hoped for a growing season worthy of such numerical significance and Mother Nature delivered.

According to Édouard Féret, there was a cold spell from 1 to 15 March that retarded vine growth. Clement weather conditions commenced from 15 April when the temperature reached 27°C (80°F) and by the end of that month, the Tastet-Lawton archives report that vines already looked "magnificent". Flowering from 6 to 15 June passed quickly and evenly without much coulure, portending the most bountiful crop since 1893. July was hot with temperatures regularly reaching 35°C (95°F) to 37°C (99°F) and there was a further hot spell from 15 to 25 August. On 22 August, Théophile Skawinski, *régisseur* at Léoville-Las Cases, prayed for rain to engorge berries and his prayers were answered with four days of much-needed showers between 26 and 29 August before heat returned on 30 August. At Cheval Blanc, Fourcaud-Laussac notes how the drought particularly affected the Cabernet Sauvignon and, interestingly, how the vines un-grafted on to American rootstock were also less affected. The harvest commenced the days after a storm had crossed the region on 19 September and ramped up in earnest around five days later. Pickers on the Left Bank enjoyed ideal conditions until their cutters were sheathed around 12 to 14 October. Fourcaud-Laussac remarks in his diary that there was only a spot of rain on one day throughout picking at Cheval Blanc. It was obviously going to be a bountiful crop but during harvest, the sentiment was that 1900s would bestow light wines and this generally turned out to be the case, prompting Ian Maxwell Campbell to describe them as "soft and gentle, almost too much to age well". It was proof that lighter wines can age over the long term. Volumes were so large that just like in 1982, some estates did not have sufficient vats to accommodate incoming fruit. I suspect that there was more concentration on the Right Bank – at Cheval Blanc must weights came in at a very reasonable 12.2%. Sauternes enjoyed a bountiful crop of botrytised fruit. Yquem experienced 26 consecutive days of picking and average yields exceeded 20 hl/ha. But it would be wrong to think that Edwardian connoisseurs loaded up on 1900s. They had spent their shillings on the well-received 1899s and perversely, weak demand compelled châteaux to reduce their prices. (Some wag will aver that this was the last time that happened… not I!) One example is Mouton Rothschild, whose 1900 was sold for £7 per hogshead compared to £22 for the 1899. Generally, prices were all around one-third of the previous year. That's some dive.

André Simon describes it as the one outstanding vintage of the first 10 years of the century and, against expectations, yielded wines structured in their youth. I have a handful of cherished first-hand experiences at vertical tastings in Bordeaux that include 1900 Montrose, Rauzan-Ségla, Gruaud Larose and Batailley. They were all monumental in their own time-buckling way, each one endowed with density and fruit concentration. One particularly memorable bottle was a 1900 Deuxième Vin de Château Margaux poured at a munificent friend's 40th birthday in London – in fact, the same friend who had cracked open the 1870 Lafite Rothschild. Pre-dating its renaming as "Pavillon Rouge", it was endowed with dazzling density, structure and longevity. God only know what the legendary Grand Vin must taste like. The best of all my experiences is a compelling 1900 Latour that was firing on all cylinders at 119 years of age. The only example from Sauternes was a 1900 Suduiraut that evidences a great vintage for Bordeaux's sweet wines.

Event
Sigmund Freud publishes
The Interpretation of Dreams

The founder of psychoanalysis actually published his most influential book, known in German as *Die Traumdeutung*, at the end of 1899 though it was dated 1900. Just 600 copies were printed but they took eight years to sell. According to Freud, dream analysis leads to better understanding of the unconscious activities of the mind. It's a good job he was never privy to my dreams, which often feature 1900 Château Margaux in large formats.

Film
Grandma's Reading Glass
– George Albert Smith

This 80-second silent film features a young boy using a large magnifying glass to study objects such as a watch and his grandmother's eye. It was one of the first to deploy cuts between medium shot and close-up. The original was destroyed in a fire in 1912 but a print was discovered in Denmark in 1960, which led to a dispute about whether the film is British or Danish.

1900
(Continued)

Music
Finlandia
– Jean Sibelius

Written the previous year, Sibelius premiered his tone poem *Finlandia* on 2 July 1900 in Helsinki. Sibelius's dig at the Russian Empire's draconian censorship meant that it had to be performed under alternative names in order to avoid the very subject it protested about. Its rousing scores evoke not only the majesty of the Finnish landscape, but also the struggle of its people and national identity. Words were later written for its hymnal finish. Sibelius retired at 59 because he was certain that he could never surpass his Seventh Symphony.

Nineteen hundred and one had the unenviable task of following two excellent vintages. Winter and spring were humid and following a stuttering start to the vines' growth cycle, shoot growth was rapid, as if trying to make up for lost time. On 17 May, there was a five-minute hailstorm that wrought widespread damage in Saint-Émilion. The summer was hot, up to 36°C (97°F) with frequent thunderstorms and hail causing widespread mildew from 23 June to the end of July, a month that also saw invasions of crickets and red-winged grasshoppers, though these were more severe in the Palus, the marshy ground close to the river. Fourcaud-Laussac wrote in his diary that the weather was abominable. The berries at Cheval Blanc already showed signs of rot without ripeness in the first days of September because of the humid conditions. There was also widespread eudemis botrana, commonly known as grape moth, whose caterpillars love nothing better than munching away the pulp of grape berries that have become gorged by moisture. A bumper crop harvested from 15 September was woefully uneven in quality, many purportedly thin, flavourless and anaemic. The weather remained poor, with Fourcaud-Laussac picking over 23 days, of which only two were clement. The Cabernet Franc was so blighted by rot that nary a bunch was picked. In Sauternes, the first pickings in mid-September offered plenty of sugar-rich fruit and after rain, there were around two weeks of harvest to create what Yquem felt was a "beautifully rich vintage" and a summer it describes as "quasi-tropical". Because of the reputation of the reds and its overshadowing by 1900, 1901 seems totally forgotten as a fecund vintage of sweet wines.

No Bordeaux wines from this vintage tasted.

Music
Piano Concerto No. 2
– Sergei Rachmaninoff

While Rachmaninoff's first concerto met tepid reviews that precipitated his long depression, his second was well received and it went on to become one of his most popular pieces. He dedicated it to physician Nikolai Dahl who had helped him recover from depression.

Film
Drama at the Bottom of the Sea
– Ferdinand Zecca

This rather morose minute-long silent film features dead bodies floating among a shipwreck where two divers find sunken treasure. The nice thing to do would have been to share the bounty. But in this drama, one diver kills the other with an axe. The end.

1901
(Continued)

2020

Event
Queen Victoria dies aged 81

The monarch's reign had lasted 63 years and as such, despite age and waning health, the nation received her passing incredulously when at 6.30 a.m. on 22 January, Superintendent Fraser pinned a notice on the bulletin board outside the entrance of Osborne House to announce that she had "breathed her last". She had been surrounded by family and her beloved Pomeranian, Turi. Four year earlier, Victoria had had the foresight to write down her wishes for the service and ceremony, instructing that there would be no lying in state and despite having worn mourning black after her husband's death, she would be buried in a white gown and wedding veil. So much time had passed since the previous royal funeral that factions of the royal household and government bickered about the details. In the end, on 2 February, Londoners lined the route from Victoria to Paddington station to obtain their final glimpse of their queen, and of an era.

Reading Féret and other coeval wine literature, 1902 was apparently blemished by a cold and wet summer. On the other hand, the Tastet-Lawton archives suggest intermittent spells of torridly hot weather, which is supported by Fourcaud-Laussac at Cheval Blanc who noted that three or four hot days at the beginning of July led to scalding of berries. Looking at the overall picture, there was a lack of sunshine and the nights were fresh with regular storms that caused outbreaks of rot and retarded vine growth. Fruit struggled to reach maturity as it remained cool throughout harvest in September and October – many estates sent their pickers out prematurely as they feared a repeat of the previous year's disaster. Consequently, the musts of Cabernet Sauvignon only reached around 9% potential alcohol. Tastet-Lawton notes that pickers started around 23 September while at Cheval Blanc they began the following day. Unfortunately, Fourcaud-Laussac's usual team from Périgord failed to turn up and so he had to conduct the entire crop with an in-house team of workers plus a few helpful neighbours. He found the weather during harvest more benevolent with just a few rainy days, including a particularly soggy day on 7 October that caused some rot. The harvest was large but as early as November that year, the 1902 vintage was seen as mediocre with green, under-ripe fruit. Down in Sauternes, they were gifted the rain to cause botrytis in early October but due to the cold temperatures, the berries could never achieve concentration.

Lawton makes an amusing comment about this vintage, opining that the 1902s were "too small and too cold" for oenophiles in Holland and Belgium, but "ought to please the Germans". A 1902 Lafite Rothschild is the only example I have tasted from this year – an outlier vintage at the First Growth's vertical to celebrate 150 years of Rothschild ownership. Given the growing season, it was better than expected, though frail. Unless perfect provenance is guaranteed, bottles will be long past their mortal coil.

1902

1870

Event
Mount Pelée erupts in Martinique

The eruption of Mount Pelée was the worst volcanic disaster of the 20th century. Almost 30,000 lost their lives within minutes as the town of Saint-Pierre lay in the direct path of the blast flow. The volcano is still active today.

2020

1902
(Continued)

Music
The Entertainer
– Scott Joplin

The son of a Texan slave who became the "King of Ragtime", Scott Joplin composed this famous piano rag in 1902, registering the copyright on 29 December, along with two other compositions. Ragtime, like many musical genres of the time, had emerged from bars and bordellos in cities' tenderloin districts, where whites and blacks mixed freely. It laid a cornerstone of 20th century music with its use of syncopation – adding an irregular beat that made it swing, made it uplifting, made you want to dance. Listen to *The Entertainer* now and it still lifts your spirit. One of modern music's first great casualties, Joplin died in 1917 in a mental institution at the age of just 48 and was buried in a pauper's grave. Yet his legacy lives on and he achieved posthumous fame after the song featured in 1973's *The Sting*, with Marvin Hamlisch's Academy Award-winning adaptation of *The Entertainer* becoming a Billboard hit.

Film
Voyage to the Moon
– Georges Méliès

Georges Méliès was one of the first directors to understand the creative possibilities of cinema and incorporated fantasy and comic burlesque into over 500 films. He introduced special effects, jump cuts, double exposures, stop-motion photography and fade-ins/fade-outs, even hand-colouring some of the frames. His most famous film is *Voyage to the Moon,* and the rocket sticking out of the eye of Méliès' anthropomorphic moon remains the iconic image of what many consider the first science-fiction film. Its editing, stylised theatricality and creativity were all hugely influential. If only the actual moon landing in 1969 had featured insect aliens chasing astronauts back to their spaceship. Sadly, Méliès' business folded in 1913. Four years later, his studio was requisitioned by the French army and his films melted down to make shoe heels. He died poverty-stricken in 1938.

This is yet another vintage that must have prompted winemakers to consider alternative vocations – anything less stressful than growing grapes. Mid-April saw frost episodes and sub-zero temperatures. Haut-Brion's *régisseur* estimated that three-quarters of the crop was lost when temperatures fell to -4°C (25°F), while Fourcaud-Laussac writes in his notebook that his vines were "heavily frozen" on 23 and 24 April. Inclement weather spoiled flowering that only got going upon the arrival of warmer temperatures on 23 June. July was hot, then a hailstorm on 17 July devastated large swathes of the Médoc with a cyclone at Brane-Cantenac felling the largest trees in its park. "*Nous sommes anéantis*" ("We are wiped out") is the dramatic post-storm conclusion in the Tastet-Lawton archives. August was overcast and beset with stormy weather. Fourcaud-Laussac found the summer humid when it rained two out of every five days, the mercury breaching 30°C (86°F) on only two or three days that month. Harvest began on 28 September and sunny and warm conditions nudged must weights upwards to 11–12%, a Pyrrhic victory since the resulting wines were poor and irregular. At Cheval Blanc, one-third of the crop was lost to grape moths and obliged a long and laborious sorting, a practice uncommon at the time. Sauternes suffered a topsy-turvy season with wildly erratic weather and much like the previous year, while rain encouraged botrytis, the fruit lacked concentration.

No Bordeaux wines from this vintage tasted.

Music
Hiawatha (His Song to Minnehaha) – Neil Moret and James O'Dea

Though written two years earlier, James O'Dea added lyrics to *Hiawatha* in 1903, along with the subtitle *His Song to Minnehaha*. It is based on Henry Longfellow's epic poem of 1855 and is one of the best-known of the Native American-themed love songs that were in vogue at the time, with the sheet music selling 500,000 copies.

Film
The Great Train Robbery – Edwin S. Porter

Despite not being critically revered, Porter's *The Great Train Robbery* was an unprecedented success and while not the first Western per se, it might be considered the first action blockbuster. Not averse from depicting violence, it ends with a grim-faced cowboy breaking the fourth wall and shooting directly at the audience, which must have made a few jump out of their seat.

1903

Event
The Wright brothers take
to the sky

On 17 December 1903, Orville
and Wilber Wright tossed a coin
at Kitty Hawk in North Carolina
to decide who would make the
first air-powered flight. It had
taken four years of research
during which they tested three
gliders. The first flight of *The
Wright Flyer* biplane, powered by
a 12-horsepower four-cylinder
engine, lasted 12 seconds,
travelling a distance of around
36 m (118 ft). They made four
flights in total, the longest lasting
just under a minute. They did not
earn any air miles.

The 1904 vintage may well be the best between 1900 and 1920 even if the dearth of decent growing seasons damns it with faint praise. It did not begin well. Rainy squalls in mid-February led to flooding and families had to be rehoused in barracks. The growth cycle began on 20 March encouraged by springtime warmth and while April saw a couple of rainy spells, May was benign. After a delayed start, flowering finally kicked off when temperatures reached 30°C (86°F) on 7 June. Up until the end of that month, the region was beset by rather wet conditions that caused outbreaks of mildew. But the weather turned better from the end of July and it remained warm and sunny, the mercury hovering in the low thirties throughout the entire summer. At Cheval Blanc, Fourcaud-Laussac notes even more tropical conditions, between 35°C (95°F) and 37°C (99°F) from 20 to 30 July, though cool night-time temperatures between 16°C (61°F) and 18°C (64°F) gave the vines some respite. The harvest generally began around 19 September. Fourcaud-Laussac posits that wide diurnal variations in temperature led to incomplete maturity in some bunches and notes two or three days of rain and fog during the picking. Thankfully there was no cochylis. Instead there was widespread eudemis botrana or grape worm that affected the Merlot, costing him around one-quarter of the harvest. Tasting in October, Daniel Lawton was impressed by the colour and aromatics. Even though alcohol levels were a respectable 12.5%, he hoped for a little more phenolic maturity. Quantities were higher than in previous years, which was good news for merchants who needed to refill their coffers. Growers in Sauternes enjoyed a benevolent warm summer with light September showers provoking botrytis. Further showers and dry spells allowed them to create rich Sauternes that, like those of 1901, have largely been forgotten since they so rarely appear.

According to André Simon, the 1904s were "light and firm" upon release and most failed to age gracefully. Féret was more enthusiastic, especially in early editions of the guide where the vintage was compared to 1899 and 1900. To date, the only examples I have tasted are 1904 Batailley and 1904 Langoa Barton. One cannot draw conclusions from a single pair of wines, yet they contradict Simon inasmuch as they both drank beautifully, full of stuffing after more than a century. Bottles with impeccable provenance may still give pleasure, although they are rarely seen.

1904

1904
(Continued)

Event
Japan and Russia go to war

The one-and-a-half-year Russo-Japanese War marked the first time that an east Asian country defeated a Western power. Under Tsar Nicolas II, Russia had pursued an expansionist policy and on 8 February 1904, fearing that Russia might impede upon its territory, the Japanese army attacked Port Arthur without a declaration of war. US President Theodore Roosevelt brokered a treaty the following year with Japan's status as a military power enhanced, sowing the seeds for the attack on Pearl Harbor 37 years later.

Music
Madame Butterfly
– Giacomo Puccini

Madame Butterfly was premiered at La Scala on 17 February 1904 but reception was poor since Puccini had completed writing his opera late, leaving little time for rehearsals. He split the opera into three acts instead of two and this seemed to do the trick. Despite ensuing success, he did not stop tweaking the work and the most commonly performed version is the one written three years later.

Film
Bullet Piercing a Soap Bubble
– Lucien Bull

Bull grew up in Dublin but moved to France in adulthood. He was a pioneer of chronophotography and this short one-minute film does what it says on the tin, using a new technique called "slow-motion".

After a prolonged but relatively dry winter, a delayed but even flowering meant a large crop was on the cards. A period of hot weather in June extended into the next month, but a series of storms was followed by a rapid and devastating outbreak of coulure. Summer saw high temperatures up to 35°C (95°F) interspersed with regular storms, though from 25 July, Fourcaud-Laussac at Cheval-Blanc reported the first sighting of dreaded grape worm, though not to the extent of previous years. Temperatures cooled towards the end of the month and it remained dry until 20 August when two days of torrential rain in Saint-Émilion revived the vines and restarted ripening. On the negative side, the berries began to expand as roots soaked up the water. The weather remained "menacing" throughout harvest, to use Lawton's vernacular, with the bulk of the picking taking place from 22 September. Some musts reached 12–12.5% potential alcohol but many struggled to reach 10–11%. By October, it was clear that this would be a large volume of wine. Despite optimism that they might surpass the previous vintage, the 1905s were ultimately deemed a bit feeble and dilute, some exhibiting greenness. Sauternes fared little better and a September deluge diluted and damaged the fruit. Many had low alcohol levels.

The only Bordeaux I have tasted is the 1905 Lafite Rothschild at the Rothschild family's dinner celebrating 150 years of ownership. In accordance with the general reputation of the vintage, it came across as frail, yet just about drinkable.

Music
Clair de Lune
– Claude Debussy

Impressionist French composer Claude Debussy had begun his four-movement *Suite Bergamasque* 15 years earlier when he was 28 years old. Its famous third segment takes its name from a poem by Paul Verlaine, which depicts the soul as somewhere where birds sing by the light of the moon. The romantic piece is apparently easy to play, around grade six, so the challenge is to play it well.

Film
The Life of Charles Peace
– William Haggar

Like *The Great Train Robbery*, *The Life of Charles Peace* was a comparatively long single-reel film for its time – 11 minutes. It comprises 10 scenes that follow the titular Victorian thief as he graduates from burglary to murder and ultimately his execution at the gallows. The film was key in helping popularise cinema in the UK.

1905
(Continued)

Event
Einstein publishes his theory of
special relativity

Einstein's dictum that nothing
could travel faster than the speed
of light was the pretext for
10 years of nigh-obsessive
research to find out how gravity
worked. "I am exhausted. But the
success is glorious," he announced
after completing his general
theory of relativity in 1915.
During my research for this book,
I began reading Einstein's theory
and after the first page concluded
that a "B" in Physics O-Level was
not enough to understand what
he was going on about.

1906

After frost episodes early in the season, inclement weather led to a prolonged and uneven flowering. Tastet-Lawton's archives confirm a warm growing season when temperatures peaked at 36–37°C (97–99°F), but the main feature of the 1906 vintage was the lack of rainfall. At Cheval Blanc, Fourcaud-Laussac reports in his diary that it hardly rained between 1 May and 5 October and that he had never witnessed such "*sécheresse*" or dryness. Lawton noted a similar period with respect to the Left Bank, something to consider when contemporary winemakers talk of *unprecedented* drought-like conditions. Not only were vines affected, but the drought also wiped out the crop of vegetable and fruit, creating a far more pressing problem for families who relied on the land. Fourcaud-Laussac notes that grape worm was endemic, particularly in Saint-Émilion and in the Graves. That was not the only challenge. Harvest commenced on 17 September and glucometer readings measured up to 14% potential alcohol due to the hot summer. Yet as early as November, they found that the musts were soft and exhibited unpleasant harshness. Clearly, the stressed vines had shut down due to the drought and denuded the wines of phenolic ripeness. The problem was compounded by the fact that vast tracts of Bordeaux were now populated by younger vines that struggle in dry conditions. Some commentators such as David Peppercorn described them as "beefy" in style in their youth, suggesting high levels of brettanomyces, while Maurice Healy found they exhibited a "burnt taste", like the flavour of crème brûlée. (Healy also found this trait in the 1921s and 1926s.) According to Haut-Brion records, the wines took 25 years to come round and one Hew Brown, a companion of Healy, described one as "a first class Claret with a dollop of first-class Port in it". Sauternes is an entirely different matter – this is a marvellous vintage for Bordeaux's sweet wines, at least for those that escaped a devastating frost on 25 March. Despite the dry conditions, there was widespread botrytis, which created small quantities of exceptionally rich Sauternes.

Maurice Healy averred that the only decent 1906 was Château Margaux, though alas, I have never encountered a 1906 red. But two Sauternes confirm that it was a phenomenal vintage for its botrytised wines. First was an exquisite and decadent 1906 Lafaurie-Peyraguey tasted at a vertical in December 2018 at the château with proprietor Silvio Denz. Second was a 1906 Château d'Arche Crème de Tête that followed a Madeira tasting in London. Perturbingly deep in colour, it yet revealed astonishing freshness and concentration.

1906
(Continued)

Event
The San Francisco earthquake

At 5.12 a.m. on 18 April 1906, an estimated 7.9-magnitude earthquake struck San Francisco, caused by the slipping of a 270 mile (435 km) long section of the San Andreas Fault. The tremors destroyed over 80% of the city, much of it set ablaze after the rupture of gas mains that swept from the business area to Chinatown and North Beach, eviscerating 500 blocks and 28,000 buildings. Over 3,000 people lost their lives and 250,000 lost their homes, with camps of the dispossessed building up in Golden Gate Park.

Film
The Story of the Kelly Gang
– Charles Tait

At over an hour long, Tait's film could claim to be the world's first full-length feature. Shot around Melbourne, it was released in Australia on Boxing Day in 1906. The reel length was around 1,200 m (3,900 ft), but most of it was damaged in storage and, as a consequence, only around 15 minutes remain today.

Music
You're a Grand Old Flag
– Billy Murray

Written for stage musical *George Washington, Jnr*, *You're a Grand Old Flag* is an American patriotic march. It became the first song to sell over one million copies of sheet music. There are many subsequent versions, some appearing under the title *The Grand Old Rag*.

After a relatively mild winter, 1907 was a very difficult season beset with constant low depressions in the early months. Hail devastated Saint-Julien on 15 May. Storms continued through June, causing an uneven flowering, and into the summer, the combination of rain and warm temperatures extinguishing flickers of optimism as mildew and oidium spread from early August. Fourcaud-Laussac at Cheval Blanc writes in his notebook that the rain/rot plus infestations of grape worm "wreaked havoc" among the vines and denied what on paper could have been a bumper crop. September saw better weather, dry and sunny, but it was too little too late. The harvest really got going on 28 September but the musts struggled to reach 11% potential alcohol, Latour scraping 10.7% alcohol for its bottled wine. At Cheval Blanc, the picking started on 30 September and dragged on to 20 October under what Fourcaud-Laussac described as "torrential rain", except on 5 October. He praises his hard-working *Salardais vendangeurs* who struggled on, but it was so wet that he found it virtually impossible to sort the fruit entering the winery. Wines were light in colour, rather green and feeble – Ian Maxwell Campbell described them as "plain and rather vacant". The Sauternais fared little better due to 35 days of continuous rain. The valiant team at Yquem made 17 attempts to pick over a three-week period, eking out just a tiny crop, mainly from over-ripe grapes at the end of September.

I have not encountered any dry red Bordeaux from this vintage and they are most likely to be long past their best. Sauternes faired more favourably and a 1907 Lafaurie-Peyraguey at its December 2018 vertical was singing.

Film
The Haunted Hotel
– J. Stuart Blackton

The Haunted Hotel is one of the earliest movies to feature animation intermixed with live-action comedy. It is quite effective, especially the stop-motion sequence of the guest's breakfast, which prefigures films such as *Jason and the Argonauts* and Wes Anderson's *Isle of Dogs*.

1870

2020

1907
(Continued)

Event
Sir Robert Baden-Powell
forms the Boy Scouts

On 1 August 1907 Baden-Powell took 20 boys, 10 from the Boys' Brigade in Poole and 10 from public school, to Brownsea Island for an eight-day camping trip. Having used boys to help troops during the Boer War, his idea was to teach them some of the skills they had utilised – tracking, cooking, lighting fires and so forth. Scouting was born. (This author was a recipient of the Chief Scout's Award almost 80 years later and can still tie a bowline.)

Music
Frog Legs Rag
– James Scott

James Scott was a Missouri-born music plugger for the Dumas Music Company and a piano prodigy born with perfect pitch. In 1905 he travelled to St. Louis to play his idol Scott Joplin his composition *Frog Legs Rag*. The sheet music was published by John Stark in December 1906 and became a bestseller, second only to Joplin's own *Maple Leaf Rag*, throughout 1907. Scott went on to publish 24 rags over the next 16 years. Listen to this and you can imagine yourself sat in some smoky saloon bar in some southern state of America.

Weather-wise, the 1908 vintage got off to a sluggish start, which retarded the growth cycle. The vines did not really begin budding until early May when producers realised that frost on 22 and 24 April had killed some of the nascent buds. At Cheval Blanc, Fourcaud-Laussac notes in his diary that this frost seemed to affect those vines on their original French rootstocks more than those re-grafted onto American. Flowering coincided with some storms and cochylis was widespread, with oidium and mildew hot on its heels by mid-June. Add to the mix the appearance of *altise*, otherwise known as flea beetle, and you understand that vineyard managers had a lot to contend with. As Fourcaud-Laussac notes in his diary, the winter had been extremely mild, a phenomenon more associated with recent years and climate change that means bugs are not killed off and flourish the following summer. Some texts state that it was a cool and rainy summer – Yquem's records say the only warm spells were in May and then autumn. Tastet-Lawton's archives paint a slightly different picture, reporting that while there were no heat spikes, temperatures remained reasonably warm. There were also fewer storms compared with the previous year, but they were clustered towards the end of August and into September, dashing hopes of a small but quality vintage. The harvest began in earnest from 21 September. One interesting observation in Fourcaud-Laussac's notebook is that the fruit tasted unsatisfactory during the first pickings and "left something to be desired". But benevolent weather, with temperatures hovering around 24–25°C (75–77°F), provided a final spurt of sugar accumulation and nudged the fruit at Cheval Blanc towards phenolic ripeness. His only setback was, yet again, the dreaded grape worm that he estimated almost halved his production. In general, according to Tastet-Lawton, the initial tastings of the must indicated green and rather lean wine. Perhaps still reeling from the measly degree of alcohol the previous year, Latour decided to chaptalise the vintage – a first for the estate. Generally, the 1908s were irregular in quality, more tannic examples allegedly bridled with a little more longevity. Because of the lack of demand, a swathe of 1908s were still languishing in barrel three years later. This is yet another growing season from the decade that favoured those in Sauternes. A dry September allowed pickers to harvest at leisure and much of the fruit at Yquem had high sugar levels, completed by a superb *trie* in mid-October.

I have tasted two First Growths. The 1908 Lafite Rothschild displayed what I described as "Burgundy-like allure" when poured blind *chez* Domaine de Chevalier. Then, a 1908 Latour, shared with friends in Hong Kong, was just as drinkable, though both First Growths needed walking frames to help them along. A 1908 Lafaurie-Peyraguey was respectable with 110 years on the clock, suggesting that it was indeed a better vintage in Sauternes. If provenance is guaranteed, you might be surprised; otherwise, opt for Vintage Port, which enjoyed a legendary growing season.

1908 *(Continued)*

Event
First Ford Model T is produced

The car that put the world on wheels rolled off the production line at Henry Ford's Highland Park Plant. Ford himself road-tested the vehicle on a hunting trip to Wisconsin. The first was delivered on 1 October 1908 and contrary to folklore, it was available in colours that weren't black: blue, red, grey and green.

Music
I Got the Blues
– Anthony Maggio

Maggio was a classically trained Sicilian musician. On the New Orleans ferry to Mississippi, he heard an elderly black gentleman playing guitar and when he enquired about the song, the man replied "I got the blues". Significantly, this is the first piece of sheet music to incorporate that word and though the 12-bar blues chord progression is found in older popular songs that are rhythmically structured around a ragtime two-step, this was the first to write it down.

Film
The Kiss of Judas
– Armand Bour and
André Calmettes

Though often quoted as opening in 1909, Bour/Calmette's *Le Baiser de Judas* in fact premiered on Christmas Eve 1908. The film stars Albert Lambert, Jean Mounet-Sully and Albert Dieudonné. As the title suggests, it depicts the treachery of Jesus's disciple and its consequences. In the film, Judas has a vision of Jesus's forgiveness and compassion and wracked with remorse, hangs himself from a tree. Not the cheeriest festive flick for cinema-goers.

Everything was going swimmingly this growing season. Similar to the previous winter, it was not cold, just very wet. Despite inclement weather in May and June, flowering was good and surprisingly, despite the rain, the vines were not too badly affected by coulure. July raised hopes of a decent vintage but on 8 August, a vicious storm ripped through Saint-Julien, Pauillac and Saint-Estèphe and hail destroyed much of the crop. August saw some hot spells that burnt some of the berries' skins, especially on gravel soils at Cheval Blanc. In a repeat of 1908, the warm winter meant bugs thrived, and flea beetles were a constant problem, according to Fourcaud-Laussac. *Véraison* was extremely drawn out, with many grapes remaining green on the Left Bank, says Tastet-Lawton. Pickers entered the vineyard from 26 September and at Léoville-Las Cases, berries were sorted one by one, a level of fastidiousness uncommon in this era. Picking was later at Cheval Blanc, running from 4 to 20 October under what Fourcaud-Laussac describes as "superb weather". I wonder if his grapes benefited from this last-minute spell of heat, as he comments that the fruit was generally healthy? The reds were mostly light and uneven in quality, with Peppercorn suggesting they were akin to the 1907s but with a bit more stuffing. Sauternes suffered a cool summer after which the second pass through the vineyard produced some botrytised fruit, though subsequent rain plagued final passes and compromised the sweet wines.

This vintage is hardly ever seen. My solitary red is a 1909 Château Margaux, bought ex-cellar at auction and served by the "Sexy Muscles" tasting group in Hong Kong (I have no idea about the origin of the name and don't like to ask). The First Growth was simple but improved with aeration, weak but hanging in there by its fingernails. I also drank a 1909 Lafaurie-Peyraguey at the December 2018 vertical, which I deemed more fatigued than its other vintages of that era.

1909

1870

2020

1909
(Continued)

Event
Bakelite spawns the plastics industry

Born in Ghent, Leo Baekeland moved to New York in 1889. After inventing photographic paper, he moved into the field of synthetic resins and in 1909 announced the invention of a hard mouldable plastic: Polyoxybenzylmethyleng-lycolanhydride. Thankfully, it was renamed Bakelite and became crucial for the nascent plastics industry, soon being widely used in telephones, kitchenware, toys and other products.

Music
Shine on Harvest Moon
– Ada Jones and Billy Murray

Though it had debuted the previous year in the Ziegfield Follies on Broadway, 1909 marked the release of this Tin Pan Alley standard on cylinder, sung by Ada Jones and Billy Murray, though other recordings were also published at the time. Nora Bayes and Jack Norworth, a husband-and-wife vaudeville act, are credited as its composers, though it was more likely penned by their pianist Dave Stamper, who had failed to gain copyright. It cost him considerably, since there have been over 100 cover versions, including ones by Vera Lynn, Rosemary Clooney and Tottenham Hotspur FC (on 1981's *Tottenham Hotspur Party Album*).

Film
Les Lunettes Féeriques
– Émile Cohl

The title of Cohl's curious five-minute film translates as "The Magic Eyeglasses" and it revolves around a gathering of people – a young girl, a glutton, a gambler, a lover and a miser – who don a magic pair of spectacles that through the power of animation reveal their desires and personality. One assumes that if the film had featured a Bordeaux winemaker of the time, it would have shown a healthy bunch of grapes.

1909
(Continued)

The
1910s

Even before the outbreak of the First World War, the succession of pitiful vintages left the market in a bleak state. Entries in Tastet-Lawton's diary fester with concern about sales and how business was languishing in the doldrums against a backdrop of simmering tensions between European countries that ultimately led to war.

In the vineyard the re-planting of American rootstock continued apace so that by 1913, some 64% of vines "spoke with an American accent", equivalent to 87,300 hectares out of a total of 135,600. Philippe Roudie makes an interesting observation that uptake was faster on the Right Bank than on the Left, with Médoc owners less acquiescent, hoping that insecticides or an innovation would obviate upheaval. Those that did re-graft onto American stock, including some of the most famous estates, were now burdened by young vines susceptible to disease and unable to bestow fruit of real pedigree. Perhaps this underlies Michael Broadbent's belief that benevolent growing seasons such as 1911 and 1918 produced promising wines that soon fatigued in bottle. Writing in his *Wine of Bordeaux*, Edmund Penning-Rowsell asserts that the first complete post-phylloxera vintage in terms of re-grafted vines was 1918. I suspect it was even later than that.

What is "Bordeaux"? Not being facetious, but if you scribbled "Bordeaux" on a blank label and glued it onto a bottle, does that make it a Bordeaux wine? Of course not. Yet this unscrupulous practice had been common for decades, since no legislation prohibited anyone wishing to pimp up non-Bordeaux wine from carrying it out. On 18 February 1911, laws were introduced that delimited the area where vines were classed as Bordeaux in order to stamp out fraud. This inevitably precipitated numerous counterfeit claims: 352 were lodged between January 1912 and September 1916. In fact, most were not about fake Bordeaux. Four-fifths concerned *mouillage*, the practice of watering down wines by as much as 25% of their volume in order to increase revenue – immoral but understandable when many châteaux faced such a bleak outlook during the war. These rules were refined on 6 May 1919 with laws that defined the *appellation d'origine*, effectively inserting borders, but grape varieties, yields and winemaking practices remained unregulated, leaving plenty of room for fraud to continue.

Before detailing the growing seasons, I confess a long-held assumption that this decade was a continuation of the last, insofar as there are no standout vintages. Connoisseurs such as André Simon and Michael Broadbent do not single out any season for praise. Taking a closer look, it would appear that Mother Nature was more benevolent towards the end of the decade with potentially great vintages in 1917, 1918 and 1919. Unfortunately, war denied

Bordeaux (and other wine regions) manpower, experienced hands with the necessary skillsets, rudimentary materials and a market. This conspired to create a downward spiral of declining revenues and withering investment. Coupled with small production, often due to mildew, and the prosaic fact that the decade is becoming covered by the sands of time, this era's bottles are hardly ever seen, much less so than those of the following decade. It is a decade of what could have been, were it not for the devastating repercussions of an assassination.

*Harvest time at La Conseillante
in Pomerol, children and adults
lending a hand. The exact date of
this photograph is unknown, though
believed circa 1910.*

1910

Ghastly from start to finish, and not only Bordeaux. The whole of France suffered awful weather that poleaxed not just vines but essential cereal and fruit crops needed to feed the population. It simply rained the entire year and so rot was rampant. Vineyard managers sprayed sulphur on the vines up to 12 times at Rauzan-Ségla to no avail and 11 times at Cheval Blanc. "*Toujours la pluie!!!*" writes an exasperated Lawton during this *annus horribilis*. Albert Fourcaud-Laussac echoes the sentiment in his personal diary at Cheval Blanc: "This year, there was neither winter, nor spring nor summer. It rained practically all of the year." He notes little powdery mildew but a serious invasion of flea beetle. The season was not a total write-off since he notes that conditions improved after 25 August, which explains the late harvest that generally began from 10 October.

Yields were so small and so feeble that many did not bother to harvest at all. I have read that Lafite Rothschild sold off its entire crop as a *vin rouge*, though according to the château's 150th anniversary almanac, a small quantity was made, perchance for private consumption. (As an aside, one newspaper article reported that the whole of Chablis produced just 200 *feuillettes*, about 3,000 cases.) At Cheval Blanc, harvesters did not enter the vineyard until 12 October and picked over the following 19 days until the last day of the month. So much fruit was affected by grape worm that it discarded half the yield after a rigorous sorting. Despite losing practically all the Merlot and Malbec, the fruit that did survive was, in fact, large and healthy. The Gilbey family, owners of Château Loudenne, remarked: "It is necessary to go back a hundred years in the history of the Médoc to find a vintage as poor as this year." Its only proponent was writer Maurice Healy, apparently with a penchant for poor years, who was a strong advocate of the 1910 Haut-Brion. He would serve it blind and ask mavens to guess the wine, then when they got it wrong, demand them to apologise to the '10 vintage for being mean.

It was just as miserable a vintage in Sauternes, which saw 40 days of continuous rainfall, nixing any chance of Yquem – and, doubtless, wine from any other Sauternes château – being released.

No Bordeaux wines from this vintage tasted.

Event
Russell and Whitehead publish the first volume of *Principia Mathematica*

The three-volume *Principia Mathematica* published by Alfred North Whitehead and Bertrand Russell forms a cornerstone of modern mathematical logic. And that's about all I can tell you because it goes well beyond my comprehension, just like the theory of relativity (page 110). Neither are necessary for the job of a wine writer.

Film
Frankenstein – J. Searle Dawley

Based on Mary Shelley's novel, Edison Production's silent horror movie was shot in the Bronx in January 1910. The monster itself was revered as "the most remarkable ever committed to film". The original nitrate film was thought lost until 1980, when a collector realised he had the only surviving copy.

Music
Come Josephine in My Flying Machine – Blanche Ring

Published in 1910, *Come Josephine in My Flying Machine* was written by Fred Fisher with words by Alfred Bryan. It was originally recorded by Blanche Ring. As you might guess, it was inspired by the Wright brothers, but who, pray tell, is Josephine? She is, apparently, the remarkable Josephine Sarah Magner, who claimed to be the first American woman to make a parachute jump in 1905. The lyrics convey the excitement in the fledgling days of aviation: "Whoa, dear! Don't hit the moon! No, dear. Not yet, but soon!" The song became a standard and can be heard in everything from *The Waltons* to *The Simpsons*. In fact, it was supposed to feature in James Cameron's blockbuster *Titanic*, Kate Winslet and Leonardo DiCaprio singing the tune as they promenade along the deck at night. Can't remember it? Alas, the scene never made the final cut.

1911

In 1911 the vines got off to a slow start after what Fourcaud-Laussac described as a "cold and long winter" – in contrast to the relatively warm winters of the previous two years. Bordeaux estates managed to escape frost episodes in April unscathed. Warm weather coincided with flowering and raised hopes of a decent-sized crop, but temperatures plummeted on 10 June when the Right Bank was in full bloom and four days of rain disrupted flowering, leaving winemakers facing a small yield – not what was needed after the disastrous previous year. Temperatures soon picked up from the middle of the month but the nights of 16 and 17 June saw hail that further depleted fruit in Pauillac and Saint-Estèphe, the First Growths losing between one-third and two-thirds of their crop. What survived benefited from warm temperatures in July that reached 37°C (99°F). Storms at the end of July whittled yields down ever further on the Left Bank, less so on the Right, then warm weather prompted a quick *véraison* around the first week of August. Some vines suffered during a dry period prior to harvest, but picking began on 20 September. When the fruit was still fermenting in the vat, bids were already coming in to purchase the vintage due to the poor quality of recent seasons and small yields. Merchants needed something to sell. In his notebook, Fourcaud-Laussac is pleased that his 1911 Cheval Blanc manages to fetch the same price as Second Growths in the Médoc, indicating how even the most prestigious Right Bank estates ranked below those on the Left. In Sauternes, many vineyards were plagued by grape worm as a result of the steamy environment, though some were able to make a couple of successful passes through the vines in mid-October that provided decent sugar levels, though quality was generally deemed average.

The 1911 vintage has been forgotten not because of the quality of its wines – reputedly a little hard in their youth – but because production was so small that it never received a wide audience who might appreciate its virtues. Tasting them in the sixties, Peppercorn claims they had charm but never reached the standard of the best 1909s. Today 1911s are hardly ever seen. I have only encountered two, both Sauternes: the 1911 Suduiraut and the 1911 Lafaurie-Peyraguey. Both were drinkable, but not memorable and rather fatigued.

Event
Marie Curie wins the Nobel
Prize in Chemistry

Born Marie Sklodowska in
Warsaw, Marie Curie had already
shared the Nobel Prize in Physics
in 1903. In 1911 she became the
first person to be awarded the
Nobel twice – for her research in
radioactive elements, especially
radium. Her work ultimately led
to the ability to treat tumours.
During the First World War,
she helped develop mobile X-ray
units, known as "Petites Curies",
travelling close to the front line
with her daughter to X-ray
injured soldiers.

Film
A Tale of Two Cities
– William J. Humphrey

This epic three-reel silent
movie, loosely based on the
Dickens' novel, starred the
so-called "dimpled darling"
Maurice Costello as Sidney
Carlton. Before signing with the
Vitagraph production company,
Costello inserted a clause in his
contract that relieved him from
carrying out certain production
tasks, such as building sets, that
actors were then expected to fulfil.
Actress Drew Barrymore is his
great-granddaughter.

Music
Alexander's Ragtime Band
– Irving Berlin

According to musician and
author Bob Stanley, Irving Berlin
wrote one of his most famous
compositions while killing 20
minutes waiting for a train in
Palm Beach, Florida. Meeting
indifference upon release, the
song gained popularity when
New York-born contralto
vaudeville singer Emma Carus
began singing it on a tour of
the Midwest. A grateful Berlin
credits Carus on the song sheet
that went on to sell a million
copies in the United States
and become a global sensation.
Scott Joplin purportedly loathed
Berlin's take on ragtime. Apart
from accusations that Berlin had
plagiarised the song, it also lacked
ragtime's syncopation and the
novelty hit did nothing to help
Joplin's quest for ragtime to be
treated as a serious art form.

1912

Nineteen-twelve witnessed a capricious growing season: heat one month, cold the next. Winter was unseasonably warm so that some vines on the Right Bank commenced their growth cycle around mid-February. This was retarded by a cold April marked by a severe and damaging frost on 3 April. At Cheval Blanc, Fourcaud-Laussac describes how on 17 April a rather innocuous cloud suddenly unleashed a 20-minute hailstorm. Sauternes was also affected, although Yquem escaped due to its elevation, despite suffering coulure. May was warmer and this helped vines recover, though flowering was uneven due to rain that caused widespread coulure at the end of June. Despite some hail, July was better with warmer temperatures up to 30°C (86°F), though there was intense mildew pressure at Cheval Blanc due to prevailing wet conditions from 15 June all the way through to mid-September. For much of August, temperatures struggled past the low twenties and this retarded sugar accumulation and ripeness until September. Some estates such as Branaire-Ducru and Brane-Cantenac commenced picking around 17 September though most began later on 26 September. Despite this relatively late date, André Simon insists the grapes were picked before they reached phenolic ripeness, even though the Tastet-Lawton archives note that musts reached 12–13%. The public were not convinced and complained of wines tasting hollow, a view shared by Maurice Healy who found them "light in texture" and "lacking body". His friend and oenophile Ian Maxwell Campbell had a soft spot for the 1912 Clos Fourtet that possessed "an almost Oriental smell", though Edmund Penning-Rowsell opined that the wines were excessively acidic. In Sauternes, some châteaux suffered an influx of grape worms and grapes that tended to be over-ripe but not botrytised.

I have tasted three dry reds from this vintage. The 1912 Ausone was the oldest wine at the vertical in London and was ossified but not totally undrinkable, while a 1912 Lafite Rothschild had just reached the end of its mortal coil. A 1912 Château du Lyonnat in April 2022 prompted speculation around the table that there had been a bit of outside assistance from imported grapes, and despite volatility, this Lussac Saint-Émilion was worth swallowing. I have a solitary note for Sauternes, namely 1912 Climens, a bottle that should have been drunk earlier, perchance between the wars? Sound provenance and large format are prerequisites for anything remotely drinkable, though the odds will be stacked against the wines surviving.

Event
The sinking of the Titanic

Even though the disaster happened over a century ago, the sinking of the *Titanic* has lost none of its potency, etched on collective minds like few catastrophes before or since. It is not just the tragic loss of around 2,220 passengers in icy North Atlantic waters on the night of 15 April 1912 that continues to resonate, but the symbolism of this grand ocean liner sunk on her maiden voyage, the unequal odds of survival depending upon wealth and station, the tales of heroism and valour. These have all been perpetuated in books and particularly films, including the bizarre *Raise the Titanic!* from 1981, which my father took me to see at the cinema as some kind of punishment.

Film
The Mask of Horror
– Abel Gance

Édouard de Max plays a mad sculptor seeking the perfect "mask of horror" in this silent short film. He decides to smear himself with blood, swallow poison and watch the effects on himself in a mirror. Cheery stuff. Gance's use of colour filters made this avant-garde film genuinely frightening entertainment for its audiences.

Music
Love Is Mine
– Enrico Caruso

The Italian tenor was one of the first classical singers to issue his recordings in physical form. He recorded *Love Is Mine* on 27 December 1911 and it was released on a shellac 78rpm the following year. In a musical career that stretched from 1895 to 1920, Caruso appeared 863 times at the New York Met and is considered one of the century's greatest opera singers.

1913

The 1913 vintage began slowly, cold temperatures retarding the vines' growth cycle and frost on the night of 14 April particularly affected the Graves, as well as down in Sauternes. Damage was mitigated thanks to the use of smudge pots – wax candles distributed across vineyards to warm ground temperatures and limit frost damage. Afterwards, a hot spell saw vines burst into action, albeit irregularly depending upon location. May was erratic, marked by temperatures up to 32°C (90°F) at the end of the month but a warm and clement June ensured even flowering. Intermittent showers combined with heat led to outbreaks of mildew in July, as well as oidium and cochylis. The latter was a constant threat throughout the entire growing season. A severe storm on 30 July came with a side order of damaging hail. August was warm but marred by heavy storms and yet more localised hail. There was also some cochylis on the Right Bank along with mildew, necessitating constant spraying in the vineyard. September was marred by further storms and hail at the end of the month, preventing fruit from reaching phenolic maturity. Conditions appear better on the Right Bank – "beautiful and warm" according to Fourcaud-Laussac at Cheval Blanc, where the harvest began on 29 September. However, Fourcaud-Laussac had labour problems to sort out after hiring 43 pickers from Corréze, led by, in his words, a "scoundrel", who tried to blackmail their paymaster. It's rather odd but the "scoundrel" refused to respect the tradition of not eating meat on Friday, a crime for which Fourcaud-Laussac retaliated by threatening to fire the entire team of pickers. Blackmails notwithstanding, it had been a traumatic roller-coaster of a growing season with little to show at the end of it. In Sauternes, mid-September rains triggered botrytis and a dry period from 22 to 29 September allowed concentrated grapes to be picked. Subsequent rain failed to manifest more botrytis and according to Yquem's records, sugar levels never exceeded 17% potential.

Like 1911, the only wines from the 1913 vintage that I have encountered are Sauternes. Alas, neither the 1913 Lafaurie-Peyraguey nor the 1913 Suduiraut offered much to write home about.

Event
Suffragette Emily Davison throws herself under King George V's horse

On 4 June 1913 at the Epsom Derby, suffragette Emily Davison threw herself under Ansam, King George V's horse. She died four days later from her injuries. While interpreted as a courageous act of martyrdom, Davison was more likely attempting to attach a suffragette flag on to the horse in order to highlight the ongoing campaign for women's rights. The jockey, Herbert Jones, laid a wreath at the funeral of leading suffragette Emmeline Pankhurst in 1928, 10 years after women had won the right to vote in the UK.

Music
The Rite of Spring
– Igor Stravinsky

Composed for the Ballets Russes company, Igor Stravinsky's *The Rite of Spring* was first performed at the Théâtre des Champs-Élysées on 29 May choreographed by Vaslav Nijinsky. As one of the first modernist pieces that incorporated ground-breaking tonality, metre and dissonance, it was hugely influential throughout the century.

Film
Fantômas
– Louis Feuillade

Feuillade's silent series of crime adventures was released as five episodes in 1913 and 1914, each one ending on a cliffhanger. They were based on the *Fantômas* novels by Marcel Allain and Pierre Souvestre and in some ways can be seen as precursors to the Bond franchise.

1914

After a stuttering start, a clement April saw the vines burst into green. May was warm except for a northerly wind that sent the mercury tumbling at the end of the month and initially retarded flowering. Things got back on track with a warm June, July and August maintaining sanitary conditions in vineyards. In fact, this was certainly the best summer in recent years, even though potential yields were down. The harvest commenced on 20 September and weather conditions remained quite benign. On paper, 1914 is a great vintage, the wines deeply coloured and powerful. Yet early on, some merchants claimed that they missed some maturity and apparently fatigued just after a few years in bottle. Of course, there is the backdrop of the First World War breaking out and in all likelihood, barrel ageing did not proceed ideally given that winemakers and their families had far more pressing matters at hand. Sauternes was likewise all set up for a good season when harvest began around 23 September, with Yquem reporting 22 days of leisurely picking. But returning downpours dashed hopes of a decent crop and two-thirds of the fruit had to be discarded.

The only red Bordeaux I have tasted is a 1914 Gruaud Larose that held up well enough at the infamous "Worst. Bottle. Ever." dinner in Clapham, London when guests/victims were invited to proffer their most dodgy bottles. The spittoon had never seen so much action. I have also sampled a quartet of Sauternes. The first was a 1914 Château d'Arche Crème de Tête that sported golden raisin and quince on the nose, and a little oxidation on the palate – worthy of applause just for lasting the distance. The best I have encountered is an astonishing 1914 Lafaurie-Peyraguey at the vertical in December 2018, which eclipsed both the 1914 Suduiraut and the 1914 Climens I tasted in Switzerland at respective verticals.

Event
Start of the First World War

The assassination by Gavrilo
Princip of Archduke Franz
Ferdinand and his wife on
28 June 1914 was the catalyst for
the First World War. Austria-
Hungary declared war on Serbia
and like falling dominoes, other
European countries also took
up arms. The next four years
would see 20 million military and
civilian deaths and 21 million
wounded. That is a lot of death
from one bullet.

Music
Saint Louis Blues
– W.C. Handy

The Father of the Blues published
his most famous piece when he
was already 40 years old, inspired
by the anguish of a woman
walking through St. Louis and
despairing her husband's absence.
It was subsequently recorded
by giants such as Bessie Smith,
Louis Armstrong, Django
Reinhardt and Dizzy Gillespie,
among many others. It also found
royal approval. King Edward VIII
requested his Scottish pipers to
play it at Balmoral Castle and
Queen Elizabeth II called it one
of her favourite songs.

Film
Cabiria
– Giovanni Pastrone

A classic of early Italian cinema,
Pastrone's *Cabiria* incorporated
a new level of *mise-en-scène*,
pioneering the use of trolley and
dolly-mounted cameras to create
tracking shots. Author Gabriele
d'Annunzio collaborated on the
script and filming in Turin took
six months. The lead role was
played by Bartolomeo Pagano,
a Genoan ex-docker renowned
for his muscular physique. At
two hours in length, *Cabiria* is
considered by many to be the
world's first epic movie.

1914
(Continued)

1870

2020

1915

Mother Nature and war extirpated this vintage from birth. According to the Tastet-Lawton archives, the rain was almost constant until around the end of May. Any respite was short-lived. Flowering was rapid thanks to high temperatures but further deluges caused widespread mildew both on leaves and nascent bunches. Brown rot was endemic by July and towards the end of that month, many properties were throwing in the towel, forewarning merchants that any harvest was doubtful. *Véraison* was irregular and insects affected whatever bunches had survived since there was little to treat infestations. Remarkably, potential alcohol was up to 14% for the Merlot, yet tumbling temperatures during September meant the later-ripening Cabernets struggled to reach full ripeness. Harvest began around 22 September but the resulting crop was the smallest since 1886 since many estates declined to release any wine. In Sauternes, a series of heavy showers in late September ruined the harvest and apparently the potential alcohol levels never reached a measly 13%. As an aside, despite this *annus horribili*s in Bordeaux, Burgundians enjoyed one of the best growing seasons ever.

No Bordeaux wines from this vintage tasted.

Music
I Didn't Raise My Boy to Be a Soldier – Peerless Quartet

Composed by Al Piantadosi but, most crucially, with lyrics by Alfred Bryan, *I Didn't Raise My Boy to Be a Soldier* is considered one of the first anti-war songs and became a hit in 1915 before America entered the First World War. Several versions – and parodies – were released, the most popular by Peerless Quartet, the most commercially successful group of the decade.

Film
The Birth of a Nation – D. W. Griffith

Griffith's *The Birth of a Nation* is a cinematic landmark of the silent era. Its technical innovations, epic battle recreations, lengthy running time, popularity and profitability prompted many sceptics to start treating film as a serious art form. Based on the novel *The Clansman*, it told the story of the American Civil War and its effects upon two families on opposing sides. Though hailed as one of the pioneering films of cinema, one cannot overlook its overt racism and favourable portrayal of the Ku Klux Klan, so much so that it prompted a surge in its membership.

Event
First zeppelin raid over London

Until this point, Britain had relied on coastal defences. But German airships, the so-called Zeppelins, could switch off their engines and silently drift over enemy territory at 3,350 m (11,000 ft) like deadly clouds. The first of them, Zeppelin LZ.38, appeared over Stoke Newington in north London on the night of 31 May 1915, nine months after war had been declared. Why the wait? It was partly because Kaiser Wilhelm assumed that military action would be over swiftly and his close relationship with the royal family meant he had no appetite to destroy the capital's cultural heritage. However, by 1917, some 528 people had lost their lives to these silent menaces in the sky.

1916

This was shaping up to be a good vintage. The early part of the year was wet and sleety, but it began warming up from mid-March. However, vines got off to a sluggish start and flowering was strung out once it got going around 2 June. Fears of coulure never amounted to anything serious, though there were outbreaks of oidium and mildew. August was fairly clement with temperatures reaching the mid-thirties. *Véraison* was late, a warm September allowing winemakers to conduct a late harvest that kicked off around 26 September. Quantities were down, partly because of the small size of berries and although they initially showed deep colours and good body, potential alcohol levels were around 11–12%. Sauternes enjoyed a warm and hot summer and three dry weeks during October saw some concentrated fruit. Alas, rain in the final two weeks that month nixed any chance of a good vintage. The real tragedy is that as Nature inexorably pressed on, farmhands and pickers were being slaughtered in the trenches.

The best of three that I have tasted from this traumatic year is a sublime 1916 Malartic-Lagravière poured at the Académie du Vin dinner in Bordeaux. I walked up to proprietor Jean-Jacques Bonnie with a look of incredulity plastered over my face. "Tell me, how can this wine be so harmonious, so joyous?" He just smiled. This was closely followed by a fine-boned 1916 Montrose at a vertical in London exactly one century after its birth. An ex-château 1916 Mouton Rothschild opened in Hong Kong evidenced very under-ripe Cabernet Sauvignon, but the mainly female pickers doubtless had more pressing concerns at the time.

Event
The Battle of the Somme

Perhaps the most infamous battle of the First World War lasted from 1 July until the final clash on 13 November. The Allied offensive attacked 15 miles (24 km) along the Western Front, the French army another 8 miles (13 km). British Commander-in-Chief Douglas Haig was warned that the German army had far more military hardware, nevertheless, waves of comparatively unarmed men stormed into no man's land to be pointlessly slaughtered in the quagmire. Twenty-thousand troops were killed in the 60 minutes. Over 141 bloody days, the Allied forces advanced just 5 miles (8 km) and over 300,000 men on both sides lost their lives.

Music
Take Me Back to Dear Old Blighty
– Florrie Forde

Recognisable to a certain generation as the opening to The Smiths' *The Queen Is Dead*, this music-hall song composed by Arthur J. Mills, Fred Godfrey and Bennett Scott tells of three soldiers on the Western Front longing for dear old Blighty. Florrie Forde was an Australian music-hall singer known for rousing sing-along choruses such as this and *It's a Long Way to Tipperary*.

Film
Joan the Woman
– Cecil B. DeMille

De Mille's tale of Joan of Arc starred opera singer Geraldine Farrar, who had triumphed in the director's *Carmen* the previous year. There was much brouhaha over her huge salary and generous take of the profits, but her pulling power ensured the film became a box-office smash.

1917

This year started cold, the mercury plunging to -10°C (14°F) in February with snow continuing into April and delaying the vines' growth cycle, particularly with respect to the Cabernet Sauvignon. A warm May fired up vines' engines, though rain towards the end of the month brought mildew pressure that was mitigated by a hot June, temperatures reaching 35°C (95°F) and thereby ensuring a regular flowering. A storm on 18 June brought hail that affected Saint-Julien, Pauillac and Saint-Estèphe, though July and August were both hot and sunny, predicating early picking that began on 19 September under ideal conditions. "The month of September finished superbly," writes Lawton at the end of the month, then poignantly, "Without the war, it would be a pleasure to live!!" The harvest was mostly undertaken by female hands like the previous year – basically, by anyone who was available, including the elderly and the young. All in all, 1917 was a benevolent growing season with the potential to bestow excellent wines. However, there were few experienced cellar hands in the winery to turn that promising fruit into wine, while the market had been snuffed out by war. Maurice Healy, writing in *Stay with Me Flagons*, adopts a more negative stance and writes, "Oddly enough, 1917 was a very unsatisfactory year in most districts; but the Pomerol wines were all successful, and, although I have my doubts of their ability to stay the course, they had every other attribute a wine should have." André Simon blamed the failure of the vintage squarely at the war rather than Nature. Sauternes châteaux enjoyed a small crop of high-quality wines after 37 mm (1½ in) of rain had provoked botrytis and allowed some profitable passes through the vineyard in September, though later rainfall compromised the quality of subsequent ones.

The only wine I have tasted from this vintage is a fabulous 1917 Lafaurie-Peyraguey in Sauternes, glistening like a polished diamond after 101 years when poured at the memorable vertical. Admittedly, I considered eloping with that bottle, but I don't think my fellow attendees would have been amused.

Event
The Russian Revolution ousts
Tsar Nicholas II

With Russia having been ruled
by the Romanov family for three
centuries, Tsar Nicholas II was
an unpopular leader. Riots broke
out in St. Petersburg on
8 March 1917 and soldiers
refused to obey his orders,
forcing him to step down
on 15 March. A provisional
government was installed
but a second revolution the
following October saw Lenin
lead the Bolsheviks to power.
Communism became the
new political system, laying
the foundations for fractious
international relations between
East and West throughout
the century.

Film
Cleopatra
– J. Gordon Edwards

The first Cleopatra film starred
Theda Bara as the Siren of
Egypt. It was one of Hollywood's
most lavish productions to date
with some 2,000 hands hired
to work on the set. It was also
noticeable for its risqué costumes,
particularly Cleopatra's snake-
design breast plates, which
meant it was subject to cuts by
censorship boards. Despite the
edits, the film was a box-office
smash, though the last two
prints were destroyed in a fire
in 1937 and only fragments of
it now survive.

Music
Dixie Jass Band One-Step
– Original Dixieland Jass Band

On 26 February 1917, five
musicians from Chicago entered
the studio to cut two songs for
a 78 rpm disc, *Livery Stable
Blues* and *Dixie Jass Band One-
Step*. Originating from Afro-
Americans in New Orleans
several years earlier, jazz was so
novel that its spelling had yet to
be determined. Prime contender
for the title of first jazz record,
the track was ironically recorded
by white musicians, prefiguring
the appropriation of rock 'n'
roll decades later. Its sound was
revolutionary – loud and raucous,
centred on cornet, trombone
and clarinet, which all pointed
to the ceiling when they hit the
high notes. Bob Stanley rightly
hails the Original Dixieland Jass
Band as the first modern pop
group and the record sold over a
million copies – a stepping stone
from ragtime to jazz that altered
popular music forever.

1918

Nineteen-eighteen began with low temperatures and a cold snap between 20 and 23 April burnt the young buds. Winemakers, who had endured four years of war, now feared they had lost one-third or even half the crop. Temperatures began rising in May and remained clement at the beginning of June during flowering, which was nevertheless strung out over a month. There was no coulure this year, but localised millerandage. July and August were hot and dry, temperatures peaking at 36°C (97°F), so that vines began to suffer hydric stress. This long dry period, often referred to by the French as *canicule*, extended into September, though relief came courtesy of rain on 8 September, which encouraged late *véraison*. Harvesting began on 24 September under good conditions and it was potentially a fine but small vintage, if variable due to lack of manpower and expertise after four years of war. Sauternes was a case of "almost there" – 71 mm (2¾ in) of rain in mid-September provoked widespread botrytis, albeit with low sugar levels, and a cold snap meant that potential alcohol levels struggled between 15–18%.

I have encountered two wines from this vintage. Firstly, a surprisingly perky 1918 Citran served blind by Olivier Bernard at Domaine de Chevalier, and then a commendable 1918 Siran that proprietor Édouard Miailhe cracked open at his numerically themed "Eight" dinner. Disappointingly, no After Eight mints were offered.

Event
Outbreak of Spanish flu

Despite its name and a lack of concrete evidence, it is widely thought Spanish flu originated in military personnel in Kansas. The first recorded case was in Philadelphia on 17 September 1918 and within a fortnight there were 20,000 more reports of people suffering similar symptoms. Without vaccines, the only means of subduing rates was via social distancing. It is estimated to have killed as many as 40 to 50 million people in its most virulent phase between 1918 and 1920, more than the number who perished in the First World War.

Music
The Planets
– Gustav Holst

Written between 1914 and 1917, Holst's *The Planets* was premiered at Queens' Hall in London on 29 September, conducted by Adrian Boult. The orchestra only saw the music two hours prior to the performance, so it was good sight-reading practice. Despite *The Sunday Times* sniffily describing it as "pompous, noisy and unalluring", it went on to become one of the most recognised and popular classical works of the century. Of course, Holst never composed music for Pluto, which was yet to be discovered (then relegated to dwarf planet status, see page 444), nor for that matter Earth, presumably because we already know what that sounds like.

Film
Tarzan of the Apes
– Scott Sidney

Based on Edgar Rice Burroughs' 1912 novel, this first cinematic outing for Tarzan starred Elmo Lincoln in the title role. It was filmed in the swamps and bayous around Louisiana and spawned several sequels. Lincoln went on to appear as an extra in two forties Tarzan movies, one starring former Olympic swimmer Johnny Weissmuller in the tree-swinging role, another with Lex Barker. Apparently, Burroughs was less pleased with these later depictions of his jungle hero.

1919

The 1919 vintage started begrudgingly and it was not until mid-April that clement weather awoke vines from their winter slumber. That said, a wet spring had rendered the ground soggy and difficult to work, turning hard and cement-like when it became warm. Some observed that after pruning, the previous year's drought caused some of the branches to become desiccated. The weather turned better from May and flowering started on 3 June under clement conditions without any coulure, though late-developing vines suffered millerandage. Rain in July precipitated outbreaks of mildew and oidium and conditions remained damp until 27 July. August was blisteringly hot with widespread drought, though thankfully showers on 27 August brought relief. September began with a return of hot weather, though there were further showers prior to harvest that commenced on 24 September. It was an irregular crop with some of the Cabernets bearing little or even no fruit due to the millerandage. In Sauternes, concentration was stymied by 156 mm (6 in) of rain in September and at Yquem, the prerequisite 20% potential alcohol was not reached until 10 October, after which sugar levels dropped away.

The wines of 1919 were potentially fine but apparently affected by some volatility and generally failed to last the course. I have encountered two from the Left Bank. Two bottles of 1919 Montrose at two different verticals demonstrated how this vintage could bestow long-lasting wines even in the most challenging seasons. Both bottles were superior to a 1919 Talbot, the oldest vintage at its centenary vertical in December 2018 and a little fatigued. A splendid 1919 Lafaurie-Peyraguey, served just a couple of days earlier, suggests that Sauternes fared better, though it remains the only example of sweet wine that I have tasted from this vintage.

Event
Start of Irish War
of Independence

After winning the general
election in 1918, the separatist
Sinn Féin party declared
an Irish Republic, sparking
confrontation with the Dublin-
based British administration.
Violence escalated on both sides
the following year, including
on Bloody Sunday, when 15
civilians were shot dead at a
football match at Croke Park. By
the time a truce was declared in
1921, over 2,500 had been killed.

Film
Daddy-Long-Legs
– Marshall Neilan

By 1919, Toronto-born Mary
Pickford, "America's sweetheart",
had become one of Hollywood's
major stars. Silent comedy-
drama *Daddy-Long-Legs* was
produced by United Artists, the
company she co-founded with
Charlie Chaplin, D.W. Griffith
and future husband Douglas
Fairbanks. It was seen as a risky
move and yet it revolutionised the
way films were distributed. Her
pulling power ensured *Daddy-
Long-Legs* was a box-office hit
and throughout the twenties she
starred in and produced a string
of hits before the talkie era ended
her acting career. She continued
to produce films and acted as a
shrewd businesswoman, finally
selling her shares in 1956.

Music
The Alcoholic Blues
– Louisiana Five Jazz Orchestra

The Alcoholic Blues was recorded
in June 1919 and released three
months later. Written by Albert
Von Tilzer and Edward Laska, it
was one of a number of records
written about Prohibition in the
US. Other versions at the time
were recorded by Billy Murray
and Vernon Dalhart.

1919
(Continued)

1870

2020

THE

1920s

This was the first decade since the 1870s that was bejewelled with bona fide great growing seasons and wines, though wine aficionados little knew that the Roaring Twenties would turn out to be the best decade until the eighties. The decade put Bordeaux on a steadier keel after the ups and downs since phylloxera and oidium. After those crises, it can be argued that it was this decade, rather than 1899 and 1900, that proved Bordeaux could create world-class wine using grafted vines. By the end of the twenties, almost the entire region had been re-planted, the success of 1928 and 1929 dispelling any remaining doubts about compromised quality. Some notable estates held on to their beloved un-grafted vines. In his *A Book of French Wines*, P. Morton Shand describes Ausone as "...among the very longest to be grown wholly from old un-grafted French vines". That was written in 1928. I wonder when the Dubois family finally bit the bullet?

In wineries, perhaps the most significant innovation was the spread of concrete vats – lined with ceramic tiles if money was available, which made them easier to clean. One of the first was installed at Château Loudenne. Over at La Mission Haut-Brion, they were even further ahead of the curve. Assisted by his two sons, its proprietor Frederic Woltner in 1926 installed enamel-lined steel vats with a vitrified inner coating that facilitated temperature control.

The Right Bank remained in the shadow of the Left Bank, especially bucolic Pomerol. Alexandre Thienpont once described to me how Vieux Chateau Certan was run down and uninhabitable at the start of the decade. When it was put up for sale in 1923, Antoine Moueix, uncle of Jean-Pierre Moueix, opted to buy Château Taillefer instead because it was closer to the station, proximity to amenities taking precedence over quality of the vineyard. At least it opened the gate for Georges Thienpont to buy Vieux Chateau Certan and ultimately transform it into one of Bordeaux's finest estates.

This was the final decade in which the sweet wines of Sauternes were as coveted as Bordeaux's elite reds. A series of great vintages in 1921, 1924, 1927, 1928 and 1929 gifted Sauternes lovers with a surfeit of fabulous noble rot-affected wines, many longer-lasting than the most revered reds, not least the peerless 1929s whose alumni astound almost a century later. The next time Sauternes would enjoy such a fecund run would be after the Second World War, though by that time tastes had begun to shift away from sweet dessert wines, while the market was still recovering.

Another development this decade was the emergence of Raymond Baudouin, founder of the magazine *La Revue du Vin de France* in 1927. He became an influential critic who denounced frauds and encouraged more châteaux to bottle their own wines. Indeed, this was the decade when château-bottling became compulsory for First Growths. Since the 18th century, châteaux had often bottled some barrels themselves, though it was a bit of a faff what with sourcing bottles and corks, labels, logistics and so forth. Why bother when merchants could take the wines off your hands and do it all for you? As time went by, the First Growths in particular did more bottling themselves. At the turn of the century, Lafite Rothschild was bottling around half of its production and occasionally, in great years, the entire production, partly in response to the thriving industry of fakes in Russia. Baron Philippe de Rothschild, who took over then-Second Growth Mouton Rothschild in 1922, is the man whose diplomatic guile and persistence persuaded the First Growths to start bottling themselves in a rare instance of co-operation between rival estates. Château-bottling was introduced in 1923 at Château Margaux and Haut-Brion, 1924 at Château Mouton Rothschild and 1925 at Château Lafite Rothschild and Latour. In a sense, this marked the beginning of a transfer in power from merchants to châteaux, the start of a transitional process that would last until the end of the century. By then, the leading châteaux were calling the shots.

Workers stop to pose for a photograph in the winery at Château Haut-Brion in 1924. Standing in front of the basket press is head winemaker Georges Delmas, grandfather of present winemaker, Jean-Philippe Delmas.

1920

The most fecund decade for Bordeaux in years kicked off with a vintage that in some ways was a rehearsal for 1928.

The season began with rapid vine growth, but the initial spurt was retarded by a cold snap and frost on 9 and 10 March. This was not such a bad thing. Vineyard workers were on strike, which meant that early-season tasks were not being carried out and the dispute was only resolved in May. By that time, the vines' growth had accelerated a fortnight in advance and flowers were seen in the vineyard from around 23 May. Flowering was irregular due to passing rain and only towards the end of June did the region enjoy more settled weather. July was cold with a brief hailstorm in Saint-Julien and rot became a constant menace. August was rather overcast with cool nights due to northeasterly winds. As a consequence, some bunches were still green by the end of that month. September was warmer although the dry conditions meant that the thick-skinned berries contained little juice, partially remedied by showers in the second half of the month that reconstituted some of the berries' pulp. Most of the pickers were out from 22 September and despite the nippy July and August, the sunny September resulted in a small crop of high-quality wines. Sauternes was hampered by berries struggling to achieve decent sugar levels; Yquem used only 20% of its fruit.

Maurice Healy kept changing his mind on the 1920s. He notes that this vintage was "trumpeted" upon release, but found they were "full of tannin and slow to come around". In 1934 he lambasted it as a "treacherous vintage" but then discovered they had improved by the early forties. Penning-Rowsell was a fan and despite their dryness said they were quite refined and "clarety". I have encountered several wines from this vintage, sadly not the Latour that was always the most celebrated. Most have been impressive, solid and clearly born with longevity in mind. The first 1920 I tasted was from Pontet-Canet, bottled by Castel rather than Cruse, which bottled a majority of the production in those days. It was impressive with deep colour and meliorating in the glass, just a touch of piquancy urging you back for another sip. The 1920 Montrose and 1920 Lafite Rothschild are both magnificent, the latter with vestiges of a sturdy backbone that had since softened to create an exquisite First Growth. In April 2022, the 1920 Pichon-Lalande, Gruaud Larose and Domaine de Chevalier all had plenty in the tank, structured, almost broad-shouldered wines revelling in antiquity. Somehow, I managed to identify blind a rickety 1920 Château de Sales at another of Olivier Bernard's soirées *chez* Domaine de Chevalier. The only Sauternes I have tasted is a 1920 Climens that was creaking at the seams, yet perfectly drinkable if you could abide its dry finish.

Event
Prohibition introduced in
the United States

The passing of the
18th Amendment made
the manufacture, sale and
transportation of alcoholic
beverages illegal in the United
States from 1920. It resulted in a
flourishing bootlegging industry
and speakeasies, many run by
local gangsters, most notoriously
and flamboyantly, Al Capone.
The act was repealed in March
1933 under President Franklin
Roosevelt by which time it was
patently clear that Prohibition
had done absolutely nothing to
quell American's taste for liquor.
But it did provide fodder for
some great gangster movies.

Music
Crazy Blues – Mamie Smith
and Her Jazz Hounds

Recorded on 10 August 1920,
Crazy Blues had been written
two years earlier by Afro-
American bandleader Perry
Bradford. Mamie Smith was
a Cincinnati-born vaudeville
singer who sang on numerous
hits for the Okeh label
throughout the twenties.
Crazy Blues is a music landmark.
It was the first blues record
sung by an African-American
artist to sell a million copies and
presaged a line of female blues
singers who would dominate
throughout the decade. But
Smith suffered the same tragic
outcome as far too many blues
artists, dying penniless in 1946
and interred in unmarked
ground. Shamefully, it was not
until 2013 that a monument was
erected in her honour.

1920

Film
The Cabinet of Dr. Caligari
– Robert Wiene

The Cabinet of Dr. Caligari is essentially Wiene's attempt to translate German expressionism into a silent horror film. He succeeded brilliantly. How? Firstly, thanks to the stunning canvas backdrops designed by Hermann Warm, Walter Reimann and Walter Röhrig with their disorientating oblique angles, not unlike a funfair's crooked house, both childlike and grotesque. Secondly, uncommon for the time, because it was filmed entirely in the studio, which enhances the sense of claustrophobia and theatricality. Thirdly, there's the disquieting, manic performance of Werner Krauss in the title role, not to mention Conrad Veidt's turn as the supposedly murderous somnambulist. The final twist in the sixth act flips the narrative and begs the question of exactly where insanity lies. It must have shocked audiences after premiering in Berlin on 26 February 1920. Cineastes revere it as one of the first arthouse films and it influenced many directors, but it was also a mainstream success.

Like 1967, this is a vintage renowned for its sticky Sauternes rather than dry reds.

Nineteen twenty-one commenced with a fairly dry early spring. Having survived a minor skirmish, five days later on 21 April, temperatures dipped below zero causing wider frost damage. Things began warming up in May and flowering went well as the mercury crept upwards, despite some millerandage. June's heat spike peaked at 34°C (93°F) and when the hot weather broke, storms wrought hail damage in Margaux and Saint-Julien, Gruaud Larose losing approximately one-third of its crop. July and August were balmy and the lack of rainfall threatened to shut down vines until showers brought relief in mid-August. Clement weather followed from the end of the month and the harvest really got going around 15 September. Some Merlots had reached 15–16% potential alcohol, portending difficult vinification in days before temperature-regulated vats. With daytime temperatures hovering around 28–29°C (82–84°F), the cool nights were a blessing. It remained stubbornly hot into October and, according to Edmund Penning-Rowsell, blocks of ice were often thrown into the vat to control the fermenting must, though a few had the nous to gently dunk the ice blocks in bags to prevent any dilution. Those vats in which fermentation spun out of control led to many unbalanced, volatile and acetic wines and that includes Lafite Rothschild, which Penning-Rowsell claims turned vinegary in a single night and nearly all of it was sold off as generic Pauillac. This might have been because, as a relatively large vineyard, it found sourcing sufficient ice to cool all those vats unfeasible.

Sauternes enjoyed not just a great growing season, but a legendary one, despite the frost during bud break and persistent drought conditions. The 38 mm (1½ in) of rain on 1 September provoked botrytis and the early harvest continued for several weeks since parcels were deemed to be at various levels of ripeness.

Charles Walter Berry was never a fan of the vintage. "Too big. Tastes of burnt skins, owing to the excessive heat," he says without mincing his words. André Simon was so enraptured by the 1921 Cheval Blanc that he splashed out on other '21s, only to find they hardly matched up, bereft of charm and balance. Bottles of this vintage are now rarely seen and as yet, I have never tasted the legendary Cheval Blanc that propelled the estate to the highest echelon where it has remained ever since. Both my experiences with the 1921 Gruaud Larose and the 1921 Montrose at respective verticals indicate wines that have lasted the course, yet were besmirched by a feral element, suggesting both estates struggled to control alcoholic fermentation. Better was a 1921 Siran served by Édouard Miailhe in December 2021: a touch of chlorine on the nose that dissipated, the palate surprisingly fruit-driven and substantial given its age. The 1921 vintage is stupendous in

1921
(Continued)

Sauternes, a golden treasure trove of precocious, decadent, unctuous wines that blossomed over decades. My solitary encounter with the 1921 Yquem, siphoned off by the sommelier who had decanted a bottle for pop star Madonna, was memorable – just a couple of sips enough to confirm its legendary status. Thank you Ms. Ciccone. She appeared to be enjoying it just as much. Subsequent encounters with 1921 Climens and a stellar 1921 Lafaurie-Peyraguey prove how the best wines were refulgent and golden.

Event
Coco Chanel introduces
Chanel No. 5

Saumur-born Gabrielle "Coco" Chanel was already a successful businesswoman and owned boutiques around Paris by the time she revolutionised perfume in 1921. Wanting to create a fresh, clean scent to appeal to modern women like herself, she challenged perfumer Ernest Beaux to come up with a fragrance. After a few months he presented several numbered samples for her assessment and she chose number… well, I am sure you can guess. No. 5 contained more aldehydes, allegedly added in serendipitous error by Beaux's lab assistant. I hope he got a cut of the profits.

Music
Margie
– Eddie Cantor

This standard was written the previous year by Con Conrad and pianist J. Russel Robinson, who was part of the Original Dixieland Jazz Band. Named after Cantor's five-year old daughter, it gained popularity after he introduced it into his repertoire at the Winter Garden Theatre in 1921. Cantor had made his debut in the Ziegfeld Follies four years earlier and recorded it for Columbia Records in the early twenties. He became one of the era's most popular entertainers despite turning down the lead role in *The Jazz Singer*.

1870

Film
The Kid
– Charlie Chaplin

Chaplin was such a perfectionist
that over nine months he
filmed more than 50 times the
amount of footage he used in
the completed picture. The title
role was played by seven-year-old
Jackie Coogan, who enjoyed a
short period of celebrity before
finding himself a penniless
teenager after his parents
mismanaged his earnings. His
plight led to the Coogan Act,
which was designed to protect
child actors. Coogan eventually
got his life back on track, playing
Uncle Fester in *The Addams
Family* TV series. *The Kid* was
a box-office triumph for the
greatest comedy actor of the
silent era and is widely regarded
as his masterpiece.

2020

1922

This is a vintage that delivered in terms of volume, but sadly not so much in terms of quality.

Following a cold start to the year when temperatures dived to -9°C (15°F), winter dragged on into March, predicating a sluggish growth cycle. April brought rainy and quite stormy conditions, then the weather turned on its heel so that the following month was unseasonably warm. These pendulum-like conditions acutely affected the Cabernet Sauvignon during the disrupted flowering, with coulure and millerandage widespread. July saw alternating spells of dry warm weather and showers. August began more clement but turned rainy at the end of the month, encouraging some châteaux to pick before further damage was done – berries had swollen to bursting point, at least according to some eye-witnesses. Some properties like Pontet-Canet began around 11 September, but the harvest really got going around 19 September and finished about a month later. Ripeness levels were irregular with musts generally showing 11–12% potential alcohol. Sauternes was stymied by the cool conditions and despite promising initial *tries* through the vines, much of the fruit failed to reach required levels of concentration. Quantity was large – 7.2 million hl compared with 3.8 million hl in 1921 – principally because of the pre-harvest rain bloating the fruit and the vintage swamped the market with excess wine.

I have tasted only three red Bordeaux from this vintage, the first two from Margaux. A Burgundy-like 1922 Château Margaux encountered in Hong Kong, despite ex-château provenance, was rickety and exhibited dilution. Meanwhile, a 1922 Siran tasted with Édouard Miailhe implied a stuck ferment and residual sugar. Despite its initial ersatz sweetness, this oddball was just about drinkable for an open-minded oenophile and seemed to cohere in the glass. It certainly deserved more than the derisory one-star from Michael Broadbent. Just one week later, a 1922 La Conseillante from a Danish cellar shared over dinner in Pessac-Léognan was ethereal and though nearing the end of its drinking plateau conveyed elegiac harmony. Far better were a pair from Sauternes. The 1922 Lafaurie-Peyraguey was a sensational showing at the vertical in December 2018, while a 1922 Suduiraut was not in the same league, but put in a decent showing given its antiquity.

Event
Gandhi imprisoned for sedition

On 10 March 1922, "Mahatma" Gandhi was arrested in Bombay (Mumbai) by British officials for sedition. "I wanted to avoid violence," he told the judge when asked whether he would question his sentence. "Non-violence is the first article of my faith. It is also the last article of my creed. But I had to make my choice." He served two years of his six-year sentence before being released and continuing a lifetime of peaceful process against British rule, which ultimately led to his assassination in January 1948 in New Delhi.

Music
The Fives
– Hersal and George W. Thomas

Recorded for Okeh Records, the Thomas brothers' *The Fives* is generally regarded as the first boogie-woogie record, certainly the first in print. It was composed by the brothers in 1921 and officially published by George Thomas's publishing company the following year. The left hand pummelling out the rhythm on the piano symbolised the clickety-clack of a train and the unmistakable boogie-woogie inflection hardly changed over following decades. The title refers to the number of the train and its time of arrival at Frisco.

Film
Blood and Sand
– Fred Niblo

In the early twenties, Rudolph Valentino set many a cinema-goer's heart a-flutter. In *Blood and Sand*, he plays a matador who embarks upon a torrid affair with a widow. Prior to the film's release, the star found himself accused of bigamy under Californian law and spent several hours in custody, though the scandal did not prevent *Blood and Sand* becoming one of the biggest box-office draws of the year.

1923

This was a tricky season with the caprice of Mother Nature in full effect.

Nineteen twenty-three began with rainclouds overhead, with spring not arriving until late March. A cooler April retarded bud break and intermittent cold spells put the brakes on the growth cycle. Winemakers were resigned to a late harvest. The inclement weather caused a delayed and irregular flowering with widespread coulure that particularly affected the Merlot, berries apparently littering the ground. Saint-Émilion lost around half its potential crop. July was warmer, but stormy, with some mildew and localised oidium before August saw heat spikes that peaked at 34°C (93°F) at the beginning of the month. This forced some vines to shut down and across Bordeaux observers could see yellowing leaves falling to the ground. *Véraison* was irregular and spun out and in September the weather remained unpredictable with intermittent storms engorging the berries. The late harvest got underway on 1 October with temperatures lifting just after a week later. Sauternes was a rather mixed bag, with rain from 13 – 22 September provoking botrytis, though the fruit struggled to reach decent sugar levels. Only small lots picked towards the end of October reached a high standard and bolstered what otherwise would have been rather anaemic sweet wines.

André Simon notes that the 1923 vintage was delicious upon release, "fragrant and sweet", so it was disheartening that the best faded in bottle to what Simon describes as "sugar-and-water". The only two Bordeaux I have tasted are, first, a 1923 Gruaud Larose that was timeworn but holding on in there when poured at the annual vertical on en primeur eve. The other was a bottle served blind by the irrepressible and much-missed Harry Gill at The Arches wine bar in London. "What d'ya fink it is? Go'on…" he cajoled in a thick cockney/Greek accent as I marvelled at a clearly timeworn, degraded yet enjoyable claret. I cannot recall my wildly incorrect reply, but he laughed in a mocking way reserved for wine critics supposed to know their Bordeaux from their Beaujolais and revealed a 1923 Soutard. Down in Sauternes, both 1923 Suduiraut and Lafaurie-Peyraguey suggest that it was a better vintage for anyone affected by noble rot. Generally, 1923 is a lesser-spotted vintage because the wines were allegedly light and elegant, and so a majority were consumed in their youth.

Event
Great Kanto earthquake
destroys Tokyo

On 1 September 1923, an
earthquake with a magnitude of
7.9 struck Tokyo. It was lunchtime
and many families were cooking
meals over gas burners inside their
wooden houses. Almost as soon as
the trembling stopped, fires broke
out and swept across a vast swathe
of the city. The conflagrations took
two days to extinguish, by which
time over 100,000 people had
perished in their tinderbox abodes.
Traditionally a peaceful city,
Tokyo descended into anarchy to
the extent that order could only be
restored by the army.

Film
The Hunchback of Notre Dame
– Wallace Worsley

Lon Chaney's astonishing turn as
the tortured, love-sick Quasimodo
underneath layers of prosthetics
and make-up remains one of
cinema's greatest performances,
conveying a sensitivity and pathos
that entrance audiences to this
day. The film is arguably the finest
adaptation of Victor Hugo's novel
and Universal Pictures lavished
$1.25 million on its production,
ultimately earning returns of
$3 million and spawning a
decade of horror films that drew
audiences throughout the decade.

Music
The Charleston – James P. Johnson
and Cecil Mack

Sharing its title with the dance
that symbolises the Roaring
Twenties, the song first featured
in the black Broadway musical-
comedy *Runnin' Wild*, which ran
at the New Colonial Theatre in
Manhattan. James P. Johnson
wrote the music and Cecil Mack
penned the rarely sung lyrics.
Johnson's inspiration came
from hearing the "ring-shout"
rhythms of South Carolina
longshoremen and improvised
a piano refrain to match the
claps and hollers. Though not
proven, this may explain its title
– black populations migrated up
to New York from cities such
as Charleston. The dance had
already appeared earlier that
spring in another black musical,
Liza, and was at first mainly
adopted by boys – described by
one newspaper as "street urchins"
– who would perform it for a
penny in the hat. From the streets,
the Charleston rapidly became a
global dance craze, though it
was banned from some ballrooms
and ratskellers for its sexual
innuendo and exposure of
excessive female flesh.

1924

This is one of those 'so near, yet so far' growing seasons.

Perusing the Tastet-Lawton archives, I noticed how entries for the first three months hardly talk about the growing season and concentrate upon the market. Finally, vines are worthy of mention in May, which had begun cool and overcast, then warmed up and accelerated vines' growth. Flowering began on 1 June with some outbreak of eudemis and cochylis, then the middle month saw heavy rain and severe hail damage in some of Bordeaux's satellite regions. Four sunny days from the summer equinox revived winemakers' spirits, temperatures reaching 33°C (91°F) by the end of the month and eradicating mildew pressure. But July was unseasonably cool and overcast with occasional storms and outbreaks of black rot. August started with heat spikes yet turned rainy towards the end of the month. The season was saved by a sunny and warm September, except for pre-harvest storms around 8 September. With potential alcohol reaching 12–12.5%, picking was underway from around 19 September and it stayed warm and sunny with cool nights until October. After a bit of a roller coaster season, the result was an abundant crop of decent reds that lacked the staying power of 1926, 1928 or 1929. Sauternes came within a whisker of producing a great vintage after two spells of rain in September and October caused widespread botrytis and more showers in late October led to further infection. The problem was not the level of botrytis, more that much of the fruit failed to reach adequate levels of sugar concentration.

Over the years, I have been fortunate to taste several clarets from this vintage, which is reputed to be best in Saint-Émilion and the Graves. Yet without doubt, the finest has been from Pauillac, the 1924 Latour, tasted on two occasions several years apart: pure, refined and yet aristocratic. Bottles with sound provenance will still give pleasure, and do not be afraid to decant. This was not my first encounter with a First Growth. That honour belongs to a 1924 Lafite Rothschild, a purchase when you could buy these bottles for tuppence. Opened for a Christmas knees-up in London with an old university friend, it could not match the Latour and felt rather fatigued. Yet at that stage it was the oldest vintage I had ever tasted and, in retrospect, was a catalyst for my love of mature Bordeaux. The 1924 Château Margaux suggests that many Left Bank wines did not have a long shelf-life, though a 1924 Montrose at an epic vertical in June 2016 was marvellous, solid yet fresh and resoundingly complex. One bottle of 1924 Léoville-Las Cases felt heavily chaptalised, fleshy but rapidly falling victim to oxygen. In Sauternes, I have encountered a very fine 1924 Climens (despite an unwanted tinge of cork taint) and a sprightly bottle of 1924 Filhot that provided the perfect finish to a vertical at the château.

Event
Hubble discovers the
Andromeda galaxy

On 30 December, Missouri-
born Edwin Hubble announced
that what hitherto was thought
a nebula was in fact, a galaxy.
Astronomers had considered the
Milky Way to be an island of
stars beyond which lay infinite
nothingness (a bit like the Essex
countryside). After months
observing Andromeda through
a 100-inch Hooker telescope
at Mount Wilson Observatory,
Hubble identified a star that he
labelled V1 that lay beyond our
galaxy – two million light years
away to be exact. This landmark
discovery expanded our concept
of the universe. There was much
more out there than we thought
(unlike the Essex countryside).

Music
Rhapsody in Blue
– George Gershwin

Rhapsody in Blue contains one of
the most striking openings of any
20th-century composition: its
clarinet glissando never ceases to
stop you in your tracks. Gershwin,
though, didn't write it. His lead
clarinettist elongated the opening
notes as a joke and Gershwin
immediately told him to make
the glissando wail as much as
possible. He had started to piece
together *Rhapsody in Blue* in his
head while on a train to Boston,
the name later suggested by his
brother Ira Gershwin after he
visited an exhibition of Whistler
paintings that mentioned colours
in the titles. It premiered on
12 February 1924 at the Aeolian
Hall in Manhattan to an audience
that included the renowned
composers mentioned in this
book's entries for 1893 and 1913
(pages 81 and 131).

1924
(Continued)

Film
The Navigator
– Buster Keaton

The Navigator, co-directed with Donald Crisp, premiered at the Capitol theatre in New York on 13 October 1924 and went on to become the silent movie star's biggest commercial success. Keaton plays Rollo Treadway who ends up boarding the same ship as the former paramour who had rejected his marriage proposal. The film was shot on the passenger ship USAT *Buford* and the cast and crew lived aboard the vessel for 10 weeks of filming. Underwater scenes were shot in swimming baths whose retaining walls had to be heightened, though the water pressure broke the bottom of the pool. Keaton had to pay for the repairs out of his own pocket.

The 1925 vintage is not one of the decade's finest growing seasons.

A chilly March prompted vines to shut down, reawakening at the beginning of a clement but fresh April. Saint-Émilion, and to a lesser extent Pomerol, were struck by hail on 19 April. Poor weather at the end of the month retarded the vines' growth cycle and changeable weather extended into May. June was warm and flowering occurred at the same time as the previous year, plagued by disruptive storms. Nevertheless, the vines were in healthy condition. July saw intermittent sunny days interspersed with storms that predicated brown rot towards the end of the month. August was beset with heat spikes that caused some burning of grape skins. Rainclouds refused to disperse and exacerbated an uneven *véraison*. It was almost as if Mother Nature was teasing winemakers, every sporadic ray of sunshine followed by yet another rainstorm hot on its heels. A northerly wind kept temperatures down in September and the grapes struggled to reach full maturity. Unsurprisingly, it was a tardy harvest that started around 3 October, though with potential alcohol languishing around 11–11.5%, some châteaux avoided risk and picked a couple of weeks earlier. Quality was patchy: the wines pale, rather weak and a little green. Though they meliorated during their barrel maturation, merchants ignored them. It was a middling vintage in Sauternes. The 37 mm (1½ in) of rain in September caused ample botrytis and although many vineyard teams picked right through until 24 November, including at Yquem, the fruit never achieved satisfying potential alcohol levels.

This is a rarely seen vintage and my only tasting notes derive from Sauternes: a 1925 Lafaurie-Peyraguey, which was still going strong at the vertical in December 2018 and showing better than a slightly oxidative 1925 Climens poured in Zurich several years earlier.

1925

1925
(Continued)

Event
F. Scott Fitzgerald publishes
The Great Gatsby

Fitzgerald's tale of enigmatic millionaire Jay Gatsby and his old lover Daisy Buchanan with its glitterati of socialites and lavish parties on Long Island is the quintessential twenties novel. You can almost hear the jazz band playing as you turn its pages. Published on 10 April 1925, it met with mixed reviews and was initially a commercial failure compared to Fitzgerald's previous books. It only started to gain widespread popularity after his death in 1940 and obituaries eulogised the novel. It has now sold in excess of 25 million copies.

Music
Saint Louis Blues
– Bessie Smith

In the twenties female blues singers ruled and Bessie Smith was the Beyoncé of her time. Her definitive version of W.C. Handy's blues standard (page 133) features no less than Louis Armstrong on cornet and their interplay is so intoxicating that it sounds more like a call-and-return duet. Born in Chattanooga to poverty after her parents died young, she sang for the first time as a teenager, apparently sauntering on stage in her street clothes, knowing her powerful voice was all that was necessary. Smith learned her craft under Ma Rainey, recording records for Columbia from 1925 and becoming the highest-paid black entertainer. Gaining the nickname the "Empress of the Blues", she travelled the country in her own private railroad car and starred in the film *St. Louis Blues* in 1929. However, her career took a nosedive after the Depression and she eschewed opportunities to move into jazz. She died in a car crash in 1937.

Film
Phantom of the Opera
– Rupert Julian

After his outstanding performance as the hunchback, Lon Chaney again spent hours in make-up to play the deformed phantom who skulks around the catacombs beneath the Paris Opera House in the film adaptation of Gaston Leroux's *Le Fantôme d'Opéra*. In the 1910 book, the character's grotesque facial features are the result of flesh-eating ants that were set upon him after he fell out of favour with a Persian Sultana. Given this might put cinema-goers off their popcorn, it was edited out of the movie version. The skull-like make-up was self-applied by Chaney. Preview audiences reacted negatively and so Universal reshot some scenes to add more romance and comedic interludes before the premiere in New York on 6 September 1925. Audiences allegedly screamed when the phantom's mask was ripped away since it had been kept secret until its release. Good job they didn't know about the flesh-eating ants.

1926

"Not a cloud in the sky!" declares Lawton in March in the family archives, perhaps with a sense of misplaced optimism.

The year got off to a warm and sunny start and by 22 March, those out in the vineyard reported explosive vine growth that surely prompted concerns about frost. Temperatures of 26–28°C (79–82°F) encouraged vines to develop, though Théophile Skawinski, the *régisseur* at Léoville-Las Cases, noted that plunging temperatures on 7 April stopped the sap from rising. Still, comparisons were being made with the hot growing season of 1893, at least until the end of that month when a northerly wind brought cold temperatures and localised hail. The weather swung either way in May and though temperatures were low, there was little frost. The pendulum-like conditions affected flowering, which was irregular and poor fruit set predicated a small crop, some areas losing 30% to 40% to coulure. Though others elsewhere reported that July was cool, Lawton states that temperatures were high and peaked at 34°C (93°F) mid-July. August witnessed heat spikes of 35°C (95°F) and there were concerns about hydric stress with little relief for vines. The first three days in September saw violent storms each afternoon, after which it stayed overcast until 14 September, when a southerly hauled temperatures back up to 30°C (86°F), according to the owners of Château Talbot at the time. It remained dry until the first pickers ventured out on 27 September, though some of these would have been to clean the vineyard of unripe bunches before the harvest really got going on 4 October. One interesting anecdote from Tastet-Lawton is that the sale of the 1926 Cheval Blanc took place on 7 October by sealed envelope, which must have been intriguing to witness. It rained on and off during picking, which finished around 16 October under sunny skies. It was a small crop, 4.4 million hl, around 35% down on the previous year. Château Latour was picked at a measly 7 hl/ha but was apparently a stellar wine (though my solitary encounter came riddled with cork taint). Not so much because of the diminished crop but rather because of the revaluation of the French franc, the wines were expensive on release and Ian Maxwell Campbell noted that consumers ignored these rather "coarse" clarets. In Sauternes, there were hopes that rain on 31 August would ignite botrytis, but it failed to really infect the vines until further showers on 6 October. Unfortunately, the following downpours washed away hopes of a good crop of sweet wines.

Rarely seen due to the small harvest, I have had only three encounters with the 1926 clarets. A broad-shouldered magnum of 1926 Talbot at its centenary vertical had held up well, though had a bucolic heart. The best, a magnum of 1926 Canon, chosen when invited to pick anything from their considerable cellar, suggesting an admirable Right Bank vintage, holding up and blossoming throughout an alfresco supper. Of two Sauternes, the 1926 Lafaurie-Peyraguey was impressive and swarthy after 92 years, whereas a bottle of 1926 Climens several years earlier was decrepit.

Event
Agatha Christie disappears

On 3 December 1926 Agatha Christie's Morris Cowley was found abandoned at Newlands Corner in the Surrey Hills. Like a scene straight out of her detective novels, the author's whereabouts were a mystery and made newspaper headlines. One-thousand police officers combed the area and Sir Arthur Conan Doyle gave a medium one of her gloves to help track her down. Eleven days later, the author was found safe and sound in a hotel in Harrogate. She never explained what had happened, though speculation is that she had suffered some kind of nervous breakdown following an acrimonious divorce. Newlands Corner lies just 10 minutes from my home and flowers are still left to mark her vanishing.

Music
Black Bottom Stomp – Jelly Roll Morton and the Red Hot Peppers

Black Bottom Stomp was composed in 1925 and released on the Victor record label the following year. Morton was a legendary ragtime pianist who claimed to have invented jazz back in 1902. Indeed, he had a bit of a chip on his shoulder and frequently claimed to have been robbed of royalties (not unlike Chuck Berry throughout his career). His hubris should not diminish his status as one of the leading innovators of the New Orleans sound. This particular song was backed by the Red Hot Peppers, who included influential jazz trombonist Kid Ory. Listen and try not to tap your feet.

Film
Battleship Potemkin
– Sergei Eisenstein

Eisenstein's epic tells the true story of a crew's mutiny aboard an Imperial naval vessel that spills over onto the streets of Odessa as it enters port. The famous massacre on the Odessa Steps, filmed by cinematographer Eduard Tisse, was not in the original script but added during production. Such is the power of the movie that it was banned in many countries for fears of inciting communism or worker insurrection, including in Russia where the ban was only lifted after Stalin's death in 1953. *Battleship Potemkin* is now rightly regarded as a cinematic masterpiece.

1927

This was an anomalous horrible growing season of the twenties.

March saw persistent rain from which there was only some relief on 1 and 2 April. That month's cool spells discouraged bud break and May was changeable. The first flowers could be spotted around 25 May, but non-stop torrential rain on 12 June augured the rest of the season. Millerandage was endemic, nascent berries falling off or stunted in growth. Humid conditions prevailed and those working in the vines had to combat oidium and mildew. Margaux was hit by hail on 1 July. Waves of storms criss-crossed the region, some with hail that plagued châteaux for the rest of the month. Consequently, rot was difficult to control. A lack of sunshine meant sugar accumulation was slow so that by the end of August, châteaux had all but given up hope of anything near a decent harvest. It probably didn't matter that the rain did not cease throughout September. There was no point in waiting and harvesters went out around 27 September and finished around 10 October. The wines were pale and feeble, tasting of "dried leaves", according to Lawton when sampling from vat in December. André Simon was more positive, even if he cautioned that the wines were "too light to last", while Ian Maxwell Campbell remarks that he hardly saw any '27s in the English market and put them on par with 1919 and 1925. "Very poor wines," rues Michael Broadbent in his *Vintage Wine* tome about his birth year. "At least I survived." Brilliant. In Sauternes, winemakers suffered cool conditions from June. Late September rain brought some botrytis but also some sour rot that needed to be eradicated. Dry weather concentrated the fruit and further passes through the vines were made in the second half of October.

Unsurprisingly, many 1927 clarets were consumed in their youth and were almost immediately eclipsed by the following two vintages. I have not tasted any dry reds, but by all accounts, the rainy conditions were perfect for botrytis formation. I have had two encounters with Sauternes: a fabulous 1927 Lafaurie-Peyraguey that I could have drunk all night at the vertical in December 2018 and a very commendable, quite dainty 1927 Climens at the vertical in Zurich. Better to search for 1927s in the Douro Valley where Port houses made a General Declaration.

Event
Babe Ruth scores 60 home runs

Music
Dark Was the Night, Cold Was the Ground – Blind Willie Johnson

Considered the greatest baseball player of all time, "The Bambino" scored a record 60th home run of the season on 30 September 1927. It came in the New York Yankees 4-2 win over the Washington Senators, the final game of the season, whereupon jubilant spectators threw their hats and torn paper into the air to celebrate. Ruth was part of the so-called "Murderer's Row" line-up that also included Lou Gehrig, Tony Lazzeri and Bob Meusel, though Ruth was always in a league of his own.

Texas-born Blind Willie Johnson, who unlike some blues singers *was* actually blind, having lost his sight as a young child, recorded this masterpiece on 3 December 1927. The title comes from an English hymn written in 1792 by Thomas Haweis. The crackly recording was released on Vocalion and consists solely of Johnson's ethereal slide guitar together with his hums and moans, which translate its transcendental emotive power. In 1945, Johnson died penniless after his house had burnt down. The song is currently spinning through the cosmos at 37,000 mph (60,000 km/h) since it is one of the recordings on the *Voyager I* space probe. To quote comedian Steve Martin, Martians will reply with the message: "Send more Blind Willie Johnson."

1927 *(Continued)*

1870

2020

1927
(Continued)

Film
Metropolis – Fritz Lang

Fritz Lang's expressionist masterpiece produced some of the most memorable cinematic images of the 20th century. It was filmed over 17 months on a huge budget for the time, 5.3 million German marks – not surprising given the thousands of extras and elaborate set designs and special effects involved. Actors reported that production was long and hard: lead actress Brigitte Helm fainted inside the robot costume during the famous transformation sequence because it took so many hours to film. *Metropolis* received a cool and occasionally disparaging reception, even from H.G. Wells, who you'd think would have a penchant for such dystopian sci-fi. It did have one fan, though: Adolf Hitler, who loved it so much that he overlooked Lang's Jewish heritage. Decades later, *Metropolis* can be seen as one of the most audacious and influential films ever, whose lessons are perhaps even more pertinent today as they were back then.

1928

The reputation of the 1928 vintage is richly deserved – one of the great inter-war growing seasons that produced a treasure trove of outstanding and long-lived wines, the first of a pair that finished the decade on a high.

February saw a fortnight of incessant rain that caused minor flooding, then the weather turned clement for the rest of the month. The vines' growth cycle got off to a quick start thanks to splendid weather and unseasonably warm temperatures in the first half of March, though winter made a brief return, the mercury plummeting to -3°C (26.5°F) on 12 March. This cold snap continued for three days and burnt some of the buds, though not too seriously. April was cold and rainy with minor frost episodes on 17 and 23 March, the latter more damaging, especially in the Graves. May was decidedly cool, the Tastet-Lawton entry on 18 May ruing that there had not been a single warm day for three weeks. Talk was of a disastrous vintage. But the weather turned more favourable at the end of May when the thermometer reached 27°C (80°F) and it hovered around that figure throughout June. The flowering, which reached *pleine fleur* on 15 June, lasted 15 days with just a little millerandage. July simmered nicely, warm and dry so that vineyards remained in healthy sanitary condition, while August saw temperatures reach 35°C (95°F) with rainfall on 4, 15, 21 and 29 August preventing hydric stress.

The clement weather continued unabated and the first pickers entered the vineyard from 18 September with must weights around 12.5–14%. Cool nights kept a lid on alcohol levels and rainfall on 25 September took some of the heat away at the opportune moment as the harvest ploughed ahead and fruit entered vat-rooms. Without temperature-controlled vats, these more moderate conditions meant there was less risk of volatility and spoilage. Picking finished between 12 and 17 October and initial tastings from vat portended a great vintage albeit with some occasionally rugged tannins. Meanwhile, in Sauternes, winemakers benefited from a warm and dry summer followed by 50 mm (2 in) of rain in early September that provoked widespread botrytis. The first pass through vines provided concentrated berries. Following 100 mm (4 in) of rain on 9 October, there were fewer dry windows to pick and so later passes through the vines were far less consistent.

Ian Maxwell Campbell initially preferred the '28s over the '29s, describing them as "well-balanced and well-bred, full to the taste and, at the same time, supple… There was a touch of tannin and roughness about them, it is true, but it seemed to me to be counterbalanced by a sufficiency of fruit and sugar." He confesses that he misjudged the tannins, which did not soften nearly as quickly as he predicted. Indeed, the '28s were renowned or chided, depending upon your level of patience, for their glacial pace of maturity. Michael Broadbent famously remarked that Latour took half a century to reach its drinking window.

The 1928 vintage is the oldest in which I could claim modest experience, having accreted more than 30 tasting notes over the years. Each and every encounter is cherished. Approaching any bottle of '28 is always preceded by heightened anticipation, in no small part because their longevity means that decades on, these are no curios from a bygone age, rather wines that continue to cruise at high altitude. There is no vintage for which the word "ageless" is more apt. Over the years I have tasted all the First Growths, including Mouton Rothschild, lest we forget, still seething at its Second Growth status. The 1928 Latour was Michael Broadbent's "star of the vintage" and after years of it evading me, I finally got to taste a magnum served over lunch in Hong Kong. Despite its age, it demanded 90 minutes to unfold and reveal its multi-dimensional magnificence, even if the 1929 has the edge. The Latour overshadows the strangely anaemic 1928 Lafite Rothschild, which represented my first encounter with the vintage at a dinner held at Doisy-Védrines. I was seated next to estate director Charles Chevalier, who was disparaging about his own contribution and confirmed Penning-Rowsell's assertion that the wine had been pasteurised to stabilise it from the heat, a process that denudes it of class. The 1928 Château Margaux has held up well, though two bottles of the 1928 Palmer suggest that it stole top honours in the appellation that year – ethereal, floral and bewitching. The 1928 Lascombes was also chugging nicely along when opened in 2022. The 1928 Mouton Rothschild, served blind in Bordeaux, curiously seemed to lack depth and intensity. My solitary encounter with the 1928 Haut-Brion at the London retrospective was so precocious that looking back, I question its authenticity (purportedly another wine that was pasteurised), while the 1928 La Mission Haut-Brion at dinner in Hong Kong in 2018 was more poised and balletic. Moving through the hierarchy there are many standouts, though one that sticks in my memory is a magisterial 1928 Gruaud Larose that had an entire room of tasters in the palm of its hand in London. It showed better than a slightly weary yet pleasurable 1928 Ducru-Beaucaillou served at the annual Grouse Club lunch with Lord Bruce in 2020, while the 1928 Léoville-Las Cases displayed impressive concentration with just a soupçon of volatility that I could easily abide. I have fond memories of a soulful 1928 Domaine de Chevalier poured by Olivier Bernard at the château and a grippy 1928 Cos d'Estournel that was firing on all cylinders at the château after 90 years. Other notable '28s include Brane-Cantenac, a briny Branaire-Ducru, a very convincing Batailley, a tobacco-tinged Siran, a cedar-infused Pontet-Canet and a 1928 Poujeaux mischievously served blind by proprietor Mathieu Cuvelier. We all piped up that it must surely be an '82. Right numbers – wrong order. It epitomises the time-defying acrobatics of the vintage.

I have far less experience on the Right Bank, which was still playing second fiddle to the Left Bank. I have fond memories of both 1928 Pétrus and Cheval Blanc, the latter sublime if faded compared to the best wines on the Left Bank. Sauternes enjoyed an exceptionally strong season crowned by a breathtaking 1928 Yquem. Lafaurie-Peyraguey, Suduiraut, Doisy-Daëne and Doisy-Védrines continue to drink well. Perhaps I was expecting more from the 1928 Climens given the stellar wine it produced the following year.

Event
Walt Disney introduces Mickey Mouse

Walt Disney was riding a cross-country train from Manhattan to Hollywood when an idea popped into his head for an animated anthropomorphic mouse. Disney was at a low ebb. His business was foundering after the acrimonious departure of Charles Mintz, who had taken cartoon characters with him to rival Universal. He developed his idea with Ub Iwerks and Mrs. Disney suggested the name "Mickey". The first two cartoons, *Plane Crazy* and *The Gallopin' Goucho*, were poorly received when previewed. Fortunately, audiences were far more receptive when he appeared in *Steamboat Willie*, which premiered at the Colony Theatre in New York on 18 November 1928. It was one of the first cartoons to combine animation with synchronised sound. The $1,000 received for a fortnight run saved the fledgling studio and Disney never looked back.

Music
Mack the Knife
– Kurt Weill and Bertolt Brecht

Mack the Knife was written by Kurt Weill for *The Threepenny Opera*, the lyrics composed by Bertolt Brecht. "Mack" refers to the murderous title character, Macheath, and its original title was "Murder Ballad". This last-minute addition to the opera was supposed to be accompanied by a barrel organ, but the instrument broke on the night and the pit orchestra had to improvise. Translated into English, the lyrics are far less graphic than in the original. Numerous artists have released their own versions, including Louis Armstrong, Frank Sinatra and Robbie Williams. Out of all of them, Bobby Darin's 1959 take is probably the most popular.

1928
(Continued)

Film
The Passion of Joan of Arc
– Carl Theodor Dreyer

Maria Falconetti shed so many
tears as the Maid of Orleans
that she could have extinguished
the flames herself as they licked
around her feet. Her performance
in the Danish director's biopic
is one of the most moving
ever committed to the silver
screen and she never utters a
single word. The camera focuses
unrelentingly on Falconetti's face,
which expresses terror, anguish
and futility to devastating effect.
Dreyer instructed the actress to
forego any cosmetics and in one
scene has her hair brutally cut
close to her scalp. Censorship
ordered by the Archbishop of
Paris led to numerous edits
and the original version was
not shown until 1981. It was
Falconetti's second and final role,
yet it remains one of cinema's
most revered performances.

Nineteen twenty-nine saw the first back-to-back successful vintages since 1899 and 1900. However, the resulting wines are cut from a different cloth to 1928 and until I examined the season closer, I never realised that it was fraught with so many challenges. It is a miracle the wines achieved such heights.

February was bitterly cold. The mercury plunged to -8°C (17.5°F), the cold weather lingering into early March. Hardly a spot of rain fell until the spring equinox and this delayed the vines' growth cycle. Consecutive days of frost severely damaged the early buds, some estates losing three-quarters of their potential crop. There was almost total evisceration at Cantemerle. Only Sauternes was let off the hook. Plagued by frost and then hail, Paul Skawinski at Léoville-Las Cases declared that his "vintage was done" as early as 28 April! Prevailing northeasterly winds kept temperatures low during May, though intermittent torrential rain replenished underground reserves. Rainclouds continued to hang overhead and disturbed June's flowering, followed by a period of warm and humid weather that increased the mildew pressure. "I cannot dream of such poor weather for the vine," laments Daniel Lawton in the archives on 6 July. But the following day turned warm and dry and temperatures reached 36°C (97°F) just a couple of weeks later. The first 10 or so days of August were stormy, though *véraison* was rapid and the rest of the month saw plenty of sunshine and warm temperatures, to the extent that there was some *grillure* at the beginning of September.

The first half of that month witnessed heavy storms and humidity, but the vintage kicked off around 19 September at Latour, despite scepticism that the season would yield quality wines. Fermentations were tricky and yet early on, the suppleness of the wines, especially compared with the tannic '28s, was already evident. Lawton reports that the '29s were impressive as early as November but, to quote the entry on 17 November, nobody was interested in buying them since global stock markets were in free fall. In the very first Tastet-Lawton entry of the thirties, the merchant describes the disquieting absence of activity on the market and that 80 million hl of 1929 was available. Who was going to drink them?

Sauternes enjoyed a dry season whereby the heat gradually increased as the weeks rolled by. Yquem's weather station recorded 14 days over 30°C (86°F) in September. Conditions remained textbook throughout the harvest allowing teams to pick at the optimal moment, just checking that sugar levels did not become excessive. At Yquem, which picked from 24 September to 8 November, potential alcohol reached 26%.

1929
(Continued)

I have not tasted the 1929s as extensively as the 1928s. Apart from the fact that the wines have mostly been drunk, it was a small vintage, negligible for some châteaux. The 1929 Latour is stunning and perhaps, against consensus, I found it superior to the 1928 when it was poured at dinner in Hong Kong. The 1929 Mouton Rothschild is one of Baron Philippe de Rothschild's early successes, utterly sublime when generously poured blind over lunch in London, transparent and graceful. I have not had the pleasure of the other Firsts. The most memorable wine from this vintage was the last remaining Marie-Jeanne of Clos de l'Église-Clinet, opened by Denis Durantou at a dinner. Made by his grandfather, this ancient Pomerol was frail, yet provided glimmers of enjoyment. A 1929 Latour à Pomerol served in London was tertiary on the nose, rustic and a bit unclean. The best 1929s I have tasted are Cos d'Estournel and Ausone. Others, including Batailley, Léoville Poyferré, Beychevelle, Rauzan-Ségla and Canon, have all been impressive, but I had the nagging feeling they were past their peaks. Sauternes knocked the ball out of the park in 1929 – it is bejewelled with spectacular sweet wines that can astound after almost a century. The 1929 Yquem, the culmination of a bacchanal in Kowloon, was pure and penetrating, a pyrotechnical display of aromas and senses undimmed by passing decades. Not to be outdone (and, my word, I would love to taste them side by side), the Climens and Lafaurie-Peyraguey bottles I have encountered were also sheer perfection, while Suduiraut was not far off in quality.

Event
The Wall Street crash

The Roaring Twenties came to an abrupt halt on 29 October 1929, otherwise known as Black Tuesday. An overheated Wall Street stock market had seen not just bankers, but ordinary American citizens use their savings and re-mortgage their homes in order to plough everything into shares. The bubble burst and shares began to slide, inciting a frenzy of mass selling, despite the Hoover administration's futile attempts to quell the panic by insisting it was a short-term blip. The Treasury Secretary assured them that "prosperity lay just around the corner". What did lie just around the corner was the Great Depression, which would define the following decade.

Music
Ain't Misbehavin'
– Louis Armstrong

"Fats" Waller and Harry Brooks wrote the score for a Broadway musical, *Connie's Hot Chocolate*, that premiered at the Hudson Theatre in June 1929 and featured the early swing tune, *Ain't Misbehavin'*. Trumpeter Louis Armstrong led the pit orchestra and encouraged by the audience began to mount the stage during the intermission to play the trumpet solo to great applause. It turned Armstrong into one of America's most beloved and influential stars. Waller himself re-recorded the song for the 1943 film *Stormy Weather*.

Film
Double Whoopee
– Lewis R. Foster

Double Whoopee saw Laurel and Hardy finish the silent age of film in typically hilarious style, though not without scandal. In its famous scene, 18-year-old Jean Harlow's dress becomes caught in a taxi door and when the vehicle drives away, Harlow is left in her underwear. She strides into a packed hotel blithely unaware of her deshabille. *The Jazz Singer* had ushered in the age of sound, though thankfully for fans of Stan and Ollie, the duo adapted better than other silent stars to the new era.

The
1930s

The thirties saw the implementation of legislation that codified pre-existing rules and established a framework for winemakers to follow that remains in situ to this day. Better late than never. On 30 July 1935, the French government passed a law that bolstered rules set in 1919 that had defined Bordeaux's appellations (page 121). Any label bearing the name of the appellation had to originate from within its boundaries. Crucially, grape varieties would be regulated. Georges Bord's survey in 1932 listed "fine" and "ordinary" varieties cultivated in Bordeaux's vineyards, with the latter including oddities such as Grappu, Pardotte and Panereuilh (the last should have been outlawed for being unpronounceable). Bord's work provided the foundation for the separation of principal and secondary varieties that vineyards should cultivate. The decree similarly legislated on pruning methods, minimal alcohol levels (11.5% for Saint-Émilion Grand Cru Classe, 10.5% for Saint-Estèphe, Pauillac, Saint-Julien, Moulis, Listrac, Margaux and Pomerol, 10% for the Graves, Haut-Médoc and the Médoc) and maximum yields, set at 40 hl/ha, though this figure could be modified by authorities. Regulations were to be overseen by the newly created Comité National des Appellations d'Origine, renamed the Institut National des Appellations d'Origine (I.N.A.O.) in 1947. The first vintage subject to these new rules was 1937. The following year also saw chaptalisation legalised, even though it was already common practice to add sugar during the alcoholic fermentation in Burgundy (obtaining sugar in the years leading up to the war was another question, however). Separate to this, in 1932 the first classification of Crus Bourgeois du Médoc was made, allowing properties existing outside the influential 1855 Classification to be part of a qualitative hierarchy at lower price levels for, as its name implies, the bourgeoisie.

Unfortunately, these laws and classifications seeking to improve quality coincided with a miserable run of growing seasons and a global economic slump, all in the shadow of Nazism's insidious rise across the border in Germany. In retrospect, the decade represented a nadir and Bordeaux's wines were acutely sensitive to the malaise. Consumers did not have money to fritter away on a luxurious beverage and poor quality gave them no incentive to open their wallets, not that there was much in them.

Apart from 1934 and to a lesser extent, 1937, Bordeaux endured one forgettable summer after another. Many châteaux did not release any wine for three consecutive years in 1930, 1931 and 1932, leaving coffers empty. That had grave consequences. At Vieux Château Certan, proprietor and father of six young children, Georges Thienpont was deprived of a livelihood and in 1935 was forced to sell Troplong Mondot. That same year, a 10-year-old Francis

Nicolas never forgot a fateful evening at his family's Pomerol estate, La Conseillante. On the eve of harvest, his father Henri opened the front door to find hailstones the size of chickens' eggs strafing the vines. Later on that night, for the first time in his life, he saw his father weep. No wonder, like many others eking a living off the land, Nicolas encouraged his children to pursue alternative careers – winemaking could no longer support a family.

Lack of income and lack of investment meant many vineyards, including famous Grands Crus Classés, began to deteriorate. Superannuated vines were either unproductive or simply died and left gaping holes across the blanket of serried vines. The number of hectares under vine shrunk and wineries made do with antiquated equipment. With little means or motivation to improve frequently lean and under-ripe wines, prices inevitably suffered. For example, the 1929 Léoville-Las Cases had fallen by one-third of its release price by November 1931 and others doubtless experienced even steeper falls. It was a vicious circle.

Examining the Tastet-Lawton archives, one notices how the ominous political changes in Germany impinged upon Bordeaux winemakers before the outbreak of war. For example, in January 1937, Lawton remarks how it is becoming more difficult and expensive obtaining goods from overseas. Still, there were glimmers of hope in terms of wine, always rubies in the sand. Some 1934s matured beautifully in bottle, while 1937 yielded highly regarded Sauternes.

Taken in the early 1930s, this evocative photograph depicts the Borie family, before their ownership of Ducru-Beaucaillou. Holding his straw hat is Francis Borie with son, Jean-Eugène Borie, in shorts in front. Smartly-attired in the fedora is Francis's brother Marcel, with his daughter Denise next to him. The image belies a stricken region suffering poor harvests and dwindling demand.

1930

So began the first of four vintages that took many winemakers to the brink.

The year started very rainy with 690 mm (27 in) from mid-September to February, an omen of things to come – 1930 would be the wettest year until 1960. Spring-like weather towards the end of February was swiftly followed by deluges in March so severe that they caused flooding and fatalities in the Gironde. Vines began to leaf at the end of the month and a fortnight's settled weather expedited growth. Alas, in the first half of May, barely a day passed without the need for umbrellas and yet curiously at Latour, long-standing *régisseur* Daniel Jouet was feeling positive about the season. Flowering was late and continuous rain – some 113 mm (4½ in) in June – predicated a strong attack of mildew with severe coulure the following month. Winemakers had not witnessed vines in such a poor state and could not recall such an inclement July. They were already calling 1930 "*un nouveau 1897*". Downpours were relentless, though there was a three-week spell of warmer weather that, to quote Jouet again, "salvaged what remained of the crop". The mercury continued to climb to 35°C (95°F) at the beginning of September and ironically, after such terrible weather, some of the grape skins were burnt. Clement conditions in mid-September were little, too late. The harvest commenced around 1 October under perfect conditions, as if to rub salt into wounds. Édouard Féret describes the wines as "light and mean", while Charles Walter Berry can barely contain his ire in his *In Search of Wine*: "If ever there was a bad vintage, here you have it." He goes on to lament the quality of the 1930 Latour, suggesting that even this renowned First Growth had produced a wine that might dissuade Bordeaux lovers from ever drinking its products again. It was no better in Sauternes. After a dry August and September that precluded botrytis formation, 275 mm (11 in) of rain fell in October, which meant that, despite pickers going into the vineyard for 28 days over six weeks at Yquem, nothing was deemed worthy of the label. I doubt anyone else produced any sweet wine in 1930.

One hardly ever sees this vintage. Most of the wines were probably consumed in their youth during the thirties. However, I have come across two. Firstly, an ancient and long-defunct Pomerol, 1930 Clos du Commandeur, which Olivier Bernard served blind at one of his Domaine de Chevalier soirées and was perfectly drinkable, if possibly cut with some 1929. The other was a Pauillac, 1930 La Tourelle, which turned up at lunch at La Trompette in Chiswick. It was just a little anaemic, but not undrinkable.

Event
Uruguay wins the first
FIFA World Cup

On 30 July 1930, Uruguay beat
Argentina 4-2 in the first FIFA
World Cup final at the Estadio
Centenario in Montevideo. FIFA
President Jules Rimet helped
organise the competition, which
had no qualifying games, but
was unable to persuade many of
Europe's top teams to attend –
partly because unemployment was
climbing and many players feared
they would have no job to return
to. As a consequence, England,
Italy, Spain and Germany
declined to participate.

Film
The Blue Angel
– Josef von Sternberg

Marlene Dietrich shot to stardom
as cabaret singer Lola Lola
in Sternberg's *The Blue Angel*,
which premiered on 1 April
1930 in Berlin. The actress had
been spotted by the director in a
Berlin revue and he insisted she
play the role, mesmerised by her
sexuality and her world-weary
attitude during a test screening.
Dietrich's stealing of the limelight
so incensed her male co-star,
Emil Jannings, that he threatened
to throttle her on set. Dietrich
and Sternberg had an affair that
caused scandal in the papers, but
they ignored the brouhaha and
went on to make several more
films together.

Music
Preachin' the Blues
– Son House

Delta Bluesman Son House
led a conflicted double life.
Growing up in the Deep South
he regularly attended church and
became a pastor in Mississippi
by the age of 20. Out walking
one day, he overheard a guitar
and transfixed by its sound,
bought his own, which had one
missing string and a hole in
the back. He patched it up and
perfected his art as a gigging
bluesman while continuing his
religious work. This dual life,
leading sermons while playing
what his parishioners termed "the
devil's music", created an inner
conflict that inspired *Preachin' the
Blues*, which was released on the
Paramount label in 1930.

1931

The dire state of the market is mentioned in the opening entries of Tastet-Lawton's records in January '31. "*Les affaires sont dans la marasme…*" – business is in a slump. It was little better meteorologically speaking.

February set the tone with a fortnight of rain that continued into March, though sporadic spells of dryness encouraged vines to awaken. April and May were both very changeable and wet, and warmer temperatures at the end of May caused mildew. Flowering was disrupted by storms at the beginning of June, but a window of dry sunny weather from 9 to 11 June offered hope until July brought further deluges. August was cool and saw three weeks of downpours that totalled 195 mm (7½ in), approximately quadruple the average. Hope springs eternal for many winemakers, but by this point they were downbeat as the rain refused to let up. The harvest did not commence until 25 September and things were looking up for the first five days until the weather deteriorated once again. While October saw outbreaks of sun, it was too late. The first tastings in November indicated the wines were light, rather green and acidic with comparisons made to 1922 and 1925. In Sauternes, July to September was "glacially" cold at Yquem with hail reported on 6 August. Remarkably only a single barrel reached 20% potential alcohol at the estate, even after one of the tardiest starts to the harvest on record – around 14 or 15 October – and 39 days of work in the vineyard.

One hardly ever sees this vintage because quantities were not large and most would have been drunk young. While the dry reds have evaded my palate, I did encounter an absolutely delicious and vivacious 1931 Yquem in June 2016, which implies that the late harvest and hard work in the vineyard bore fruit in the end, literally and figuratively.

Event
Al Capone is sent to jail

Al Capone, a.k.a. "Scarface", achieved unparalleled notoriety as a mafia kingpin, the leader of the Chicago Outfit during Prohibition. Capone relished his celebrity status – the dapper, cigar-chomping, pin-striped mobster in his tilted fedora was cheered as he attended baseball games. Booze-starved citizens revered him as a Robin Hood-like figure. On the other hand, Robin Hood would not have ordered the St. Valentine's Day massacre. This killing in broad daylight woke many up to his ruthlessness and newspapers dubbed him "Public Enemy No.1". On 17 October 1931, after federal agent Eliot Ness and his team of "Untouchables" had begun successfully dismantling his bootlegging business, Capone was found guilty of tax evasion and sentenced to 11 years in prison.

Film
The Public Enemy
– William A. Wellman

James Cagney shot to fame with his visceral performance as underworld hoodlum Tom Powers in *The Public Enemy*. The most famous scene, in which Powers mashes a grapefruit in actress Mae Clarke's face, was actually an unscripted joke in front of the film crew that director Wellman decided to keep. Apparently, Clarke's husband enjoyed it so much that he returned to the cinema several times to see it. *The Public Enemy* set the template for violent gangster movies and remains one of the best.

1931
(Continued)

Music
Minnie the Moocher – Cab
Calloway and His Orchestra

The most famous call-and-
response song of all time was
recorded on 3 March 1931.
Calloway based *Minnie the
Moocher* on the turn-of-century
vaudeville hit *Willie the Weeper*
and introduced the scat after
forgetting the words during a
live radio concert. The audience
participation ("Hi De Hi De Hi
De Hi"/"Ho De Ho De Ho De
Ho") became an integral part of
the song when Calloway, who cut
a distinctive figure with his pencil
moustache and long-tailed suit,
performed it around Chicago's
clubs. Released on the Brunswick
record label, it became one of the
first jazz records to surpass one
million sales. How many of its
listeners understood its lyrics?
It is a miracle that it escaped
censorship. "Kick the gong
around" is jive patois for passing
opium and a "kokie" is a person
who takes cocaine. Calloway's
final, show-stealing performance
was in John Landis's 1980 caper
The Blues Brothers.

Could things get worse? Business continued to languish in the doldrums. Tastet-Lawton signals the state of the market when it reports how 60 *tonneaux* of perfectly decent 1930 Montrose was sold off as generic Saint-Estèphe in tank wagons. The growing season was not about to plant seeds of hope.

January and February were cold but settled, March fresh and dry with showers at the end of the month, then a cold snap mid-April fortuitously did little damage since the vines' growth cycle was so delayed. In May, the weather worsened, discouraging the vines from developing, with only a brief respite on 11 and 12 May. Consequently, the first sightings of flowers were not until mid-June. "In early June," observed Charles Walter Berry during his tour of the region, "there were few leaves and very little fruit on the vines." Mildew ravaged the vineyards as the rain continued through July and August saw wide swings of heavy rainfall, brief days of torrid hot weather and hail damage on 11 August. Unsurprisingly, *véraison* was slow and tardy due to the continuing downpours and by early October, châteaux found it difficult to find anyone to pick the fruit from their beleaguered vines. It was one of the latest harvests ever, with pickers finally trudging into the vines around 15 October under overcast and rainy skies, finishing around 28 October. Despite such tardy picking, many wines were pale and feeble, green with meagre alcohol levels around 8–9%. The late-picked Sauternes likewise offered little reward for their efforts. One can speculate how many châteaux released a Grand Vin and I suspect much of the year's output, like that of Montrose, was sold off as generic Bordeaux.

No Bordeaux wines from this vintage tasted.

1932

1932
(Continued)

Event
Charles Lindbergh's son is kidnapped

On 1 March 1932, the 20-month son of aviator Charles Lindbergh was kidnapped from his home in New Jersey. Ransom notes were sent, postmarked Brooklyn, demanding $70,000 for his return. A go-between, Dr. Condon, negotiated with the unknown kidnapper via a series of cat-and-mouse meetings. Eventually, the child was found by accident near Martha's Vineyard, killed two months earlier via a blow to the head. The investigation took two years and the kidnapper, a carpenter named Richard Hauptmann, was eventually caught by tracking the bills used to make ransom payments.

Film
Grand Hotel – Edmund Goulding

Greta Garbo, John Barrymore and Joan Crawford starred in MGM's all-star movie, which premiered on 12 April 1932 in New York. It broke the mould by featuring more than two big names, which obliged careful handling of egos and Garbo's infamous reclusive and aloof personality. The Swedish star refused to attend the spectacular premiere. She wanted to be alone. Instead, co-actor Wallace Beery appeared as Garbo in drag, a skit that went down like a lead balloon. Despite Garbo's non-appearance, the film became a huge box-office smash.

Music
Brother, Can You Spare a Dime? – Rudy Vallée

No song encapsulates the desperation of the Great Depression like *Brother, Can You Spare a Dime?*, written for the musical *Americana* by Jay Gorney and E.Y. "Yip" Harburg, who had turned to song-writing after his electrical appliance company went bust. The melody was based on a Jewish lullaby that Gorney had heard growing up in Russia and its title came during a spell of writer's block. Taking a walk in Central Park to seek inspiration, a stranger approached Gorney and asked, "Buddy, can you spare a dime?" The song was one of the few to directly address the effects of the Depression, and crooners Rudy Vallée and a young Bing Crosby recorded the most popular versions at the time.

1933

The 1933 season could be the one that got away. It commenced with a cold snap in January, temperatures falling to -10°C (14°F). February and March were relatively benign and dry, though frost damaged young buds on 1 April. Frost continued to be a constant threat but what the vines really needed was water. Instead, on 2 May they got hailstorms causing severe damage in Margaux. The weather improved and the first flowers were spotted around 18 May, yet conditions remained unstable and flowering irregular due to the wind. June was rainy, especially on 15 June, which witnessed a 50 mm (2 in) deluge. Coulure affected the vines and millerandage acutely damaged the Merlot. Matters improved in July and hopes were raised for a better vintage than the previous three. The mercury reached 37°C (99°F) towards the end of the month and some of the berries were burnt. The heat wave continued into August and stressed the vines. Apart from light showers around 21 August, their throats remained parched and it wasn't until 6 September that rain came to relieve them. However, it brought further storms and hail damage in the Graves and Barsac. The harvest commenced around 22 September but a series of heavy downpours plagued the pickers. Winemakers were surprised when musts entered the chai at just 11–12% potential alcohol, indicating that hydric stress had shut down the vines – some Cabernets diluted by rain barely reached double figures. Those vines picked later around 8 or 9 October begat riper fruit, some up to 14% potential alcohol. These were the exceptions. It would seem the 1933s were very irregular; overall less ripe than the 1928s or 1929s. Volumes were smaller than in the previous two years. The wines were deemed better than those of the previous three vintages but forgotten once the superior 1934 vintage entered the market. Down in Sauternes, flowering was disturbed by the poor weather and following 157 mm (6 in) of rain in September, the dry spell failed to concentrate berries and few sweet wines achieved complexity.

By all means, not a growing season without challenges, but one that might have yielded some exceptional claret if winemakers had had access to contemporary knowhow and technology. The wines are not often seen, though the handful I have tasted often surpassed low expectations both in Bordeaux and in Burgundy. Two bottles of the 1933 Montrose needed a walking stick (or two) when tasted in 2016 and yet suggested a fine Saint-Estèphe that was just past its prime. A bottle of 1933 Cos d'Estournel from the château fared better in 2018, a pleasant surprise. I also have two notes for Sauternes, though neither the 1933 Suduiraut nor the 1933 Lafaurie-Peyraguey showed particularly well.

Consensus is that the 1934 vintage is the best of a dismal decade for Bordeaux wine.

1933
(Continued)

Event
Harry Beck's London tube map is published

Electrical draughtsman Harry Beck realised that the current maps showing the geographical locations of London's tube stations were hard to read. So in 1931 he drew a simplified version with straight lines that allowed travellers to work out their routes more easily. The cartographic masterpiece was such a radical innovation that it was initially rejected, but positive feedback meant that, after a couple of alterations, Beck's map was adopted by London Transport from 1933. It has been modified as new stations and tube lines have been added, but it will always be Beck's design.

Film
King Kong – Merian C. Cooper and Ernest B. Schoedsack

Animator Willis O'Brien used six 46-cm (18-in) high rabbit-fur-lined models of a gorilla to create one of cinema's most iconic monsters: King Kong. Audiences queued around blocks to see the giant ape scaling the newly built Empire State Building, desperately swatting away biplanes as he tries to protect his beloved, played by Fay Wray. The stop-motion animation evoked enough pathos to get the audience rooting for the fated and abused King Kong. It was also the first film to include a feature-length original score.

Music
Goodnight, Irene – Leadbelly

Huddie "Leadbelly" Ledbetter wrote his signature song while in prison on a murder charge. He had always had a short fuse. Imprisoned again in 1930 at Angola State Penitentiary in Louisiana for taking part in a knife fight, he was visited three years later by music historian John Lomax and his son Alan, who were recording songs by Afro-American convicts on their Edison cylinder machine to preserve in the Library of Congress. Leadbelly sang *Goodnight, Irene,* whose lyrics dwell on that age-old tale of a married man gone astray. Upon release, Lomax promoted Leadbelly as a singing jailbird, forbidding him to wear anything but prison garb on stage and pocketing a third of the takings. He was ruthlessly exploited. Leadbelly later pursued his own career under the wing of the less exploitative jazz historian Fred Ramsey, recording a clutch of blues standards that became pillars of rock 'n' roll.

The year started with a very dry January and February, rain finally replenishing underground reserves mid-March with some deluges causing localised flooding. Winter was dragged out by a very cool April that deterred vine growth, though temperatures began to rise as the month continued, reaching 28°C (82°F) between 14 and 16 April. May witnessed scattered showers, which were thankfully followed by fine conditions that ensured a perfect early flowering and, later, an early *véraison*. June saw warm temperatures, up to 34°C (93°F) and Bordeaux simmered in July to the extent that the tropical conditions predicated an invasion of crickets and grasshoppers around Cantenac. During early summer hardly a drop of rain fell, though finally on 21 July the weather broke and rain quenched the vines' dry throats. This was followed by a violent storm in Sauternes that brought hail, damaging vines in both Yquem and Guiraud. The first half of August was rather rainy and cool. Fortunately, the weather turned sunnier from 17 August, but it was a brief respite. Rainclouds gathered once again on 23 August so that ultimately twice the average precipitation fell that month and average temperatures were over a degree less than normal. Winemakers must have feared a rerun of previous vintages.

Fortunately, after a somewhat inclement start, a warm and sunny September saved the vintage. It was a large harvest that began 14 September, potential alcohol levels coming in at around 11.5–12%. Initial reactions were a little lukewarm – many '34s went through a dull period before blossoming in bottle. In Sauternes, downpours on 31 August triggered botrytis and many estates commenced picking soon after – Yquem's harvesters went out on 7 September. Thankfully, the weather conditions remained ideal and many picked through to the beginning of October. Finally, after four lamentable seasons, Sauternes had something to offer wine lovers apart from the reds.

This is a vintage I would dearly love to taste more often, though as with many pre-war vintages, wines of sound provenance are increasingly rare. I am fortunate to have tasted and compared a dozen or so 1934s in London when Linden Wilkie organised a memorable horizontal. These, and the handful of other bottles I have tasted, confirm 1934 as a vintage with much to offer. The 1934 Latour and 1934 Montrose, two of the Médoc's most lasting clarets, were solid and steadfast after many decades, with substance and pedigree, unlike the 1934 Beychevelle, which has faded in recent years. The 1934 Branaire-Ducru, the wine that inspired one of Roald Dahl's vinous-themed short stories, might not garner superlatives, yet has the legs to last a few more years. I have not tasted the Gruaud Larose. A shame, for this was the year that the estate's proprietor, Désiré Cordier, and the mayor of Saint-Julien organised a Fête de la Longevité to celebrate wine's life-extending properties after tracking down 14 couples in Saint-Julien who had been married more than 50 years.

1934
(Continued)

Sadly, I have very little experience on the Right Bank. A bottle of 1934 Trotanoy had clearly held up well in 2014, although compared to post-war vintages, it could not disguise its rustic personality. Without doubt, my fondest memories of the vintage stem from Saint-Émilion. A bottle of 1934 Cheval Blanc at the horizontal tasting remains one of the greatest inter-war wines I have tasted: vibrant, profound and complex – quintessential Cheval Blanc undiminished by time, even if another tasted three years later failed to reach the same heights. Not to be outdone, the 1934 Ausone was superb at Jordi Oriols-Gil's vertical in January 2018. I also have fond memories of two or three bottles of 1934 Petit-Village, surprisingly youthful and confit-like when last tasted in Germany, while the 1934 Vieux Château Certan had a terracotta-tinged nose and a surprisingly plump palate. Despite suffering hail damage, the 1934 Yquem that Pierre Lurton served over lunch in June 2021 was sublime and the late Professor Denis Dubourdieu generously poured a vibrant magnum of Doisy-Daëne at the Académie du Vin dinner in Bordeaux. The 1934 Climens faltered at the epic vertical in Zurich, though another bottle in London was magical, gaining intensity in the glass with electrifying acidity. Generally, the 1934 Sauternes are overshadowed by their 1937 counterparts.

Event
Bonnie and Clyde ambushed in Louisiana

Few robbers have become as iconoclastic as Bonnie and Clyde: their lives a conflation of crime, romance and violence that came to a bloody ending. The pair are thought to have committed 13 murders, including those of two police officers, not to mention a spate of robberies and car thefts. They constantly evaded capture and must have felt untouchable until they were ambushed near Sailes in Louisiana on 23 May 1934 and died in a hail of bullets. It seems perverse that such merciless killers subsequently became romanticised in film.

Film
Dames
– Busby Berkeley

Though directed by Ray Enright, Busby Berkeley created and staged the film's iconic musical numbers. He choreographed troops of flamboyantly or scantily dressed women to dazzling effect and filmed them using innovative camera angles – particularly from above to create kaleidoscopic formations. Berkeley's films offered brief escapism from the drudgery of life in the poverty-stricken decade, but his golden period would soon end. The following year he was acquitted of causing a car accident that cost two lives and never quite recaptured his magic touch.

Music
I Get a Kick Out of You
– Cole Porter

Though Sinatra's 1954 version is perhaps the best known, it was Ethel Merman who first sang this Cole Porter classic in the Broadway hit *Anything Goes* in 1934. Porter's original line: "Some get a kick from cocaine" was altered to "Some like the perfume in Spain". Porter wrote countless standards throughout the thirties, including *Night and Day* and *I've Got You Under My Skin*.

1934
(Continued)

1870

2020

1935

If the previous vintage had given winemakers hope that the second half of the decade would compensate for the first, then 1935 snuffed it out.

After a cold start in March, vine growth kicked off towards the end of the month. But on 3 April winemakers woke up to a widespread frost that lasted until the next day. Some claimed not to have seen anything as severe in 40 years. The entire Médoc, Graves and Sauternes were affected with some properties losing three-quarters of their crop, though the Right Bank suffered less damage. May was mostly cold and saw another light frost on 16 May. June was cool and rainy up until the end of the month when yet another hailstorm, this time in the commune of Soussans, struck on 25 June. Flowering was late and a heat spike at the end of the month saw the mercury reach 37°C (99°F). After a sunny and hot July and August, hopes were for a tiny crop of concentrated wines. But on 3 September a violent storm traversed the region with severe hail that spared the Médoc but wrought havoc in Saint-Émilion. "*Cheval Blanc est hâché!*" exclaims the entry in Tastet-Lawton, which I guess you could basically translate as "the vines were mincemeat". Rain showers persisted and delayed picking until 30 September but the weather did not improve and harvesters had no option but to plough on under wet conditions. In Sauternes, 90 mm (3½ in) of rain in late August provoked botrytis, but hopes for a worthy follow-up to 1934 were nixed by constant showers. Despite all this trauma, the wines were received better than the 1931s or 1932s and comparisons were made to 1922, probably due to the benevolent July and August. "Our 1935 will in the future occupy a very honourable place among the range of vintages appreciated by the connoisseur," opines Latour owner Comte de Beaumont in an example of euphemistic interwar puff. However, merchants had a more realistic take – sales were sluggish and Latour remained unsold. Merchants still had the superior '34s on their shelves and in any case, their customers had barely recovered from the Depression.

The only dry red I have tasted is a 1935 Domaine de Chevalier at the Académie du Vin dinner during en primeur that was only just drinkable, but deserved a light round of applause. I also met a rather monotone 1935 Filhot at its vertical in Sauternes. Otherwise, it is a vintage to give a wide berth.

Event
Sir Malcolm Campbell breaks
the land speed record

Former pilot Sir Malcolm
Campbell broke nine land
speed records in his career.
On 3 September 1935 on the
Bonneville Salt Flats in Utah, he
reached 301 mph (484 km/h),
becoming the first man to exceed
300 mph (483 km/h) on land.
After this he turned to breaking
water speed records, achieving
141 mph (227 km/h) on Coniston
Water in 1939. Unlike many men
and women addicted to speed,
he died not in an accident, but of
natural causes in 1948.

Music
Cheek to Cheek
– Fred Astaire

Composed by Irving Berlin,
Cheek to Cheek features in the
most famous scene from musical
screwball comedy *Top Hat*. Since
Berlin did not read music, he
composed the tune on a specially
designed piano with a mechanism
that could transpose keyboard
fingering. As astute businessman,
he negotiated a contract by which
he kept the copyright to the score
and a share of the profits. In the
film, Astaire sings the song to a
feathery Ginger Rogers as they
glide around the ballroom. He
later recorded the song with the
Leo Reisman Orchestra and it
soon topped the charts.

Film
A Night at the Opera
– Sam Wood

A Night at the Opera was the
Marx brothers' first film for
MGM and one of the year's
biggest box-office hits. Chico,
Harpo, Groucho, Gummo
and Zeppo had started as a
vaudeville comedy act and
became famous for their
sharp satire and improvisation
(Zeppo eventually left the
group and became a successful
agent). *A Night at the Opera*
dialled down their brand of
anarchic comedy – producer
Irving Thalberg felt it made
them unsympathetic – and
introduced a stronger storyline.
Originally, the film was
supposed to begin with each
Marx brother mimicking
the roar of the MGM lion,
but studio boss Louis B.
Meyer vetoed the idea as he
felt it diminished the brand.
Audiences lapped up their
much-needed humour and
along with their previous
Duck Soup, *A Night at the
Opera* is seen as a critical and
commercial high point in the
Marx Brothers' career.

1936

This was another woeful growing season.

An abnormally warm February encouraged vines to wake from winter dormancy so that by March their growth cycle was already three weeks ahead of schedule. This warm period ended on 9 April when the wind swung north. May was changeable with occasional torrential downpours towards the end that caused outbreaks of mildew. Flowering was irregular due to rain and cold temperatures followed by a double dose of hail on 23 and 29 June, the latter particularly violent and damaging. The rain did not let up and inevitably July saw more mildew, especially after three days of heavy rainfall from 12 to 14 July. The volatile atmosphere, not unlike that seen in 2021, provoked yet more hail on 17 July. Overall, the month saw over 150 mm (6 in) of rain in some places. The weather improved in August, though it remained overcast. By the end of the month, the mercury was reaching 34°C (93°F) before tumbling in September, which had particularly cold nights. The first pickers were out with their secateurs around 26 September, although it was bitterly cold in the morning, only just above freezing on 30 September. The general harvest took place between 1 and 4 October under ideal conditions, though it was far too late to salvage the vintage. In Sauternes a lack of rain, just 30 mm (1 in) between 18 August and 4 November, precluded botrytis formation so that berries became over-ripe instead of botrytised.

Wines from the 1936 vintage were "thin and acidic", according to André Simon. Even the Lafite Rothschild was being sold as "Pauillac" by Averys in Bristol for six shillings and sixpence in 1942. Like many wines from the decade, 1937s are rarely seen. The only claret acquainted with my palate is a 1936 Léoville Poyferré that was part of a Christmas "party-pack" of odds and sods. It went straight down the sink. In Sauternes, bottles of 1936 Suduiraut and 1936 Lafaurie-Peyraguey at verticals were decrepit and passable respectively. I also encountered an odd bottle of 1936 Climens, which seemed very confected and over-chaptalised.

Event
King Edward VIII abdicates

A constitutional crisis enveloped the nation when King Edward VIII decided that if he intended to marry divorcée Wallis Simpson, he had no option but to abdicate the throne. The king had wanted Simpson to be made queen consort, but faced fierce opposition from the government, while the Church of England forbade them from marrying in church since Simpson's former spouse was still alive. Society was scandalised, with many convinced Simpson was motivated by money, rather than love. The king wrote his letter of abdication on 10 December and addressed the country via a BBC radio broadcast the following day from Windsor Castle. Looking back, the unsympathetic public were wrong to doubt the couple's feelings and the two remained married until the Duke of Windsor's death in 1972.

Music
Peter and the Wolf
– Sergei Prokofiev

Commissioned by Moscow's Central Children's Theatre to compose a musical symphony for children, Prokofiev set about creating his most famous work. Each instrument or class of instruments represented an animal – for example, oboe for a duck, clarinet for the cat, percussion for the hunters and the string section for Peter himself. Premiered on 2 May 1936, the piece achieved worldwide popularity and was released as a sound recording, turned into a ballet, and made into a film by Walt Disney.

Film
The Trail of the Lonesome Pine
– Henry Hathaway

Based on the novel of the same name, *The Trail of the Lonesome Pine* starred Henry Fonda, Fred MacMurray and Sylvia Sidney. Though the movie itself is not regarded as a classic of the thirties, it was the first to use three-strip Technicolor to depict exterior landscapes such as mountains, vast plains and farmsteads and set a precedent for the age of colour.

1937

Apart from 1934, this is the decade's only vintage that offered some cheer to beleaguered Bordeaux winemakers – the last favourable vintage until 1945. It was also the first Bordeaux vintage made under AC rules and the last to be shipped and bottled to Europe before war broke supply chains.

The growing season began with unseasonably dry conditions that were an omen for the coming months. February finally saw some much-needed heavy rainfall, then a warm spell between 3 and 8 March encouraged vines to wake from their winter slumber. April was initially changeable but settled towards the end of the month, though May saw a return to inclement weather and cold nights, albeit with no frost risk. At the end of May, the mercury shot up to 33°C (91°F) as the first flowers appeared and flowering progressed well until a violent storm hit the southern Médoc and the Graves. Vineyards were damaged by hail and the rain was so torrential that cellars were flooded. The rest of June was warm and dry and these conditions continued into a balmy and dry July and August. Towards the end of August there were concerns about lack of water and *négociant* Louis Eschenauer feared another 1887. According to Lawton, vines suffered more in Pomerol than in the Médoc, though one would have thought its clay soils would have stood it in good stead. The summer portended a great vintage, but temperatures plunged, reaching an uncharacteristically nippy 15°C (59°F) on the afternoon of 11 September, the air chilled by a brisk northerly. This prompted some châteaux to commence picking, though heavy showers posed a lingering threat.

Fortunately, skies cleared and the harvest started in earnest from 20 September, the weather overcast but with warmth and light showers. Potential alcohol levels were surprisingly low considering the heat of the summer, around 11–12%, probably due to the dryness shutting down the vegetative cycle. The pickers finished in early October and though the quality was promising, quantities were small. As time went by, the positivity towards the wines was tempered by some of the reds, which lacked a bit of weight and depth, pulling up short. It was a different story in Sauternes. Those September showers produced ample botrytis and a three-week dry spell enabled harvesters to pick almost perfect fruit. They just had to avoid patches of sour rot. The Sauternes were blessed with rich musts with high sugar levels, putting the 1937 in the same line as 1967 and 1997, years when botrytis-affected vines ruled.

We should discuss the Sauternes before the dry reds because they are remarkable. The 1937 Yquem is one that I have tasted three times, including one bottle at the château. It is a fabulous, intense Sauternes that bowls you over with its power and complexity, though I am not quite as eulogistic as some, who hail it as one of the finest ever. I have enjoyed two bottles of the 1937 Climens, which is almost on par with the Yquem. A flight of Sauternes served blind by Olivier Bernard attested that quality spread across the appellation: Suduiraut, Coutet, Rayne Vigneau and Guiraud were all immensely pleasurable after eight decades. With regard to the reds, wine writer Alexis Lichine thought they were "exceptionally stubborn" and only just reaching their prime by the late sixties. The 1937 Latour had an intriguing curry-leaf tincture on the nose when encountered in 2017 but continues to drink well, though my preference is towards the burly 1937 Mouton Rothschild. The 1937 Pichon Baron was elegiac and fungal, frayed yet enjoyable when opened at the estate in March 2022. Other notable bottles include a "solid" 1937 Domaine de Chevalier and a very respectable if swimming pool-tinged 1937 Palmer. Right Bank wines are hardly seen because of smaller production. When I was researching my Pomerol tome, erstwhile proprietor Paul Goldschmidt opened a 1937 Vraye Croix de Gay for me at the château that, to use my own words, was "hanging on in there", while a Belgian-bottled 1937 Latour à Pomerol evidenced a proportion of Malbec and felt lumbering and ferrous.

Event
The *Hindenburg* airship explodes over New Jersey

At 7.25 p.m. on 6 May 1937, the passenger airship LZ 129 *Hindenburg* caught fire as it made its final approach for landing and exploded over New Jersey, killing 13 passengers and 22 crewmen. Captured in newsreel footage, the sight of the giant airship engulfed in flames as it fell to the ground became one of the defining images of the decade, later immortalised on the cover of Led Zeppelin's debut album. Several theories circulate about the cause of the fire, but none are conclusive.

Film
Snow White and the Seven Dwarfs – Walt Disney

America's first full-length cell-animated film continues to delight children and adults alike decades after it premiered at the Carthay Circle Theatre in Los Angeles on 21 December 1937. Originally, Snow White had a sexy image with long eyelashes and pouting red lips, probably because the artists were the same ones who had drawn Betty Boop. Disney altered her look to make it more wholesome and family-friendly. Two-million illustrations using 1,500 shades of paint came at tremendous cost, but the film had raked in four times as much as any other 1937 release by the following year.

1937
(Continued)

Music
Love in Vain
– Robert Johnson

Robert Johnson recorded *Love in Vain* in the second of just two studio sessions. The Mississippi-born Delta bluesman was ostensibly a travelling musician, a busker. Johnson laid the song down in Dallas in June 1937 and died the following August aged just 27, though his record company Vocalion did not release it until 1939. Apocryphal stories of his death abound: murdered by a jealous husband or possibly poisoned. Posthumous rumours circulated that he owed his mastery of the guitar to a pact with the devil in exchange for his soul – a legend that helped guarantee Johnson's status as a mythical figure. His handful of recordings laid the blueprint for the blues and continue to be a major influence upon what became rock 'n' roll.

The 1938 vintage has been ostensibly forgotten, a year of ordinary wines that would be lost in the fog of war.

The year kicked off with a cold snap, the mercury plunging to -12°C (10.5°F) and February remained bitterly cold. The vines awoke around the middle of March and despite the previous cold conditions, their growth cycle was in advance of previous years. There were minor skirmishes with frost: the Côtes de Blaye was hit by a severe episode on 11 April and there was wider devastation in the Graves and Saint-Émilion 10 days later. Finally, it was the turn of Médoc and Sauternes to suffer on 21 and 22 April, when around half the buds burned and Yquem recorded a chilly daytime temperatures of -1.1°C (30°F) on the latter. Bordeaux also suffered an unusually early drought, with hardly a drop of rain for almost three months. Cold temperatures persisted and there was yet more frost damage at the beginning of May (likewise in Burgundy). Finally, temperatures rose from mid-May but in tandem with rainy conditions. Despite the inclemency, flowering went well and vines that had survived the frost seemed eager to compensate for the prospective shortfall. The rest of June remained warm, though July was decidedly cooler and stormy, if warmer towards the end of the month with intermittent deluges. August was changeable, with cool night temperatures and hail affecting the Médoc on 6 August. An inclement September delayed picking. While 12 and 13 September brought much-needed sunshine and warmth, it was too late for the dry whites, which suffered rot. Pickers tentatively entered the vineyards around 27 September and finished on 12 and 13 October, though hopes of a decent small harvest were dashed by rain. Potential alcohol was around 12–13%. Sauternes is intriguing this year. Heavy downpours on 28 and 29 September provoked botrytis and ensuing dry conditions were ideal for picking, though several passes were needed at Yquem, including one when the vines were purportedly frozen. The *Féret* guide describes the reds as "ripe, elegant and harmonious", but despite initial flattery, it was generally agreed that the wines lacked substance. As the market for Bordeaux languished in the doldrums, many 1938s were not shipped until after the war.

My only two encounters are with a frail 1938 Pichon-Lalande that turned up at a BYO lunch at La Trompette. All that was missing was a Zimmer frame. Estate manager Nicolas Audebert inserted a 1938 Rauzan-Ségla at the vertical in 2018 but it was just a couple of steps from the morgue. Most wines from this vintage will be of curiosity value only.

1938

1870

2020

1938 *(Continued)*

Event
Action Comics #1 introduces Superman

Is it a bird? Is it a plane? No, it's the first appearance of Superman in issue one of *Action Comics*. Created by Jerry Siegel and artist Joe Shuster, who received just $130 in exchange for the exclusive rights, the character was the catalyst for a multi-billion-dollar superhero industry that ultimately begat the Marvel franchise. Published in June, the first comic simply explained the origins of the Man of Steel: how he ended up on Earth and adopted the name Clark Kent. In April 2021, one of the few surviving original comics sold for a cool $3.25 million.

Music
A-Tisket, A-Tasket
– Ella Fitzgerald

Based on a nursery rhyme, *A-Tisket, A-Tasket* was co-written by Fitzgerald and Al Feldman. Fitzgerald suffered a traumatic childhood. Her mother died when she was 15 years old and she was allegedly mistreated by her stepfather. Seeking refuge in music, she shot to fame for her show-stopping performances at the Savoy Ballroom with bandleader Chick Webb and gained national exposure when *A-Tisket, A-Tasket* became a huge radio hit. Fitzgerald went on to become one of the defining voices of the 21st century.

Film
Jezebel
– William Wyler

Bette Davis plays impetuous Southern belle Julie Marsden, who scandalously wears a red dress to the ball. Unmarried women were expected to wear white and her paramour, played by Henry Fonda, is not amused. Davis's marriage was breaking down at the time. She had an affair with director Wyler, whom she later called "the love of my life" and after they rowed she seduced Fonda – a fling nipped in the bud by a phone call from Fonda's pregnant wife. By the end of filming, Davis herself was pregnant by Wyler. A bit of life imitating art? No wonder there was simmering tension on set. But Davis's bravura performance deservedly won her an Oscar and she received nominations for the next four years.

The 1939 growing season could be viewed as trifling given the upheaval in Europe and the suffering that ensued. However, the cycle of Nature continued.

The vines were tardy in awakening from their winter hibernation, as if they knew what lay ahead. "We are still in winter," is the Tastet-Lawton entry on 27 March. Shoots finally began to grow at the beginning of April, but it remained bitterly cold and temperatures struggled to rise during a very inclement May. Finally, it began to warm just before June and the first flowers dotted the landscape around 3 June, before the weather settled towards the end of the month. However, a rainy and hot July led to outbreaks of mildew and conditions deteriorated as August approached, with three days of persistent rain. August saw higher temperatures but *véraison* was spun out by constant rainfall that lasted throughout the month. When war was declared on 3 September, the weather was appropriately warm but stormy. The Tastet-Lawton archives record how Jean Faure and Daniel Lawton left for their mobilisation units in the town of Tarbes. Meanwhile, the grapes were stubbornly slow in achieving ripeness as a northerly wind kept a lid on temperatures. The harvesters went out on 2 October even though some of the grapes remained green. Rain persisted throughout the picking, not ceasing until early November. The musts clearly missed body and ripeness, though the whites seemed to fare better. Sauternes suffered a severe and damaging frost on 11 June and the season was generally cool, 1–2°C (34–36°F) below average at Yquem throughout the season and with above average rain in August. Although weather conditions remained dry during picking, potential alcohol levels struggled and never breached 17% at Yquem.

The only two reds I have tasted were a 1939 Rauzan-Ségla, part of a vertical organised at the estate, which appeared to be drying out. Also, a 1939 Cheval Blanc was poured at dinner *chez* Berry Brothers & Rudd with the château's assistant winemaker Pierre-Olivier Clouet, who explained that its entire measly production was bottled by Bordeaux merchant Mähler-Besse. In 2016, a 1939 Yquem tasted at Club 1243 in Beaune was proffered for Aubert de Villaine to celebrate his birth year. He could not attend but it was opened anyway and like many off-vintages of Yquem, it was utterly delicious – unlike a 1939 Climens in Zurich a few years earlier that had fallen apart.

1939
(Continued)

Event
The Second World War is declared

At 11 o'clock on 3 September 1939, families huddled around their radios to hear Neville Chamberlain's address. The British prime minister had spent months trying to appease Hitler and was now requesting that he withdraw German occupying troops from Poland. Chamberlain gravely intoned: "I have to tell you no that no such undertaking has been received, and that consequently this country is at war with Germany." So began a tumultuous six years of global conflict and bloodshed.

Music
Strange Fruit
– Billie Holiday

Few songs have had the impact of *Strange Fruit*. Lyrics such as "Black bodies swingin' in the southern breeze" chill to this day. They were written by a civil rights activist and communist Jew, Abel Meeropol, after he saw a photo of two lynched black men in Indiana. Holiday was moved by the words, particularly since her father had died after being refused hospital care because of his skin colour. Federal Bureau of Narcotics commissioner Harry Anslinger, a known racist, forbade Holiday from singing *Strange Fruit* and when she refused, framed her for heroin abuse and she spent 18 months in prison. After her release Lady Day's career was nixed when her cabaret performer's licence was withheld. Withered and emaciated, her voice just a rasp, Holiday died in 1959 and yet the potency and relevance of *Strange Fruit* has not changed and her legacy has only enhanced with time.

Film
The Wizard of Oz
– Victor Fleming

Released on 25 August 1939, *The Wizard of Oz* shot 16-year-old Judy Garland to global stardom, eventually leading to struggles in her personal life. The fantasy musical featured innovative special effects and was filmed in Technicolor, although the Yellow Brick Road required some adjustment in production as it initially appeared green. The film is chock-full of classic songs, but MGM almost cut out the heart-tugging *Somewhere Over the Rainbow* because it made the Kansas sequence too long. Other scenes *were* left on the cutting-room floor, including several with the Wicked Witch, played by Margaret Hamilton, which were deemed too frightening for children. When Garland got the giggles in the scene when she slaps the Cowardly Lion, Fleming took her aside and, after sharp words, slapped the teenager, who then went back on set and did the scene in one take. The director later said he was ashamed by his behaviour. When Garland overheard his remorse, she went up and gave him a kiss on the nose.

1939
(Continued)

1870

2020

The
1940s

It is almost impossible to extricate the growing seasons in the first half of this decade with the tumult of the Second World War, though as I wrote in the introduction to this book, vines pay little heed to conflict. Come what may, they reawaken the following year. On the other hand, war directly impacted the running of vineyards and deprived estates of manpower and skill. It also created dire shortages of raw materials such as sulphur to protect the vines and glass to bottle the wine, which is why many wartime bottles are clear or brown in colour, whatever was to hand. Military action meant markets in the UK and the US immediately vanished, leading the Germans to create what the French called *weinführers* to maintain a functioning wine industry and profit from reselling French wines in Germany. Nearly all of Hitler's inner circle were oenophiles, in particular Hermann Göring, who had a penchant for Lafite Rothschild. In 1940, 47-year-old Heinz Bömers was assigned the region of Bordeaux. His family had owned Smith Haut Lafitte prior to the First World War and he was already acquainted with many château owners, so Bömers trod a fine line keeping on good terms with both his Nazi overlords and local French winemakers. One decision he did make was to buy up all the unsold claret from the thirties, relieving the Bordelais of unsold, poor-quality stock.

In Don and Petie Kladstrup's indispensable *Wine & War*, Bömers is portrayed as an erudite wine lover with anti-Nazi beliefs, which led to accusations that he was too pally with the French merchants and château owners. One of his accusers was Göring, in part due to the acrimonious relationship that had festered between him and Bömers' father. During the German occupation, the fortunes of individual merchants and proprietors varied. Louis Eschenauer's relationship seemed so close and profitable that he was found guilty of collusion, whereas Jewish owners, not least the Rothschilds, soon realised their lives were at risk. Baron Philippe de Rothschild remained as long as possible at Mouton Rothschild until forced to flee, smuggled across the Pyrenees to Spain on foot. The Vichy government sequestered Lafite Rothschild as a property of the French state in order to prevent it falling into the hands of Göring and allegedly Hitler, who entertained the idea of seizing the First Growth and offering it to his successor. Its trove of historical vintages that date back to 1797 were secreted away to other estates for protection. Many chateaux were billeted by German troops, who ransacked cellars. Some estates concealed their precious bottles behind fake walls or by moving them to less prestigious châteaux. Up in the attic at Palmer, you can still see graffiti carved into wooden beams by German soldiers. For a temporary period, its owners Louis and Édouard Miailhe concealed two Italian Jewish families behind a kitchen wall until they could smuggle them out under cover of night.

As the war dragged on, matters worsened. Vineyards were left untended and the German army requisitioned all horses in 1942, leaving only oxen to both work the land and provide milk. Some châteaux tried to rectify things by using more sulphur to protect wines from spoilage, though this was soon rationed, making it even more challenging to mitigate against rot in the vineyard and stabilise the wines during vinification.

In trying to appease the Germans' thirst for Bordeaux, the Vichy government implemented an anti-alcohol campaign to reduce domestic consumption and, to the dismay of quality-driven winemakers, encouraged watering down and the use of prohibited grape varieties. Meanwhile, Bordeaux's importance as a port meant the region was bombed by Allied forces and when anti-aircraft guns were installed in many properties, they immediately became targets. At Montrose, soldiers established shooting ranges where vines once stood. Over at La Conseillante, the Nicolas family pulled up precious vines to provide grazing for cows and sheep, so their children would not go hungry. One night the Nicolas's walnut trees mysteriously lost their fruit and it wasn't until half a century later that a remorseful elderly neighbour confessed that she had stolen the walnuts to feed her starving family.

German troops finally left Bordeaux on 28 August 1944. Naturally, there was jubilation, but their departure left a vacuum of law and order. There was not so much a sense of anarchy, rather outbreaks of lawlessness. Baron Philippe de Rothschild had joined de Gaulle's Free French Forces in 1942, though his non-Jewish wife had remained. She was dragged away by the Gestapo and perished in the Ravensbrück concentration camp. Mouton Rothschild's vineyards were in good condition, though the buildings and winery were in a ruinous state. La Lagune was whittled down to just 10 hectares of vine, while d'Issan was so dilapidated that the wines had to be made at Rauzan-Ségla. Baron Philippe discovered that German soldiers had been imprisoned nearby and, ever-resourceful, used them to repair the damage and rebuild the surrounding gardens.

During wartime, Mother Nature did not bestow winemakers with an unequivocally great vintage, though 1942 and 1943 provided opportunities to make decent wine. Instead, she timed it to perfection, delivering a bone fide classic to coincide with the end of the war, as if to reward those who had survived. The 1945 season provided an opportunity to make magnificent, in many cases, legendary wines, though in reality many chateaux had been reduced to a terrible state after the stagnation of the thirties and German occupation. The likes of Château d'Issan survived by a thread:

A splendid photograph of young and old tending the harvest at Château Marquis St-Exupéry in the famous 1947 vintage.

Therefore not everyone could exploit the 1945 vintage and many dilapidated estates took years to patch themselves up.

The second half of the decade is completely different: a trio of beatified vintages in the form of 1945, 1947 and 1949 plus a half-decent 1948. One would presume that winemakers were overjoyed in the peaceful afterglow of war, yet it had taken its toll financially. Many countries had years of austerity ahead. Rationing was not withdrawn in the UK until 1949 and similar austerity measures were imposed by the Vichy government. Consequently, there were few buyers for something as luxurious as fine wine. It is sobering to read that in July 1946, Lawton found it impossible to secure orders for any of its 1945s. Compounding winemakers' woes, the French government devalued their currency in 1947 and 1949, stymying trade further. Future *régisseur* at Latour, Jean-Paul Gardère, then a broker in Margaux, remarked that Bordeaux château owners "feel now that the prosperity born of the war was only illusory". The wine market was at a standstill and the many legendary wines birthed by the golden post-war era languished unsold, remaining freely available until the seventies.

Taken outside the winery reception of Château Marquis St. Exupéry in 1947, the two children are Jacqueline Zuger on the left and Jean-Claude Zuger, the great-aunt and great-uncle of present winemaker Lea Zuger. (The gentleman is likely an employee at the château.) Bottles are lined up outside enticing passers-by to stop and purchase wine, common practice back then.

1940

In another timeline, one where there was no Second World War, 1940 could have yielded some useful claret.

January was bitterly cold, the coldest since 1917 according to the Tastet-Lawton archives, although it became more spring-like towards the end of February. This encouraged buds to swell, though further growth was retarded by a cold March and April saw little rise from freezing temperatures. Mid-May witnessed an influx of French and Belgian refugees who might have seen the first flowers at the end of the month. Full flowering was reached on 7 June under clement, quite warm conditions. On 25 June, the Tastet-Lawton archives refer to the armistice signed with the German army and the inevitability that Bordeaux would soon be occupied. This transpired on 28 June, commencing four years of German occupation. July saw mildew attack the bunches and the rest of the month was changeable. The German army ransacked Léoville and Langoa Barton on 19 July. The mercury climbed to 31°C (88°F) in August just as the RAF bombed petrol storage facilities in Pauillac and Blaye.

Warm and dry conditions continued into September and the first pickers went out into the vines at Montrose around 17 September, though a small harvest was on the cards. That was no bad thing since châteaux found it difficult recruiting pickers. The heart of the harvest was from around 26 September. Interestingly, Lawton reports a large acquisition of wine via an intermediary: three million bottles of Médoc and two million bottles of Pomerol and Saint-Émilion, perhaps the aforementioned unsold stocks from the previous decade. The picking must have taken longer than normal due to the lack of manpower and extended into October when the weather turned sour, the last bunches coming in around 9 or 10 October. Still, the first tastings in November were more promising than expected thanks to the benevolent August. In Sauternes, concentration was stymied by cold and wet conditions, though the first passes at the end of September looked promising. However, constant rain through the following weeks ruined the crops and a measly amount of Sauternes was produced.

On paper, 1940 is not a bad growing season, but it was poleaxed by the difficulties posed by the occupying army and a lack of manpower and equipment both in the vineyard and the winery. Lawton's archives express satisfaction with the quality. Nowadays, bottles are rarely seen. I have only had three encounters with the reds over the years. The first was a 1940 Léoville-Las Cases, frail and prompting discussion about whether it had been able to complete its malolactic fermentation. Second was a 1940 Clinet that proprietor Ronan Laborde opened for me when I was researching my Pomerol tome. Sadly, this war veteran was of curiosity value only, but thank you anyway Ronan. The best? An ethereal 1940 Pichon-Lalande over dinner with winemaker Nicolas Glumineau that possessed a sorbet-like freshness that belied its antiquity. Also, a 1940 Suduiraut that was clinging on in there for dear life.

Event
The Battle of Britain

After Dunkirk, Hitler planned to invade Britain. All that was needed was the mighty Luftwaffe to remove the RAF's fighter planes protecting the skies above southern England. But the Führer underestimated the potency of the RAF's Hurricanes and Spitfires, the effectiveness of radar defences and the observation-post network, and the bravery of whom Churchill called "The Few", which it should be pointed out included those of different nationalities. Having met stiff resistance to take out Fighter Command, the Luftwaffe redirected its efforts upon London. It was a tactical error because, despite causing huge civilian casualties, it gave the RAF breathing space to regroup and inflict unsustainable losses on the enemy. After Europe had fallen into Nazi hands, the Battle of Britain marked the start of a fightback.

Music
In the Mood
– The Glenn Miller Orchestra

The music that soundtracked much of the war was big band swing and *In the Mood* is perhaps its signature tune. Its origin is rather vague, essentially an amalgam of three or four songs from the thirties, an era when copyright was lax. It was first recorded in 1938 and band leader and trombonist Glenn Miller laid down his version a year later, speeding up the tempo and inserting a saxophone "face-off" between Tex Beneke and Al Clink and a trumpet solo by Clyde Hurley. In 1940 it became one of the biggest-selling hits of the year on the newly introduced Billboard charts. Glenn Miller's big band entertained legions of troops during the Second World War until his plane disappeared flying over the English Channel on 15 December 1944.

Film
The Grapes of Wrath – John Ford

Henry Fonda stars in this adaptation of John Steinbeck's best-selling Pulitzer Prize-winning novel that was initially banned by farmer associations, who labelled it "communist propaganda". Directed by John Ford, the film is a human parable of the Joad family, who lose their farm during the Depression and end up as struggling Dust Bowl migrants in California. Wanting to capture the visceral nature of the story, Ford allowed little rehearsal and shot many scenes in one take. The cinematography was by Gregg Toland, who went on to work on *Citizen Kane* (page 213).

1941

"The war will be long and cruel," reads Lawton's entry on 3 January 1941 before lamenting food shortages and long queues at shops.

February witnessed violent storms among the aerial bombardment. March was rainy, then April saw a northerly wind bring down temperatures. This resulted in a damaging frost on 10 April and over the following days, which was most acute in Margaux, Graves and Sauternes. It remained wintry until mid-May and then flowering was interrupted by violent storms and rain, so the first flowers were delayed until mid-June. July saw temperatures reach 35°C (95°F) but there were outbreaks of rain that caused mildew and oidium. Little sulphur was available to treat outbreaks, nor workers to apply it, and black rot was endemic by the end of July. Even the top estates were affected. Latour needed 100 kg (220 lb) of copper sulphate to tackle the rot but struggled to obtain 40 kg (88 lb). August was changeable, marked by 14 hours of uninterrupted downpours at the end of the month – a short cold spell that helped slow the spread of rot. After a warm but inclement September, the inevitably late harvest began on 3 October, with teams comprising whoever could pitch in. They had to work with a shortage of supplies, but after a terrible growing season, the weather turned fine for the harvest. Haut-Brion reported potential alcohol levels of a respectable 12%, though it also spoke of widespread rot, which is why many expedited picking, which finished around 11 October. Quantities were small, many producers losing around one-third of their average yield. Interestingly, Tastet-Lawton compares the growing cycle with that of 1891 in terms of similar dates. The wines were rather simple and hollow – Lawton describes them as a cross between 1922 and 1925. In Sauternes, temperatures struggled throughout the season and at Yquem the harvest only commenced in November, with frost reported from 24 to 26 October and from 1 to 8 November when daytime highs never exceeded 3°C (37°F).

The only Bordeaux I have tasted is a 1941 Latour opened by Olivier Bernard at Domaine de Chevalier. It was just about drinkable but rapidly faded in the glass.

Event
The bombing of Pearl Harbor

Music
Take the "A" Train – Duke Ellington and His Orchestra

Just before eight o'clock on 7 December 1941, the United States Pacific Fleet, docked at Pearl Harbor, suffered a surprise aerial attack from the Japanese Air Force. Over two hours, almost 30 vessels and 300 planes were destroyed with 2,403 military and civilian fatalities. The Japanese strategy to disable the United States' means of retaliation was not wholly successful, since its aircraft carriers were out at sea and its shipyards and repair shops were left mostly intact. The following day, Congress approved Roosevelt's declaration of war against Japan and the theatre of conflict became global.

Take the "A" Train became Ellington's signature tune. The jazz standard had been penned by long-time collaborator Billy Strayhorn two years earlier, referencing the New York subway line that connected Harlem with Manhattan Island. It was inspired by directions Ellington wrote down for Strayhorn to get to his house in Sugar Hill in Harlem. Legend has it that Strayhorn threw the score into a dustbin because he was convinced it sounded like another arrangement and it was salvaged by Ellington's son, Mercer. The most famous recording was made on 15 February 1941 for the Victor record company.

Film
Citizen Kane – Orson Welles

"Rosebud". The final utterance of newspaper tycoon Charles Foster Kane and we're off on a cinematic tour de force that breaks all the rules. In fact, it had already broken one before this by eschewing any opening cast credits. Welles dominates *Citizen Kane*. It was his vision. But it was most definitely a team effort, one where everyone was at the top of their game: cinematographer Gregg Toland, co-writer Herman J. Mankiewicz, editor Robert Wise, composer Bernard Hermann and the actors from the Mercury Theatre. Welles fought for creative control and his contract with RKO banned any interference from its executives. Despite critical praise, the film failed to attract audiences upon opening on 1 May 1941 in New York and Welles himself commented that the theatre was almost empty when it premiered in Chicago. But *Citizen Kane* is often cited as one of the greatest films ever made and has stood the test of time.

1942

Who would want to be a growing season in the middle of a global war?

Nineteen forty-two kicked off with a sharp snap in January when the mercury plunged to -10°C (14°F) and arctic conditions continued until 22 February. Thereafter, temperatures struggled to climb so that the vines only began to emerge from dormancy at the end of March. April saw the weather turn volte face, reaching 25°C (77°F) around the middle of the month. Rain in May, not least a deluge on 16 May, increased the risk of mildew. Flowering began on 4 June and finished almost a fortnight earlier than the previous year thanks to clement, warm conditions and the remainder of the month swung between warm and rainy spells. July was much the same, though it warmed up nicely towards the end of the month. Nevertheless, downpours plagued the region and oidium was widespread, reducing the potential crop by approximately one-third. It could have been more, but some estates began to apply permanganate of potash, which worked as an effective substitute for copper sulphate. Fortunately, temperatures held up and winemakers hoped for ripe fruit when pickers began to enter vineyards on 14 September and en masse five days later. Potential alcohol levels hovered around 12% though Mouton Rothschild reported 13–14%. Alas, the weather deteriorated in the final few days of the month and it remained inclement until the end of picking around 2 October. Yields were very small on the Left Bank, not quite so meagre on the Right. The one bright spot was an outstanding clutch of dry whites and very good Sauternes, Tastet-Lawton going as far as to suggest they might surpass the '37s. This was thanks to heavy rain in mid-September that triggered botrytis, followed by four settled, dry weeks that led to very even botrytis formation. Many Bordeaux wines were bottled after the end of the Second World War since demand was so weak and consequently they can sometimes taste quite woody.

This is not a vintage one comes across often, especially on the Left Bank. The first I ever encountered was a very dark but not unpalatable 1942 Mouton d'Armailhacq (a precursor to Château d'Armailhac). I was pleasantly surprised by the quality of the 1942 Ausone at the vertical in London in January 2018, rustic yet with a modicum of grip. There was also a 1942 Vieux Château Certan poured at another retrospective in London, an odd bottle with Médoc-like traits, and my neighbour Alexandre Thienpont questioned its authenticity. Then again, a bottle of 1942 Petit-Village at the Académie du Vin soirée displayed similarly "souped-up" traits and still had something to offer. I suspect many reds will be past their prime. I have tasted three Sauternes. I was not smitten by either the 1942 Lafaurie-Peyraguey or Climens at their respective verticals. But a 1942 Doisy-Daëne tasted with Jean-Jacques Dubourdieu showed splendidly in June 2021. (It was just a shame that his grandfather Pierre could not join us as scheduled, since he could have told us about it first hand. Sadly, he passed away just a few weeks later.)

Event
First transmission of
Desert Island Discs

Many people sought momentary refuge from the war by listening to the radio. On 29 January 1942, they were introduced to a weekly show on the BBC Forces Programme called *Desert Island Discs*. The first guest was comedian Vic Oliver and the show was recorded in the bomb-damaged Maida Vale studios. The format was straightforward: choose eight songs to take to your notional castaway island along with a survival pack that includes the Bible, the *Complete Works of Shakespeare* and one further book of your choosing. Devisor Ray Plomley presented 1,791 editions before he passed away in 1985. The show continues to draw large audiences and famous guests to this day. The most popular choice? Beethoven's 9th Symphony.

Music
White Christmas
– Bing Crosby

Irving Berlin's *White Christmas* was written for the film *Holiday Inn*. America's biggest star and crooner Bing Crosby debuted *White Christmas* on the radio on Christmas Day 1941 and recorded it for Decca Records five months later. Sales were initially sluggish. But it topped the charts the following year, its plangent, melancholy tone striking a chord with displaced servicemen thinking of home and family. They would often break down upon hearing Crosby sing it. *White Christmas* went on to become the biggest-selling single of all time, with accumulated sales of various versions topping 50 million. According to Bob Stanley, the original recording stamper was used so much that it eventually wore out and the song had to be re-recorded in 1947.

Film
Bambi – David Hand et al

If you want to teach a child about mortality, you can either sit them down for a heart-to-heart or you can watch *Bambi*. Audiences accustomed to Disney's fantasy world were shocked by the animated depiction of death and apparently even Walt Disney's wife rebuked her husband and asked why the mother had to die. The lead artist on the project was Chinese animator Tyrus Wong, who used softened backgrounds to draw the eyes towards characters. The rotating antlers were particularly difficult to animate, so artists created a plaster cast that was filmed from various angles and then rotoscoped on to animation cells. Released at the height of the war, *Bambi* initially took less at the box office than was hoped, only turning a profit after the conflict.

1943

Discounting 1945, 1943 is seen as the best vintage of the Second World War, although the business was in dire straits – Lawton's archive entry in January states that it had nary a barrel to sell.

February was cold and then March was quite dry with cold mornings, the vines awakening in the last week. Their parched throats were not quenched until a storm on 21 March, though by then Saint-Émilion had suffered frost damage. May commenced with changeable weather although it settled towards the end of the month with higher temperatures accompanying flowering from 19 May. After a dry first-half of June, there was a splash of rain before dry and warm conditions returned for the rest of the month. July began very dry until a violent storm on 6 July, strong enough to fell trees, brought hail damage that particularly affected Saint-Estèphe. The storm ruined many of the fruit trees; disastrous when civilians' food was strictly rationed. The rest of the month was hot and saw a heat spike of 38°C (100°F). Intermittent storms meant rot was a constant threat, though fortunately brief warm and clement weather kept it in abeyance. This was crucial because many estates had little sulphur available to protect vines – Latour applied one-third of the usual number of treatments. Any more rain and rot would have spun out of control. A mid-August heat wave predicated an early picking, *vendangeurs* first entering vineyards around 9 September and starting across most of the region 10 days later under humid conditions. Hail in Sauternes ruined the vintage in the final furlong: Yquem lost around 70% of its crop, though the fruit that survived was laden with botrytis. For the reds, according to Henri Woltner at La Mission Haut-Brion, the fruit ripened in the last eight or 10 days, but the picking was over by 1 October. Interestingly, Tastet-Lawton felt that the 1943s were better than the 1942s when tasting the musts and this was confirmed upon tasting from barrel in December. The wines were said to be comparatively rich upon their eventual release after the war with some '43s containing excess residual sugar that risked re-fermenting in bottle.

This vintage is rarely seen although I have fond memories of both 1943 Haut-Brion, opened at a bibulous soirée at the Saint-Julien restaurant in the namesake town, and also a very fine, perhaps more elegant 1943 La Mission Haut-Brion. The 1943 Figeac was the most venerable bottle poured at proprietor Thierry Manoncourt's 90th birthday celebration in Paris: solid, ferrous but compelling. Nearby, a 1943 Vieux Château Certan at the vertical in London in January 2020 offered hints of aniseed on the nose, and though the palate was still standing, it indicated a wine that had spent a little too long in wood. In Pomerol, a bottle of 1943 Petrus, reconditioned in 2015, was sumptuous and warmed the cockles of the heart when poured blind at Oswald's in London in 2022. A magnum of 1943 Grand-Puy-Lacoste was stocky, rustic and brawny at one of Linden Wilkie's earliest verticals in London, though more recently, the 1943 Pichon Baron was startling, almost Burgundy-like with ample red fruit on the persistent finish.

I have had three encounters with Sauternes. Firstly, a slightly feral yet captivating 1943 Yquem that was being poured by the glass at Noble Rot restaurant in London in August 2021. Toffee apple and mandarin on the nose, maybe a little one-dimensional and slightly volatile on the finish, it was still a wartime veteran that deserves a hearty round of applause. A few weeks earlier, I had drunk my second bottle of 1943 Doisy-Daëne, with Jean-Jacques Dubourdieu – the first had been with his late father a few years earlier. A beautiful and quite Germanic Sauternes, it is still going strong today. Finally, there was a wonderful 1943 Climens at the Zurich vertical, which provided further evidence that Sauternes fared well this year, and a 1943 Coutet, which was perhaps even better, displaying spine-tingling race when opened at the property. Incidentally, 1943 was the maiden vintage of Château de Fargues after Bertrand de Lur Saluces had begun planting vines in the thirties.

Event
Dambuster raids on
German dams

Music
We'll Meet Again
– Dame Vera Lynn

The 617 Squadron's moonlit raid on three dams in the Ruhr valley was one of the most audacious attacks of the Second World War. British engineer Barnes Wallis developed the bouncing bombs that were dropped at a height of 18 m (60 ft) and a speed of 232 mph (373 km/h) from 19 specially modified Lancaster bombers. The aircrew, under Wing Commander Guy Gibson, needed immense skill and bravery. Of the 133 men who flew out, 53 died and three were taken prisoner. Two of the three targeted dams collapsed, inflicting damage in the German industrial heartland and giving Allied Forces a much-needed morale boost.

Few songs capture the anguish of the war like *We'll Meet Again*. Popularised by the namesake film in 1943, it was actually recorded in 1939 when Lynn was just 22 years old. Loosely based on Anton Rubenstein's *Melody in F*, her version utilised a Hammond Novacord, an instrument that could replicate several instruments, which strangely makes *We'll Meet Again* one of the first synth-based pop songs. Every Sunday night, on the radio show *Sincerely Yours*, Lynn read out letters from soldiers back to their sweethearts, always finishing with this wistful tune. Sadly, for countless servicemen hoping that they would meet again one sunny day, it wasn't to be.

1943
(Continued)

Film
Casablanca – Michael Curtiz

Humphrey Bogart and Ingrid Bergman star in a film that has lost none of its power since its nationwide release on 23 January 1943. Based on the play *Everybody Comes to Rick's*, it was almost entirely shot in the studio, including the tear-jerking final scene. Yes, the backdrop is a cardboard cut-out plane. Bogart revelled in his role as disillusioned ex-pat Richard Blaine, who runs one of the city's nightclubs. Though the on-screen chemistry between him and Bergman transfixed audiences, the actors exchanged little conversation during shooting. Naturally, the film struck a chord when it was released in November 1942. Many of the extras playing Nazi officers were Jews who had escaped persecution and swept away tears in the scene where *La Marseillaise* is sung over *Die Wacht am Rhein*. Of course, it is well known that no one ever actually utters the immortal line "Play it again, Sam".

Many vintages in this book are eclipsed by one that followed 12 months later, but here the eclipse is almost total.

The 1944 vintage began with almost spring-like weather, 15°C (59°F) reported in mid-January before freezing temperatures set in from mid-February. After a cold snap in early March, the rest of the month was settled, dry and warm, but the lack of moisture retarded the growth cycle and a persistent northerly wind kept the vines' throats dry until substantial rain on 19 May. The first flowers could be spotted around one week later, though the dry conditions persisted until intermittent downpours at the end of June. Despite some oidium, the flowering portended a large crop and July saw warmer temperatures. But heavy rainfall meant rot was a constant risk for vineyard teams still without the manpower or equipment. August was an eventful month. It saw heat spikes of 34°C (93°F), though those were the least of everyone's worries since over 250 were killed or injured in bombardments in Pauillac. A sign the war was reaching an end came when most of the German army boarded trains and left Bordeaux city on 22 August. The rest of the month saw warm temperatures and on 28 August, the bells rang out to celebrate the last of the occupying army leaving the city. After a clement first few days in September, Mother Nature could have perhaps conspired to banish the clouds and give the Bordelais a vintage with which to celebrate their newfound freedom. While mid-September saw good weather, the picking was delayed due to irregular ripening and, I suspect, an inability to really organise the harvesters. In October, the mercury fell and the weather became unsettled with particularly heavy storms in the middle of the month. Sauternes generally saw an early harvest from mid-September to mid-October that featured cold temperatures and intermittent frost.

The 1944 clarets were purportedly light and attractive in their youth but lacked potential to last. Most were consumed early and are now rarely seen. They were almost immediately overshadowed by the following vintage. The only two I have encountered were a frail and hollow 1944 Gruaud Larose, opened at the famous Tsubaki wine bar in Tokyo in November 2007, and a 1944 Suduiraut that was pure but sharp before it faded rapidly in the glass. Nearly all will be long past their best.

1944

1944
(Continued)

Event
D-Day

The liberation of Europe by Allied Forces began on a 50-mile (80-km) stretch of Normandy coastland on the morning of 6 June 1944. The invasion was supposed to go ahead in May but was delayed by poor weather. Over 156,000 American, British and Canadian troops poured out of amphibious landing vessels to face a barrage of machine-gun fire from the heavily defended coastland, planted with some four million landmines. It took five days to capture all five beaches and over 4,000 Allied troops were killed at Normandy. But it was a decisive turning point in the war, the beginning of the end.

Music
This Land Is Your Land
– Woody Guthrie

"This machine kills fascists" was the message emblazoned across Guthrie's acoustic guitar. It was not directed at Hitler, though I am sure Guthrie would not mind the misinterpretation. He wrote *This Land Is Your Land* in 1940 as a riposte to Irving Berlin's *God Bless America*, which he found nauseating to constantly hear on the radio. It was a song about the people rather than the country, an anthem for the humble working-class populace, but he shelved it for four years until a recording session with Moe Asch. It went through a couple of revisions, in particular a sanitised recording for a children's album in 1951, so there is no definitive version. But it became ingrained upon the American psyche and is often referred to as "America's alternative national anthem".

Film
Henry V – Laurence Olivier

Laurence Olivier hit the ground running as both director and lead in his rousing *Henry V*. Recreating Shakespeare's play was fraught with challenges. Firstly, there was the Luftwaffe bombing London, which delayed the shooting of one battle and forced filming to relocate to County Wicklow. Then there were privations of materials, which obliged the use of second-hand clothes for costumes and painted scraps of metals to serve as weapons. The famous Battle of Agincourt scene took six weeks to shoot, using 500 soldiers on foot plus another 200 on horse – a feast for the eyes when filmed in Technicolor. Released in Britain on 22 November 1944, the film won Olivier a special Oscar for his achievement.

No Bordeaux vintage will ever surpass the *réclame* of 1945. It marks a unique conjunction of a benevolent growing season, the end of the Second World War and a clutch of stellar wines. May-Éliane de Lencquesaing, former proprietor of Pichon-Lalande, described the 1945 vintage as a "gift from God". Despite its haloed reputation, it was not an easy growing season and one must remember that though liberated by Allied Forces, blood continued to be spilled across Europe.

The year commenced with heavy snow and temperatures that plummeted to -10°C (14°F), followed by a prolonged dry spell until March. Then came a blisteringly hot April when, according to Tastet-Lawton, temperatures reached a positively balmy 28°C (82°F) on 19 April. Parallels started to be made with 1893, though rain towards the end of the month alleviated the heat. These conditions encouraged vine growth, however, which carries the risk of a damaging frost and that is exactly what happened. On 30 April, the mercury plunged to around -2°C (28.5°F) and the next two days saw widespread frost and even some snow. The region as a whole suffered 60% damage – vines closest to the estuary were less impacted, and the Merlots were affected more than the Cabernets. Temperatures soon picked up and tipped 30°C (86°F) by mid-May, allowing the second-generation buds to advance and partially compensate for the loss of the first. Flowers speckled the landscape from 12 May, one of the earliest ever. June was warm and showery with a hailstorm on 19 May damaging vineyards in the Margaux appellation. July witnessed a heat wave as the mercury reached 36°C (97°F) on 21 July with oidium now widespread. August was slightly cooler and intermittent showers helped ripen remaining bunches towards perfect maturity for when harvest began on 10 September – the elation they must have felt picking during peacetime! Bunches were picked under nigh-perfect conditions. Yields were around 15–20 hl/ha at many properties, and berries were concentrated with some potential alcohol levels touching 14.5–15%. Harvest was completed early on or around 17 September but persistent high temperatures meant alcoholic fermentation was fraught with danger as vats could easily overheat. Indeed, the archives at Latour confirm that the vinification was "tricky" and indicated some volatile acidity. The total crop in Bordeaux amounted to just 1.48 million hl, the smallest since 1915. Winemakers tended towards longer-than-usual skin maceration in order to produce rich and deeply coloured wines, which were apparently hard and unyielding in their youth due to the tannins and yet effortlessly counterbalanced by intensity of fruit.

Sauternes was blessed with a great vintage, though it had obstacles to overcome. The frost was a little later here: -2°C (28.5°F) was recorded at Yquem's weather station on 2 May, damaging the upper sections of vines but sparing the flower clusters, according to its vineyard team. Summer was hot and dry, with only 13 mm (½ in) of rain recorded between August and October. The harvest at Yquem was intense: five passes through the vineyard over six weeks between 10 September and 20 October. Sugar levels were high at around 22% potential alcohol, and would likely have been similar at many Sauternes estates.

To drink a Bordeaux 1945 is always a memorable, moving experience. Any bottle is preloaded with such symbolism that exercising objectivity can be hard, and even feel immoral given the backdrop. Over the years, I have done my best to retain impartiality in order to ascertain the most successful wines. Not all of them were victorious. I have fortuitously accrued notes from most of the major Bordeaux estates, on more than one occasion with some wines.

The most iconic is the 1945 Mouton Rothschild, partly because of its *Année de la Victoire* label, partly because of Baron Philippe de Rothschild's Jewish heritage, but mostly because he returned to his homeland to oversee a sensational wine. The four bottles I have tasted over the years all convey its trademark minty nose, which is intense and opulent, the palate plush and ineffably complex, utterly delicious even after many decades. The minty tincture is shared by the 1945 Latour, not dissimilar in style but with less breeding and refinement. The 1945 Lafite Rothschild is more elegant, the 1945 Château Margaux perhaps compromised by that year's hail and summer heat. Two wines that challenge the supremacy of the Mouton Rothschild are 1945 Haut-Brion and 1945 La Mission Haut-Brion, both profound when served side by side in Hong Kong on a night when I ticked off more the 15 bottles from this fabled season. The 1945 Pichon Baron, served blind by estate director Christian Seely, was astonishing, so youthful and vigorous I foolishly declared that it must be the best 1989 Pichon Baron I had ever drunk. This bottle epitomises how this vintage could enter an ethereal realm (although according to Michael Broadbent there is significant variation – we just got lucky that night). Among the Left Bank wines tasted, favourites include Gruaud Larose, Pichon-Lalande and Cos d'Estournel – the first 1945 I ever drank, at a hedonistic festive supper *chez* moi with Christmas crackers and paper hats. Batailley, Lynch-Bages and Rauzan-Ségla are wonderful, though perhaps just beginning to tire, while d'Issan (made at Rauzan-Ségla due to the ruinous state of the winery) had definitely seen better days.

Right Bank wines are much harder to come by. The 1945 Pétrus is a wine I could have tasted with the Christie's wine department, Michael Broadbent and winemaker Jean-Claude Berrouet up in the boardroom had I not declined their invitation to catch the 10.30 p.m. train home to West Norwood. Idiot. Thankfully, another was served blind as a mystery bottle at Jordi Oriols-Gil's epic Pétrus dinner, which was not transcendental like the '47, but did taste wonderful. My pick from Pomerol is the 1945 Vieux Château Certan, which heralds an unrivalled series of sensational wines under Georges Thienpont. Pure, finessed and mind-boggling complex, it shows no sign of fatigue after more than seven decades. Two bottles of 1945 La Conseillante, one served in London and the other in Hong Kong, were equally fabulous a decade apart and a 1945 Certan de May was so voluptuous I questioned its veracity, even if it did chime with Robert Parker's commentary.

Do not overlook a clutch of otherworldly Sauternes. The 1945 Yquem opened by Pierre Lurton at the château left me speechless and a 1945 Château de Fargues, served by the much-missed wine merchant Dylan Paris at the St. John restaurant, was a revelation and perhaps my botrytis-affected eureka moment, putting me on a mellifluous slope to everything noble and rotten. Proprietor Jean-Jacques Dubourdieu served the 1945 Doisy-Daëne at a vertical in June 2021 and it was also stunning.

Event
Atomic bombs destroy Hiroshima and Nagasaki

On 6 August at 8.15 a.m., *Enola Gay*, an American B-29 bomber, released its cargo, dubbed "Little Boy", above the Japanese city of Hiroshima. It was the first time a nuclear bomb had been used in warfare. The explosion instantly killed 70,000 civilians and tens of thousands more later died from radiation and resulting injuries. Two-thirds of the city was eviscerated, the heat such that the ground was permanently scorched with victims' shadows. Three days later, an even more powerful nuclear bomb was dropped over Nagasaki. The Japanese government finally surrendered and the Second World War formally ended on 2 September.

Music
Sentimental Journey – Les Brown and his Orchestra (ft. Doris Day)

Les Brown and His Orchestra had been performing *Sentimental Journey*, written by Brown and Benjamin Homer, for a couple of years before they recorded it in November 1944. The lyrics by Bud Green dwelled upon renewing old memories and setting hearts at ease, thereby striking a chord with demobilised soldiers returning from war. It became the biggest hit on the Billboard charts in 1945 and introduced the world to Doris Day, who was featured vocalist. Day pursued a solo career two years later and became one of the biggest film and music draws of the next two decades.

1945
(Continued)

Film
Brief Encounter
– David Lean

David Lean directed this
quintessential British romantic
drama, based on Noël Coward's
one-act play *Still Life*. Trevor
Howard and Celia Johnson
play the doctor and housewife
struggling to repress their
mutual feelings. As their ardour
deepens, the cost of a full-blown
affair ultimately forces them to
make a choice and sacrifice their
happiness. Howard and Johnson
excel. But the magic of *Brief
Encounter* derives just as much
from the exquisite lighting of
the railway station and Lean's
masterful direction, not to
mention its ingenious change
in perspective and devastating
denouement.

Nineteen forty-six was predestined to lie in the shadow of 1945 and subsequent superior vintages. It is forgotten and nowadays hardly ever seen.

March began with a cold snap until the middle of the month when spring arrived and buds dappled the landscape from around 24 March. It had been quite dry, so early April downpours expedited vine growth. Vineyard managers were concerned about the risk of frost, indeed, there was localised damage in Saint-Julien and the southern Médoc from 27 to 29 April, then in Pauillac on 12 May. The rest of the month was changeable and flowering in the first half of June was concurrent with showers and a deluge on 12 June. These were followed by unseasonably cool temperatures until summer finally arrived at the end of the month. Somebody turned the oven up too high however and a heat spike of 38.4°C (101°F) on 2 July led to coulure, wiping out almost one-third of the fruit. July was warm and August began well, but temperatures fell in mid-August when the vines needed warmth to even out ripening. By the end of that month, winemakers were already pessimistic about the chances of a decent crop. September alternated between heavy downpours and brief warm spells, delaying the picking that got going around 30 September (though Latour commenced five days earlier). Apart from night-time deluges on 4 and 5 October the harvest took place under ideal conditions and these final few days in late September/early October offered some relief. The secateurs were put away around 18 October. In Sauternes, the dry summer led to a late harvest that did not start at most properties until the beginning of October and when it did begin, intermittent showers stymied sugar levels. Much of the crop at Yquem was picked in November and the secateurs were out until the 19th, patchy quality obliging strict selection in the winery.

Unsurprisingly, the quality of the 1946 vintage was uneven and it was eclipsed by coeval seasons. In any case, consumers could ill-afford the luxury of fine claret during post-war austerity. Most of the wines in this vintage would have been consumed in their youth so one hardly ever sees them. The only two bottles I have encountered come from adjoining Saint-Émilion estates. First, a 1946 Cheval Blanc poured in Hong Kong that was a little green around the edges but pleasant. Better was the 1946 Figeac poured at a dinner to celebrate the opening of its new winery in April 2022. Numerous bottles were served from a cache of 300-odd impeccably preserved 1946s found at the château and served blind as a mystery vintage by proprietor Marie-France Manoncourt. A hint of chlorine on the nose, sour cherry and molasses on the palate, it was quite delicious and in remarkably fine fettle. Having rhapsodised its virtues on social media the following day, a friend later reminded me that the same mystery vintage was to be served at a second dinner. This might explain why around half the guests nailed it as a 1946 the following night.

1946

1870

2020

1946
(Continued)

Event
ENIAC, the first computer,
is unveiled

The computer age arguably began on 14 February 1946. On that day, *The New York Times* announced the invention of ENIAC (Electronic Numerical Integrator and Computer), a calculating machine with no mechanical parts. Instead it comprised some 17,000 vacuum tubes, which had to be constantly replaced every two or three days. Built between 1943 and 1945 in the basement at the University of Pennsylvania at a cost of over $400,000, it measured 15 x 9 m (50 x 30 ft) in size and was capable of executing 5,000 additions per second. One of its first tasks was related to the construction of the hydrogen bomb. If only Control-Alt-Delete had been available.

Music
Choo Choo Ch' Boogie – Louis Jordan and His Tympany Five

This jump-blues standard was recorded on 23 January 1946, topping the charts in August that year. It's proto rock 'n' roll – just listen to the piano riff and the sax solo. Formed in 1938, the group had been on Decca's "race" label until 1941, when the company transferred them to its so-called "Sepia Series" for groups that appealed to both black and white audiences. Louis Jordan became one of the most popular and influential rhythm 'n' blues artists of the era. Try listening to *Choo Choo Ch' Boogie* without snapping your fingers and seeing the future.

Film
The Big Sleep
– Howard Hawks

Humphrey Bogart stars with Lauren Bacall in this adaptation of Raymond Chandler's novel. The plot was secondary to atmosphere and script. Nobody but Bogart could play P.I. Philip Marlowe and he relished the hard-boiled dialogue with its sexually charged subtext and double entendres. Bogart drank heavily on set as his marriage crumbled and his affair with the young Bacall intensified, despite Hawks' disapproval. By the time they convened a few months later to reshoot some scenes, Tinseltown's golden couple were husband and wife.

The 1947 vintage is often namechecked as an example of how a hot growing season can yield great wines, becoming a blueprint in later years when ripeness was paramount.

It commenced with a cold snap, a bone-chilling -12°C (10.5°F) recorded at the end of January and cold weather continued until mid-February, which saw a brief warm spell. March was warmer but rainy, and vines budded at the beginning of April. Warm weather throughout the month accelerated growth – 28°C (82°F) at the end of April augured what was to come. May was warm but some vines began to suffer hydric stress. Pomerol and Sauternes suffered hail damage on 21 and 26 May. The mercury remained high as the first flowers appeared on 27 May, and flowering was regular and even, portending a large crop. Apart from a couple of heavy downpours, there was no relief for the vines as the thermometer topped 38°C (100°F) at the end of June and 39°C (102°F) on 26 and 27 July, burning and shrivelling exposed berries. Finally, winemakers breathed a sigh as the mercury dipped from 5 August and the Médoc and the Graves enjoyed much-needed rain four days later, though not a drop fell on the Right Bank. The hot weather then returned, peaking at 38°C (100°F) on 19 August.

There were a couple more showers at the beginning of September and, unsurprisingly given the constant heat, the first pickers entered the vineyards around 8 September, though most waited until the following week. Musts entered the vat-rooms at almost 15% potential alcohol and combined with the unrelenting warm weather and lack of temperature regulation, fermentations spun out of control. Blocks of ice were dunked into vats to prevent them from boiling over and rendering wines volatile. Figeac co-proprietor Marie-France Manoncourt recalled to me how her husband had driven into Libourne to purchase ice from butchers or fishmongers, finding them reluctant to make a one-off sale to a local winery, preferring to keep blocks for regular customers. Only three or four of the leading wineries bothered cooling the vats. Unlike Thierry Manoncourt, who had a scientific/engineering background, most winemakers were farmers with only a basic understanding of alcoholic fermentation and temperature control. The 1947 crop was much larger than in 1945, with 2.7 million hl produced. Sauternes enjoyed a bumper year, the hot summer leading to highly botrytised fruit that was powerful and high in sugar.

Over the years I have tasted many of Bordeaux's major 1947s, including two-dozen of them at one memorable dinner at The Square in London. The wines that evening reflected a vintage with mind-boggling highs and distasteful lows. In my experience, the high alcohol levels and volatility resulted in wider inter-château variation than in 1945 and 1949, not to mention potential variations between one bottle and the next. Provenance is crucial for old claret, but especially for any 1947. Caveat emptor. The vintage is better-known for its Right Bank rather than its Left Bank wines. That might be a surprise given that Pomerol and Saint-Émilion are populated by earlier-ripening, heat-sensitive Merlot, but remember that far more Malbec was cultivated before the 1956 freeze, even in the most auspicious vineyards. At best, a great 1947 is larger than life, decadent and rich, Bordeaux with Mediterranean flair, teetering on the brink of imbalance yet upholding a sense of coherence and focus. I suspect they were more fun to drink from the fifties to the seventies than now.

The 1947 vintage is a famous/infamous vintage put on a pedestal by a single Saint-Émilion. To my regret, I have never tasted a château-bottled 1947 Cheval Blanc, which is often cited as an exemplar of a legendary wine in a hot vintage. The alcohol level was 14.4%, high for the time but lower than many 2018s and 2019s, technically faulty given its volatility. The closest I have come is a Vandermeulen bottling that some say is more "tamed" than the château bottling and indeed, I found it less Port-like than expected. Alas, only a handful remain at the property. The 1947 Figeac is divine and showed less volatility than fellow Right Bank wines when poured from large formats in 2015 at the château. Apart from a suspect 1947 Ausone, I have fond memories of a 1947 La Carte before it was absorbed into Beau-Séjour Bécot. Over the years, I have tasted quite a few Pomerols. The best has been the 1947 Vieux Château Certan, three bottles over the years, so precocious on the nose with an intense, confit-like palate to die for. Two bottles of the legendary 1947 Pétrus were magnificent if perhaps a few years past their peak, ditto a *négociant*-bottled peppermint-scented 1947 Trotanoy. The final remaining bottles of 1947 La Croix de Gay from the Raynaud family's cellars defied time, likewise a 1947 La Conseillante that evoked images of a roaring log fire on the nose. The 1947 Lafleur bottled by Vandermeulen was a faded behemoth and 1947 Clos du Clocher, which came from the Bourotte family's cellar, could sadly muster only remnants of fruit. The Left Bank is inconsistent to say the least. My two most memorable experiences are a stunning 1947 Mouton Rothschild that threatened to eclipse the 1945 in November 2017, crystalline and shimmering with energy, and a regal 1947 Château Margaux. I prefer this to my encounters with Latour, Lafite Rothschild and Haut-Brion, which were compromised by the merciless heat. I have very positive notes for 1947 Cos d'Estournel, Pichon Baron and Branaire-Ducru, and the 1947 Talbot was shining at its centenary vertical in December 2018. In Margaux, the 1947 Château d'Issan and Rauzan-Ségla were rickety with age, though the 1947 Siran coped with its volatility, teetered on falling over, but remained standing. One of my fondest memories is a 1947 La Tour Haut-Brion, intense and nutty on the nose, blazing for 10 minutes before it was dismantled by oxygen.

Sauternes can be superb, my pick perhaps the 1947 Climens and a bewitching 1947 Château de Fargues served blind by Comte Alexandre de Lur Saluces that caused me to run out of superlatives. They are often rich and decadent compared to their 1949 counterparts.

Event
UFO "found" at Roswell, New Mexico

After the Second World War, there was an obsession with UFOs, especially in the United States. In summer 1947, William Brazel awoke to find wreckage on his ranch in New Mexico, north of Roswell. Around the same time, several sightings were reported of an object flying faster than any Air Force jet. Within days newspaper headlines were talking about a "flying saucer" from outer space. The US Army debunked the theory, but there are still those who claim a cover-up and that staff at the Roswell Army Air Field glimpsed three alien bodies.

Music
Golden Earrings – Peggy Lee

Peggy Lee, née Norma Deloris Egstrom from Scandinavian heritage, recorded the smouldering *Golden Earrings* on 24 September 1947 backed by Dave Barbour and His Orchestra. The platinum blonde jazz singer had cut her teeth in the early forties with Benny Goodman's band where she had fallen for guitarist Barbour. Unlike many female singers of the era, she composed over 200 songs and controlled most aspects of performances, including staging and costume. Yet she always remained a bit of an enigma, her songs never revealing much about herself (Bob Stanley refers to her as pop's Mona Lisa). Renowned for her alluring tone, Lee was no powerhouse singer, rather a masterful and nuanced interpreter over her seven-decade career.

Film
It's a Wonderful Life – Frank Capra

Capra's timeless heart-tugging classic is the Christmas gift that keeps on giving. James Stewart was perfectly cast as suicidal bank manager George Bailey in his first role after returning from military service. Just as Bailey is about to jump from a bridge on Christmas Eve, he is visited by a guardian angel, who through a series of flashbacks, shows him how his hometown would have been had he not existed. Though regarded as a festive flick, the film was shot in the summer during a heat wave – including the scene where Stewart runs through snowy Bedford Falls. Going on general release on 7 January 1947, it was not a box-office hit and became so forgotten it fell out of copyright. Subsequently, TV stations constantly showed the film at no cost and it gradually achieved its cherished status.

1948

Like 1946, 1948 finds itself sandwiched between two lauded vintages. However, it has much more to offer – the dark horse of this period.

A spring-like January was almost a continuation of the torrid heat that defined 1947 and warm conditions lasted until mid-February when temperatures tumbled to -9°C (15°F). The cold snap did not last long and warmer temperatures in the first week of March provoked buds to swell. Lawton alludes to the 1937 vintage as the warmth continued and vines grew as if they had to meet a July harvest deadline. Lower temperatures from mid-April put the brakes on and winemakers feared a frost episode. There was a skirmish in the Graves on 4 May but the mercury had risen by the time flowers appeared a fortnight later. It then began to rain heavily, which coupled with cooler temperatures caused widespread coulure and oidium. June was quite stormy and winemakers now had to contend with mildew pressure and became pessimistic. Thankfully, the weather settled from 19 July, becoming warm and dry, only to deteriorate in August, which caused uneven *véraison*. The vintage was saved at the last moment thanks to hot weather and a cessation of downpours from 17 September. Encouraged by the settled weather, pickers entered vineyards around five days later under ideal conditions that remained throughout harvest. The potential alcohol at Pontet-Canet was 13.5% when the harvesters completed their task around 13 October, though many were 25% to 30% down in quantity. The harvest in Sauternes took place in dry conditions, the berries apparently ripening slowly.

The 1948 is not particularly well-known, crowded out by 1945, 1947 and 1949, though its Right Bank wines are highly regarded among cognoscenti, even if they are rarely seen nowadays. Without question, the finest I tasted was a 1948 Cheval Blanc served blind in London for a small party that included Édouard Moueix. Both of us were convinced this magnificent, precocious wine must be the 1982 Cheval Blanc. I was astonished when its vintage was revealed, giving credence to those convinced the 1948 is superior to the 1947. Three bottles of 1948 Vieux Château Certan have been wonderful. The first came when I spotted a mis-priced bottle on a merchant's list and exchanged it for a place at a VCC vertical. It was stout and sturdy, yet supremely well balanced with layers of black fruit. Around the same time I encountered a rather gruff and obdurate 1948 Pétrus, though I preferred the VCC. Left Bank wines can be a bit hard and charmless. That said, a 1948 Langoa Barton showed well in 2009, and put a big fat grin on the face of Anthony Barton. It is a vintage that châteaux rarely show and even during my comprehensive Pichon Baron vertical, it was the only omission from that era.

I have had very few encounters with Sauternes from this vintage, save for a chlorophyll- and crushed-flower-tinged 1948 Coutet opened at the château, shaded by an accompanying 1943.

Event
HMT *Empire Windrush* docks at Tilbury

On 21 June 1948, the *Empire Windrush* docked at the Port of Tilbury in Essex. On route from Australia to Britain, it had docked at Kingston, Jamaica. The vessel was not full and a newspaper advertised cheap travel, £28 to be exact, for anyone who wanted to work in the UK. Nobody knows the exact figure, but around 500 Jamaicans boarded, looking for a better life abroad. The passengers included Sam Beaver King, future mayor and a co-founder of the Notting Hill Carnival, and were the first of a group of migrants who would become known as the Windrush generation.

Film
Bicycle Thieves – Vittorio De Sica

The seminal *Bicycle Thieves* tells the story of a poor father searching for his stolen bicycle with his son, Bruno. It's a tale of injustice and frustration, of how modern life·can crush one's confidence. De Sica shot the scenes around Rome and used amateur actors to add realism. The anxiety expressed by lead actor Lamberto Maggiorani was genuine since he had no confidence in his acting ability. After filming ended, he found it difficult to find employment. This masterpiece of Italian cinema influenced a number of directors and is rightly cited as one of the defining films of the 20th century.

Music
I Can't Be Satisfied – Muddy Waters

In 1948, blues guitarist Muddy Waters laid a cornerstone of rock 'n' roll with one of his earliest releases, *I Can't Be Satisfied*. Waters had recorded for folk archivist Alan Lomax several years earlier and then travelled north to Chicago to pursue a career as a musician. The song is essentially a 12-bar Delta blues, but Waters' innovation was to express it through slide on his electric guitar. Released on Aristocrat Records, later to become the renowned Chess label, it became a template for the Rolling Stones' (*I Can't Get No) Satisfaction*.

1949

Nineteen forty-nine is the last of a post-war triumvirate, but the beginning of the growing season did not bode well.

January was tempestuous and stormy, then February was unseasonably dry and deprived the vines of much-needed rain. March began with a cold snap and the mercury finally began to rise from 10 March. The vines burst into green from 23 to 28 March but their throats were still parched. Instead of rain, temperatures soared with 26°C (79°F) recorded on 13 April, before gradually cooling towards the end of the month and 24 April saw welcome downpours. May was changeable with sporadic showers before the first flowers were spotted around the 27th. The weather remained mercurial throughout flowering in June and, combined with hot spells, caused widespread coulure – Rauzan-Ségla lost around half of its potential crop. July was picture perfect, with temperatures bobbing along in the low thirties so that, by 29 July, Lawton notes that some places had not seen a drop of rain for 60 days. Outside, it was a balmy 36°C (97°F). August remained warm and dry, though crucially without the heat spikes seen two years earlier.

But the vines still needed rain and they had to make do with intermittent showers until early September, the sirocco wind raising temperatures to 36°C (97°F) once more. Finally, the heavens opened on the night of 5 September, continuing throughout the next day, before a second spell of rain reinvigorated vines on 15 September. After more rain on 23 September, the first pickers went out into the vineyards, though at Mouton Rothschild they began over a week later.

In Sauternes, the season had been dry. The showers in May and June relieved some of the stress and early September rain provoked botrytis to such an extent that only two passes through the vineyard were required at Yquem. Though yields were small, quality was high.

This is one of my favourite Bordeaux vintages, and the handful I have tasted are paragons of mature claret. They are cut from a very different cloth to the rich and opulent 1947s. They exude panache and class and have a sense of precision, like notes being carefully placed upon a stave. Sichel & Co opined that they would peak around 1955, when in fact the 1949s across the board matured with style uncommon for the time.

Among the First Growths, the 1949 Mouton Rothschild is impeccable, the third wine within five years under Baron Philippe de Rothschild that flirts with perfection and mocks its Deuxième Cru status. If someone argued that it is better than the more iconic 1945, I would not argue against them – a Pauillac sculpted by the finest chisel in the set. The 1949 Latour is similar to Mouton Rothschild in the sense that it eases off the gas, surfeit with elegance, poise and breeding. In my experience it's the best of its post-war triumvirate, more substantial than the 1949 Lafite Rothschild that on both occasions I felt lacked a bit of mass and grip. Pedigree is not exclusive to the top rank. Other impressive Left Bank wines include a multi-layered 1949 Batailley served two or three times by proprietor Philippe Castéja at the château, a fine-boned Montrose and a heavenly 1949 Cos d'Estournel, a highlight of a vertical in 2018. I have never tasted either Haut-Brion or La Mission, though Jean-Jacques Bonnie served a sublime 1949 Malartic-Lagravière rescued from a cache found in a Swiss cellar in 2021. So fresh and poised, it gained depth as it blossomed in the glass over lunch, much like a 1949 Pichon Baron that meliorated with aeration just a few weeks later. One not to overlook is the 1949 Beychevelle, shared with TV presenter-cum-oenophile Phillip Schofield and wine celebrity Oz Clarke (one of the finest Bordeaux tasters I have met). The Right Bank is also studded with brilliance, though they are difficult to find. The 1949 Pétrus is so beautiful it could bring a man to tears, so have a handkerchief handy if you are ever lucky to be graced with one. It is almost matched by an ethereal 1949 Figeac poured from double magnum just before the Manoncourt family demolished their old barrel cellar in 2018. A 1949 Lafleur, served at a vertical tasting overlooking Attersee in Austria, was testament to the Robin sisters' knack of creating wonders from their Pomerol jewel. The 1949 Ausone is one of the estate's high points of the post-war era, brimming with energy in January 2018. Cheval Blanc is better this year than in 1945, though does not have the sheer concentration of the preceding vintage. Its neighbour in Pomerol, La Conseillante, was full of breeding in 2010, though is now almost impossible to find. In Sauternes, I am waiting to taste the highly touted 1949 Yquem, though I will make do with memories of a crystalline 1949 Climens, which I found superior to a 1949 Suduiraut that was marred by some volatility.

1949
(Continued)

George Orwell publishes *1984*

Despite the success of *Animal Farm*, George Orwell had suffered traumatically in the final years of the war: his house had been destroyed by a doodlebug and his beloved wife had died during a routine operation. Grief-stricken, the author upped sticks to live an ascetic life on the Isle of Jura without electricity and sleeping on a camp bed. He battled with tuberculosis while working on his novel, changing the title from *The Last Man in Europe* to *1984*, and entertaining suicide as he tried to meet his publisher's deadline. Hitting the bookshops on 8 June 1949, it was hailed as a dystopian masterpiece. Churchill was so taken that he read it twice. The novel introduced several words into the common English language, including "Big Brother", "thought police" and "newspeak", while "Orwellian" entered the lexicon to describe a bleak future. Orwell died the following January.

Music
The Fat Man
– Fats Domino

On 10 December 1949, 21-year-old "Fats" Domino entered the studio to record his take on the 1940 New Orleans piano blues number, *Junker Blues*. Renamed *The Fat Man*, it was distinguished by Domino's piano triplets and its driving beat, essentially a blueprint for rock 'n' roll before the term had been invented. Released by Imperial records, *The Fat Man* became a hit across the US the following month and went on to sell a million copies.

Film
Kind Hearts and Coronets
– Robert Hamer

Alec Guinness was so taken with the script for *Kind Hearts and Coronets* that he asked to play eight members of the D'Ascoynes family instead of four: The Duke, The General, The Banker, The Parson, The Admiral, Young Ascoyne, Young Henry, The Old Duke and Lady Agatha. One by one they meet their demise at the hands of Louis, avenging his deceased mother by restoring the dukedom denied his family. Though Guinness's multiple cameos are a delight, the centrepiece of this blackest of Ealing comedies is Dennis Price's performance as Louis. Revel in his perfect RP as he plots murders with Tarantino-like equanimity, not forgetting Joan Greenwood's Machiavellian Sibella.

1949
(Continued)

1870

2020

THE 1950s

The upheaval of the Second World War was in the rear-view mirror and yet its aftereffects continued to ripple through daily life. Post-war countries could only gradually rebuild their shattered and mostly debt-ridden economies. Ration books were still being used at the beginning of the decade across Britain and in other countries. Against this backdrop, the fifties witnessed some outstanding vintages, though demand was stymied by lack of disposable income and prices languished accordingly. Many châteaux were in various states of disrepair following the Great Depression and privations of war, denied revenues that would have enabled them to sew vineyards back together or repair damaged and dilapidated wineries. In a sense, there was a two-speed financial recovery among estates. While the elite were mostly able to return to a small profit by the time of the decidedly average 1951 vintage thanks to a buoyant en primeur campaign, many small and less illustrious estates, especially those severely damaged by war, struggled to break even.

The decade saw the introduction of two significant official classifications. In 1953, the Syndicat de Défense de l'Appellation des Graves requested the I.N.A.O. for a classification of its châteaux. To keep it simple, there was no hierarchy and there would be no revisions. Sixteen estates, all within Pessac-Léognan were classified, including Haut-Brion, making it the only château to be categorised twice. The classification came into effect in February 1959. Another classification, this time on the Right Bank, was born in 1954. More complicated than the Graves list, it followed the 1855 Classification by forming a hierarchy headed by the two Saint-Émilion Premier Grand Cru Classé "A" producers, Ausone and Cheval Blanc, with 10 Saint-Émilion Premier Grand Cru Classé "B" and numerous Saint-Émilion Grand Cru Classé estates beneath. Unlike the immutable 1855 Classification, this was to be revised every 10 years, thereby encouraging châteaux to maintain quality or improve and seek promotion. That was clearly well-meaning, though writing in early 2022, it sowed the seeds for its undoing, prompting a flurry of lawsuits and its top châteaux – first Ausone and Cheval Blanc, then Angélus and La Gaffelière soon after – choosing not to apply for the 2022 classification. Post-fallout, the credibility of the classification remains to be seen.

This was the final decade during which authorities tolerated less noble varieties – anything other than Cabernet Sauvignon, Cabernet Franc, Merlot, Malbec, Petit Verdot and rarely cultivated Carménère. Up to 10% of them were permitted until 1953, but the ban was moot as nearly all had been uprooted the previous decade. It was also the last decade in which Malbec played a key role in blends. The grape was shunned by most châteaux after the

1956 freeze mandated whole-scale replanting. Malbec had been particularly prevalent on the Right Bank, but it was perceived as a less noble variety. From my experience of tasting pre-1956 Pomerols and Saint-Emilions over the years, I must confess I appreciate Malbec's contribution. There is a valid argument that, in the light of climate change, Malbec could play a similar role to Cabernet Franc insofar as it is better adapted to hotter summers than Merlot. Too late now. Another important change came in 1951 when chaptalisation was legalised. Initially, permission to chaptalise was supposed to be on an ad hoc basis, though it had become so endemic by the early sixties that it was permitted every year instead of just when it was needed.

Perusing the introductory chapters of the 1949 edition of the *Féret* guide, I was interested to read its analysis of vintage quality over 132 seasons between 1795 and 1926. It concludes that 90 out of 132 vintages provided wines described as "satisfying". These figures are rather skewed by the definition of "satisfaction", which in those times could be read as merely "drinkable". In reality, even by this point in Bordeaux's timeline, winemakers anticipated two or maybe three genuinely good vintages per decade where they might make a profit – not a given since this depended on them being able to sell their wines and not their quality. There might be three fair-to-middling vintages and the rest would be write-offs. Technology and practices had changed little since the beginning of the century despite advances in the understanding of winemaking, such as Professor Jean Ribéreau-Gayon's research into the hitherto mysterious process of malolactic fermentation.

Bordeaux châteaux welcomed benevolent vintages such as 1953, 1955 and top of the heap, 1959. The last is crucial to Bordeaux, arguably even more so than 1961, since it bestowed both quantity and quality. Ask any winemaker which one they coveted more in those straitened times and it would be quantity, simply to balance the books. This decade contains some other decent, if more challenging and patchier, growing seasons, such as 1952 and at a stretch, 1957. The 1954 is neither here nor there, ditto 1958, whereas 1951 was a write-off.

The infamy of 1956 stems from the unprecedented and devastating winter freeze that killed off swathes of vines, especially on the exposed Right Bank (page 256). Not only did it eviscerate that year's potential crop before it had even left the starting blocks, but it necessitated widespread replanting, encumbering vineyards with immature vines for a number of years, assuming they could be re-planted immediately. Many growers never returned after 1956. The previous year, just under 56,000 declared their 1955. In 1956 it was 46,701 and that continued to fall as estates were consolidated, down to about half that number by 1980.

Faced with large swathes of Bordeaux needing replanting, the I.N.A.O. decided to champion Cabernet Sauvignon over Merlot, probably because it was later-ripening and so less prone to such extensive frost damage. "After the frost, the French government offered grants for replanting if the variety was Cabernet Sauvignon, which in their infinite wisdom they viewed as preserving the character of Bordeaux," Bill Blatch informs me. "Then, the entirety of cooler vineyards, the ones that were prone to frost, were planted with Cabernet Sauvignon that never ripened properly, which accounts for those green wines of the sixties and seventies, at least until they were replanted with Merlot. There was a second problem too: the tardy-ripening Cabernet Sauvignons were often planted on the more frost-prone foot of vineyards, where they ripened even less well."

———————

1950

The fifties kicked off with a Janus vintage, deified in some parts of Bordeaux but criticised in others.

The year commenced with a typically chilly January before warming up, though a spring-like February saw the mercury reach 20°C (68°F). Vines began their bud burst at the end of March and April was fresh and rainy. Much of May was fairly hot with occasional storms, then flowering was concurrent with hot temperatures, up to 32°C (90°F), with *pleine fleur* on 8 June. With no signs of coulure, prospects were for a large volume. But on the 13 June, Sauternes was hit by a significant hailstorm that wiped out half the crop at Yquem and two days later, severe hail affected Saint-Julien and south of Pauillac – André Delon at Léoville-Las Cases estimated he lost 90% of his potential crop. Curiously, next door at Latour, hail damage was reported as "negligible". It precipitated minor outbreaks of coulure among the Merlot. There was more hail damage in Listrac five days later and then Sauternes was struck on 22 June, some châteaux losing up to 70% of their crop. This was followed by a heat spike of 38°C (100°F) in some places that continued into early July. August was warm and mainly sunny, the sirocco wind keeping temperatures up in the low thirties. Despite hail damage, many were optimistic that this could bring about a small crop of high-quality wines. The first pickers ventured out around 18 September but the harvest was plagued by outbreaks of heavy rain between the sunny spells.

In Sauternes, light showers led to a wave of botrytis and picking began around 20 September, the following passes through the vineyard lasting until 27 October at Yquem.

The 1950 vintage has always been renowned on the Right Bank thanks to frequent eulogies by Robert Parker. Saint-Émilion and Pomerol had a small advantage because, examining the Tastet-Lawton entries, the weather seems slightly more settled there in September when the earlier-ripening Merlot was picked. This has been borne out by a handful of ethereal Right Bank wines I have tasted. Both 1950 Pétrus and Lafleur are magical, like multifaceted diamonds, elegant and refined after many decades – that's if you can find one with sound provenance, as many fakes abound. The 1950 Vieux Château Certan continued Georges Thienpont's dazzling run that had begun in 1945, a formidable and fabulous Pomerol on the two occasions it has blessed my palate, the last bottle with a distinctly tobacco tinge. Proprietor Christian Moueix cracked open a half-bottle of 1950 La Fleur-Pétrus following one of our interviews for my Pomerol book. Ferrous and slightly volatile aromatically, it showed quite a bit of piquancy on the palate. Three bottles of 1950 Cheval Blanc have been wonderful (two château-bottled and one equally fine Berry Brothers' bottling) – sumptuous, precocious with just a touch of volatility giving it a kick up the bum. Figeac also produced a masterful 1950 even though, according to proprietor Marie-France Manoncourt, it took two decades before it was sumptuous, sweet and mouth-filling. Both Cheval Blanc and Figeac are better than the 1950 released by Ausone, which was beginning to lose form in that period.

I have only tasted a few Left Bank wines: a surprisingly vigorous magnum of 1950 Latour, which picked 80% more than the 10-year average, and a 1950 Pichon Baron, which convinced me the Médoc could produce wines of note. The 1950 La Mission Haut-Brion poured in December 2018 in Hong Kong was interesting, if rather short and dry on the finish. Sauternes can be delightful. The 1950 Yquem is intense and weighty, while Climens had a lovely nutty, gingerbread element in 2009. I also once drank a 1950 Saint-Amand, a Sauternes I'd never heard of, which still had a glint in its eye after 65 years.

Event
Fangio wins first Monaco Grand Prix

Hailed as one of the greatest racing drivers of all time, Argentina's Juan Manuel Fangio won the Monaco Grand Prix in the maiden Formula One World Championship season. He managed to avoid a pile-up on the first lap that was bizarrely caused by a freak wave flooding the circuit. Upon reaching the crashed cars on the next lap, he gallantly pushed one of the obstructing cars away to continue. In an era when serious injuries and fatalities were not uncommon, Fangio spent the next few days assisting the recovery of two colleagues who had suffered burns and personally drove them to hospital. He went on to dominate motor racing throughout the decade.

Music
Mambo No. 5
– Pérez Prado

Cuban bandleader, composer and arranger Dámaso Pérez Prado was the undisputed "King of Mambo" with a string of popular releases throughout the fifties that popularised Latin music outside of Hispanic communities. Mambo replaced the rhumba as the dancehall craze in the late forties. Prado was so prolific that when stuck for a title, he simply went for a number. The song received a new lease of life when it was sampled by Lou Bega in 1999, though personally, I would stick with the original.

1950
(Continued)

Film
Rashômon
– Akira Kurosawa

Kurosawa's masterpiece remains one of the most influential cinematic works of the century. This film about the murder of a samurai and the rape of his wife retold through multiple perspectives rewrote the rules of storytelling with its conflicting narratives and lack of a resolution, leaving viewers to interpret events for themselves. Toshiro Mifune is mesmerising as the bandit Tajōmaru and the actor collaborated with Kurosawa in 16 films between 1948 and 1965. *Rashômon* received wide critical acclaim, so much so that some believe it coerced the Academy into introducing the best foreign-language film Oscar.

Nineteen fifty-one has the ignominy of being considered one of the worst vintages of the century.

The growing season was marked by wretched weather conditions throughout a rain-drenched spring with warmer climes only arriving around mid-April. Hail in Sauternes on 3 May destroyed around half of the potential crop, then it was rainy and humid during a late flowering, with *pleine fleur* on 19 June. Mildew, cochylis and, in July, oidium followed, the latter becoming widespread during a series of storms across the region. The 4 August was like autumn, according to Lawton, and the rain did not let up throughout the month, retarding *véraison*. September did not come to save the day and the weather remained inclement with rays of sun in short supply up until 22 September. What survived this soggy growing season was picked from the beginning of October with the heart of the harvest around 9 October. Nearly all the red wines were heavily chaptalised to compensate for the lack of sugar. Essentially, it was a write-off and anyone spotted drinking a '51 claret had either misread the vintage as '61 or was completely mad. It was no better in Sauternes. Remarkably, flowering did not take place until July with *véraison* in September. Basically, there was nothing to pick come harvest and no Yquem saw the light of day, ditto nearly all other Sauternes.

Count me among the mad. It took many years to come across a 1951 because the tiny crop was mostly consumed in its youth, but I finally got to encounter a 1951 Mouton Rothschild when future wine scribe William Kelley cracked one open in the student halls at Oxford University after I had tutored a Pomerol tasting for the Oxford University Wine Circle. It was undeniably skeletal but not undrinkable. A second was poured at the fifth edition of "Grouse Club", an informal annual lunch after 12 August to savour the game bird. Coming from a full case acquired by Lord Bruce, the 1951 Latour cocked a snook at its birth-year's reputation. Yes, a green tincture on the nose, yet the palate boasted plenty of fruit and it felt velvety smooth – a pertinent reminder not to prejudge wine by vintage, though Latour does have a propensity to excel when its back is against the wall. Having read my effusive write-up, the château poured a second bottle for me there a few weeks later and it was just as fine.

1951

1951
(Continued)

Event
Dennis the Menace debuts in *The Beano*

On 12 March 1951, British comic *The Beano* introduced a new character, the world's naughtiest boy, Dennis the Menace. The name came from a music hall song that featured the line: "I'm Dennis the Menace from Venice". He got his trademark black-and-red-striped jumper two months later. One of the longest-running comic-strip characters in the world, Dennis is still terrorising the "softies" to this day with his pea-shooter and catapult, accompanied by his faithful hound, Gnasher.

Film
A Streetcar Named Desire – Elia Kazan

Marlon Brando shot to stardom in Kazan's adaptation of Tennessee Williams's most famous work. Brando had graduated from the Actor's Studio as a student of method acting and had starred as Stanley Kowalski in the theatre production since 1947. Nine members of the cast reprised their roles for the silver screen. Williams wrote the screenplay and toned down some of the sexual elements, but the film still has an edgy feel with an undercurrent of violence stemming from Brando's brutish and mumbling portrayal. Kazan cleverly reduced the size of Kowalski's apartment in order to enhance a feeling of claustrophobia.

Music
Rocket "88" – Jackie Brenston and His Delta Cats

Often cited as the first rock 'n' roll record, *Rocket "88"* was in fact recorded by Ike Turner and his Kings of Rhythm. Brenston was the band's saxophonist and sang vocals. Though he was also credited as songwriter, many believe Turner composed this ode to the Oldsmobile Rocket 88 car. Musically, it was ahead of its time in the sense that Turner made jump blues more visceral, wilder and sexier. The song introduced fuzz guitar, allegedly after Willie Kizart's amplifier was damaged by falling out of the band's car on the way to Memphis. *Rocket "88"* was a huge jukebox hit and topped the R&B chart on 9 June 1951.

This is a rather overlooked vintage with plenty of caveats, yet with much to offer if you look carefully.

The 1952 growing season began cold in January and February and March was inundated with rain that delayed the vines' growth cycle. Temperatures fell on 7 April, burning some of the nascent buds, particularly the Merlot. Warmer temperatures towards the end of the month encouraged growth and the first flowers were spotted around 22 May. Flowering was a little earlier than normal and clement conditions meant it was regular, portending a decent-sized crop. June was warm, though a terrible storm on 17 June wrought hail damage in Sauternes so severe that 1952 is a rare no-show for Yquem. The mercury kept rising, reaching 37°C (99°F) towards the end of the month with small outbreaks of oidium and July remained warm with welcome rain on the 7th. Temperatures remained high throughout August, though 5 August saw hail in Saint-Estèphe and Listrac. With sporadic showers and heat, 1952 was heading for a fine harvest, but September was much cooler and changeable when pickers unsheathed their secateurs around 11 September, rainfall particularly heavy on 15 and 17 September when the harvest was in full swing. The wet conditions had improved little by the end of the harvest around 29 September. The summer heat had produced satisfactory sugar levels, musts coming in with 12.5–13.5% potential alcohol.

Sichel compares 1952 with the 1950 vintage and felt the wines' charm on release would deceive inexperienced tasters into thinking they would not last. The season favoured the earlier-picked Merlots harvested before the rains and also those on the well-drained gravel soils of the Graves. Lawton writes of "ripe, supple, flowing wines" in its records and alludes to a crop that might have mirrored 1929, if only it had not rained during harvest. Maybe the wines were pliant in their youth? My limited experience of the Left Bank has shown the wines to be rather tannic and "serious", missing the flair common among the '53s. The best wines from this vintage have originated from the Right Bank and include a gorgeous, if chlorophyll-tinged 1952 Pétrus bottled by Vandermeulen. But my finest Pomerol is the 1952 Vieux Château Certan from an era when Georges Thienpont (still) could not put a foot wrong and it was just as charming and vigorous when revisited in January '20. In Saint-Émilion, I recall a pure chestnut-tinged 1952 Magdelaine that lit up a dinner in Kowloon as New Year fireworks thundered overhead and made the entire building tremble, while a 1952 Canon-la-Gaffelière had plenty of stuffing, but was just beginning to dry on the finish. On the Left Bank, the 1952 Latour was rather austere but, intriguingly, I chanced upon the same wine but with Réserve des Propriétaires printed across the label. This was a private cuvée made by the owners at the time, the de Beaumont and de Flers families. Unquestionably, it had much more fruit than the regular bottling and was utterly entrancing. The 1952 Montrose showed well at two verticals in 2018, though two bottles of the 1952

1952

1870

2020

Haut-Brion were musty and uncharacteristically rustic, likewise the 1952 Gruaud Larose and Pichon Baron, structured and ossified after six decades. The only Sauternes I had tasted was a volatile Climens until two more Barsac wines appeared at Olivier Bernard's "2" soirée. The 1952 Doisy-Daëne was ethereal and beguiling in its purity, suggesting that it escaped the storm unscathed, while the 1952 Cantegril was more evolved yet with remnants of appeal.

Event
Pea souper kills over
4,000 Londoners

Londoners had become accustomed to pea soupers – when thick fog mixed with smoke belching from factory chimneys and domestic coal fires. Between 5 and 9 December, a particularly dense pea souper settled on the capital and reduced visibility to a few metres (feet). People were advised to stay inside and transport virtually ground to a halt. An estimated 4,000 to 12,000 people died of respiratory illnesses and it led to the Clean Air Act of 1956 that made smokeless fuel mandatory in heavily populated urban areas.

Music
Here in My Heart
– Al Martino

The early fifties was ruled by crooners such as Italian-American singer Al Martino. Not only did *Here in My Heart* reach the top of the charts in the US, but it was the maiden number one in the newly inaugurated UK Singles Chart on 14 November 1952, where it sat for nine weeks. It was Martino's solitary chart-topper. He became better known as Johnny Fontane, the singer pleading for favours in *The Godfather*. In a case of life imitating art, Martino allegedly had to use his mafia connections to lean on Francis Ford Coppola to get the role after the director had already given the part to Vic Damone.

Film
Singin' in the Rain
– Gene Kelly

Film musicals reached their peak with *Singin' in the Rain*. Gene Kelly was a perfectionist and a disciplinarian who drove co-stars Debbie Reynolds and Donald O'Connor to their physical and mental limits. Nineteen-year-old Reynolds, who had no formal dance training, was regularly left in floods of tears and both actors ended up in hospital recovering from injuries and exhaustion. Despite the off-stage trauma, Kelly's taskmaster approach yielded magical sequences, not least the title song featuring Kelly splashing through the rain twirling his umbrella and doing his utmost to disguise his 39°C (102°F) fever.

1953

Nineteen fifty-three is in some ways stylistically dichotomous to 1947.

It began with a cold but clement January. It was dry, though reserves had been topped up by December's torrential downpours. March was also dry but spring was in the air and despite the vines needing water, they began to bud around 24 – 26 March. Finally, the first two days in April saw the pitter-patter of much-needed rain, though the middle of the month was cold and frost severely damaged exposed vineyards. May started cool but warmed up after a few days with the first flowers dotting the landscape from 23 May, followed by a mini-heat wave that saw 32°C (90°F). Flowering finished by the end of the month and its regularity augured an abundant crop despite localised outbreaks of coulure. June was warm with occasional showers and some stormy weather towards the end of the month. July saw constant warmth, nothing excessive, albeit with hail causing some damage in the appellation of Margaux. But from 1 August, warm and dry conditions prevailed, ensuring a quick *véraison*. Temperatures reached 34°C (93°F) by the end of the month and fell only a couple of degrees at the beginning of September. What the vines desired was a bit of rain and their wish came true from 15 September – Latour recorded 10 days of rain until 25 September. Harvesters began entering vineyards in Margaux around 22 September and three days later at Haut-Brion. Picking began in earnest under benevolent conditions from 27 September and those that expedited their harvest missed the downpours on 13 and 14 October. The suppleness and delicacy of the fruit was noticed early on in barrel, though some misguidedly advised that the wines would not last. It was a large crop – Latour's 190 *tonneaux* was double the previous 10-year average. Winemaker Jean-Paul Gardère praised the wines full-body and ripeness, likening them to a mixture of '49 and '52. Meanwhile, having tasted the nascent 1953 Mouton Rothschild that October, Lawton compared the vintage to the 1924. The aforementioned downpours in mid-October triggered botrytis down in Sauternes, leading to a generally late harvest. Picking at Yquem lasted from 2 October to 10 November and the resulting wines were well received, even if not particularly sweet and unctuous.

Though some initially doubted their longevity, many 1953s evolved beautifully over the years and bestowed far more drinking pleasure than those of the previous vintage. They became particularly popular in Britain, appealing to writers and merchants of the time, to the extent that 1953 is often referred to as a typical "Englishman's vintage". Bottles of 1953 were common when I started my career in the late nineties, but they have since become rare birds. Quality is evenly distributed on both the Left Bank and Right Bank, not forgetting in Sauternes. Among the First Growths, the 1953 Lafite Rothschild is not just the best wine of the vintage but its finest offering of the post-war era, astonishing in terms of its precision and intensity when tasted after three corked bottles in 2017. The 1953 Haut-Brion and

La Mission Haut-Brion are concentrated and almost Pauillac-like, while the 1953 Mouton Rothschild is ethereal and elegant. How many stupendous wines did Baron Philippe have to make to persuade authorities to promote Mouton to a First Growth? There was a rare misstep from Latour: its 1953 just lacking breeding, while the gutsy 1953 Pichon Baron is marked by a touch of volatility. Among a dozen or so others, my pick would be the 1953 Ducru-Beaucaillou, an absolute charmer at the vertical tasting in June 2021, not forgetting a splendid 1953 Montrose. Others have been a little inconsistent, especially in Margaux, which might well be because of the summer hail. The Right Bank yielded some gems. Jacques Thienpont once handed me a glass while I turned the steaks on a barbecue at his home next to Le Pin. Only after dishing out the meat did he nonchalantly reveal that it was 1953 Vieux Château Certan and I wished I hadn't gulped it down so eagerly. Both the 1953 La Conseillante and Figeac are splendid, likewise a 1953 Clos de l'Église-Clinet that the late Denis Durantou martyred for the sake of my Pomerol tome. A 1953 Angélus opened at the château was elegant and "charmingly bucolic", though my one encounter with Ausone was nothing to write home about. It is not such a renowned vintage for Sauternes although I have fond recollections of the 1953 Climens and Doisy-Daëne.

Event
Edmund Hillary reaches
Everest's summit

On 29 May 1953, New Zealand mountaineer Edmund Hillary and Sherpa Tenzing Norgay ascended the highest point on Earth, though news of the feat didn't reach London until the morning of Queen Elizabeth's coronation on 2 June. They got to the summit at 11.30 a.m., took some photos and buried sweets and a small cross in the snow before descending. There was some speculation about who set foot on the summit first, Hillary or Norgay, but in his memoir Norgay confirmed it was Hillary.

Film
From Here to Eternity
– Fred Zinnemann

Burt Lancaster and Deborah Kerr star in the steamy adaptation of James Jones' even steamier novel about life in Hawaii just before the Pearl Harbor attack. The actors were romantically involved during filming, lending the famous tumble in the surf even greater sexual frisson. Frank Sinatra, whose career was at its nadir, pleaded for the role of G.I. Maggio and accepted a knockdown salary. The film was a hit with critics and audiences alike, with some New York cinemas playing the film 24/7 to cope with demand. It won eight Oscars the following year.

1953
(Continued)

Music
Your Cheatin' Heart
– Hank Williams

Written by Hank Williams after his divorce from Audrey Mae Sheppard, *Your Cheatin' Heart* came from a phrase he uttered while driving to his new fiancée Billie Jones's parents in Nashville. He immediately recognised that it would make a great title for a country song – accusing, venomous even. Williams asked Jones to jot down lyrics in the car. He recorded the song on 23 September 1952 with Chet Atkins on lead guitar, but years of liquor and morphine abuse had taken their toll. Williams died of a heart condition just a few weeks later. His signature song became a posthumous hit in early 1953, enshrining the myth of one of the greatest, if most troubled, country singers.

This is a rather forgotten vintage, not as derided as 1951 or 1956, but lost between the well-received 1953 and 1955 growing seasons.

The year began with a cold snap in January when temperatures plummeted to -8°C (17.5°F) and it was not until mid-February that the mercury finally began to rise. March was changeable but settled towards the end of the month and this triggered buds to swell. However, growth was instantly retarded by cold spells in April as the wind swung round to the north. May was changeable with intermittent sunny weather and the first flowers did not appear until 4 June, much later than the previous year. Flowering was interrupted by one or two showers and early July saw oidium in the Médoc and the Graves, coulure in Sauternes. Afterwards, it was cool and quite humid, but temperatures shot up to 33°C (91°F) at the beginning of August during *véraison*. Unfortunately, hopes of a good vintage were scuppered by persistent rain and cool nights that struggled to reach average summer temperatures. September offered little respite from rain so that harvest kicked off late, on 10 October, after a benign warm week. Picking took place under ideal conditions, with an unusual 27°C (80°F) recorded on 16 and 17 October and a couple more showers by the time harvest finished around 25 October. Harvest was later in Sauternes for the second year in a row due to the inclement September – Yquem did not complete its picking until 16 November after several passes through the vineyard. The challenging vintage dissuaded many Sauternes properties from releasing any wine.

Bottles are rarely seen and were mostly consumed in their youth. No less than three encounters with the 1954 Clos de l'Église-Clinet (renamed l'Église-Clinet the following year) demonstrated that this Pomerol could transcend the vintage, the first bottle in particular surpassing all my expectations. My only other note is for a rather mealy, heavily chaptalised 1954 Pichon Baron that was part of its vertical in March 2022.

1954
(Continued)

Event
Roger Bannister breaks the four-minute mile

A man couldn't run a mile in under four minutes… could he? On 6 May 1954, 25-year-old medical student Roger Bannister worked his shift at St. Mary's Hospital, caught the train to Oxford for a light lunch with friends, met his teammates Christopher Chataway and Chris Brasher at the Iffley Road track and, despite unfavourable weather, ran the distance in 3 minutes and 59.4 seconds, collapsing into the arms of his pacemakers after crossing the finish line. Having completed this literal milestone achievement, Bannister promptly retired from athletics and enjoyed a distinguished medical career.

Music
Three Coins in the Fountain
– Frank Sinatra

Following the success of his role in *From Here to Eternity* (page 249), Sinatra signed a deal with Capitol Records that predicated an astonishing career comeback after his adoring bobby soxers had grown up and moved on. Crucial to this second coming was Nelson Riddle, who arranged numerous Sinatra classics up until the early sixties. *Three Coins in the Fountain* was written by Jule Styne and Sammy Cahn for the namesake film and refers to the Trevi Fountain in Rome. It went on to win the Oscar for Best Original Song the following year. Ol' Blue Eyes was back.

Film
Creature from the Black Lagoon
– Jack Arnold

Science fiction-horror films packed cinemas in the fifties. The idea for this film originated from a Mexican myth about an Amazonian half-fish/half-human creature that producer William Alland overheard at a dinner party when filming *Citizen Kane*. Ricou Browning, a professional swimmer, played the "Gill-man" for the underwater scenes during which he had to hold his breath for up to four minutes. The film was released in primordial 3D, with audiences donning paper glasses to marvel at the fish swimming around their heads.

Nineteen fifty-five might well be the most underrated Bordeaux vintage. It is one whose virtues I have expounded since the fledgling days of my career as bottles continually confirm its pedigree.

Following a chilly March that saw temperatures as low as -3°C (26.5°F), things rapidly warmed up at the end of the month when the mercury reached the low twenties. April was dry and settled, with some winemakers anxious that vines' throats were getting dry – localised hail at the end of the month added to concerns. May's weather was benign, commencing with a couple of days of welcome rain and intermittent showers keeping vines healthy. The first flowers were spotted around 24 May and flowering passed evenly by the beginning of June. The month was fairly warm and dry with occasional showers that continued into July. Two or three heavier downpours gave vineyards a soaking towards the end of the month, with Jean-Paul Gardère at Latour assuring the owners that it was just what the vines needed. "Watch out for hail!" warns Lawton in his archives on 26 July, just as the berries began to change colour. Thankfully none materialised. August simmered away nicely, nothing excessive with coolish nights – around 14°C (57°F) in the morning, according to Lawton. The absence of heat waves meant ripening was steady and did not augur an early picking. Temperatures hovered in the low thirties towards the end of August and the mercury began to fall in early September, with heavy rain on the night of the 14th. Harvest in the Médoc for early pickers began two or three days later. Everything was ideal except in the Graves, according to Lawton, which saw an invasion of wasps and flies that fed on the juicy ripe pulp and ostensibly sucked the berries dry, sour rot acutely affecting the Sémillon. Most of the Grands Crus Classés commenced picking around 22 or 23 September as conditions remained dry and warm, fresher nights towards the end of the month locking in the acidity. Harvest at Mouton Rothschild did not commence until 2 or 3 October, according to Lawton, a little later than Lafite Rothschild. A large proportion of the crop was picked on the Left Bank between 5 and 10 October, interrupted by heavy rain on 8 October, and harvest was completed around 20 October. In Sauternes, the wild swings in weather finally settled so that August was hot, though interrupted by a single heavy downpour. The first passes through the vineyard were from late September and most properties had a wide window of picking, Yquem finishing on 28 October.

The 1955 vintage produced a large crop of elegant and beautifully balanced wines that could be described as "late bloomers" insofar as they took many years to peak. It was the first vintage since the war that saw an increase in prices and yet for many years, the vintage was undervalued, partly because it lay in the shadow of 1959 and 1961. They were patiently awaiting their chance to shine. I proselytised this vintage early in my career. A sublime 1955 Lynch-Bages alerted me to its quality, transfixing my table of admittedly inebriated colleagues

1955

1955

over dinner at Saint-Julien restaurant, and henceforth I sought as many '55s as possible. The vintage's apotheosis is unequivocally the 1955 La Mission Haut-Brion, in my consideration one of the century's pinnacles. Among the four bottles I have tasted, the best was proffered by the influential Bristol merchant, the late John Avery, who was rifling around his cellar when he stubbed his foot upon an original case with bottles still wrapped in their original straw. Poured during a Southwold dinner, it was perfection: crystalline and effortlessly complex. Snapping at its heels is the 1955 Les Carmes Haut-Brion, a revelation when served blind by winemaker Guillaume Pouthier at the château: sensual and luxuriant on the nose with Saint-Émilion-like precocity on the palate. The First Growths are all impressive and paradigmatic of their respective style, the 1955 Latour and 1955 Mouton Rothschild epitomes of "classic claret" and continuing to drink well. Numerous wines from the Médoc elicit joy – my picks include 1955s from Cos d'Estournel, Pichon Baron, Batailley, Talbot and Palmer. On the Right Bank, a handful of bottles have tasted divine. My introduction came courtesy of two half-bottles of 1955 Figeac, both a little frayed around the edges but still offering plenty of fruit and not bad for a fiver each! Over in Pomerol, the 1955 l'Église-Clinet was transcendental when Denis Durantou opened his last remaining magnum, the kind of Pomerol that makes you hear choirs of angels singing hallelujah in the background. It glistened in the glass, vivacious and poised, vivid and vital. Remaining in Pomerol, 1955 Trotanoy, Lafleur and in particular Latour à Pomerol have all been utterly wonderful, as was a 1955 La Croix de Gay tasted with the Raynaud family. In Saint-Émilion, I have fond memories of Figeac and a 1955 Cheval Blanc opened in Beaune with a delicious 1955 Ripeau as its wingman. Both showed better than 1955 Angélus, which had begun to flag with age when proprietor Hubert de Boüard served two bottles on a visit in 2021. Among the Sauternes, both Guiraud, Suduiraut and Lafaurie-Peyraguey have shown well, though I should mention a vibrant and mandarin-infused 1955 Gilette Doux that was the perfect conclusion to lunch at La Pyramide.

Event
Rosa Parks refuses to give up her seat

On 1 December 1955, 42-year-old Rosa Parks caught the bus back from her work at the Montgomery Fair department store. A white man boarded. All the seats in the "white" section of the segregated bus were taken and so the driver requested four people in the "black" section to stand so he could sit down. Three obliged. Parks remained seated and was arrested for doing so. Four days later, she was fined 10 dollars for violating segregation laws. The black population began boycotting buses and started a campaign for equal rights under the newly formed Montgomery Improvement Association led by 26-year-old Reverend Martin Luther King.

Music
Tutti Frutti
– Little Richard

A-wop-bop-a-loo-mop-a-lop-bam-boom! Few intros had the earth-shattering impact of Little Richard's raucous wake-up call. Rock 'n' roll was suddenly wild and raunchy, almost unhinged. Who was this wide-eyed, camp, black singer with his outrageous bouffant and eye-liner? *Tutti Frutti*'s original lewd lyrics were cleaned up by Dorothy LaBostrie in the studio, then recorded during the final minutes of allotted studio time on 14 September 1955. *Tutti Frutti* conveys a sense of infectious and untrammelled power and aggression, a hard-rock rhythm pounded out on the piano like Richard's life depended upon it. The ultimate showman was instrumental in making popular music the property of teenagers and young adults, associating it with rebelliousness and a disregard for rules set by adults. They could enjoy Pat Boone's sanitised version.

Film
Rebel Without a Cause – Nicholas Ray

Just as rock 'n' roll was inciting youthful rebellion, so teenage cinema-goers had their anti-establishment poster-boy, James Dean, dressed in his signature white T-shirt and red leather jacket. The actor was cut several times during the movie's switchblade fight and when the director paused filming to attend to his wounds, Dean reproached him for doing so. Like Brando, who had screen-tested for the same role several years earlier, he was a disciple of Method acting and improvised many scenes, almost directing some himself. Dean died in a car accident on 30 September 1955 just four weeks before the movie premiered, enshrining the reputation summed up in the title of his most famous film.

1956

The 1956 growing season is a watershed for all the wrong reasons. It was the most catastrophic year since phylloxera plunged Bordeaux into crisis.

It began innocuously enough, January wet but not abnormally cold. On 3 February, the mercury plunged to -9°C (15°F) and then to -14°C (6.8°F) 12 days later, causing parts of the Gironde estuary to freeze over. The region endured Arctic conditions for five days, buried under deep snow on 21 February. The freeze was unrelenting: -2°C (28.5°F), -12°C (10.5°F) and -5°C (23°F) on the mornings of 22, 23 and 24 February and, after a brief respite, -3°C (26.5°F), -4°C (25°F) and -4°C (25°F) on 26, 27 and 28 February. It was not just the degree of cold but the duration that inflicted widespread damage. Bordeaux had not seen such a cold winter since 1709. Lilian Barton-Sartorius at Léoville Barton remembers her uncle Ronald Barton waking one morning to hear what he thought were gunshots. In fact, it was the sound of vines' trunks rupturing and splintering as they froze to their core, killing swathes outright. Nobody escaped, though the Right Bank was eviscerated more than anywhere. Mme. Loubat, the grandiloquent owner of Pétrus, was distraught and confessed to her local priest that she felt that "life had slipped away". Taking his encouraging words to heed, instead of pulling up the vines, a treacherous act she could not countenance even in such dire circumstances, she scoured the vineyard for survivors, pruned them down to a stub (known as *recépagement*) and prayed for their recovery. Her gamble paid off because many of her vines pulled through, even though her reward was a solitary barrel of Pétrus that year. At the other extreme, I remember discussing the 1956 vintage with Jean-Pierre Boyer at Bel Air-Marquis d'Aligre. He had a slightly different approach to Mme. Loubat. "I pulled up the vines in 1956 after they were killed by the frost and I just never got round to replanting," he explained, before continuing, "I could do it, I suppose."

By the end of March, the full extent of the devastation was becoming apparent and predictions were that even if the rest of the season was benevolent, Bordeaux would produce little more than 1 million hl. As it turned out, April was changeable but the surviving vines began their delayed cycle around the middle of the month. It was only now that winemakers fully comprehended the extent of damage. The rest of the season was almost moot. May was warm with occasional showers. Flowering began on 1 June and was disrupted by more cold temperatures, 2.1°C (37.8°F) below average, and there was rain five days later. The 1 July witnessed a violent storm followed by the most severe outbreak of coulure since 1926. By now, temperatures had risen to normal levels, but two days of torrential downpours on 21 and 22 July left vineyards so muddy that it became impossible to use tractors. Mildew and oidium added to producers' woes.

Temperatures 2°C (35.5°F) below average throughout August saw more than double the usual amount of rain and led to an extremely slow *véraison*. Early September witnessed more violent storms that caused more rot towards the end of the month. Harvest began late, on 7 October, under dry conditions and finished around 23 October. It had been the most traumatic growing season in living memory and its repercussions lasted many years as many vineyards needed replanting. In Sauternes, winemakers also suffered a rainy summer and harvest began late – on 8 October at Yquem and not finishing until 21 November. Even then, it reported that grapes did not reach 20% potential alcohol until 15 October.

One hardly ever sees wines from this vintage. The average yield across the region was just 17 hl/ha compared to 41.1 hl/ha the previous year. Bordeaux was hit harder than other regions in terms of yield – Burgundy reported 21 hl/ha and Champagne 28 hl/ha the same year.

The first I ever tasted was opened by Lilian Barton-Sartorius in London in 2017, a 1956 Léoville Barton that was enervated but drinkable. It deserves a medal for simply existing after nearly six decades. The only other two encounters are with a 1956 Ausone, which according to records produced a decent amount of wine given how others fared, probably due to its location up on the côte in Saint-Émilion. It was a little dilute but surviving. A 1956 Pichon Baron was a curiosity when opened at the château, though did not disgrace itself. Many châteaux could not produce any Grand Vin and sold off the fruit they did manage to eke out.

Event
Suez Canal crisis in Egypt

Egypt's president Gamal Abdel Nasser had nationalised the Suez Canal in July 1956 and jeopardised a vital commerce route, particularly for oil. On 29 October, Israeli forces invaded the country, joined by French and English forces two days later. The crisis threatened to blow up and embroil Russia and the US. Russian President Nikita Khrushchev, who sought leverage in the Middle East and supported the Egyptian army, threatened that nuclear missiles would "rain down" in Western Europe. French and British forces withdrew the following December and the canal came under Egyptian control, symbolising France and Britain's diminished power on the world stage.

1956
(Continued)

Music
Hound Dog
– Elvis Presley

"Before Elvis, there was nothing," is one of John Lennon's most famous quotes. That's not exactly true, as proven by previous entries in this book, but rock 'n' roll was certainly inaccessible for a young lad in Liverpool until Elvis. He was the complete package: the smouldering looks, slicked-back hair, strong vocals, ace backing band and hips that elicited teenagers' screams with the merest swivel. Crucially, in 1956, Elvis unleashed a series of classic songs composed by the best writers in the business. *Hound Dog*, written by 19-year-olds Jerry Leiber and Mike Stoller, had been a smash for Big Mama Thornton in 1952. Having heard it played in Las Vegas, in early 1956, Elvis began performing *Hound Dog* on national TV shows to an estimated 40 million viewers. On 2 July 1956 he recorded his cover, adding a Habanera beat, a guitar solo by Scotty Moore, drum fills courtesy of D.J. Fontana and a delivery imbued with more aggression than his previous downtempo live performances. Released two weeks later, it sold four million copies and spent 11 weeks at the top of the Billboard charts.

Film
The Searchers
– John Ford

The Searchers is often held up as one of the greatest westerns of all time. Starring John Wayne in a career-best performance as Ethan Edwards, it tells the story of a Confederate veteran returning home and embarking on a journey of retribution after his family is massacred and his niece abducted. Apart from Wayne's performance and its dark themes, *The Searchers* was a feast for the eyes, in particular, the shots of the wild prairies filmed in Monument Valley. Legend has it Buddy Holly watched the film and used the recurring phrase "That'll be the day" as the title for a song.

The growing conditions of this vintage might be considered irrelevant since many estates had barely recovered from the previous year's carnage.

January began with a cold snap, but it began warming up in the middle of the month. February was wet but March was unseasonably spring-like, with temperatures nudging the low twenties, coaxing vines out of their winter slumber – 25°C (77°F) was recorded in the Tastet-Lawton archives at the end of the month. The mercury dipped in April, but not for long and thankfully there was little frost, save for local skirmishes on 7 May. Inclement wet and windy weather disrupted flowering, which began around 30 May and a diminished crop was on the cards. The rest of June was warm and although July began well, the weather broke and became changeable, with 84 mm (3¼ in) of rainfall recorded compared to an average 54 mm (2 in). August began with a mini-heat wave but temperatures fell around the 9th, just when warmth and sunshine was needed to ripen berries.

September saw rain but it became more settled and a warm dry spell nudged maturity onwards. Harvesters entered vineyards around 27 September at Latour, most châteaux going out with their secateurs a couple of days later. After what had been a frustratingly changeable season, picking took place in early October under perfect conditions with barely a drop of rain. In Sauternes, those same September rains invited botrytis, but despite good concentration, the otherwise dry weather resulted in little noble rot on the small amount of grapes. At Yquem, the yield was a minuscule 3 hl/ha, even though it persevered with attempted pickings until 31 November.

The wines were reputed to be rather hard and tannic when they first appeared. It is not a vintage often seen and volumes were always small, averaging 18 hl/ha, little more than the previous year. On the rare occasions they have materialised, I've been pleasantly surprised. My fondest memory is a 1957 Mouton Rothschild, opened during a fifties-themed dinner in Hong Kong, rock 'n' roll blaring from a jukebox. The wine was elegant and beguiling, proof Baron Philippe could not put a foot wrong, even in challenging seasons. Meanwhile, the 1957 Pichon Baron was perhaps the biggest surprise of that decade when served at its retrospective in March 2022, full of fruit, elegance and vivacity. Some have not lasted so well: the 1957 Smith Haut Lafitte opened at one of the Cathiard's annual verticals drying out and, likewise, a magnum of 1957 Lascombes was past its best-before date. On the Right Bank, a bottle of 1957 Canon-la-Gaffelière surpassed expectations at an Académie du Vin dinner in 2017, further evidence of how this Saint-Émilion performed well in this era. The 1957 Vieux Château Certan, served at the vertical at La Trompette in 2020, evinced what must have been a stocky Pomerol in its youth, but which revealed its elegant side after a few decades. I have tasted few Sauternes, though the 1957 Suduiraut was commendable at the Zurich vertical, edged by a vigorous, if simple 1957 Climens.

1957

1957
(Continued)

Event
Jack Kerouac's *On the Road* is published

With its references to jazz and recreational drugs, *On the Road* is the defining novel of the Beat era. The first draft of Kerouac's *roman à clef* was typed over three weeks on a 36.5-m (120-ft) scroll in April 1951 – fictional character Carlo Marx based on poet Allen Ginsberg and Old Bull Lee on author William S. Burroughs. The text was subsequently edited before publication by Viking Press. Kerouac's book became the touchstone counterculture novel and its influence went far beyond literature – you could argue the Swinging Sixties and its anti-establishment ethos began in its pages.

Music
That'll Be the Day – Buddy Holly and the Crickets

Composed by Buddy Holly and Jerry Allison, Holly's signature tune was released on 2 September 1957. Holly had originally recorded it the previous year, but his record company (Decca) was dissatisfied with the songs from the session. After Holly moved label to Brunswick, his producer Norman Petty circumvented a clause forbidding any re-recording by crediting the song to The Crickets, Holly's new backing band. During his short but prolific career, Holly pioneered the role of singer-songwriter, the use of double-tracking, and the rock-band set-up of singer, two guitars, bass and drums. He died on 3 February 1959 in a plane crash along with Ritchie Valens and The Big Bopper – the first rock 'n' roll stars to meet untimely deaths.

Event
The Seventh Seal – Ingmar Bergman

Max von Sydow's game of chess with Death, played by Bengt Ekerot, became one of the defining – and most parodied – images of cinema. Bergman's tale of medieval morality in plague-ridden Sweden was shot in just 35 days for just $150,000, taking its title from the Book of Revelation. Bergman had begun writing it when recovering from a stomach issue in Stockholm's Karolinska Hospital. After winning the Special Jury Prize at the 1957 Cannes Film Festival, Bergman shot to international stardom, a timely reminder that arthouse cinema could appeal to a wide audience.

The 1958 vintage is often overlooked – one of those neither-here-nor-there seasons in the minds of cognoscenti. In fact, it was a rather dramatic season, which beleaguered winemakers with a succession of storms.

After a benign January, February was warmer and saw temperatures touching 22°C (71.5°F). But March was cold courtesy of a brisk northerly wind that brought deep snow – 29 cm (11 in) in the Médoc on 11 March, according to Tastet-Lawton. The weather then turned warmer but was accompanied by storms that persisted into April. May commenced with a hot spell with the mercury reaching 28°C (82°F), allowing vines to make up some lost time in their retarded growth cycle, but the heat wave broke down and gales on 16 May damaged many branches. Thereafter, the weather refused to settle and another storm on 1 June caused hail damage in the Côtes de Blaye. The first flowers began to appear on 2 June, although there was insufficient warmth for an even flowering. Yet another violent storm beset Bordeaux on 26 June with torrential rain and strong damaging gusts accompanied by localised hail; another followed in mid-July. And still winemakers were not off the hook: a further violent storm battered the region on 17 August, causing severe damage in Margaux, with major properties losing up to half their potential crop. If that was not enough, vineyard managers had to constantly battle against mildew. Unsurprisingly, *véraison* was strung out, although a warm spell in September must have helped even out the ripening. A late harvest did not really get going until 6 October under generally good conditions but with cool nights. In Sauternes, 50 mm (2 in) of rain in September provoked botrytis and subsequent passes through the vines were undertaken in dry conditions, though deteriorating weather hampered efforts to create quality sweet wines.

Upon release, the 1958s were received as decent but short-lived – wines were barely out of the blocks when they were eclipsed by 1959 and then 1961. David Peppercorn posits that it was the first challenging vintage in which winemakers had the skill to overcome the problems. I have a sentimental attachment to the 1958 Latour. It was my maiden First Growth, drunk over lunch at merchant Justerini & Brooks in the salad days of my career, astonished that I was worthy of such a wine. It was an esoteric First Growth to open my account with and to date I've never drunk it again. Over the years I have accrued around a dozen tasting notes, none particularly exciting, typified by rather stolid showings of 1958 Haut-Brion and 1958 Château Margaux in 2019, and most recently, 1958 Pichon Baron – best described as a party-pooper – and its sibling, 1958 Pichon-Lalande – a dullard a month later. The best? A magnum of 1958 Certan de May and a very respectable 1958 Montrose. Most bottles will be past their low peaks, though it's not a vintage to write off and might spring a surprise.

1958

1958

Event
Manchester United players die
in Munich plane crash

Manager Matt Busby had
nurtured a formidable football
team nicknamed the "Busby
Babes". Their average age was just
22 when they were crowned 1956
domestic champions. The next
goal was success in Europe. On
5 February 1958, the Manchester
United team flew back from a
European Cup tie against Red
Star Belgrade. Flight 609 stopped
in Munich to refuel. After two
aborted attempts to take off,
the plane crashed on the slushy
runway, killing 23 passengers,
including eight players and
three members of staff. Despite
this, just 13 days after the crash,
they went ahead with a fifth-
round FA Cup tie where the
match programme's banner read:
"United will go on." Ten years
later, Busby took them to victory
at the 1968 European Cup final.

Music
Johnny B. Goode
– Chuck Berry

Chuck Berry is a prime architect
of rock 'n' roll with standards
like *Maybellene* and *Roll Over
Beethoven*. But *Johnny B. Goode*
had the most swagger and energy.
Its semi-autobiographical lyrics
tell of a "little country boy [who]
could play", though originally
he was a "coloured boy". Unlike
some singers, Berry enunciated
the words clearly in order for the
story to be heard. The guitar riff
was inspired by Louis Jordan's
Ain't That Just Like a Woman and
the break from T-Bone Walker's
Strollin' with Bones, but *Johnny
B. Goode* is all Chuck Berry –
a blueprint for rock music.

Film
Cat on a Hot Tin Roof
– Richard Brooks

Starring Elizabeth Taylor and
Paul Newman, Brooks's drama
was based on the Pulitzer
Prize-winning play by Tennessee
Williams. Williams was
apparently displeased when he
discovered that the homosexual
themes had been expunged for
the film adaptation in order to
abide by the Motion Picture
Production Code. Taylor's
husband had died on the day
shooting began when his private
plane, ironically named "Lucky
Liz", crashed. She refused to
pause filming, though the shock
of his death induced stuttering in
her speech that disappeared when
the cameras rolled.

1959

The 1959 vintage was a watershed moment for Bordeaux whose importance transcends the hedonic quality of the wines. It was the first vintage since the twenties in which estates were blessed by quality *and* quantity, enabling many to earn much-needed profit after years of stagnating prices and lack of investment. Clive Coates MW argues it was the last vintage made using pre-scientific methods, although I would contend that it might be later, since stainless-steel vats were not commonly used for several years.

The year began with typically changeable weather in January, but February augured the growing season – warm and clement with cool nights. March commenced with spring-like conditions as temperatures reached 18°C (64.5°F). The vines began their growth cycle towards the penultimate week of that month, but heavy rain persisted between 28 and 30 March. The warm and clement weather continued in April, putting vines some 15 days in advance of their cycle, portending an early harvest. After temperatures tumbled on 22 April, the Médoc escaped serious frost damage with around 5% of buds burnt. Sauternes was hit harder, though thankfully not to a catastrophic extent. May was warm and the first flowers speckled the landscape from 26 May, with perfect 28°C (82°F) temperatures ensuring *fleuraison* was regular and a large crop achievable. Hail on 18 June caused damage in Saint-Émilion when a storm crossed the region, but July was idyllic and peaked at a balmy 35°C (95°F). Fortunately, there were no other heat spikes that might have burned the berries. August was a repeat of July with just minor hail on the 9th. What vines needed was rain and they got a welcome soaking on 11 September and then again four days later. Everything was teed up nicely for harvest, which commenced around 18 September, with most pickers entering vineyard after a spot of rain on 24 September. The weather remained warm throughout harvest, posing challenges in terms of moderating temperatures during vinification. Jean-Michel Cazes was not at Lynch-Bages at the time, but once told me: "I heard that '59 was a good wine, but difficult to vinify. I heard that some properties suffered problems with the fermentation."

The rain on 24 September was just what Sauternes required to provoke widespread botrytis infection. At Yquem pickers made four passes through the vineyard, each one followed by a new wave of botrytis.

Over the years I have sampled most of the major 1959s. It's a vintage I always look forward to tasting, maybe even more so than 1961, because it doles out sensory pleasure. Whereas 1961s can seem aloof and more intent on impressing you, the 1959s have a propensity to seduce. In 2019, I was fortunate to taste numerous 1959s, many during two memorable 1959-themed soirées that confirmed both the greatness and longevity of the vintage. Quality is unevenly dispersed, even among the Grands Crus Classés, not because of growing conditions, but because some estates had undergone little investment since the thirties, which precluded their chances to fully exploit the season.

The first bottle to make a deep impression was 1959 Latour, just a couple of weeks after my maiden 1961, at Marco Pierre White's Mirabelle restaurant in Mayfair. It felt like the most gorgeous and sensual wine imaginable and more than a dozen bottles and magnums have never failed to deliver. While the 1961 might be more impressive, the soupçon of volatile that often underlies this vintage, less so in magnum, renders it more alluring and sensual by comparison. The 1959 Lafite Rothschild is superior to its underwhelming 1961 counterpart, albeit not quite as transcendental as the 1953, fine-boned and disarmingly pure. The 1959 Mouton Rothschild can leave you short of superlatives, so have some spare – it's another awesome addition to Baron Philippe's canon of work after the war. I once had the opportunity to compare not only the 1959 Haut-Brion and La Mission Haut-Brion together, but also a 1959 Domaine de la Passion Haut-Brion, the rarely seen and discontinued separate growth originating from within the First Growth's vineyard. They were all impressive and the latter held its own. The 1959 Château Margaux flirts with perfection and, like the Lafite Rothschild, is superior to the 1961, although my last bottle was drier than expected.

Some châteaux forgot to bring their A-game: the likes of Pichon Baron, albeit superior in magnum than bottle, and Rauzan-Ségla, which struggled to reach 11.8% alcohol in a warm summer, not to mention Léoville Poyferré, Montrose and Cos d'Estournel. These are all very fine, but not dazzling. On the other hand, many Left Bank wines deliver. Among the most memorable are a sublime 1959 Ducru-Beaucaillou, one of the highlights at the vertical in 2021, and a stunning 1959 Léoville-Las Cases, which has more complexity and intellect than the 1961. I also have fond recollections of Palmer, Gruaud Larose, Batailley and Haut-Batailley, not forgetting a splendid magnum of Domaine de Chevalier poured by Olivier Bernard at an Académie du Vin soirée. Matthieu Bordes poured blind a lovely terracotta-tinged 1959 Château Lagrange at the property, surely one of the only pre-Suntory vintages with something to offer, while the 1959 Dauzac acquitted itself admirably at a vertical held at the estate.

The Right Bank is studded with gems, which is remarkable given how many vineyards had been devastated by the 1956 freeze. Mme. Loubat's gamble in not grubbing up her vines meant she oversaw a sensational 1959. Three bottles of 1959 Vieux Château Certan have been divine – the last bottle served in Bordeaux at a 60th birthday celebration was sheer perfection. Both bottles of 1959 Trotanoy that I have drunk were intense and profound, and three examples of 1959 Latour à Pomerol were precocious and utterly delicious. Thierry Manoncourt oversaw a sublime Figeac that is on par with the 1959 Cheval Blanc, and both these Saint-Émilions have the upper hand against a faltering Ausone. Other gems include a vivacious 1959 Canon, one of the last great vintages before the château hit a sticky patch, plus a not-to-be-underestimated Trotte Vieille. Sometimes you have to watch for high volatile acidity levels because of the warmth that year, but not to the extent of the 1947s since winemaking had improved in the interim and temperatures were less extreme. Racking my brain, I cannot recall a Sauternes that disappointed. Though several bottles of Yquem have been excellent, my fondest memory is a riveting 1959 Suduiraut that ranks among its all-time greats, not to mention a brilliant 1959 Rayne Vigneau that chaperoned lunch at the estate. The 1959 Climens was just a little slight by comparison, ditto Coutet. Lafaurie-Peyraguey was better, with over-ripe satsumas on the nose.

Event
Britain's first full-length motorway

In November 1959, the M1 opened between St. Albans and Rugby – Britain's first full-length motorway. It is estimated that over half the workers came from Ireland. Plans for a motorway network had been made before the Second World War, but it was not until the fifties that a UK government gave them the green light. However, there was little regard for safety upon its opening, with no speed limit, lighting or crash barriers. Still, there were fancy futuristic-looking bridges designed by Owen Williams, who had worked as principal engineer on Wembley Stadium. The idea of driving without any impeding obstacles at a constant speed must have seemed like utopia to petrol-heads, though that is rarely possible today. The M1 now carries around 10 times the amount of traffic expected, which will come as no surprise to anyone who's ever been stuck in one of its traffic jams.

Music
So What
– Miles Davis

As the fifties closed, some felt the rock 'n' roll fad was running out of steam. Jazz would take over as the popular musical genre and why not, given the slew of seminal jazz albums put out in 1959. On 17 August trumpeter Miles Davis released *Kind of Blue*, an exploration of modal jazz that went on to influence John Coltrane and others. Throughout his career, Davis pushed the boundaries of the genre and helped launch numerous jazz musicians, including Bill Evans, Herbie Hancock and Coltrane. *So What*, written in Dorian mode, opens what is widely considered one of the most popular and influential albums of all time.

Film
Some Like It Hot
– Billy Wilder

Marilyn Monroe steals the
show from Jack Lemmon and
Tony Curtis in Wilder's timeless
romantic caper. Monroe, pregnant
during filming, was notoriously
insecure on set and constantly
forgot simple lines and obliged
dozens of retakes. Despite
this, she gave a career-best
performance and proved she was
a dab hand at comedy. Tragically,
she would complete only two
more films before her untimely
death in August 1962. Since then,
the fascination with Monroe
has never waned; if anything,
enhancing posthumously.

The

1960s

Music and fashion defined the Swinging Sixties. It was a revolutionary decade – literally on Parisian boulevards in 1968. With respect to the Bordeaux wine industry, it's perhaps an exaggeration to say it was changing on its axis as it did in the eighties. Rather, as David Peppercorn describes, it was a decade of "reconstruction and growth". Buoyed by revenues from the 1959 and 1961 vintages, estates finally had the means to start stitching together tears in the vineyard inflicted by war. But the decade did witness two fundamental changes.

Firstly, livestock – horses and oxen – were gradually pensioned off and replaced by *tracteurs enjambeurs* (overhead tractors), allowing operators to drive over the vines without damaging them. Working vineyards became far more efficient, even if machinery was less romantic and ecologically friendly. Bruno Borie is one who rued the disappearance of beasts of burden at Ducru-Beaucaillou. But if Borie assumed the sound of hooves would never again be heard in Bordeaux vineyards, he was wrong, with many top estates having reintroduced horses in recent years.

Secondly, the sixties saw the implementation of stainless-steel vats. La Mission Haut-Brion had already introduced enamel-lined steel vats back in 1926. Stainless-steel, though, is more inert, easier to clean and more hygienic, leading to far less microbial spoilage, especially compared with ancient, often dirty wooden vats. However, only a small number of châteaux could afford such technology. There was no immediate rush and some viewed stainless steel with scepticism – after all, wooden vessels had been used since time immemorial. Who would take the plunge and invest in this new technology? Step forward Jean-Bernard Delmas, who installed stainless-steel vats to ferment the 1961 vintage at Haut-Brion and produced a quite brilliant wine as a result. A handful of others followed suit: Latour introduced 12 stainless-steel vats just one day before picking commenced in 1964, raising the roof to accommodate them. However, both Lafite Rothschild and Mouton Rothschild were more hesitant and when André Mentzelopoulos took over Château Margaux in 1977, he stayed loyal to wooden vats.

Châteaux also began introducing mechanical *égrappoirs*, or de-stemmers, to remove stalks before grapes entering vats, a process previously undertaken by hand. But all these innovations were predicated on having the money to invest. Just one example of the poverty at the time comes from Jean-Michel Cazes, who once told me that his grandfather at Lynch-Bages used potato bags as a raincoat, as did his pickers. This was at a time when a potato field occupied the middle of the vineyard, in what is now one of the estate's most propitious parcels. Needless to say Lynch-Bages no longer uses potato bags to keep dry and there are no potatoes for sale.

There might have been a third fundamental change, but it never came to fruition. Alexis Lichine was part of a committee formed to decide whether to reclassify the châteaux under the supposedly immutable 1855 Classification – Lichine himself was a proponent of altering the hierarchy. In 1960, the I.N.A.O. was called in to arbitrate but two years later concluded that a reclassification would be too complex and controversial. I wonder how Baron Philippe de Rothschild felt about that? He was still doggedly campaigning for Mouton Rothschild's promotion, but he would have to wait longer.

The sixties was a decade that saw changes in overseas markets, not least that of the most powerful economy in the world, the United States. According to Edmund Penning-Rowsell, exports increased from 25,600 hl in 1961 to 47,900 hl by 1967. The difference between exports to the UK and the US was that the latter consisted entirely of wine bottled in Bordeaux, whereas UK merchants continued to import casks and bottle in their own cellars.

The pedigree of the decade relies on the reputation of the 1961 growing season, the solitary vintage revered across the entirety of Bordeaux. Many proprietors must have hoped that it was an augury for the decade, but Mother Nature had other plans and unleashed growing seasons so miserable that many châteaux declined to release any Grand Vin in 1963, 1965 and 1968. You could say that when a Bordeaux vintage was bad in the sixties, it was dire. Even the once-mighty Château Margaux was forced to put out a declassified multi-vintage, something scarcely believable today. Other vintages such as 1962, 1967 and 1969 saw only partial success, which meant prices bobbed along at a low level, stymying investment in outmoded wineries.

Looking at the decade in a more positive light, it did offer more than the 1961 vintage. Nineteen sixty-six provided classically styled Bordeaux wines on both banks that matured with style and grace. The 1964 Right Bank is splendid, producing a bevy of sensual and rich wines that remain gorgeous half a century later. The Left Bank was less consistent but not without gems in the northern Médoc. In Sauternes the class of 1967 are rightly hailed as benchmark wines unsurpassed for many years, while the 1962s, overshadowed by the previous season, were insiders' wines, at least until word got out that they too provided some marvellous fare (*mea culpa*).

Harvest time at Château Figeac in Saint-Émilion, where much of the picking was conducted by gypsies. Proprietor, the late Thierry Manoncourt, is in the grey V-neck jumper just in front of the tractor, his daughters Claire and Blandine are on the far right of the front row.

1960

You must feel a degree of sympathy for the 1960 vintage, sandwiched between two of the most-lauded seasons of the post-war century. As such, its reputation is perhaps lower than it truly deserves.

January began with a cold snap, but soon warmed up and February ended with a balmy 22°C (71.5°F). March was typically changeable, ditto April, which finished with widespread frost on 29/30 April. There had not been rain for three weeks when the heavens finally opened on the night of 14 May. Regretfully, the downpour came with a nasty side-order of hail that damaged the Graves and Saint-Émilion. Early flowering at the end of May prompted some estate managers to claim it was the most perfect they had ever seen. By the end of flowering, the vines were eight days ahead of 1959 in their growth cycle. A clement and June prompted Lawton to suggest another 1955 was on the cards, but July saw some rain and cool nights. The season hit a hurdle with a very rainy August, which gorged and inflated berries, but temperatures held up and winemakers held out hope that a warm September would see them through. It was not to be. The month saw heavy showers relieved by three warm days from 10 to 12 September. Harvest began on 15 September after downpours the previous night and despite intermittent spells of settled weather, Bordeaux continued to be plagued by showers and there was a severe storm on 27 September. The final pickings of Cabernet Sauvignon at the beginning of October were undertaken under poor and very wet conditions, washing away vestiges of hope that 1960 would produce great claret. Lucien Lurton of the family dynasty, owners of several Bordeaux estates, found the wines "hard and mean", conversely, André Portet, estate manager at Lafite-Rothschild, opined that it was "a year for Merlot" and admired the wines' roundness. Sauternes was plagued by heavy rain: 146 mm (5¾ in) in soggy September and 196 mm (7¾ in) in soggier October, resulting in over-ripe rather than botrytised berries.

I have drunk a handful of wines from this vintage, including decent if rather unexciting bottles of 1960 Montrose, Pichon Baron (twice), Batailley, Gruaud Larose and La Mission Haut-Brion. Most have been interesting but past their sell-by date. Best might be a 1960 Les Carmes Haut-Brion served blind by winemaker Guillaume Pouthier in 2016: briny, rough around the edges and, who knows, maybe blended with a soupçon of 1959. Whether it was or wasn't, my glass was soon empty. On the Right Bank, the 1960 Pétrus served blind in London was leafy and easy-going with an "abstract sense of pride" to quote myself. Just two sweet wines to mention: a *négociant*-bottled Climens that was not disastrous but of curiosity value only, and a 1960 Yquem that was not a complete write-off – then again, Yquem never is.

Event
To Kill a Mockingbird
is published

On 11 July 1960, Harper Lee published her debut novel, *To Kill a Mockingbird*. Loosely based on an event that occurred in her hometown in 1936, its themes of loss of innocence and racial injustice in sleepy Alabama struck a chord with readers. It won a Pulitzer Prize for fiction and to date has sold over 40 million copies worldwide, becoming a standard school text. But instead of setting out on a glittering literary career, Lee became a recluse. Almost everyone had given up hope of hearing a peep from the author when in February 2015, she released her second novel, albeit based on a manuscript she wrote in 1957. We might know little about the enigmatic Harper Lee, but most have read *To Kill a Mockingbird*.

Music
Non, Je Ne Regrette Rien
– Édith Piaf

Édith Piaf recorded *Non, Je Ne Regrette Rien* in the twilight of her career in 1960, lending its sentiment greater pathos. In his book *Édith*, journalist Jean Noli recounts how its composers, Charles Dumont and Michel Vaucaire, visited Piaf's home in Paris that October, beseeching her to record their new composition. But they found the ageing chanteuse short-tempered and impolite. Having rebuffed their request for some time, she finally acquiesced and asked them to play it at the piano. Dumont was understandably nervous. As the final note echoed around the room, there followed an interminable silence before Piaf asked Dumont to play it again. "*Formidable!*" she exclaimed, telling them it was the song she had been waiting for her entire life. She passed away in 1963, a life lived with no regrets.

Film
Psycho – Alfred Hitchcock

Psycho is a masterpiece that pivots around the most notorious scene in cinematic history. Spoiler ahead, but killing off leading lady Janet Leigh one-third of the way through the film left audiences reeling. Their shock was compounded by the brutality of the murder, which saw Leigh repeatedly stabbed in the shower. Hitchcock amplified the terror with his ingenious use of jarring jump cuts and shifting viewpoints so viewers became as disorientated as the victim. The auteur had changed the grammar of cinema once again.

1961

Many regard 1961 as the first great vintage of the modern age of Bordeaux. Whereas 1959 seems to somehow look back in time, a fabulous end to the post-war era, 1961 portends what followed.

Following a wet winter, spring was unseasonably mild. At Latour they noticed the first leaves on 10 March. Temperatures began to drop and there was localised frost damage on 25 and 29 March, fortunately too early to inflict serious damage. Nevertheless, vineyard managers were on tenterhooks as April remained cold. Although this marginally retarded growth, the previous month's warmth meant vines had energy and the first flowers were seen around 20 May. At this stage of the growing season, most must have felt relief that the risk of frost was behind them. Things began to look ominous on 27 and 28 May as the mercury began sliding and on 29 May crestfallen winemakers pulled back their curtains to find extensive frost damage. It affected the more precocious Merlot vines and therefore impacted the Right Bank more than the Left Bank, lent some protection by the temperature-regulating effects of the Gironde. Nevertheless, Philippe Castéja remembers that the frost encased the early flowers and even Latour, impervious to frost more than almost any other estate, lost around 75% of its crop, so you can imagine the magnitude of loss on the exposed clay soils in Saint-Émilion and Pomerol. Unlike in 1991, the ensuing summer was perfect. July was balmy with occasional showers nudging the disrupted vine cycle along, and August much hotter with barely a spot of rain. September saw no respite with 30°C (86°F) recorded on more than half the days. August and September witnessed just 30 mm (1 in) of rain, the lowest between 1929 and 1985 and consequently vines finally began to shut down, delaying the harvest from early September until the 19th. The surviving grapes reached physiological maturity and the fruit was harvested under a glorious autumn sun, save for an inconsequential spot of rain on 28 and 29 September. Average yields were low at 25.7 hl/ha compared with 35.4 hl/ha the previous year.

In Sauternes, it was an early harvest, yet botrytis stubbornly refused to infect the bunches due to prevailing dry conditions. Even Yquem could eke only 15 barrels over three weeks, albeit with some lots laden with a whopping 30% potential alcohol. Rain spoiled pickings in October, denying Sauternes the greatness bestowed upon the reds. Continuing high temperatures meant red-wine producers had to control the alcoholic fermentation in the vat. Fortunately, they were now far more adept at this than back in 1947, preventing volatile acidity that spoiled some wines in that vintage. Of course, Jean-Bernard Delmas had his stainless-steel vats, so he must have found controlling his fermenting temperatures a breeze.

The 1961 vintage preceded my birth and so I asked merchant Barry Phillips, who has decades of experience tasting Bordeaux, how he remembers the '61s in their youth. "Knife and fork jobs," he told me in his own inimitable way. "They were very austere. But you knew that they were going to be very good." Over the years, I have been fortunate to taste nearly all the major wines from this legendary vintage. Provenance is key, not least in lauded vintages like this because so much has been traded over the years. In my experience, it is a vintage I am often able to pick out blind, primarily because of an estuarine, briny tincture on the nose, something rarely found on other coeval vintages.

My introduction to the vintage was a 1961 Latour. A friend generously proffered a bottle to dinner at Avenue restaurant in London, very early in my career. I could scarcely believe that I was in the presence of this immortal Pauillac, let alone about to drink it. It had a low mid-shoulder level but was mesmerising, everything I hoped and more. Though it was several years before I began writing, it marked my first perfect score. I never knew that a wine could possess such stature. Enthralled and a bit giddy, I handed my glass to a stranger at the next table. I had an impulse to share this experience. "It's all right," he indifferently replied. Not even a thanks. Having tasted this 1961 a dozen times thereafter, it remains a monumental Latour. Both 1961 Haut-Brion and 1961 Mouton Rothschild are majestic, but I have often been disappointed by both 1961 Lafite Rothschild (100% Cabernet Sauvignon) and definitely 1961 Château Margaux, which was losing its mojo. For many, the 1961 reaches its zenith with the 1961 Palmer. Tasted several times, blind and sighted, ex-château and otherwise, it is the reason God invented wine. Ditto the 1961 La Mission Haut-Brion, which easily matches its neighbour over the road. I've had half a dozen bottles over the years, each and every one beguiling. Others that have impressed on the Left Bank include the leviathan 1961 Ducru-Beaucaillou, an ethereal 1961 Giscours (a hidden gem of this vintage) and a great 1961 Siran tasted with proprietor Édouard Miailhe. A double-magnum of 1961 Lascombes was a highlight of the winery's inauguration dinner in 2022 with plenty of years ahead. Léoville-Las Cases, Batailley, Brane-Cantenac and Domaine de Chevalier have all been splendid. The 1961 Pichon Baron varies bottle to bottle, though my last in March 2022 was grippy and spicy.

Right Bank wines are less frequently seen, partly because many vineyards were still recovering from the freeze five years earlier. Two bottles of 1961 Pétrus encountered in Hong Kong were magnificent, remarkable since the owner Mme. Loubat had passed away that year leaving no one to make the wine, notwithstanding that it suffered a stuck fermentation. The 1961 Latour à Pomerol tasted at lunch in Hong Kong was precocious and reminiscent of the 1982 Le Pin, while the 1961 Trotanoy is towering. I have fond memories of a rustic but delicious and sweet 1961 Nénin while half-a-dozen bottles of 1961 Vieux Château Certan have been nectar, even though Thienpont lost one-third of the crop. The last bottle in January 2020 was the best example I have ever encountered. In Saint-Émilion, the 1961

1961
(Continued)

Ausone can be good but inconsistent, likewise the 1961 Cheval Blanc, made famous in the film *Sideways*, which lies in the shadow of the 1964. Figeac and Larcis-Ducasse also produced fine 1961s. In my experience, the 1961 Sauternes are eclipsed by the superior 1962s (even though Pierre Montégut at Suduiraut begs to differ). I just find they lack some complexity. Perhaps my most memorable encounters are with two 1961 Crème de Têtes, one from Château d'Arche, the other from Château Gilette, opened at the property after a decade maturing in concrete vats and sporting a spine-tingling acidic bite. The 1961s from Rieussec, Climens and Suduiraut were also drinking well after four or five decades, while an English-bottled 1961 Coutet at Noble Rot restaurant in February 2022 was like pure essence of marmalade squished into a bottle.

Event
Yuri Gagarin becomes the first man in space

Russia beat the United States in the space race. "Off we go!" exclaimed Yuri Gagarin like an excited schoolboy as *Vostok 1* launched at 9.07 a.m. on 12 April 1961. His spontaneous remark to mission control became an instant catchphrase across the Eastern Bloc countries. Gagarin orbited the Earth for 108 minutes before landing in Kazakhstan. He then toured the world, a hero with a cheeky smile, instilling dreams of space travel in countless children – except in the US where John F. Kennedy was piqued by the communist's popularity. Gagarin died in March 1968 in an accident during routine training.

Music
Will You Love Me Tomorrow – The Shirelles

By the early sixties, as rock 'n' roll purportedly reached the end of a cul-de-sac, a cluster of girl groups such as The Shangri-Las and The Ronettes emerged Stateside and proved hugely influential, not least upon The Beatles. *Will You Love Me Tomorrow* was composed by couple Larry Goffin and Carole King, two of the Brill Building's most preternaturally gifted songwriters. Its title alone was daring enough. She's willing to spend a night with her boyfriend, but can she be sure she's not being used? The chorus builds the anticipation in its first two lines, before that heart-wrenching shift to a minor key in the third, representing the doubt and maybe reality. None of the song's pathos has been lost since it was released at the tail-end of 1960 and topped the charts in early 1961.

1961
(Continued)

Film
West Side Story – Robert Wise
and Jerome Robbins

Robert Wise directed this critical
and commercially successful
update of the Bard's *Romeo and
Juliet*. Its innovative sets, stunning
choreography and, of course,
Leonard Bernstein and Stephen
Sondheim's memorable songs,
including *Maria* and *America*,
guaranteed it would become a
classic. Audrey Hepburn was
originally offered the role of
Maria, but as she was pregnant
she turned it down and Natalie
Wood stepped into her dancing
shoes. Talking of which, more
than 200 pairs were worn out
during the dance sequences and
countless trousers were torn.
The musical went on to win
10 Oscars.

1962

Overshadowed by the previous year, 1962 was an overlooked Bordeaux vintage that has belatedly gained kudos.

The year began rather rainy and warmer than normal, but in February through to mid-March, temperatures hovered just above zero and delayed the vines' growth cycle. By 26 March, Lawton observes hardly any growth. It finally warmed up in the last week and yet by April, the vines lagged three weeks behind normal growth, prompting Lawton to compare the season with 1917. Finally, in early May warm spells allowed vines to make up lost ground, but inclement weather kept the brakes on. Come June, the vines were still 15 days behind schedule. The month was more settled and the mercury began to rise, with the first flowers spotted at Mouton Rothschild on 8 June. Sunny climes meant flowering was regular and even. July was hot, 34°C (93°F) recorded on 24 July with a sirocco wind intensifying heat, though two days later Margaux and Côtes de Blaye suffered hail damage. August was hot and dry, the lack of water vexing winemakers who noticed stress as vines began shutting down. Nevertheless, hopes began to rise by the end of the month and talk of a new 1928 or 1945 began to circulate. The heat wave continued into September with temperatures reaching the mid-thirties, before falling in the middle of the month. Much-needed rain finally quenched vines' thirst on 25 September. The first pickers were dispatched on 1 October, but the following night a storm brought hail across the Médoc, most acute in Saint-Julien. Afterwards, the weather became more benign. Must weights were not particularly high considering the summer warmth since a lack of water had halted vines' accumulation of sugar. The harvest finished around 22 October. The aforementioned rain in September kick-started botrytis in Sauternes, though bunches were initially missing some concentration. Later pickings from mid-October were much more beneficial and rich, the harvesters out at Yquem through to 15 November. All good things come to those who wait.

Maybe it is my penchant for rooting for the underdog, but I have always had a soft spot for the 1962 vintage. Bottles used to litter wine lists at affordable prices when I commenced my career. Generally, my experiences have been very positive and many bottles surpassed expectations. The 1962 Latour can be brilliant, four encounters over the years have shown it to be a strong follow-up to the mighty '61, precocious and almost Right Bank in style. The 1962 Mouton Rothschild is excellent and though I have not had them side-by-side, my recollections of the 1962 Lafite Rothschild glow a little brighter than the 1961. My solitary encounter with the 1962 Château Margaux evidenced a wine that lacked distinction as the First Growth entered a period of inconsistency. Several encounters with the 1962 Haut-Brion were better. A slightly raisin-ed 1962 La Tour Haut-Brion showed well at one of Linden Wilkie's epic verticals – my last encounter in 2020 deceived me into thinking it was 20 years younger. I have fond memories of a sublime 1962 Ducru-Beaucaillou cracked open at home when I needed to chase the blues away and it did the trick, sparkling with vivacity. Subsequent bottles, including one at the château, have never quite replicated that performance. The 1962 Gruaud Larose is quite medicinal but delicious, while two bottles of Léoville-Las Cases have been uncommonly fine-boned with flesh à la '59. In Pauillac, a magnum of 1962 Batailley at the Académie du Vin soirée was atypically sensual and the 1962 Lynch-Bages was a match for the 1961. The 1962 Grand-Puy-Lacoste was unassuming and harmonious and 1962 Pichon Baron was fleshy and like the Gruaud Larose, tinged with menthol. The 1962 Palmer has never quite lived up to expectations although it has its admirers. A quintet of '62s were lined up for inspection at the Académie du Vin soirée in April 2022, of which the best was a splendid magnum of 1962 Chasse-Spleen, the 1962 Poujeaux and Domaine de Chevalier superior to Pontet-Canet and Malartic-Lagravière. On the Right Bank, perhaps the best I have encountered is a fabulous 1962 Latour à Pomerol, breath-taking in poise and elegance, though rarely seen these days. The 1962 Trotanoy, bottled by Grafé Lecocq, managed to shake off a bit of cork taint on the nose to show well enough after 50 years, while the 1962 Lafleur, tasted in Hong Kong after almost 50 years, was blessed with an entrancing bouquet of roasted chestnuts. The 1962 Vieux Château Certan is sprightly for its age, graceful. Before broaching any sweet whites, I should say it was also a great vintage for Bordeaux's dry whites with a quite profound 1962 Laville Haut-Brion and a decent 1962 Domaine de Chevalier Blanc opened in Bordeaux by Olivier Bernard. Unlike 1961, 1962 is a great vintage for Sauternes, with an abundant crop of wines only surpassed that decade by the 1967s in terms of production. The 1962 Yquem is excellent despite a slightly muffled nose, though I have encountered superb '62s from Climens, Coutet, Rieussec and Suduiraut. Most should continue to drink well.

1962 *(Continued)*

Event
The Cuban missile crisis

The world came to the brink of nuclear war during a 13-day stand-off after the Soviets installed medium-range ballistic missiles on Cuba, just 90 miles (145 km) from the Florida coast. Fidel Castro led a coup in 1959 and the United States retaliated with a blockade, making Cuba reliant on Russia for economic and financial aid. On 14 October 1962, a U-2 spy plane photographed launch pads being assembled, alarming the American government. President John F. Kennedy addressed the nation, promising to neutralise the threat. What did that mean exactly? Military action was only narrowly avoided when Khrushchev agreed to remove them with the guarantee that the US would not invade the island.

Music
Twistin' the Night Away
– Sam Cooke

In 1962, everyone was shaking their hips and doing the twist. A number of smash hits were dedicated to the latest dance craze, though *Twistin' the Night Away* had the most joyous, life-affirming melody and the most soulful vocals. Cooke began his career as a tenor in the gospel group The Soul Stirrers before a series of solo classics in the late fifties, such as *Wonderful World* and *Cupid*. Written by Cooke and backed by the legendary Wrecking Crew, *Twistin' the Night Away* was a smash hit on both sides of the Atlantic. Two years later, just as he was becoming one of the leading civil rights activists, Cooke was tragically shot dead in his motel.

Film
Jules et Jim – François Truffaut

Directed, written and produced by Truffaut, this 1962 French New Wave classic is your typical love affair between a woman and two men, based on Henri-Pierre Roché's novel, which Truffaut had allegedly chanced upon in a bookseller's discount bin back in 1955. Jeanne Moreau plays the wilful Catherine whose affections are torn between Jules and Jim. You just know it's not going to end happily ever after. The movie was shot on a shoestring to the extent that Moreau, the quintessential French actress (at least until Christian Seely informed me that her mother hailed from Oldham), had to bail out the production and even lent a hand with the catering. Truffaut's revolutionary camerawork and narrative editing portended a new genre of filmmaking.

Nineteen sixty-three is like that embarrassing uncle you try to keep away from family gatherings. Bring a 1963 claret to dinner and you are unlikely to be invited back.

You have to look back to December 1962 to see how this *annus horribilis* began. A portent of what was to unfold, the winter was cold – Santa Claus would have had to have donned a second layer of thermal underwear as temperatures plummeted to -12°C (10.5°F) on Christmas night. A prevailing northerly meant the mercury barely rose above freezing. It got worse in February, with -18°C (0.5°F) recorded up in Lesparre in the northern Médoc. By the end of the month, vineyard managers were anxious that vines could suffer permanent damage, just as they had in 1956. March was warmer but changeable and unsurprisingly the vines only commenced their growth cycle around 8 April. The rest of the month saw intermittent rain, but vineyards emerged unscathed after their deep winter freeze. May was rainy and overcast with deluges on the Right Bank, the first clement day not until 25 May, according to Lawton. Hail in Pessac-Léognan on 2 June and again seven days later in Saint-Julien – which caused Gruaud Larose to lose 30% of its crop – preceded late flowering from 13 June under humid and rainy conditions, followed by moderate temperatures when coulure affected the Merlot. July was changeable with average temperatures for the time of year, finishing with a settled and warm week at the end of the month, up to 34°C (93°F). Any hopes of a more benevolent season were dashed by August's downpours, which led to outbreaks of black rot and oidium, rain persisting throughout the month and causing a strung-out *véraison*. From April to the end of August there had been 299 mm (11¾ in) of rain, and September was little better as mildew pressure increased.

With no sign of improvement, pickers went out around 18 September to harvest the early-ripening Merlot. As well as secateurs, they needed umbrellas and waterproofs. At Château Latour, it rained persistently until 8 October, pickers entering the vines two days later. Must weights were a pathetic 8.5–9% and so every château would have readied bags of sugar to chaptalise the wines. Come October and there was finally some improvement in the weather, but it was too little, too late, bunches either ripe or rotten, particular the Cabernets. New Zealand winemaker John Buck, owner of Te Mata Winery, did the vintage that year and once told me about the quagmire he waded through and the smell of rot in the air. The picking of the Cabernets began from 8 October and finished around 10 days later under sunny skies, just to rub salt in winemakers' wounds.

In Sauternes, the botrytis just could not contend with the unrelenting rainfall and eventually most of the grapes were picked in November, much of them bloated and diluted. Picking wasn't finished at Yquem until 20 November. The '63s that dribbled onto the market were tiny

1963

1963 (Continued)

in quantity, though many cut their losses and sold off what they had as generic Bordeaux. The wines were light, acidic and green, but with 1959, 1961 and 1962 to buy, consumers simply ignored them.

Unsurprisingly, you hardly ever see bottles of 1963 Bordeaux. "I remember 1963 very well, when it rained all the time," Philippe Castéja once told me at Batailley. "I think we still made wine, but there were only one or two that did. With the new methods today, we could all have released a 1963." My solitary experience was the 1963 La Mission Haut-Brion, which reeked of boiled cabbage, despite coming directly from the château cellars and the French wine writer next to me singing its virtues.

Event
The assassination of J.F.K.

The assassination of the President of the United States at 12.30 p.m. on 22 November 1963 as his motorcade passed through Dealey Plaza in Dallas left the world's most powerful country mourning its leader. It was not just the brutality of the murder. The facts that it happened in broad daylight, among cheering, flag-waving crowds, and left his wife covered in blood seared horrific images upon a nation, one that had seen J.F.K. as a symbol of a prosperous future. All snuffed out in a single gunshot. Lee Harvey Oswald was arrested 70 minutes later only to be shot dead by Jack Ruby, live on television, as he was escorted to county jail. Conspiracy theories linger to this day. All that we can be sure is that the world lost a charismatic leader.

Music
She Loves You
– The Beatles

She Loves You marks the moment when the Fab Four became a nationwide phenomenon, completing the first chapter of their journey, from dingy Hamburg bars to the tabloids' front pages. Composed by Lennon and McCartney in their hotel room after a concert at the Majestic Ballroom in Newcastle upon Tyne, it was finished the next day at McCartney's home, not before his father chided him for its American slang. Thankfully he rebuffed his suggestion to change the chorus to "Yes, yes, yes". Recorded on a two-track on 1 July in a five-hour session at Abbey Road's Studio 2, *She Loves You* was released on 23 August 1963 with half a million advanced orders, making it a shoo-in at the top of the charts. When they played the London Palladium, 15 million tuned in. Beatlemania swept the country and pop music was never the same again.

1963
(Continued)

1870

Film
The Great Escape
– John Sturges

With its all-star cast led by
recalcitrant P.O.W. Steve
McQueen, *The Great Escape*
was a glitzed-up retelling of
how prisoners tunnelled their
way out of Stalag Luft III
camp in Poland on the night
of 24 March 1944. Some of
the actors, including Donald
Pleasance and Hans Reiser,
had actually been imprisoned
during the war. McQueen
briefly ended up behind bars
when caught speeding with
several crew members. His
attempted motorcycle jump
over the barbed wire fence
at the film's finale failed, so
a stuntman had to be used.
You probably have the theme
from *The Great Escape* running
through your head by now.

2020

1964

If 1961 takes the gold medal in the sixties, then 1964 probably takes silver after a photo-finish with 1966, edging it thanks to the stellar quality of its Right Bank wines.

January temperatures swung one way to the other and February was rainy. March was changeable with spring-like spells. Cold days at the end of the month extended into early April and delayed vines' growth. Finally, warmer temperatures mid-April encouraged shoots to grow, but a cool and rainy second half augured a late picking. Or did it? May was warm, the mercury reaching 31°C (88°F) on 12 March, and vineyards began requesting rain. The Tastet-Lawton archives note there were 22 days without so much as a drop. The heavens eventually opened on the night of 22 May followed by a 48-hour downpour, heavy enough to disrupt flowering. The 30 May saw an afternoon deluge with hail brushing the Médoc, most severely in Listrac and Saint-Julien. The first flowers began to appear on 1 June and though conditions were initially unsettled, warm and sunny days from 6 June meant that overall nobody could complain about flowering. July was mostly hot, with temperatures reaching 38°C (100°F), and the month finishing with localised violent storms. The heat wave continued into August, though hydric stress ensured *véraison* was slow. Showers on 7, 18 and 29 August gave vines a boost of energy, while more moderate temperatures towards the end of the month left winemakers feeling upbeat.

September started well despite four days of heavy rain from 3 to 6 September, after which temperatures returned to 31–34°C (88-93°F), encouraging harvesters on the Right Bank to commence picking around the 21th in ideal sunny and dry conditions. The weather broke towards the end of the month with heavy downpours, though many estates in Saint-Émilion and Pomerol had their fruit safely in vats by then. On 4 October, Lawton speculates that Bordeaux could have a 1924 or 1947 on the cards. But on 8 October heavy rains plagued the region and continued for 10 days, ruining the later-picked Cabernets on the Left Bank by diluting the fruit. "Nineteen sixty-two was a great success but 1963 was a terrible vintage," Jean-Michel Cazes explained during a vertical of Lynch-Bages. "In 1964, rain plagued the harvest. My grandfather's theory was to harvest late, which is why his wines were different. He was very stubborn. He waited for total ripeness of the fruit, which was unusual back then. People did not want to take the risk. Those that did made better wines. However in 1964, it all went sour. He said he would wait one week until after Château Latour had picked, but the rain came just when he started picking and so he waited and waited and waited until he had no choice and picked in the rain, finishing the picking on 24 October, one of the latest ever. The 1964 was to be his last vintage."

It was a terrible season in Sauternes. Three weeks of unrelenting rain, some 255 mm (10 in), prohibited many from producing any wine, including Yquem.

Any bottle of 1964 from the Right Bank is a bottle to get excited about since it was a textbook growing season for Pomerol, Saint-Émilion and indeed satellite appellations. Several bottles of 1964 Pétrus have been mind-boggling in quality, the last at the annual Grouse Club lunch at Otto's was almost ineffably complex, even if a glug was used to reduce the sauce. This legendary Pétrus was conjured by a 22-year-old winemaker hired by Jean-Pierre Moueix straight out of oenology studies, Jean-Claude Berrouet. I dubbed him "the sorcerer from the Basque region" because despite being thrown into the deep end, he oversaw a raft of brilliant Pomerols, which, as well as Pétrus, include a flamboyant Latour à Pomerol, a Trotanoy of beguiling symmetry and a sublime La Fleur-Pétrus. The Robin sisters made a bucolic but equally captivating 1964 over at Lafleur while *régisseur* Pierre Lasserre oversaw a superb, Left Bank-leaning l'Église-Clinet. The 1964 Vieux Château Certan was captivating when last tasted in January 2020, the best of several bottles drunk over the years. Some Pomerols such as La Conseillante were not at the standard achieved today, though a few Pomerol minnows still give pleasure, not least the 1964 La Croix de Gay and a respectable Clos du Clocher. Saint-Émilion is crowned by a stunning 1964 Cheval Blanc, picked between 22 September and 9 October, one of the greatest ever crafted. The sensual 1964 Figeac can challenge Cheval Blanc's supremacy on a good day. I also have positive notes for La Tour Figeac, Larcis Ducasse, Clos Saint-Martin and Grand Mayne.

After the harvest rain, the Left Bank is a mixed bag, but do not dismiss it out of hand. Saint-Estèphe is a cut above other appellations with several excellent bottles of 1964 Cos d'Estournel, Montrose and Lafon-Rochet, perchance because they contain a little more Merlot and also because, at Montrose, the pickers finished before October's downpours. Down in Pauillac, the 1964 Latour also transcends the vintage because it managed to harvest from 25 September to 7 October, before the heavens opened. This fabulous and atypically decadent wine was firing on all cylinders when poured at another Grouse Club lunch in 2018. Elsewhere, it is up and down, with some wines exhibiting dilution and hardness. Even the 1964 Haut-Brion is rather simple and chaptalised. My first bottle of 1964 Haut-Bailly was past its best although another tasted in 2016 was magnificent. Léoville-Las Cases is smooth if leafy, nowhere near the pedigree of its finest vintages. I also have fond memories of a 1964 Poujeaux at the Lion d'Or restaurant in Margaux, my French colleague aghast that I chose an ancient wine. It was quite lovely.

The only Sauternes I have met are a decent Climens with a muffled bouquet yet quite honeyed on the finish and a 1964 Rabaud-Promis, which indicated the estate had not prevented grey rot getting into the vats. In terms of dry whites, the 1964 Laville Haut-Brion and 1964 Haut-Brion Blanc evolved beautifully in bottle.

1964
(Continued)

Event
The Beatles debut on
The Ed Sullivan Show

Remarkably, *She Loves You* sold barely 1,000 copies on its first release on the Swan label in the US. But America's teens pricked up their ears as Beatlemania spread like wildfire in Britain. Legend has it TV host Ed Sullivan first noticed The Beatles when he witnessed legions of screaming fans as he was departing London airport. In fact, he had already seen them in 1963 and negotiations had taken place for their arrival on American soil. On 9 February 1964 at eight o'clock, The Beatles debuted on CBS. An incredible 73 million viewers tuned in to watch Sullivan read out a congratulatory telegram from Elvis, before they ripped through *All My Loving*, *Till There Was You* and *She Loves You*. As the camera focused on their individual faces, their names appeared at the bottom of the screen, one warning that John Lennon was married. They shook their mop tops and sang over the screams. The Beatles were catharsis for a nation in mourning for Kennedy and instantaneously inspired an entire generation to pick up a guitar.

Music
Dancing in the Street
– Martha and the Vandellas

The horn riff that opens *Dancing in the Street* was a clarion call for Motown's commercial success throughout the sixties and into the following decade. Composed by Marvin Gaye, William "Mickey" Stevenson and Ivy Jo Hunter in Stevenson's attic, the song was inspired by Stevenson's childhood memories of dancing under an opened fire hydrant. Gaye sang a rough demo in a slower, jazzy style with Kim Weston in mind, but asked former Motown secretary Martha Reeves to sing a guide vocal. Reeves' up-tempo take made an immediate impression, but unfortunately the studio engineer forgot to press the record button. Annoyed, she sang it again with more aggression and Hunter added grit to the Funk Brothers' instrumentation by whacking a crow bar on the concrete to the beat. *Dancing in the Street* became the summer anthem of 1964.

Film
Goldfinger
– Guy Hamilton

The film adaptations of Ian
Fleming's spy novels had begun
with *Dr. No* the previous year.
But *Goldfinger* is when Sean
Connery's 007 is fully realised.
Connery had machismo and
charm in spades. He also had
the Aston Martin DB5 with
optional machine-gun and
women falling at his feet. (How
did they get away with the name
Pussy Galore?) *Goldfinger* was
the Bond film that introduced
the explosive finale. It also had
Dame Shirley Bassey's lung-
busting theme tune (featuring a
teenage Jimmy Page on rhythm
guitar) and John Barry's dramatic
score. There was a villain par
excellence whom Fleming had
rather waspishly named after his
neighbour, Modernist architect
Ernö Goldfinger. Incidentally, in
the first few months of my wine
career I dined with Goldfinger's
daughter and naturally asked the
question I am sure she is asked *ad
nauseam*, for which I apologise.

1965

Nineteen sixty-five fights it out with 1963 for the ignominious title of "worst vintage of the sixties".

January was its usual wintry self, as was February, which saw a cold snap in the middle of the month. March was variable but finished with a sunny dry spell that lifted winemakers' spirits. Alas, April was mainly cold and retarded vines' growth cycle, though at least there had been no frost. The start of May was inclement but a week of dry and warm weather encouraged rapid vine growth, stymied by a cool and overcast remainder of the month. June began rainy and cool – just 7°C (44.5°F), according to the Tastet-Lawton archives – which delayed flowering until 7 June. Warm weather meant flowering was fairly quick as the mercury climbed to 31°C (88°F). After a brief dry spell, the weather broke towards the end of the month with heavy rain inflicting coulure among the Merlot and Petit Verdot vines by early July. Between 14 and 20 July it was cool and rainy and this intensified coulure, temperatures languishing around 20–22°C (68–71.5°F). What the vines needed was some warmth and August tried to address matters as the mercury hit 31°C (88°F). Unfortunately, the burst of heat was brief and cooler temperatures, particularly during the night, delayed *véraison*.

September commenced with yet more rain and a lack of warmth, many bunches remaining green and affected by rot. According to Lawton, Jean-Pierre Moueix commented that some wines would be half their normal crop and that he was "very pessimistic" about quality. By 12 September, Lawton was realistic, writing that only a miracle would save the vintage. Despite a brief respite, more torrential showers swept across Bordeaux and were particularly heavy in the northern Médoc on 26 and 27 September. After a small window of drier conditions at the beginning of October, the harvest began on 5 October and several rain-free days and warm temperatures offered some relief, though all it succeeded in doing was ensuring the wines weren't quite as wretched as the '63s. Edmund Penning-Rowsell observed how plumes of grey dust rose into the air as grape loads were tipped into crusher-de-stemmers because rot was so widespread. Some producers apparently placed bunches in open cauldrons above fires in a vain attempt to concentrate the must. After the disastrous 1963 vintage, several estates attempted to pick out rotten berries. One could see this vintage as a more concerted effort to sort berries, but to be honest, there was so much rot that efforts were futile. Sorting was more successful when applied in 1968.

In Sauternes, the cool growing season precluded phenolic ripeness. The 100 mm (4 in) of rain in late September was followed by warm weather that allowed some to make a couple of profitable passes through the vines in early October, yet hardly any fruit contained sufficient concentration.

Like 1963 Bordeaux, 1965 claret is hardly ever seen. In fact, this is one of the few vintages that was poor in almost every wine region around the world. I have only tasted three examples: first, a 1965 La Mission Haut-Brion at the 2009 vertical. To say it was slightly better than the 1963 is damning it with faint praise since it did not yield one iota of joy. Then within a fortnight of each other, a 1965 Pichon-Lalande opened by Nicolas Glumineau that teased a glimmer of pleasure before crumbling, and a 1965 Poujeaux, a bottle I had bought in Burgundy for a measly sum. Turbid in colour, it wasn't wretched on the nose, but the palate was heavily chaptalised and a sip was more than enough to assuage my curiosity. The fact our mischievous host served it blind against a fabulous 1959 Lafite Rothschild probably did it no favours, either.

Event
First US troops sent
to Vietnam

Film
The Ipcress File
– Sidney J. Furie

War in Vietnam escalated in March 1965 when President Lyndon B. Johnson ordered the start of a bombing campaign in North Vietnam. Operation Rolling Thunder aimed to slow down the advances that communist-supported Viet Cong had made in the country. That same month, 3,500 US combat troops landed at beaches close to Da Sang: the first army boots to arrive on Vietnam soil and not the last. In response, the first major anti-war march of up to 25,000 students was organised on 17 April, though Johnson simply sent further reinforcements. During the first major battle that November, 300 soldiers were killed and hundreds injured, though this was just the opening chapter.

Based on Len Deighton's 1962 novel, this thriller provided the breakout role for Michael Caine as Harry Palmer. Sporting thick-rimmed spectacles and an even thicker Bermondsey accent, Caine plays a pawn caught up in Cold War espionage, an anti-Bond who cooked his own meals and made his own coffee – things 007 would never do. The film was praised for its gritty realism, much of it shot in dimly lit down-at-heel London. Scenes were often shot through open doors or over people's shoulders to enhance the clandestine feeling, ratcheted up by John Barry's inspired theme that was played on a cimbalom, an instrument that sounds as if it were invented solely for sixties spy flicks.

1965
(Continued)

Music
Subterranean Homesick Blues
– Bob Dylan

Few songs pack as much into two-and-a-half minutes as Dylan's *Subterranean Homesick Blues*. What do the lyrics mean? Who knows. They are paradoxically meaningful and meaningless, open to listeners' interpretation. *Subterranean Homesick Blues* looks backward in its oblique references to the Beat Generation and civil rights movement while prefiguring how songs could sound thanks to Dylan's deadpan delivery and the iconic promo video shot by D.A. Pennebaker in an alley behind the Savoy Hotel in London. The Greenwich Village folk laureate-turned-Judas looks effortlessly cool in his waistcoat and fuzzy hair, barely keeping pace with his own quasi-rap as he tosses away cue cards. So good it made Lennon wonder whether he could ever compete, *Subterranean Homesick Blues* is Dylan making genius look easy.

For this writer, 1966 runs 1964 close for the second-best vintage of the sixties. Unlike 1964, the year's strength bestowed both the Left and Right Bank with wines that can entrance.

The year began with a bitterly cold January when temperatures plunged to -10°C (14°F), though the month finished with three spring-like days, according to the Tastet-Lawton archives. February was unseasonably warm, while March was variable and quite dry with little rain between the 5th and 23th. The vines awoke from their winter dormancy at the end of the month and growth was encouraged by a wetter April and three blissful sunny days that saw in May. Temperatures reached 27°C and hovered there for the remainder of the month. The first flowers could be spotted from 29 May and *pleine fleur* was on 6 June, some coulure affecting the Merlot. Clive Coates MW attests that the flowering was spun out over a month, though other literature suggests it was more like two-and-a-half weeks. July began warm but ended with one or two cold spells and overcast days, followed by a wet and humid start to August that provoked mildew. Lawton notes that 9 August was the first time that he had seen sunshine since 24 July. Afterwards it was pleasantly warm rather than stiflingly hot, the nights not as fresh as winemakers would have liked.

The vines needed consistent hot temperatures to nudge on sugar accumulation and it never quite came, except for three days from 6 to 8 September when thermometers reached 33°C (91°F). Thereafter, temperatures tapered off a little and on 21 September, Jean-Pierre Moueix called Daniel Lawton to forewarn him that yields could be half those of the previous year. The first pickers were by now descending upon the vineyards and went out en masse from 27 September, coinciding with 48 hours of rainfall that relieved some of the vine stress. Harvest was completed around 4 October on the Right Bank, though the Left Bank was far later – Lafite Rothschild only commenced on 6 October. Most were finished by 11 October. Fermentations generally went smoothly and the wines were initially well received, notable for their deep colours and compactness. Edmund Penning-Rowsell notes that many estates chaptalised their wines by around half a degree.

With regard to Sauternes, the weather conditions slowly improved, but picking was arduous – Yquem worked 48 out of the 55 days between 15 September and 9 November to eke out botrytised fruit.

The 1966 vintages produced classic wines – fresh, structured and correct – though Edmund Penning-Rowsell notes they received a lukewarm reception and their reputation slowly grew over time. The 1961s possess more power and complexity and the 1964 Right Bank much flair and flamboyance – perhaps what 1966 misses is a single transcendental wine that knocks your socks off to give it a higher reputation. But it is a favourite among those with a predilection for well-crafted, traditional,

1966
(Continued)

straight-down-the-fairway claret without bells and whistles. Among the First Growths, the 1966 Latour is an exemplar: a blue-blooded, structured, "proper" Pauillac that I have enjoyed from both magnum and bottle. It ploughs along in formidable fashion to this day. The 1966 Mouton Rothschild is a vintage I have only encountered once and it felt relatively one-dimensional. Better is the 1966 Lafite Rothschild, each one of the three bottles I have sampled was harmonious, elegant and understated. A 1966 Château Margaux served blind in June 2021 was fresh as a daisy, the last great wine from the estate until the 1978. The 1966 Haut-Brion is sturdy and maybe a little dour, but the Graves excelled this vintage. The 1966 La Mission Haut-Brion is outstanding, structured and beautifully balanced, Domaine de Chevalier is firm and with impressive depth, and the 1966 Haut-Bailly was shining when Véronique Sanders poured one of the last bottles in its cellars upon completing its new winery in 2021. Saint-Julien performed well with fine contributions from Léoville-Las Cases, Gruaud Larose and Branaire-Ducru, while the brilliant 1966 Palmer would be more fêted were it not for the ethereal 1961. The 1966 Pichon Baron can vary, though offers classic mint-like aromas without the frills.

The Right Bank has its fair share of gems. The best has been a spellbinding magnum of 1966 Lafleur tasted in Austria, maybe just pipping a noble and quite tertiary Pétrus. I also have complimentary notes for 1966s courtesy of l'Évangile and Trotanoy, while others such as Nénin, l'Église-Clinet and Latour à Pomerol felt a little fatigued by comparison. Proprietor Ronan Laborde poured a delectable 1966 Clinet in December 2021, its salinity and freshness rather embarrassing the 1990 that was served in tandem. In Saint-Émilion both Cheval Blanc and Figeac produced utterly refined, quite magical wines, much better than Ausone, which was misfiring on all cylinders in this era. The 1966 Laville Haut-Brion Blanc continues its trend of triumphing in numerically even vintages and is the only dry white I've tasted. In Sauternes, the 1966 Lafaurie-Peyraguey was a hidden gem when tasted with proprietor Silvio Denz and Denis Dubourdieu. Suduiraut sported that chlorine-like aroma and the 1966 Climens just showed a little dryness when encountered at the Zurich vertical, clearly surpassed by its follow-up, while the less said about a 1966 Coutet kindly opened by owner Philippe Baly the better.

Event
England win the
FIFA World Cup

At time of writing, the men's
England football team's only
international title came with their
dramatic 4-2 victory over West
Germany at Wembley Stadium
on 30 July 1966. The game
provided many iconic images:
Geoff Hurst's controversial was-
it-over-the-line third goal, his
hat-trick completed as spectators
began streaming on to the pitch
– "They think it's all over... it is
now" – Bobby Moore receiving
the Jules Rimet Trophy from her
beaming Majesty and being held
aloft on his teammates' shoulders,
and Nobby Stiles' jubilant dancing
around the side of the pitch. One
can look at it philosophically and
say that winning once is better
than having never won at all.
Isn't it?

Film
Blowup
– Michelangelo Antonioni

You might have assumed a
British filmmaker would have
best captured the zeitgeist of
"Swinging London". Instead it
was Italian director Michelangelo
Antonioni in *Blowup*. David
Hemmings plays a mod
photographer, loosely based
on David Bailey and Terence
Donovan, who unwittingly
photographs a murder in a park.
Or does he? The film caused
a furore with its debauched
drug-fuelled parties, existentialist
tennis matches and a cameo
by The Yardbirds, even though
Antonioni had originally wanted
The Velvet Underground.
Released in the United States at
the end of 1966, *Blowup* was a
box-office success and remains a
flawed time capsule.

Music
God Only Knows – The Beach Boys

God Only Knows is often cited as the apotheosis of modern pop music.
Recorded between 10 March and 11 April, it is the pinnacle of Brian
Wilson's otherworldly musical genius, pushed to its limits after hearing
The Beatles' *Rubber Soul*. Wilson enlisted 20 session musicians to piece
together his complex vision, which included French horns, harpsichord,
sleigh bells and clarinets, before adding the angelic multi-tracked vocal
harmonies led by Carl Wilson. Often described as "baroque pop", it
sounds like the most gorgeous musical sigh imaginable.

1967

Michael Broadbent MW masterfully describes this psychedelic year as "a peroxide blonde of a vintage; initially attractive but the black roots began to show." So brilliant, so Broadbent.

After a dip in temperatures to -10°C (14°F) in the second week, the rest of January was fairly warm with the same conditions continuing into February. Things cooled down towards the end of March as vines woke from their slumber. The 6 and 7 April saw frost damage on the Right Bank, though the weather gradually improved throughout the month. May was more unsettled with occasional storms, three cold and humid days finishing the month on a down note. The first flowers appeared around 1 June and after a couple of rainy days, it stayed clement until the end of flowering, when temperatures reached 24°C (75°F). The rest of June was warm and sunny as the thermometer reached the mid-thirties. July provided more of the same until the vines began showing signs of hydric stress. Lawton records there were 27 days without rain in July. The heavens finally opened on 8 August, followed by a succession of sunny days with temperatures around 30°C (86°F). So far, so good.

But September was fresh and persistent spells of rain caused outbreaks of rot. It improved from 23 September, with the first pickers entering vineyards two days later. The weather remained clement for picking, which was completed around 12 October. The region that relished 1967 was Sauternes. After the dry and hot summer, the rainy spells that beleaguered the reds were a godsend for those seeking botrytis. Sure enough, pickers in Sauternes could start work from the end of September as infection spread through the vines and most estates were able to pick concentrated, heavily botrytised berries throughout October, most of them safely in the vat by the end of the month. It was the best Sauternes vintage since 1959, the difference being that in 1967 – with apologies to Pomerol (see opposite) – Sauternes did not have to share the limelight.

I was under the impression that 1967 was a pretty average year for Bordeaux, especially on the Left Bank, but growing season summaries give no particular reason why. There was no catastrophe and it remains a mystery why the wines did not turn out better. The only explanation is that the dry conditions that persisted throughout the summer prevented sugar accumulation, which producers tried to remedy through zealous chaptalisation.

Let's begin with those sweet elixirs in Sauternes. The 1967 Yquem is legendary, though my first encounters, including one at the château, did not quite match the eulogies. Finally, a bottle served blind at Hide restaurant in London in 2019 revealed a wine that was ineffably complex, brimming with energy and concentration. I drank two so-so bottles of 1967 Climens that suggested victory had slipped through their fingers, but then two more bottles in 2022, one poured by

Bérénice Lurton at the estate, proved the Barsac producer had in fact created a stunning wine that is tensile, profound and utterly delicious. Four bottles of 1967 Suduiraut over the years have been excellent, the last, served blind in March 2022, was filled with mandarin and orange rind. The 1967 Doisy-Védrines is holding up well, though Rieussec is a little flat by comparison.

Sauternes aside, the other place to head this year is Pomerol. The 1967 Pétrus was the first vintage I ever tasted – at The Square restaurant in London back in 1999 – and I remember looking on in disbelief as the sommelier poured the bottle for my table. It was everything I hoped for, though it was another two decades before I retasted it. I found it sensual, rustic and beginning to fray around the edges… yet still compelling. Other great Pomerols from this vintage include the 1967 Trotanoy and a magnum of La Fleur-Pétrus, opened by Édouard Moueix as a "test run" for the forthcoming Académie du Vin dinner. A bottle of 1967 l'Église-Clinet at Oswald's club in January 2019 was an agreeable surprise and still emitting pleasure, though a 1967 Vieux Château Certan felt fatigued by 2020. My handful of encounters with Saint-Émilion have been less memorable, though the 1967 Ausone had a lovely leathery nose and Larcis-Ducasse a divine Earl Grey-tinged finish. My experience with the Left Bank is patchy, though two wines stand out, both tasted in March 2022. First, a fleshy and almost Burgundy-like 1967 Palmer was elegiac and charming, the oldest bottle in a vertical held by CEO Thomas Duroux at the property. Three days later, CEO Frédéric Engerer poured the 1967 Latour, which still brimmed with slightly piquant red fruit and minty notes from head to toe. The 1967 Haut-Brion has bucolic charm and 1967 Smith Haut Lafitte was satisfying when I bumped into it at the château in 2018.

1967
(Continued)

Event
The Summer of Love

The summer of '67 was a brief moment in history when counterculture flirted with the mainstream. It was a convergence of drugs (especially hash and LSD), fashion (long hair, flairs and paisley), music (*Sgt. Pepper*, Pink Floyd, The Doors and Jefferson Airplane), psychedelia, free love, a rejection of consumerist values and war, plus that oft-forgotten ingredient, sunshine. An estimated 100,000 young people descended on Haight-Ashbury in San Francisco, the epicentre of the hippy movement, having initially been attracted by the Monterey Folk Festival. Everyone was seeking Utopia, but by autumn, the sun had vanished and the movement soured and disintegrated. Nonetheless, its ideals and fashions have never gone away.

Music
Purple Haze
– The Jimi Hendrix Experience

The Jimi Hendrix Experience released their second single, *Purple Haze*, in the UK on 17 March 1967, a confluence of blues and Middle Eastern modalities. Hendrix and producer Chas Chandler used studio trickery to create the sound, including an Octavia effects unit to add an upper octave. Many interpreted the lyrics as referring to hallucinogens, though Hendrix insisted it was a love song. *Purple Haze* captured the psychedelic zeitgeist but also prefigures heavy metal – the tape sent to his American record company included the instructions: "Deliberate distortion, do not correct."

Film
The Graduate – Mike Nichols

Several films broke taboos in 1967 and perhaps the most commercially successful of them was *The Graduate*, starring newcomer Dustin Hoffman as the young man unable to resist the advances of an older woman, played by Anne Bancroft. Bancroft was only six years older than Hoffman and only eight years older than her screen daughter, Katharine Ross. Hoffman was convinced he had failed the screen test, but Nichols felt he conveyed the panic he sought in the character. With its catchy Simon & Garfunkel soundtrack, *The Graduate* went on to become one of the biggest box-office draws of the year.

The 1968 vintage is an also-ran year forgotten by even the most ardent Bordeaux lovers.

The year began in benign fashion with changeable weather in January and February. March was warmer than usual, a high of 22°C (71.5°F) coaxing buds to swell at the end of the month. It was a false dawn. The wind swung to the north and temperatures dropped, blanketing the Médoc in snow on 6 April. It warmed towards the end of the month before dropping again in early May. The pendulum-like weather delayed flowering, with the first petals appearing around 7 June. According to some texts, flowering was even, although that contradicts the Tastet-Lawton archives, which noted generally warm conditions interrupted by heavy rainfall on 18 June. This was followed by a heat wave that saw the mercury reach a blistering 38°C (100°F) on 30 June. The first half of July was variable, but more settled weather in the second half raised hopes. But August began wet and then Saint-Estèphe suffered hail damage on 3 August, followed by overcast and rainy conditions that dragged on through September, accompanied by cold nights that stymied ripening.

Rot was obviously becoming a serious risk, expediting some properties such as Pontet-Canet and d'Issan to bring forward picking. Lawton reports that Montrose proprietor Madame Charmolue phoned on 27 September to forewarn that must weights were only 9.5–10%. The harvest really got going from 1 October under initially clear skies, only for more rain to fall on 7 October. Pickers finished around the middle of the month. This was the first vintage in which producers made some effort to sort incoming berries, which marginally raised quality.

Matters were little better in Sauternes. After a cool and wet September, picking began circa the end of the month and yet the fruit lacked concentration and downpours on 24 and 25 October halted the harvest. Yquem made one final pass through the vines at the end of November and used anything picked after to make their dry Y de Yquem. Half of the fruit was rejected for its sweet wine.

The 1968 vintage is one you do not see often and is not held in high regard. Penning-Rowsell observed that some Right Bank wines such as Cheval Blanc and Lafite Rothschild began browning not long after they had been bottled. A 1968 Domaine de Chevalier opened to celebrate my photographer friend Johan Berglund's half-century was ferrous and a little dry, though surprisingly vigorous on the finish. Also, a 1968 Haut-Brion that I drank in Beaune when a bottle neck accidentally smashed and the owner hastily invited anyone present to take a sip was drinkable but callously made me wish they had broken a '61 instead. A 1968 Latour at the Académie du Vin soirée from two bottles was a little tired and dour, though kudos for opening such an off-vintage, while a 1968 La Mission Haut-Brion was one for completists only.

1968
(Continued)

Event
Martin Luther King Jr. is assassinated

Civil rights leader and Baptist minister Martin Luther King Jr. was assassinated on 4 April 1968 in Memphis, Tennessee while standing on the second-floor balcony of the Lorraine Motel. The night before he had made a typically powerful and prophetic speech when he cried: "I've seen the Promised Land. I may not get there with you." King's murder provoked riots and looting across the US. Several weeks later the police apprehended the suspect, petty criminal James Earl Ray, at Heathrow Airport in London. Though he initially pleaded guilty and received a 99-year jail sentence, Ray later recanted and denied the charge for the rest of his life, his conspiracy theories never proven.

Music
I Heard It Through the Grapevine – Marvin Gaye

Norman Whitfield and Barrett Strong had co-written *I Heard It Through the Grapevine* two years earlier and Gaye was the second artist to release it, after Gladys Knight in 1967. It took more than a month to record as producer Whitfield painstakingly layered Gaye's plaintive vocals, the Funk Brothers' instrumentation and the Detroit Symphony Orchestra's strings. Astonishingly, Motown boss Berry Gordy initially vetoed its release, only acquiescing in October '68 after DJs began playing the track from its parent album, *In the Groove*. It went on to top the Billboard charts for seven weeks and became Motown's biggest seller to that date.

Film
2001: A Space Odyssey – Stanley Kubrick

Kubrick's cinematic landmark left some of its audiences a bit confused. "Will someone tell me what the hell this is about?" complained actor Rock Hudson as dozens streamed out of the premiere early and co-screenwriter Arthur C. Clarke fought back tears, distressed that his voice-over narration had been cut out. Nevertheless, its scientific rigour in speculating a possible future, combined with allegories of human birth, life and death and Douglas Trumbull's dazzling visual effects transfixed a young and perhaps more open-minded audience. Clarke could eventually dry his eyes as the film became a financial as well as a critical success.

The Swinging Sixties ended with yet another forgettable vintage.

January was changeable, February much colder, March zigzagging between warm spells and snow. April was calmer, although the vines were slow out the starting blocks due to lack of consistent warmth and rain. Three warm and clement days from 10 – 13 May gave the vines encouragement, though the mercury fell and struggled for the rest of the month. At least there was no frost. Flowering did not start until 9 June and unsettled conditions led to coulure, while the morning of 16 June brought a damaging frost that knocked Pauillac off course. July saw some much-needed warmer temperatures, up to 34°C (93°F), raising hopes of a good vintage to finish the decade. August complied with winemakers' wishes – warm and sunny with temperatures in the high twenties with little rain. Could '69 produce a small crop of high-quality wines like '61?

September answered that question when rain soaked vineyards at the start of the month and temperatures tumbled on the 12th. A torrential deluge followed two days later. Despite one or two brief spells of clement weather, it remained unsettled and wet – perfect conditions for grey rot, particularly after two days of constant rain on 18 and 19 September. By the end of the month, Lawton is ruing that September had seen 20 days of poor weather, dashing hopes of a good vintage. It was only marginally less rainy than it had been in sodden 1965. The first pickers had ventured out on 23 September and the main harvest commenced six days later. There was not a great deal of fruit to harvest, many châteaux reporting half the normal crop by the time the secateurs were put away around 12 October. The final growing season of the decade was a damp squib. In Sauternes, examining weather conditions, it seems like great wines were feasible after September's heavy rains were followed by dry weather. But the fruit lacked concentration and despite two brief windows of opportunity to pick in early October, four weeks of constant rain from late October precluded most Sauternes winemakers from making quality sweet wine.

This is not a vintage seen often, due to quality and quantity. Over the years I have gathered notes from a dozen or so wines. The best was in Sauternes, a respectable 1969 Suduiraut opened by Christian Seely to finish one of several vertical tastings undertaken over the years. I also remember a 1969 Doisy-Védrines opened early in my career to curry favour with a Japanese buyer who was born that year. The following day she confided that her birth year was in fact 1970. Oh well – we had celebrated her year of conception. The best I could write about the 1969 Yquem was that it was "inoffensive" and possibly surpassed by an excellent Climens that sported a beguiling tangy finish in our only encounter. Among the dry reds even Pétrus struggled to make a good Pomerol, the three bottles I have encountered were turbid and bucolic (incidentally, this was the final vintage from the original

1969
(Continued)

vineyard, before augmenting vines acquired from Gazin). Ausone, La Conseillante, Vieux Château Certan and Cheval Blanc were past their low peaks and the 1969 La Mission Haut-Brion was harsh and dry. Only the 1969 Montrose surpassed low expectations at the vertical in 2016. Otherwise, this is a vintage to give a wide berth.

Event
Neil Armstrong sets foot on the moon

The 20 July 1969, 10:56 EDT: in what is widely regarded as the first global live televised event, an estimated half-a-billion people watched awestruck as astronaut Neil Armstrong climbed down the ladder of the *Eagle* lunar module and set foot on another world, uttering the immortal line: "That's one small step for a man, one giant leap for mankind." Buzz Aldrin joined him and they spent two-and-a-half hours exploring and collecting samples, leaving behind an American flag. Four days later they splashed down off Hawaii having pulled off one of mankind's greatest achievements.

Film
Easy Rider – Dennis Hopper

You can almost smell the motor oil and hash as you watch *Easy Rider*. Peter Fonda and Dennis Hopper play hippy bikers Wyatt and Billy on their search for "real America" in this era-defining counterculture flick. It was the first to use pre-recorded music rather than a score, mainly because it was shot on a shoestring budget. This meant shooting without a completed script, inviting passers-by and friends to film scenes themselves, and spending much of the time drinking, smoking marijuana and bickering. Jack Nicholson steals the movie as alcoholic lawyer George Hanson, not least delivering his extra-terrestrial monologue around the campfire as he puffs grass for the first time. Hopper edited 80 hours of footage into the final 95-minute version that premiered at Cannes in May 1969.

Music
Gimme Shelter
– The Rolling Stones

The Rolling Stones entered their imperial phase as the sixties darkened. Keith Richards was apparently inspired looking out the window of his Mayfair flat on a stormy day. Some say he channelled his angst over suspicions of a dalliance between Mick Jagger and his girlfriend Anita Pallenberg into the opening guitar riff. Jagger co-wrote the lyrics, which sought to capture the sense of dread that clouded the end of the decade against the backdrop of Vietnam. Producer Jimmy Miller suggested adding a female vocalist and so a four-months-pregnant Merry Clayton was duly summoned at midnight from her Los Angeles home by Jack Nitzsche, cajoled into going by her partner since she had no idea who the Rolling Stones were. She recorded a take in her silk pyjamas and pink curlers. Invited to do another and determined to show what she could do, she unleashed an astonishing take an octave higher, her voice almost cracking, before returning to bed. Tragically she suffered a miscarriage shortly after. Completed at Olympic Studios in February and March 1969, *Gimme Shelter* opened the Stones' album *Let It Bleed* and became a defining song of the era.

THE
1970s

The seventies is not a decade that Bordeaux winemakers look back upon fondly. Theoretically, it should have ushered in stability across the region. It marked the first decade in which Bordeaux focused upon its real strength, its red wines, instead of its dry whites. Whereas in 1969 around 60% of Bordeaux was planted with white grape varieties that figure had fallen to 37% by 1978. From 1970, acreage under vine began to expand rather than contract across the region.

Following a series of rot-afflicted seasons, in 1970 the French government banned new plantings of Merlot since it was more susceptible to rot than Cabernet Sauvignon. The ban was rescinded five years later, and in their hurry to add more Merlot vines, some châteaux misguidedly planted them on gravel soils more suitable for Cabernet Sauvignon, a problem that was only rectified in the nineties. Other factors compromised quality in the seventies. Many château owners prioritised quantity and used high-yielding rootstocks such as SO4. The problem might have be less acute had Bordeaux been graced with hot summers in which dispersing concentration over a higher number of bunches could have reined in any excess. But the decade never saw such seasons and many châteaux found it difficult to achieve full ripeness, producing claret that had a proclivity to taste unripe and green.

The decade was besmirched by poor vintages. Only 1970, 1971, 1975 and perhaps 1978 had something to offer wine lovers and even then, none approach the consistency or heights of 1959, 1961 or 1982. The other vintages were plagued by inclement conditions: 1972, 1973, 1974, 1976, 1977 and to a lesser degree, 1979. Small volumes of 1971 and 1972 encouraged the Bordeaux market to ratchet up prices, with Sichel noting 1972 Médoc wines were up around 450% from just two years earlier. It was a terrible move that self-inflicted damage, since 1973 and 1974 produced a glut of wine just as the oil crisis caused major market turbulence and inflation crippled Western economies. Bordeaux wine prices crashed to the extent that Château Latour decided not to place its 1973 onto the market en primeur and only the First Growths offered their '74s en primeur, at hugely discounted prices.

Pricing was not the only poor decision. This was the decade when use of chemical fertilisers, insecticides and herbicides reached its peak. In this environmentally conscientious age we might easily look back and admonish winemakers, yet you have to consider that they faced awful growing conditions and here were salesmen knocking at their door offering solutions. How ignorant they were of their impact on the biodiversity of their vineyard and the health of their vineyard workers is difficult to ascertain, but they did not live in our enlightened times.

If all that were not enough, in 1973 Bordeaux was rocked by the Cruse scandal, which went on to engulf the entire industry. Bordeaux had been experiencing a shortfall of red AOC wine. Pierre Bert, a merchant with a dubious reputation after several brushes with the law, set up an operation in an old warehouse in Saint-Germain-de-Graves. Bert's scam involved buying wine from the Languedoc in the south of France, doctoring the paperwork and reselling it to Bordeaux merchants as legitimate Bordeaux AOC Rouge. One of those deceived was the *négociant* Cruse, headed by Lionel Cruse. Examining the details, it is doubtful that it was aware of the source of Bert's AOC wine. On 28 June 1973, Cruse's office on the Quai des Chartrons in Bordeaux city was raided by the fraud squad and suddenly this distinguished merchant family was embroiled in an unseemly affair, fomenting distrust in an industry in which trust is paramount. How could consumers believe that the label guaranteed the origin of its contents? Bert, a mendacious exhibitionist and by all accounts a Del Trotter-like rogue, stoked the fires when he declared that 90% of traders and 50% of producers behaved fraudulently. After Lionel Cruse rashly compared himself to Richard Nixon, the international press dubbed the affair "Winegate" as the case went to court over the source of 20,000 hl of wine. Bert was found guilty and imprisoned for one year, while two members of the Cruse family were handed suspended sentences. There were huge repercussions. Prices tumbled back to levels last seen in the late sixties and did not really recover until the 1982 vintage. The Cruse family gradually rebuilt its reputation, but paid a significant price when it had to relinquish ownership of Pontet-Canet in 1975.

Given this backdrop, no wonder the seventies was also the decade that quashed the notion of supremacy among Bordeaux winemakers. That feeling of self-entitlement came from their history, prestige and prices, the fact that the merchants hyped even their mediocre, subpar wines. Steven Spurrier masterminded the famous "Judgment of Paris" blind tasting on 24 May 1976, which shifted the tectonic plates of fine wine appreciation. Pitting top Bordeaux and Burgundy against California wines and totting up their scores, France's most respected critics and winemakers "shockingly" dispelled the notion that fine wine was the preserve of France. California's wines were a match for the best of Bordeaux: the 1973 Stag's Leap Wine Cellars trumped 1970 Mouton Rothschild and 1970 Haut-Brion and the 1973 Chardonnay from Chateau Montelena won the flight of whites. In his memoirs, Spurrier recalled how the judges "sat in disbelief" and how Odette Khan, editor of *La Revue du Vin de France*, demanded her score cards back, which Spurrier in typically debonair manner, politely refused. The press ran with the story, of course, not least in the

Fining the 1976 Château Talbot with egg whites. Note the use of the electric egg whisk. I imagine someone making a cake is wondering who the hell stole it from the kitchen cupboard.

US where it made headline news. Aubert de Villaine, co-owner of Domaine de la Romanée-Conti in Burgundy, said the Judgment of Paris was "a kick up the bum for French wine". Bordeaux winemakers had been resting on their laurels, though they would have to wait until 1982 before Mother Nature acquiesced and presented an opportunity to remind wine lovers of the heights its wines can achieve.

After all this negativity, one positive this decade was the European Union passing legislation in 1970 that forbade the bottling of classified Bordeaux outside the region. In recent years, the percentage of Bordeaux wine bottled outside its limits had diminished as châteaux sought to control production. In some ways, this made things simpler for consumers, who could no longer be confused by different bottlings of the same wine by different sources. That said, it did not predicate an overnight improvement, since many merchants were dab hands at maturating wine in barrel and took great care over bottling. Another move in the right direction was the increasing number of wineries modernising and equipping themselves with stainless-steel vats – in 1972, for example, Lynch-Bages removed the cows from its old stables and installed six stainless-steel vats that could vinify around half its crop.

Last but not least, this is the decade that witnessed the only alteration to the 1855 classification, if one excludes Cantemerle's last-minute inclusion upon original publication. Baron Philippe de Rothschild had been incensed that the "Club of Five" – the informal tasting/social group that he had founded in the twenties – decided to exclude Mouton Rothschild and become the "Association of Four" in 1952. It had the right since Mouton Rothschild was not an official First Growth, but it beggars belief when you taste the Baron's remarkable run of wines in the post-war period. The decision lit the touchpaper for Baron Philippe's campaign. The proposal, which was discussed in secret meetings with the I.N.A.O. and Ministry of Agriculture, was not just to promote Mouton Rothschild, but for a revision of the entire classification, including the demotion of some estates. Baron Philippe had to navigate French bureaucracy, but eventually an agreement was reached to revise the 1855 classification level by level, commencing at the top. However, as Jean-Michel Cazes, whose family had much to gain as owner of Fifth Growth Lynch-Bages, told me, once the First Growths were revised in 1973 to finally include Mouton Rothschild, the Baron had achieved his goal and soon lost interest in pursuing the revision of other ranks. The petitioning quickly ran out of steam and Mouton Rothschild's promotion was the only alteration.

1970

The decade kicked off with what is widely regarded as the best vintage of the seventies, though as it turned out, the 1970 growing season was no portent.

The year began with a relatively warm January. February was slightly colder and March was benign with a couple of brief warm spells. The vines were reluctant to wake from their winter slumber, with Lawton reporting they were a fortnight behind their usual growth cycle. Bud break was around 28 March and then April saw a warm period when temperatures reached 26°C (79°F). It did not last long and the rest of the month was overcast and cooler. By May the vines were three weeks behind schedule, though the mercury had finally begun to rise and remained in the high twenties. It was just the encouragement the vines needed. Clement conditions continued into June and the first flowers speckled the landscape from around 5 June. A heat spike four days later saw a sweltering 36°C (97°F) and *pleine fleur* followed on 12 June. Flowering was even and regular and hopes were for an abundant crop after recent shortfalls. July was benevolent, warm with little rain, and the first three days of August were a balmy 30–32°C (86–90°F). Then on the afternoon of 4 August, at around 6 p.m., according to Lawton, a violent storm ripped through the region inflicting widespread damage. Six people died and there were numerous injuries. Somehow the vines survived relatively unscathed. The rest of the month was warm, with a welcome splash of rain around 20 August and no heat spikes.

September saw temperatures in the low thirties with potential must weights around 12.5%. Pickers entered vineyards on the Right Bank around 24 September and in the Médoc around four days later. The harvest took place over the next fortnight and finished around 13 October under favourable conditions with just a smattering of rain. "I have never seen such healthier, rounder grapes without a hint of rot anywhere," enthuses Edmund Penning-Rowsell. Châteaux were elated not just over the potential quality, but also the quantity since they had been deprived of a decent income. However, it is not a well-regarded vintage for Sauternes. The first passes through vineyard in late September were profitable, yet mid-October rains made the rest of the picking difficult. Nevertheless, at Yquem three-quarters of the production harvested in early November was used. Many cite 1970 as the first truly successful en primeur campaign in terms of sales and return, fuelled by compulsory château bottling that eradicated the confusing array of merchant bottling and burgeoning demand from the US.

In his essential *Grands Vins* tome, Clive Coates MW says the success of the 1970 vintage stems from the success of the Merlot, which counterbalanced the structure and firmness of the wines. I concur. In my experience, some of the traditionally more austere wines such as

Montrose come across as balanced and a little fleshier than their '66 counterparts. Much like the 1982s, when the 1970s were released some commentators doubted they would last because they were so flattering in their youth. This proved to be untrue.

Over the years, I have tasted most of the 1970s from the major châteaux, often multiple times. It is a vintage that cropped up regularly in my early days because prices were reasonable compared to 1961 and 1982. It is a good vintage, excellent in some places, though it would have been even better and more consistent if there had been stricter selection of the high-volume crop. It is also wise to remember that some famous names were hidebound to old methods that had often been carried out by the same winemaking teams since the post-war period. They were a bit stuck in their ways. Curiously, only the 1970 Latour is renowned among the First Growths and even that is notoriously inconsistent, some bottles magnificent and others rather fatigued. You never quite know what you will get. Château Mouton Rothschild, Lafite Rothschild and Haut-Brion are what you might call "solid" and lack the chutzpah of a truly great First Growth. The 1970 Château Margaux is substandard as the estate was languishing in the doldrums. Choice pickings are found in the lower ranks. On the Left Bank, seek out superb 1970s from Palmer, Ducru-Beaucaillou and Lynch-Bages, a splendid double-magnum of the latter poured at the château in December 2019 had miles left on the clock. Likewise, the 1970 Montrose, Pichon Comtesse de Lalande, Domaine de Chevalier (red and white) and Pape Clément all have plenty of staying power. Staying in Pessac-Léognan, this is one year in which La Mission Haut-Brion has the upper hand over Haut-Brion. Recent encounters suggest that some of the top 1970s on the Left Bank are beginning to fray at their edges, drying out on the finish.

Moving to the Right Bank, in Pomerol the standouts are a sublime 1970 Pétrus and a Trotanoy, though Vieux Château Certan has always failed to launch, Léon Thienpont taking his eye off the ball in this decade. Moving to Saint-Émilion, the 1970 Cheval Blanc was undervalued for a long time and I duly filled my boots, though I always thought Thierry Manoncourt conjured a superior Figeac. By contrast, I have found the 1970 Ausone rather threadbare. It is a vintage in which lesser-known names are worth investigating. I've derived a lot of pleasure from imbibing the likes of 1970 Château de Fieuzal, Bel Air-Marquis d'Aligré, Poujeaux, Greysac and Potensac, among others, in their fifth decade, most recently a square-jawed 1970 Labégorce. Sauternes is a little inconsistent. That said, the 1970 Climens might be low in residual sugar yet was pretty as a peach when served at a dinner in memory of Steven Spurrier in September 2021, perhaps superior to the 1970 Yquem.

1970

Event
Feminists disrupt
Miss World

Music
Bridge Over Troubled Water
– Simon & Garfunkel

At this time, Miss World was a major global event and enormous television draw. In 1970, the Royal Albert Hall swapped violins and cellos for bikinis and asinine questions to host the final, which was guest-compered by comedian Bob Hope. The run-up to the contest had already seen protests against apartheid-striven South Africa sending separate black and white contestants, the former representing the non-existent "Africa South". The pageant was televised live to 22 million viewers in the UK alone. At the sound of a football rattle, activists from the Women's Liberation Movement lobbed flour bombs, threw leaflets, let off stink bombs and heckled Hope, thankfully ending his cringeworthy "jokes". In a perverse twist of fate, the contest was won by Miss Grenada, Jennifer Hosten, the first woman of colour to win Miss World, with Miss Africa South runner-up.

In 1970 every home had a copy of the album *Bridge Over Troubled Water*. For the title track, Paul Simon infused gospel with Phil Spector's "Wall of Sound" production to create the duo's most hymnal, yet melodramatic anthem. The title came from an improvised line sung by Claude Jeter in the Swan Silvertones' version of *O Mary Don't You Weep* and Simon later handed Jeter a cheque for lifting his words. The song is exquisitely sung by Art Garfunkel after Simon told him he desired "that white choir boy voice", but he later rued gifting Garfunkel his most famous composition. The track topped the Billboard charts on 28 February 1970 for six weeks, but, alas, the duo's own troubled waters could not be bridged and it marked their swan song.

Film
*M*A*S*H* – Robert Altman

Donald Sutherland, Elliott Gould and Tom Skerritt star in Robert Altman's dark-humoured film about three surgeons working in the 4,077th Mobile Army Surgical Hospital during the Korean War. The film became known for its biting and often cruel satire, as well as Altman's novel use of overlapping dialogue and liberal improvisation. Altman asked his 14-year-old son Mike to compose the lyrics to the theme song *Suicide Is Painless* as he wanted something "dumb". The song was later used in the television series, which ran from 1972–83, and resulted in Altman Jr. earning far more in royalties than his father did for directing the movie.

We all have a soft spot for bottles that share our birth year. This is mine. Nevertheless, I remain impartial when I propound the virtues of 1971, but unlike the equally underestimated 1955 vintage, you really have to look in the right places.

The year started bitterly cold, with Lawton reporting a bone-chilling -8°C (17.5°F) in rural areas. February was wet and temperatures struggled to climb above freezing. The first half of March was also very cold, with -10°C (14°F) recorded on 6 to 8 March, warming slightly after. Belatedly, April saw signs of spring with the mercury reaching a balmy 23°C (73°F), provoking vines to sprint out of the blocks with rapid growth after budding on 30 March. Following a cool start, May experienced a spell of summer-like weather, though some estates reported infestations of red spiders. The remainder of the month was quite rainy, torrential at times, which made applying sulphur to limit the spread of rot difficult. The first flowers appeared around 1 June and though things were initially looking up, the weather deteriorated and it became rainy and cool. These unsettled conditions caused poor flowering and widespread coulure that particularly affected the Merlot, reducing the size of the potential crop to 40% below the previous year's. There were simply no dry windows in which growers could get out and protect the vines (much like in 2021). To make matters worse, hail damage in Pomerol on 14 June decimated around half the crop in major properties such as Trotanoy and Latour à Pomerol. Winemakers were despondent come the end of June, but that was all about to change. July and August witnessed clement and dry conditions, temperatures hovering in the high twenties and low thirties. The weather only broke on 24 and 25 August when a violent storm deluged the region, with hail in Pessac-Léognan depriving Haut-Brion and La Mission Haut-Brion of around 15% of their crop. *Véraison* was unable to even out the ripeness between bunches, but hopes were still high for a small but high-quality crop.

September began well with just light showers, but the 19th and 21st saw a series of violent storms and localised hail. These rains divided winemakers into two groups: the lucky ones who had picked their earlier ripening Merlot before the first spots of rain and those with later-ripening Cabernets, most of whom only started picking from 27 September once vineyards had dried out. The Merlots reached a respectable 11.5–12% in terms of potential alcohol, though there was some rot to parse out. Alas, rain had already spoiled the wines on the Left Bank once picking finished around 12 October. Many 1971s were afflicted by low fixed acidity levels due to the hot summer weather and were unable to last the distance. Quantities were 40% below those of the previous year – Lynch-Bages reported a measly 15 hl/ha, albeit due to missing vines that were not being replaced.

Sauternes enjoyed a very benevolent growing season. The hot and dry summer conditions followed by September rains provoked botrytis infection, though the harvest was delayed until the beginning of October and yields were minuscule. Yquem squeezed out a measly 5 hl/ha of intense fruit, despite its hard-working pickers making 11 passes through the vines in their presumedly increasingly exasperated search for botrytised fruit.

It is perceived as a weak Bordeaux vintage because the barometer of quality, the Left Bank, struggled to produce many wines of note. Yet as soon as you travel beyond the Médoc, as close as the Right Bank or as far as Australia, you find 1971 to be a treasure trove of extremely fine and long-lasting wines. Though I might be accused of being partisan, if you know where to look, this vintage can delight.

Having tasted a bevy of 1971 Bordeaux, I should commence where the vintage excelled: in Pomerol. Several bottles of the 1971 Pétrus and Trotanoy have been magnificent, although I have encountered more than my fair share of corked examples of the latter. If you ever wonder why you see few bottles of 1971 Pétrus, it is because Christian Moueix served the wine at his wedding reception. I hope his guests appreciated the gesture. Other Pomerol wines that deserve applause include the 1971 La Fleur-Pétrus, opened *chez moi* upon reaching half a century after a generous friend dispatched two bottles to me during the Covid-19 lockdown. Latour à Pomerol, La Fleur de Gay, Le Gay and, most recently, the last original bottle of 1971 Clos du Clocher residing in owner Jean-Baptiste Bourotte's cellar have all been wonderful. The 1971 Vieux Château Certan shows the 1970 how it should be done and continues to shine. Not everything came up roses in Pomerol. Neither l'Église-Clinet nor La Conseillante were firing on all cylinders at that time, while the Robin sisters dropped a catch at Lafleur. In Saint-Émilion, several bottles of 1971 Cheval Blanc disputed some poor scores from critics and I duly picked up many for a song. Figeac is also superb, lighting up a vertical in Paris where I praised its "controlled opulence" in front of a stellar gathering of wine writers. Proprietor Thierry Manoncourt beamed and Michael Broadbent nodded in approval. I felt as if I had passed a test.

Another area of Bordeaux that delivered vinous gems is Sauternes. I've rubbed a few noses the wrong way by proclaiming the 1971 Yquem superior to the '67, but that's because it just is. The good news is you can taste far and wide and stump your toe on many exceptional Sauternes. My personal pick is the crystalline 1971 Coutet, while others that have left indelible impressions include a fabulous Climens, Doisy-Daëne and Château de Fargues.

On the Left Bank, the reality is that only a handful of wines are worth seeking out. Top of the shopping list is 1971 Latour, a bona fide great First Growth and superior to Mouton Rothschild and Lafite Rothschild, which tend to be dry and austere. Elsewhere, four bottles of 1971 Palmer have been utterly divine and my last bottle at the property in March 2022 suggested that it can surpass the 1970. Alternatively, travel down to Pessac-Léognan. Two or three bottles of 1971 La Tour Haut-Brion have amazed, the first served blind at a sushi bar in Tokyo and a second in London confirming that it can surpass a very decent La Mission Haut-Brion. A bottle of 1971 Haut-Bailly opened at the estate in summer 2021 retained vigour even if it was leaning on the herbaceous side. Better was a rustic yet concentrated 1971 Les Carmes Haut-Brion – the last-but-one bottle at the château cracked open by Guillaume Pouthier. Two bottles of 1971 La Lagune opened around December 2021 proved that this was a dark horse for the Médoc estate, while the 1971 Montrose acquitted itself admirably at yet another delayed, post-lockdown bacchanal. Elsewhere, tread carefully because many of the most reputed Left Bank châteaux produced dry and austere wines, including Cos d'Estournel, Lynch-Bages and Pichon Baron, among others.

Film
Dirty Harry – Don Siegel

"You've got to ask yourself one question. Do I feel lucky? Well, do you, punk?" snarls Clint Eastwood pointing the most powerful handgun in the world at a foiled bank robber. *Dirty Harry* is Eastwood's first and best outing as cynical Inspector Harry Callahan, on the trail of a homicidal, cherub-faced sniper around San Francisco. Inspired by the real-life Zodiac killer, the film was lambasted for sensationalising violence, its portrayal of police brutality and blurred moral lines. Nevertheless, it made for compelling viewing and sealed Eastwood's tough-guy image, not least as he performed many of his own stunts.

1971
(Continued)

1870

2020

1971
(Continued)

Event
Intel unveils the world's first microprocessor

In March 1971, fledgling tech company Intel released the 4004, the world's first microprocessor. Three engineers worked on this minor side project, a commission for a new calculator manufactured by a company called Busicom. The project had ground to a halt the previous year because Intel specialised in memory chips and lacked the necessary knowhow, so a fourth engineer, Federico Faggin, was hired to create the microprocessor without any support staff. Realising the potential of its new product, Intel wisely re-negotiated its contract with Busicom to sell the microprocessor itself. "Announcing a new era in integrated electronics" proclaimed the advertising blurb and that is exactly what it was – a new era.

Music
Stairway to Heaven
– Led Zeppelin

From the moment they plugged in their amps and first jammed together in a basement in Gerrard Street, Led Zeppelin were the world's best rock band. The musical roots of *Stairway to Heaven* originate from a night when Robert Plant and Jimmy Page were residing at a remote Welsh cottage, Bron-Yr-Aur. Plant completed most of the Tolkienesque lyrics the following night around a log fire at Headley Grange while Page strummed the chords. He recorded three guitar solos on his 1959 Fender Telecaster and agonised over which one to use. When the group debuted *Stairway to Heaven* on 5 March 1971, the audience were "bored to tears", according to John Paul Jones in a BBC Radio 2 interview. Adhering to Led Zeppelin's anti-45rpm stance, it was never released as a single, but remains their signature tune.

Nineteen seventy-two was the first of three successive vintages that put the kibosh on Bordeaux.

January and February were showery but not particularly cold, then temperatures began rising in March, reaching 20°C (68°F), and coaxing vines out of their winter dormancy. The first shoots were spotted around 25 March. April was rainy, but the vines were already three weeks in advance of their normal growth cycle. Thankfully, there was no frost when temperatures dipped in April. Temperatures recovered but unsettled conditions throughout May retarded vines' growth, Tastet-Lawton noting on 17 May that it had not been this cold at this time of year since 1955. Things warmed up towards the end of the month and into June, but slow progress meant that flowering did not occur until 7 June. Swings in temperature caused uneven flowering, so a small crop was on the cards, but a settled and warm July meant that winemakers began to look on the bright side, despite coulure and millerandage. August began warm, with temperatures reaching 34°C (93°F). A series of storms and hail traversed the region between 10 and 13 August, after which temperatures tumbled to 22–23°C (71.5–73°F) and impeded *véraison*. "It rained throughout the harvest," Jean Merlaut rued when broaching his Gruaud Larose during one of its astonishing verticals. "The vineyard was so wet that a…[he hesitates to find an appropriate adjective] 'stout' female harvest worker got stuck. It took two workers to carry her to the end of the row and her boots still stuck in the mud."

Clearly, it would be a late October harvest and a much-needed prolonged warm and dry spell was not forthcoming. Picking finally began around 9 October – not until 14 October for some, according to Edmund Penning-Rowsell – under rather showery conditions. These weren't heavy, but were enough to dampen spirits until some belated autumnal warmth of 22°C (71.5°F) on 17 and 18 October. The last pickers came in around 22 October, but as late as early November in some places. Volumes were up to 20% higher than the previous year but irregular in quality. "The must was so rotten that it was chocolate-coloured," recalled Jean Merlaut. "There was no temperature regulation and the stainless-steel tanks were simply wrapped in cloth. People asked me if the wine was red or rosé." Not for the first time, nor the last, release prices paid little heed to quality and David Peppercorn does not mince his words when he comments that "the wine trade allowed itself to be sucked into a vortex of buying at absurd prices."

Sauternes likewise endured a miserable season after the poor August, which precluded ripening, and a lack of rain from 2 September to 15 November, which prevented botrytis formation. According to its records, Yquem only made 10 barrels and presumably kept them for private use.

1972
(Continued)

I have not tasted many 1972 clarets. A 1972 La Mission Haut-Brion was "fungal and funky" when encountered in 2009. Better was an ember-scented 1972 Château de Pez poured blind by Harry Gill of London restaurant The Arches in 2020, as was an unapologetically rustic 1972 Lafleur a couple of years earlier. The 1972 La Conseillante was ferrous and frail in 2010 at the vertical organised for my Pomerol tome and the death rattle emanating from a 1972 Ausone was clearly audible. The best red might well be a 1972 Léoville Barton from a Bristol cellar: a tad under-ripe yet crisp and transparent after half a century. The finest Bordeaux I have encountered is the 1972 Laville Haut-Brion Blanc, so complex and fresh in 2017 and arguably more enjoyable than all the other '72s combined. I have drunk several Sauternes, including 1972 Suduiraut and Climens, though both showed a shortfall in sweetness and freshness.

Event
Bobby Fischer wins the World Chess Championship

On 11 July 1972, Bobby Fischer took on defending champion Boris Spassky of the Soviet Union in the World Chess Championship in Reykjavík, Iceland. The Soviets had held the title since 1948 and the match was played out as a proxy battle for the Cold War. Fischer was an eccentric prodigy and failed to attend the opening ceremony, threatening to withdraw from what the media dubbed the "Match of the Century". Henry J. Kissinger purportedly telephoned and persuaded Fischer to continue in what was surely one of his most challenging diplomatic tasks. Over 21 games between July and September, Fischer beat Spassky 12½ to 8½, rocketing Fischer to global celebrity status. He declined all ensuing endorsement offers and refused to compete again for two decades, opting for a reclusive life punctured by the occasional unwelcome antisemitic remark.

Music
Ziggy Stardust
– David Bowie

His rise to stardom might have been contemporaneous with glam rock, but Bowie's preternatural creativity and extraordinary vision made him more influential than any other solo artist before or since. Ziggy Stardust, the androgynous Martian with a shock of red hair, was Bowie's most famous alter ego, landing on planet Earth on 29 January 1972 in the modest surroundings of Aylesbury's Borough Assembly Hall. His band the Spiders from Mars were tentative about dressing up in outlandish garb until they saw the audience's ecstatic reaction. Their second gig was at the Toby Jug pub in London, witnessed by author Stephen King and around 60 others. Fame lay just around the corner. Soon, the starman was shocking parents by daring to put his arm around guitarist Mick Ronson's shoulders on *Top of the Pops* and laying the foundations of the post-Beatles pop landscape.

Film
The Godfather
– Francis Ford Coppola

Marlon Brando stuffed his cheeks with cotton wool and perfected a rasping voice to bring cinema's most famous mafia boss, "Don" Vito Corleone, to life. Coppola was constantly fighting off Paramount Pictures during filming. After seeing early rushes, the studio tried to have him fired and replaced by Elia Kazan, but Brando threatened to quit if it did. Several of Coppola's family appear in the movie, including three-week-old Sofia, who plays the baby baptised during its bloody climax and would go on to direct my film choice for 2004 (page 435). *The Godfather* triumphed at the Oscars the following year: Brando won best actor despite having barely an hour's screen time – far less than Al Pacino, who was inexplicably overlooked.

1973

Examining the weather conditions, 1973 ought to be one of the best growing seasons of the decade. So why does it have such a poor reputation?

The 1973 vintage began with a cold but not freezing January, and February followed in similar fashion. Spring arrived mid-March, which was drier than usual. The cold spell continued into April, retarding the growth cycle and the first shoots were only seen around 10 April. Cold mornings combined with dry conditions continued to slow down their growth. Early May saw temperatures pick up, but a violent storm on 1 May unleashed hail that decimated Sauternes and many estates lost 50–75% of their potential crop. The rest of the month compensated for the previous cold weather, with temperatures in the high twenties and up to 32°C (90°F) as June approached. The first flowers were spotted around 2 or 3 June and settled, warm conditions ensured the flowering was even and not drawn out. With no coulure or millerandage, a large volume was on the cards. July raised hopes of a very good vintage, warm temperatures expediting vines' growth to compensate for the stuttering early season. August was more of the same, temperatures between 26–30°C (79–86°F) with plenty of sunshine. Lawton notes at the end of the month that a high-quality vintage was expected. What's the saying? Don't count your chickens before they're hatched.

September began perfectly with five hot days at 33°C (91°F), though by now the vines were showing signs of hydric stress. Some relief came with heavy rainfall on 8 and 9 September with hail in Fronsac and then it all began falling apart between the 17th and 23rd when downpours swept across the region. Some panicking winemakers hurried out into vineyards as soon as it stopped, especially on the Right Bank. Most of the Left Bank was picked in the first couple of weeks of October and the weather was fine save for a couple of showery mornings. In Sauternes, after a difficult season, pickers had a very brief window to seek botrytised fruit in the first half of October and few berries exhibited adequate concentration. Yquem managed to make a small late pass through the vines around 1 November, otherwise it was a bit of a wash-out.

This is a vintage where you must examine context. The ongoing oil crisis had withered wine markets and prices for Bordeaux plummeted. Châteaux had little financial resources and in trying to replenish their coffers, pursued excessively high yields, aided and abetted by salesmen who inveigled vineyard managers to use chemicals and fertilisers. The high yields literally diluted quality. I wager that had this growing season occurred later, when yields were controlled and there was more selection, 1973 would have been a memorable vintage. I have tasted just a handful of 1973s and generally, if forced to choose, I might opt for the prior vintage. Without question, the best is the 1973 Pétrus, which I have tasted two or three times, the final time blind at the inaugural

Grouse Club lunch. I was taken aback by its effortless refinement, as if the wine was giving me a wink to say "Bet you weren't expecting that". I also remember a half-decent 1973 La Fleur-Pétrus at The Arches in Swiss Cottage, where I offered a glass to a Master of Wine at the next table, who was offended I was presenting him with such a bad vintage. The 1973 La Conseillante was dusty and decrepit at the vertical at Chez Bruce in London in November 2010 and the 1973 Ausone just bland. The 1973 Latour at the Académie du Vin dinner in Bordeaux, served from double magnum, had an odd kidney-bean note, big-boned tannins and a slightly astringent finish, far better than a 1973 Le Pauillac de Latour that should have been opened four decades earlier. The 1973 La Mission Haut-Brion was as musty as a cobwebbed attic while a 1973 Gruaud Larose was duller than dishwater. In Sauternes, after failing to release a wine the previous year, Yquem did put one out in 1973 and yet it still struggles to give pleasure. My one positive note is for a 1973 Coutet served at dinner in June 2021, which I initially and foolishly dismissed before it magically cohered and gained substance after a couple of hours.

Event

OPEC places embargo
on oil supply

In October 1973, the Arab members of OPEC decided to place an oil embargo against any nation that they felt had supported Israel during the Yom Kippur War, quadrupling the barrel price of crude oil. This triggered a downturn in stock markets – the UK stock exchange lost 73% of its value. Overnight, there were long queues at petrol stations as fear swept across Western nations that oil would be rationed for the foreseeable future. Though the embargo was lifted the following March, ripples from the economic shock lasted throughout the decade as nations contended with high inflation and interest rates.

1973
(Continued)

Music
Higher Ground
– Stevie Wonder

Twelve-year-old prodigy Stevland Hardaway Morris, or Stevie Wonder as he is better known, had burst onto the music scene with the infectious *Fingertips* back in 1962. Having penned countless Motown classics for himself and others, Wonder reached a lofty creative plateau in the seventies, blending soul, funk and prototype synthesisers. Taken from his album *Innervisions*, *Higher Ground* was laid down in a three-hour creative burst in May 1973. Wonder played all the instruments, including a Moog synthesiser – the source of the song's unmistakable wah-wah bass-line. The lyrics concern rebirth, being given a second chance. "It was almost as if I had to get it done," he told *Q* magazine. Three months after recording *Higher Ground*, Wonder got his own second chance after a near-fatal car accident in North Carolina left him in a four-day coma.

Film
The Exorcist
– William Friedkin

Released on Boxing Day 1973 in the US, *The Exorcist* is both a horror classic and a runaway box-office success. Apparently, Linda Blair's expletive-filled delivery as the possessed girl shocked Max von Sydow so much that he forgot his lines. With the film's demonic growling, projectile vomiting, spinning heads, inappropriate use of crucifixes and edge-of-your-seat exorcisms, paramedics were constantly being called to cinemas to attend fainting audience members. Not even Mike Oldfield's hypnotic score could soothe them. Despite the subject matter, *The Exorcist* remains Warner's highest-grossing film to date (adjusted for inflation), and won William Peter Blatty, who wrote the original novel, an Oscar for Best Adapted Screenplay.

This was the third successive poor vintage, a repeat of the early thirties.

After a rather ordinary start to the year, March began overcast and changeable before improving in the second half of the month. April was also unsettled and included a skirmish with frost in Saint-Julien. May started wet before frost affected parts of the Médoc on the 8 May. Temperatures rebounded, reaching 28°C (82°F), which encouraged rapid vine growth. Flowering began around 1 June, concurrent with three blissfully sunny days, with *pleine fleur* on 10 June. By the end of the month, hopes were high and July raised them higher with warm weather that peaked at 35°C (95°F) before gradually falling. By August, the vines were beginning to show signs of heat stress and this slowed down *véraison*. There was relief when it finally rained on the 30 and 31 August and into the first days of September.

The mercury rose again throughout the month and the Bordelais were all set for a great vintage until 21 September. The heavens opened and it poured, dissuading châteaux from sending out their pickers and risking rot. The first ventured out on 24 September on the Right Bank and the Graves. Most of the pickers were out by 30 September but the weather stayed inclement, raining the entire day on 3 October and fog lingering the day after. Lawton, writing during the harvest, felt that the rains would affect those vineyards with Merlot more than Cabernet. As the harvest drew to a close, pickers had to contend with abnormally cold mornings, down to a chilly -1°C (30°F) on 15 October. September and October downpours washed away hopes of a vintage that might have compensated for the previous two years and much of the fruit was diluted. The vinification was as challenging as the growing season. "We had problems with everything," Jean-Michel Cazes rued when I blasphemed and mentioned 1974 at Lynch-Bages. But given the same weather conditions, I am certain that superior wines could have been made using contemporary techniques, not least piecemeal picking by parcel and greater selection. Even if producers had been willing, there was just no financial incentive at the time. Sauternes experienced another dire season in which Yquem declassified its wine after 35 consecutive days of rain in October. Attempts were made to pick on 26 October and even into December, but by then it was too late.

I have tasted very few wines from this vintage and most offer about as much pleasure as walking barefoot across needles. The best were several half-decent bottles of 1974 La Mission Haut-Brion, listed at The Arches for peanuts back in the day, and better than a moribund Haut-Brion when juxtaposed one lunchtime. The 1974 Montrose was thin and weedy after 42 years, clearly showing dilution at two verticals. On the Right Bank, neither the 1974 Ausone or La Conseillante passed muster.

1974
(Continued)

Event
President Nixon resigns after Watergate

On 8 August 1974, President Richard Nixon (a Lynch-Bages fan, according to Jean-Michel Cazes) resigned in disgrace after the Supreme Court ordered him to hand over tapes of conversations in the Oval Office. These would make him complicit in the June 1972 break-in at the opposition party's Democratic National Committee headquarters in the Watergate complex to steal sensitive documents and bug telephones. *Washington Post* reporters Bob Woodward and Carl Bernstein uncovered the espionage with the help of a whistle-blower known as Deep Throat, winning a Pulitzer Prize for their investigation. The crime and the cover-up led to a distrust of politicians that you could argue lingers to this day.

Music
Waterloo
– ABBA

Since 1966, Agnetha, Frida, Benny and Björn had enjoyed domestic success in Sweden as solo artists or members of other groups before forming ABBA. On 6 April 1974 they scattered pop glitter across the world singing *Waterloo* at the Eurovision Song Contest in Brighton. Composed at their island cottage on Viggsö just outside Stockholm, like *Bridge Over Troubled Water* (page 310), the song was influenced by Phil Spector's dramatic Wall of Sound and added some glam-rock stomp. *Waterloo* was not an automatic choice. The band had also considered a wistful ballad, *Hasta Mañana*, which was more in line with Eurovision tradition, but eventually went with their gut, becoming the first winners not to sing in their native language. Their garb was so outlandish that security stopped Benny and Björn from going on stage to accept the award, refusing to believe they were the song's composers. *Waterloo* launched ABBA's career and changed perceptions among British music writers who looked down their noses at "trashy" European music. Though neither of the inter-band marriages survived, the group's canon of pristine pop songs are more popular ever.

Film
Chinatown
– Roman Polanski

Jack Nicholson puts in a career-
defining performance as hard-
boiled private eye J.J. Gittes in
this neo-noir thriller set in 1937
Los Angeles. The actor appears in
every scene and even contributed
some of his own dialogue to
Robert Towne's impeccable,
Oscar-winning screenplay, partly
based on the San Fernando Valley
land grab. Gittes' investigation
is like peeling away layers of a
rotten onion until it reaches its
bleak ending. Polanski has a
cameo as the assailant who cuts
Gittes' nose, leaving him wearing
an unsightly plaster for most of
the movie.

1975

This vintage is held in higher regard than others between 1970 and 1982, though you could argue that it is the best of a bad bunch, both literally and figuratively.

The year began warmer than usual. March commenced warm and rainy, freshening from the 11th with temperatures falling to freezing-point as April neared. Some areas were under a thin blanket of snow on the final day of the month. Bud break was around 28 March but frost damage over the next two days affected the Merlot and Malbec. Both these varieties had been quick out of the blocks, though damage was less severe than in 1977. The mercury rose considerably with summer-like temperatures giving impetus to vine growth but May began fresh, with some hail damage in Saint-Estèphe on 17 May. Then three days later, summer seemed to come early with a balmy 28°C (82°F). Flowering began around 2 June and was completed in 10 or 11 days under clement conditions, with temperatures in the mid-twenties. A large crop was in the reckoning. July was dry and hot, temperatures gradually increasing to 35°C (95°F) by the end of the month and to 38°C (100°F) at the beginning of August. The conditions began to take their toll as vines started suffering heat stress, though thunderstorms on 7 and 9 August brought deluges that quenched parched throats. It remained hot for the first 10 days of the month before Mother Nature turned the gas down to an ideal 25–28°C (77–82°F). Would September spoil the party?

It began well enough, though there were storms in Saint-Émilion on 6 September and heavy downpours six days later. That was enough water. Someone needed to turn the tap off. Nobody got the memo and rain kept coming down, prompting influential consultant and professor Émile Peynaud to advise châteaux to expedite picking since a quantity of rain equivalent to the entire average for September had fallen in just five days. A dry and warm spell followed between 18 and 25 September and the first pickers headed out into the vines from 22 September, then en masse three days later. Potential alcohol levels looked promising, around 12% and 12.5% in the Merlots, though predicted quantities were down on previous estimates – by as much as 40% in Pomerol. Lawton was still optimistic in the final week of September as clement and warm weather prevailed, but at around five o'clock on 29 September, a violent storm smashed through the Médoc, hail strafing Listrac, Moulis and Arcins, with severely affected vineyards losing up to 70% of their fruit at the final furlong. The weather improved in the first week of October, allowing berries to gain must weight lost as a result of the 216 mm (8½ in) of rain that had soaked Bordeaux throughout August and September. The harvest finished around 5 and 6 October under good conditions.

Proprietors and merchants alike were optimistic about the potential of 1975. "Roger Mau was still the cellar-master at Lynch-Bages," Jean-Michel Cazes explained. "I remember him saying to me: 'Look at the grapes. Look twice because you will not see the same quality in your life.'" But few appreciated how the summer heat had thickened berries' skins disproportionately to physiological ripeness and the fact that some Left Bank châteaux had harvested their Cabernet prematurely. The lack of de-stemming machines simply exacerbated wines' astringency. François Thienpont told me that barrel-ageing the 1975s was problematic because the volatility kept going up, possibly due to the late harvest and lack of sulphur. Thinner-skinned Merlots with their fleshier constitution, in Saint-Émilion and Pomerol, among others, produced superior wines than the austere Médocs. After three consecutive poor years, Sauternes winemakers enjoyed a benevolent season. Rain in September provoked botrytis formation on grapes that had been concentrated by the summer warmth and though not huge in quantity, what had botrytised was intense and high quality. Many regarded it as the benchmark Sauternes vintage of the decade.

This vintage divided opinion for many years. Professor Émile Peynaud talked it up as one of the greatest ever while others expressed doubts, counter-arguing that many '75s were excessively tannic and dried out. Over the years, I have tasted many bottles and unquestionably this is a Right Bank vintage. Pomerol in particular boasts a cluster of fabulous wines. Several bottles of the 1975 Pétrus have been magnificent – winemaker Jean-Claude Berrouet once told me that it was the first Pétrus that he felt matched his vision. I polished off a bottle at The Fat Duck in Bray to celebrate my wife's milestone birthday in one of those "if not now, then when" moments. The memories are far more valuable than what I could have sold it for. The 1975 Lafleur is dense, rustic but utterly compelling, while the 1975 Trotanoy vies with the 1970 and 1971 as the best of the early seventies. A magnum of 1975 La Fleur-Pétrus in Holland was a peach, though La Conseillante, yet to fulfil its potential, is its best effort of the decade. Saint-Émilion also boasts a fine 1975 Cheval Blanc and a beautifully sculpted Figeac, but neither quite delivers the heady highs of the finest Pomerols.

The Left Bank is notorious for its astringent wines, the fruit drying out before the tannins had polymerised. It's not a write-off like 1973 or 1974, but tread carefully. The First Growths are quite austere: the 1975 Haut-Brion is the best since it contains more Merlot, while the 1975 Latour is tertiary and a bit charmless, and the 1975 Mouton Rothschild is dry and a little rustic. These are all eclipsed by the fêted 1975 La Mission Haut-Brion, beatified by Robert Parker. It's not a vintage I have drunk often and maybe I have been unlucky, but personally I have always preferred the 1978. Elsewhere, I have had decent bottles of 1975 Pichon-Lalande and Lynch-Bages, but others have been dried out in bottle – examples of what could have been. Much better to head down to Sauternes, which produced some great wines, including the noble 1975 Yquem and unctuous Climens, though generally I find them slightly less consistent than their 1976 counterparts.

1975
(Continued)

1870

2020

1975
(Continued)

Event
VCR recorders enter
living rooms

You can trace streaming back to the start of home video recording. Sony introduced the first Betamax machine, the LV-1901, in Japan before shipping it to the US from 10 May 1975 – the first time such technology had been aimed at households rather than media professionals. The price-tag was a wallet-busting $2,495 although that came with a television and de rigueur teak cabinet. A few months later, Sony introduced its first standalone machine. Adverts promised "an end to the war of the channels" and "the beginning of peace in the family". Since few pre-recorded films existed, VCRs were mainly used to record shows from terrestrial TV. JVC swiftly responded with its VHS recorders, which ultimately usurped Betamax and other formats, aided by slick marketing and cheaper prices. The porn industry's preference for VHS also purportedly helped it on its path to dominance, though the marketing department probably advised the company not to crow about that.

Music
Bohemian Rhapsody
– Queen

All four members of Queen were gifted songwriters, but Freddie Mercury had the chutzpah to realise his musical vision, even though he remained ambiguous about the meaning of its lyrics. Three weeks were spent over-dubbing the operatic mid-section on a 24-track machine. In various interviews, guitarist Brian May remembered how the tape was almost transparent by the time Mercury came to producer Roy Thomas Baker with the immortal line: "I've got a few more Galileos for you dear." *Bohemian Rhapsody* came in at just under six minutes and commercial radio baulked at play-listing the song. Capital Radio's maverick DJ Kenny Everett, a close friend of Mercury, thought otherwise and played it 14 times in two days. It quickly gained traction and spent nine weeks at the top of the UK charts, returning to the top again in 1992 after featuring in the film *Wayne's World*, though Mercury had tragically succumbed to AIDS the year before.

Film
The Rocky Horror Picture Show
– Jim Sharman

The Rocky Horror Picture Show
takes place in a haunted house
full of cross-dressing oddballs
– a bit like a professional wine
tasting with a splash more
gender fluidity. Clean-cut
newlyweds Barry and Janet
(Susan Sarandon and Barry
Bostwick) stumble into the
house and meet the outrageous
Dr. Frank-N-Furter, played by
Tim Curry, who apparently
based his enunciation on
the Queen and his mother's
telephone voice. The musical's
writer Richard O'Brien plays
butler Riff Raff and a pre-fame
Meat Loaf reprises his theatre
role as fated delivery boy Eddie.
Filmed near Bray, home of the
aforementioned Fat Duck, the
movie initially flopped. But a
few months later, the Waverly
Theater in New York began a
series of midnight showings
that attracted a devout legion
of outsiders who revelled in its
campness and catchy songs. The
film became as interactive as the
original theatre production, with
its shout-outs, food throwing,
and dressing up in suspenders to
do the Time Warp (again).

1976

On paper the 1976 Bordeaux vintage should have been one of the greatest of the decade. It wasn't.

January was below freezing and February wet, improving towards the end of the month to put vine growth ahead of schedule. The landscape was flecked with green leaves from around 25 March. Encouraged by warm temperatures, the vines galloped ahead during May, energised by intermittent rain. The first flowers were seen early, around the 30th, thanks to the warm and clement conditions. Flowering passed quickly and evenly, raising hopes for a large crop. But there was some consternation about the dry conditions and as temperatures bobbed along in the mid-thirties there was little relief. At the end of June, the Tastet-Lawton archives note that it had been one of the driest since the beginning of the century. July remained hot, triggering convectional storms that led to hail in Pessac-Léognan, with up to 20% damage reported at Haut-Brion. The rain was much-needed, but afterwards temperatures remained in the high twenties with a heat spike of up to 40°C (104°F) in the city of Bordeaux on 15 July when the berries were changing hue. By early August, it was clear that vines were suffering due to drought and many shut down. Finally, there was heavy rainfall across the Médoc on 23 August, but the ensuing cool and wet conditions caused rot to rip through vineyards, affecting the Merlot in particular. By the end of August the vines had sucked up water – perhaps due to the dry conditions earlier in the season – so that berries became swollen and concentration was diluted. Bruno Borie of Ducru-Beaucaillou told me that his father Jean-Eugène Borie just looked out of his window to survey four days of constant rain.

Harvest began around 13 September under good conditions with just the occasional shower and picking was wrapped up by 28 or 29 September. The berries were thick-skinned due to the summer heat, resulting in tannic wines with low fixed acidity. Like the previous year, the bright spot is Sauternes. Rain on 15 September provoked widespread botrytis, prompting pickers at Yquem to harvest for some 22 days. Further rainy episodes simply yielded more botrytised fruit, allowing pickers to finish after only two passes through the vineyard.

The 1976 does not boast a great reputation since the heat and dryness followed by the torrential rain compromised the quality of fruit. They are sometimes described as "doughnut" wines insofar as they feel a bit hollow. That said, one should not dismiss the vintage outright. On the Left Bank, the most successful wine in my experience has been the Montecristo-scented 1976 Lafite Rothschild, which showed a little more elegance and flesh compared to others on the Left Bank, such as 1976 Montrose, Cos d'Estournel, Palmer and Pichon Comtesse de Lalande, four top estates whose wines just lack fruit and vigour. Two or three bottles of the 1976 Ducru-Beaucaillou were passable around the turn of the millennium, though my last at the property in 2021 was a bit dour and drying on the finish. The 1976 Haut-Bailly offered a modicum of pleasure at 40 years of age but again felt dry on the finish, though it was preferable to the 1976 Haut-Brion served on the same evening. On the Right Bank, the 1976 Ausone is easily the best in the era prior to the Vauthier family's sole proprietorship.

The rough-hewn 1976 Lafleur pales against its 1975 or 1978, while the 1976 Beau-Séjour Bécot and La Conseillante are long past their peaks. If you must insist on a 1976, head down to Sauternes. The 1976 Yquem tussles with the 1971 as the best of the decade and continues to dish out pleasure, as do the vivacious Climens and de Fargues. I have fond memories of a tangy chlorophyll-tinged Nairac, though it must be said that some, such as Suduiraut and Filhot, seem to have dried out in recent years.

Film
Taxi Driver
– Martin Scorsese

Robert De Niro plays Travis Bickle, the delusional Vietnam veteran and loner who becomes obsessed about cleaning up the "cesspool" of New York. De Niro worked long shifts driving cabs to prepare for the role, staying in character during production and ad-libbing the iconic "You talkin' to me?" mirror scene, the phrase purportedly inspired by a Bruce Springsteen concert. Jodie Foster was just 12 years old when she played teenage prostitute Iris and was too young to attend the premier of the R-rated movie in Cannes. She never heard the boos of an audience unprepared for Scorsese's unflinching, hard-hitting film, which helped launch his stellar career.

1976
(Continued)

Event
Concorde takes to the skies

Concorde made its first commercial flight on 21 January 1976. The joint-venture between British Airways and Air France to build a supersonic passenger aircraft began in 1962 and had made a successful transatlantic crossing in 1973. Two flights took off at exactly the same time that January morning: a BA flight from London to Bahrain and an Air France plane whisking passengers to Rio de Janeiro via Dakar. The double delta-wing craft with its drooping nose was a marvellous sight. The nose expanded 15–25 cm (6–10 in) in flight due to the heat generated and had to be coated in special paint. Crossing the Atlantic in three hours, Concorde was a symbol of success and 14 aircraft entered service. The small fleet meant that servicing and spare parts because exorbitantly expensive and after one burst into flames upon take-off in Paris in 2000, its days were numbered. The last flight took place on 24 October 2003. The supersonic era was over.

Music
Anarchy in the UK
– Sex Pistols

The Sex Pistols imploded after just a couple of years and one album. But their music and attitude drew a line in the sand and helped countless musicians realise that you didn't need to simultaneously play three keyboards while dressed as a wizard to be a musician. When Queen dropped out of a television interview on Bill Grundy's *Today* programme on 1 December 1976, the teatime slot was misguidedly filled with the Pistols and their entourage. Responding to Grundy's goading questions with expletive-ridden ripostes, they made front-page news: "The Filth and the Fury!" ran the headlines. Their debut single *Anarchy in the UK* sounded dangerous, political, anti-establishment, chaotic, splenetic, but at the same time intelligent and poetic. An antidote to the excess and posturing of bloated seventies rock, the controversy, gleefully engineered by manager Malcolm McLaren, lit the touchpaper for a musical and cultural revolution.

The nadir of a wretched decade? Step forward '77.

After a cold January and changeable February, March saw the mercury reach 23°C (73°F), encouraging vines out of dormancy. Winemakers became concerned that early budding, around 5 March, risked frost damage and the nights of 29 and 30 March saw temperatures dip to -3°C (26.5°F) and -4°C (25°F). Thankfully, a brisk wind prevented frost. But they were not out of the woods and the following night saw temperatures tumble to -5°C (23°F). It was the most widespread frost since 1945 and destroyed up to two-thirds of nascent buds. The earlier-budding Merlot was acutely affected, meaning the Right Bank took the brunt, while many Sauternes estates lost one-third of their crop. The first half of April remained cold, with heavy snow reported at Latour on 9 and 10 April, warming up in the second half for the Queen Mother's visit to Mouton Rothschild. I wonder if she requested a glass of sherry? May was rainy and cool, retarding vines' growth cycle, as if they knew what was in store. Clement weather in early June revitalised some vineyards during flowering, which was very late, around 15 June, but it was a brief respite as ensuing cold weather led to uneven flowering and widespread coulure. July was continually wet and by now, even the most optimistic winemakers had written off the vintage as they strived to tackle oidium and mildew. Latour required 15 sprays to prevent rot compared with the usual 8 to 10. Temperatures struggled throughout August, which was interrupted by occasional violent storms, making *véraison* slow and tardy.

September was drier and warmer, although the dry conditions merely reduced potential yields even further. Haut-Brion began picking its whites on 3 October and the reds three days later, the same as Lafite Rothschild where Éric de Rothschild had just taken the helm. Most châteaux were out harvesting on 7 October and predictably it pelted down with rain the following day. Harvest was quick because of diminished quantities and most had completed by 18 October, ironically under ideal warm and dry conditions. Must weights were predictably low, between 10–11%, so many wines were heavily chaptalised. Tasting barrel-samples the following spring, a charitable Lawton opines that they missed a little maturity and roundness. In Sauternes, it was a late harvest, though few berries had adequate sugar levels. Many estates did not declare.

The 1977 vintage produced a gamut of claret that often tastes as bad as the weather that year. Those with masochistic tendencies might find some self-inflicted pleasure, but they might also find their senses assaulted by fetid aromatics and flavours not far from that of rotting cabbage. I have suffered a handful. It's part of the job. The best is 1977 La Mission Haut-Brion or perhaps Lafleur. Requesting Véronique Sanders to open her most challenging vintages, she obliged with a 1977 Haut-Bailly that glimmered for a few minutes before oxygen

1977

1977
(Continued)

kicked away both its walking sticks. A bottle of 1977 La Conseillante clung onto life by its fingernails. An ex-château magnum of 1977 Cos Labory at the annual Académie du Vin dinner made me wish for a smaller format, preferably one called "non-existence", but kudos for having the guts to open it. A bottle of 1977 Climens was not bad all things considering – oddly quite Germanic in style – but really of curiosity value only.

Event
Elvis leaves the building

The King took his last breath on 16 August 1977 at the age of just 42. Found unconscious by his girlfriend Ginger Alden lying face down in his pyjamas on the floor of his bathroom at Graceland, Elvis was rushed to hospital where he was pronounced dead at 3.30 p.m. The following day, the public were allowed to enter his mansion. An estimated 100,000 turned up to pay their respects before he was buried in a mausoleum with his mother at Forest Hill Cemetery.

Music
Stayin' Alive
– Bee Gees

At the centre of disco-mania is one of the biggest-selling soundtracks of all time, *Saturday Night Fever*. The Bee Gees' manager Robert Stigwood asked the Gibb brothers to provide songs for a film with the working title of "Saturday Night", though the group refused to use that phrase as they felt it overused. The lyrics are both a paean to the discotheque and surviving the then-dangerous streets of New York. The killer guitar riff has an innate ability to make ordinary people make embarrassing dance moves, while Barry Gibbs' falsetto is irresistible. *Stayin' Alive* was never intended to be released as a single. The record company only acquiesced after radio stations were inundated with requests following the movie's release. The song became the first of four US chart toppers that Barry Gibb had a hand in composing that year, when the Bee Gees ruled the world.

Film
*Star Wars: Episode IV
– A New Hope* – George Lucas

Few kids, including this one, will
forget the jaw-dropping opening
sequence as an Imperial Star
Destroyer flies above audiences'
heads for what feels like an
eternity. Lucas had the idea for
*Star Wars: Episode IV – A New
Hope* in 1971 and began writing
the screenplay two years later,
establishing Industrial Light &
Magic to create the special effects.
The film was released in the US
on 25 May 1977 and Lucas was
so sceptical of its success that
he booked a holiday in Hawaii.
Interviewed on Parkinson, Sir
Alec Guinness admitted that
he had found the dialogue
"ropey" as did Harrison Ford
who complained, "You can type
this shit, but you can't say it."
Nevertheless, Guinness accepted
the role as Obi-Wan Kenobi for
2.25% of the profits instead of
a flat fee – no doubt the right
decision since *Star Wars* went on
to become the first movie to make
more than $500 million at the
box office.

1978

The 1978 vintage is more fondly regarded than others this decade. Yet for most of the year the omens looked bad. The late Clive Coates MW sums it up nicely in his book *Grand Vin*: "Until mid-August, everything went wrong."

January was cold and February colder. March dished up more of the same until spring finally arrived at the end of the month. These cold conditions delayed the vines' growth cycle, with budding around 29 March – over three weeks later than in the previous years. Vines' growth was discouraged by temperatures that struggled above zero throughout April. By May, their growth lagged a fortnight behind and not until the end of the month did warmer conditions, around 24°C (75°F), give the vines a much-needed spurt. The first flowers were spotted around 10 June, 10 days later than usual, but conditions remained changeable, Lawton noting that it was the coolest June for half a century. There was disquiet across Bordeaux as winemakers feared another wretched growing season on the back of 1977. When Latour director Jean-Paul Gardère gathered his team, he reported that the meeting took place "without talk and with sad faces". Finally, from 7 July, summer arrived with temperatures up to 32°C (90°F), though châteaux still predicted a late October harvest. Cooler conditions followed heavy rainfall on 29 July and throughout August thermometers rarely exceeded 30°C (86°F), recording an unseasonal 16°C (61°F) at the beginning of the month. *Véraison* was slow but accelerated after settled warm weather at the end of August, but the lack of rainfall – just 51.5 mm (2 in) in August and September – kept the brakes on vines' growth.

An Indian summer essentially saved the vintage and brought forward picking dates. When Gardère reconvened his team there were "broad smiles and a cheerful brouhaha". Montrose began picking on 4 October and Jean-Bernard Delmas sent his pickers out the following day at Haut-Brion, most of the others starting either on 8 or 9 October. Coates observed that, unusually, harvests commenced around the same time on both Left and Right Banks, though slightly later on clayey soils that could retain moisture and allow ripening to continue. Conditions remained settled and warmer than usual, around 27°C (80°F), with must weights about 11.5–12%, allowing the harvests to finish on a high note by around 24 October. In Sauternes, many estates had suffered coulure earlier in the season and dry conditions from August to November stymied botrytis. It was a remarkably late picking, the team at Yquem not unsheathing their secateurs until 25 November and finishing on 7 December. Pierre Dubourdieu at Doisy-Daëne even produced a one-off Eiswein.

I have a sentimental attachment to the 1978 vintage. One of my first experiences came courtesy of several bottles of 1978 Latour sent by a *négociant* after I secured a large order for the wine for my

Japanese employer. That First Growth is emblematic: a bit tough and unapologetically tannic, yet with just enough fruit and freshness to give pleasure, particularly for those with a penchant for so-called "proper claret". Most '78s are not going to deliver fireworks and might not sate palates seeking tons of fruit, but generally the wines matured commendably in bottle. The year saw a new chapter for Château Margaux after the *négociant* Ginestet sold the estate to André Mentzelopoulos and it released its best wine since the 1966. Both Lafite Rothschild and Mouton Rothschild produced "solid" wines that lack a bit of flair. If you want real quality, head down to Pessac-Léognan. Numerous bottles of 1978 La Mission Haut-Brion confirm that the Woltners oversaw the wine of the vintage: packed full of black fruit and brimming with complexity, it was going strong when poured at a Grouse Club lunch in summer 2020. Ditto its sibling, the 1978 La Tour Haut-Brion – a hidden gem – while the 1978 Domaine de Chevalier shows little signs of decay. The 1978 Pichon-Lalande is excellent (Michel Delon of Léoville-Las Cases having made the previous three vintages) and the 1978 Ducru-Beaucaillou is the finest since the 1970. I have also encountered some delicious bottles of 1978 Palmer and Talbot, and even a 1978 La Fleur Milon, a lowly Cru Bourgeois subsequently subsumed into Clerc Milon that had Olivier Bernard at Domaine de Chevalier scratching his head when I mischievously served it blind. The caveat is that even some well-known estates were suffering from long-term lack of investment, hidebound to outmoded modus operandi that had hardly changed since the war. Brane-Cantenac and Pichon Baron are both very rustic and green, failing to reach the standards expected.

Over on the Right Bank, Pomerol has its fair share of worthy wines. The Robin sisters oversaw a sturdy, rustic but utterly compelling 1978 Lafleur. The 1978 Pétrus is leaner and pleasantly leafy, though a step down from the 1975. Bottles and magnums of 1978 Vieux Château Certan have been broad-shouldered but quite delicious, just like Trotanoy. Over the border, 1978 Cheval Blanc lacks flair and Ausone was still treading water at the time. Better is the leafy but harmonious Figeac. A bottle of 1978 Clos Fourtet was a bit rough around the edges yet pleasurable in December 2021, easily surpassed by a delicious 1978 Pavie savoured down to the last drop a month later lunching in London.

Sauternes was not a disaster, although the wines are inferior to '76 and many now seem fatigued. Sauternes are uncommon, but the 1978 Climens – despite an odd white chocolate note on the nose and conservative finish – still had something to offer after three decades and a 1978 Rabaud-Promis showed freshness and energy when opened at the property.

1978 *(Continued)*

Event
Louise Joy Brown is the first test-tube baby

Many babies were born on 25 July 1978, but Louise Brown was special: the first conceived by in vitro fertilisation (IVF). British medical researcher Robert Edwards and gynaecologist Patrick Steptoe fertilised her mother's egg in a petri dish. Monitoring the dish overnight in their laboratory, their assistant Jean Purdy was the first to peer down a microscope and witness the miracle of cells dividing. Two days later, the embryo was implanted and nine months later the world's first "test-tube baby" was born in Oldham and District General Hospital. Edwards and Steptoe suggested the middle name "Joy" because the technique would bring that to many people. At least eight million IVF babies have been born, and counting.

Music
Heart of Glass
– Blondie

Though it topped the charts early the following year, *Heart of Glass* was the highlight of Blondie's 1978 *Parallel Lines* album and came out as a 12-inch single that December. It is a nexus between the post-punk New Wave emanating out of New York's influential CBGB club and Giorgio Moroder-inspired electro – a future-past composition symbolised by its drums, which combine a Roland CR-78 drum machine with Clem Burke's live percussion. Debbie Harry and Chris Stein wrote the song and demoed it as a reggae number in 1975, before producer Mike Chapman picked up on its potential and added its unmistakable disco sheen. Blondie were accused of selling out their punk credentials, but in retrospect they were just an open-minded band splicing musical genres together. The track sounds as futuristic today as it did back then.

Film
Grease – Randal Kleiser

Summer 1978 and "Grease" was the word. John Travolta applied his Brylcreem as Danny Zuko and Olivia Newton-John perfected her virginal smile as Sandy Olsson to join the students at Rydell High School singing and dancing their way through this nostalgic box-office smash. Based on the Broadway musical set in 1958 California, *Grease* was packed with quotable lines and unforgettable ear worms such as *You're the One That I Want*, which sold over two million copies in the UK alone. Olivia Newton-John had to be sewn into her skin-tight trousers in the final scene because the zip broke.

Nineteen seventy-nine is one of those middling vintages. It is not burdened with a terrible reputation like 1972 or 1977, nor is it really coveted.

Following a mild and wet end to 1978, the following year began with Arctic-like conditions and it remained bitterly cold until the second week of April. Warmer temperatures encouraged vines out of dormancy, buds not swelling until 12 April, yet it was a brief respite and the thermometer once again touched zero at the end of the month. May saw a change with much warmer and wetter conditions, though intermittent cold spells continued. June was more settled and this clemency coincided with flowering around 12 June that was completed under ideal warm conditions. Nevertheless, châteaux still anticipated a second late harvest in a row. A warm and settled July raised hopes of a good vintage, but August was unseasonably cool and temperatures never breached 30°C (86°F). At least it was dry, with just 150 mm (6 in) of rain between June and September, so there was no rot and plenty of underground moisture from the previous winter. What the vines needed was heat because the sun had to ripen a much larger crop than the previous year. Two warm spells at the beginning and end of September, combined with the fact that much of the aforementioned 150 mm (6 in) of rain fell in the weeks preceding harvest, nudged grape maturity forward by around a week.

The first pickers entered vineyards from 2 October, most busy among the vines from 5 October. Conditions were mainly favourable except for poor weather on 13 October and the harvest finished around 24 October. It was a large crop, with average yields of 62.9 hl/ha, the largest since the war, but it meant the fruit lacked concentration, with the sun's energy distributed across more bunches than in seasons where volume had been reduced either by frost or poor flowering. Like the previous year, 1979 saw another late harvest in Sauternes, generally beginning in mid-October. While initial passes through the vines bestowed some botrytised fruit, heavy rain from 23 October reduced concentration and Yquem diverted half of its fruit to make its dry Y de Yquem.

Keep expectations modest and you might be pleased by a bottle of 1979, though the wines were not born to last long term. On the Left Bank, I have fond memories of both 1979 Kirwan and 1979 Château Margaux, the latter portending a run of successful vintages throughout the following decade. The 1979 Palmer tasted at the château was frayed at its edges and the 1979 Brane-Cantenac was commendable during a vertical with proprietor Henri Lurton. I often find the Margaux wines more pleasurable than the rather rustic offerings from Latour, Lafite Rothschild and Mouton-Rothchild, while in Saint-Estèphe I found Montrose and Cos d'Estournel a bit leaden. Perhaps seek out the 1979 Pichon-Lalande? It marks the first year of Didier Cuvelier's tenure at Léoville Poyferré, though the harvest was strung out over three weeks and his pickers buggered off back to university, so the wine is an inauspicious opening of his account.

On the Right Bank, the standout is (to borrow Ian Maxwell Campbell's adjective, page 46) the pachydermatous 1979 Lafleur, the final great Pomerol from Marie and Thérèse Robin, which looms over the slight but at least balanced Pétrus. A solitary encounter with the 1979 Le Pin in Los Angeles with proprietor Jacques Thienpont suggested that his maiden release was a bit of a test-run, Thienpont assuring me that his second effort was better. Nevertheless, it was a privilege to taste this now extremely rare debut. The 1979 Vieux Château Certan was long past its best in 2020, though the 1979 Ausone was a pleasant surprise at the vertical in 2018, superior to Figeac and Canon-la-Gaffelière. Sauternes is not top drawer but some, such as Yquem and Climens, are trotting along nicely, though nowhere near the 1971s, 1975s or 1976s.

Music
Don't Stop 'Til You Get Enough
– Michael Jackson

Don't Stop 'Til You Get Enough gave notice that the star of The Jackson 5 had plans for global stardom on a gargantuan scale. Despite his success as a preternaturally gifted child, his successful transition to adult solo artist was by no means a given, and Jackson upped the stakes further by gambling on his first self-composed song as lead single for his forthcoming album. Any doubts were silenced by that introductory trademark yelp that ignites its infectious groove. Quincy Jones's impeccable production delineates the intricate instrumentation, allowing Jackson's falsetto to soar jubilantly over. This floor-filling nexus between seventies disco and eighties dance became his first US chart-topper for seven years and laid the foundations for his enthronement as the King of Pop.

Film
Alien
– Ridley Scott

In space, nobody can hear you scream. But my screams were audible in outer space when I first watched the unforgettable scene in which the *Nostromo*'s crew gather for a celebratory dinner and John Hurt has an "upset stomach". Scott purposely did not forewarn the cast about how much blood and guts would spew from Hurt's chest so as to capture their visceral reactions. And the new-born alien's horrific screech? That was provided by popular animal impersonator Percy Edwards. This seminal sci-fi-horror launched the career of Ridley Scott, while H.R. Giger's unsettling designs ensured it was a feast for the eyes. Most importantly of all, it proved that a woman could be a fearless lead, even if Sigourney Weaver outrageously receives second billing to Tom Skerritt.

Event
Margaret Thatcher elected
prime minister

"Thatcher, Thatcher, milk
snatcher!" That was as far as
this eight-year-old's political
knowledge extended when
Margaret Thatcher was elected
the UK's first female prime
minister on 4 May 1979. Having
grown up above her father's
grocery store in Grantham,
she ascended the ranks of the
Conservative Party, abolishing
free milk for schoolchildren as
Secretary for Education and
Science in 1971. Ousting Labour
leader James Callaghan with a
43-seat majority, she famously
quoted St. Francis of Assisi as
she entered 10 Downing Street:
"Where there is discord, may we
bring harmony. Where there is
error, may we bring truth. Where
there is doubt, may we bring
faith. And where there is despair,
may we bring hope." Her policies
divided the nation but that did
not prevent her from becoming
Britain's longest-serving prime
minister of the 20th century,
finally ousted by her own party in
November 1990.

THE

1980s

The eighties was a pivotal decade. Bordeaux on 31 December 1989 was different to how it was on 1 January 1980.

There were changes afoot out in the vineyard. Producers started to control yields via early-season pruning and green harvesting in summer months, snipping off excess bunches so the vines' energy was focused on fewer grapes – something anathema to the old guard for whom quantity equated to livelihood. Both Alexandre Thienpont at Vieux Château Certan and Alfred Tesseron at Pontet-Canet recalled their fathers watching aghast as perfectly healthy bunches were cut off, littering the earth with lost income.

"You always have conflicts between generations," Tesseron told me in an interview. "My father was an excellent businessman, so he could not understand why we dropped grapes on the floor when we started to green harvest in 1989. Nobody really knew we were doing it, including my father, until the summer of 1994 when we were green harvesting in front of his bedroom window. So I could not hide it. I told him to let me do all the technical work until April and then people could see whether I was right or wrong. 'If I am wrong, I will leave,' I told my father, 'and if I am right, you will handle the financial part and I will run the vineyard.' So the following April, I went to his place in the country so that he could taste a sample of the '94. I did not know how well I had done. He told me to leave it on the table and he said he would taste it the following morning on his own. Fortunately the 1994 was recognised as one of the wines of the vintage and from then on I was able to do what I wanted."

Tesseron went on to become one of the leading practitioners of biodynamics, though the seeds of Rudolf Steiner's philosophy had already been planted this decade. In December 1988, John Cochran III and his French wife Véronique acquired Château Falfas in the Côtes de Bourg and immediately converted its vineyard to biodynamics, becoming one of the first estates to be certified. Though it made few waves at the time, it was a prescient decision that many would eventually follow.

Many wineries were little changed since the war, especially on the Right Bank. In the eighties both château buildings and equipment began to be overhauled and spruced up. I often muse on the architectural wonders that furnish today's Bordeaux landscape and then remember Denis Durantou telling me how the winery floor was bare earth when he took over l'Eglise-Clinet in 1983. At the time he was maturing his wine in rudimentary concrete vats without any cooling system, new barrels a dream he would have to wait for. The Left Bank had made more progress, yet a surprising number of celebrated names clung to outdated techniques and desperately needed investment. The château building at Pichon Baron was shabby and uninhabitable and the wine, a Second Growth, was vinified outside in storage conditions that Christian Seely once described euphemistically as "less than perfect". Pichon Baron was one of a number of estates that constructed new wineries, which were often more elaborate and aesthetically befitting their status. Coinciding with investments was increased technical knowledge of vinification. "After the 1983 vintage, there were no more difficult years as our knowledge of the fermentation had improved so much during the decade," Jean-Michel Cazes explained. "I would say that our last problems in terms of knowledge were around 1981 to 1983 and consultants such as Prof. [Pascal] Ribéreau-Gayon changed how we looked at vinification."

Pichon Baron provides a good example of how outside investors were entering the Bordeaux property market at its highest echelons. France's second-largest insurance company, Axa-Midi, purchased the château in 1987 and assiduously appointed Jean-Michel Cazes of Lynch-Bages to run its estates, which also included Cantenac Brown in Margaux. Other insurance companies also acquired Beaumont and Larose-Trintaudon. Causing more ripples was Suntory's acquisition of one of the Médoc's largest estates, Château Lagrange, for 54 million francs in November 1983. Bordeaux had always seen investment from outside of France – *sacre bleu!* – and even Latour was in British hands for a few years. But the acquisition by a Japanese beverage giant signified how internationalised Bordeaux was becoming, and was arguably a precursor to the influx of Chinese investment three decades later. Most importantly, Suntory's purchase marked the moment when a previously under-performing Saint-Julien estate began to improve and reach its true potential.

There were gradual changes in vinification. Under the influential Professor Denis Dubourdieu, pre-fermentation maceration became more widespread in order to extract extra colour and tannins. He also advocated the Burgundy technique of lees-stirring for white wines to enhance texture and aromatics. Temperature-controlled, hygienic stainless-steel vats, first implemented at Haut-Brion back in 1961, finally became more popular and blocked fermentations, volatility and microbial spoilage became less common. There was wider use of malolactic fermentation in barrel instead of tank – another practice common in Burgundy – which helped render nascent wines more velvety in barrel (always useful for when journalists descended upon Bordeaux during en primeur). Opponents felt it detracted from terroir expression and compromised longevity. Concentrators, which could remove up to 15% of water from musts and perform the same task as *saignée* or bleeding vats, crept into wineries across Bordeaux in this decade, though really proliferated during the rain-affected vintages of the nineties. Winemakers bristled whenever asked about the extent of their use since it implied a shortcoming in viticulture that had to be rectified by technology. More estates also began introducing Deuxième Vins or Second Labels, parsing away less propitious parcels and/or barrels from the Grand Vin, which improved quality. At the same time, it also lowered quantity, which made it easier to leverage up prices. Though Deuxième Vins had existed since the turn of the century (see my note on the 1900 Deuxième Vin de Château Margaux, page 99), most major châteaux had begun deselecting part of their crop to varying degrees by the end of the decade.

At the start of the eighties, Bordeaux was still coming to terms with the run of poor growing seasons, stagnating prices, scandal, economic travails, a slump in demand and an overreliance on chemicals and herbicides to boost yields at the expense of quality. The hangover carried over into the first two years of the decade, meaning winemakers found it difficult to exploit a golden PR opportunity in June 1980 when three French doctors published a paper noting that the incidence of coronary heart disease was lower in people who drank red wine, the so-called "French Paradox". The phenomenon was eventually attributed to their Mediterranean diet, but it must have been nice to think you were boozing yourself to fitness while it lasted.

Though the 1980 vintage had little to commend it, 1981 has its bright spots. But 1982 was the watershed moment, an inflexion point. First and foremost, it was the first growing season since 1959 that combined quantity and quality, demonstrating how Bordeaux wine could act as a sound and potentially profitable financial investment. The First Growths all put their 1982s on the Place de Bordeaux at 170 francs per bottle but within a year they were trading at just under 300 francs per bottle. There were also sharp increases among the Second Growths compared with the previous vintage – for example, Ducru-Beaucaillou increased from 48 francs a bottle for its 1981 to 70 francs for its 1982, La Mission Haut-Brion from 80 to 140 francs and Pichon-Lalande from 45 to 67. These revenues replenished châteaux's coffers and gave them the means to invest.

Second, it was the vintage that thrust an ambitious, hard-working ex-lawyer from Maryland onto the map: Robert Parker. He single-handedly changed the Bordeaux landscape, how its wines were assessed and communicated, and even its raison d'être. Some of his more established peers had dismissed the 1982 vintage on the assumption that quantity had come at the expense of quality. Parker was not the only commentator whose praise went against them, but he was the new kid on the block with a natural ability to communicate with his audience. When the 1982s were finally consumed, it was clear Parker was on the money, quite literally, and he was soon enthroned as the go-to critic. He could never have envisaged his all-pervasive influence upon not just consumer behaviour, but eventually winemaking practices. Logically, winemakers who sought praise from Parker began tailoring their wine to his predilections – and hiring the consultant most attuned to applying those techniques. That man was Michel Rolland, whose laboratory, co-owned with his wife Dany, in the village of Catusseau became a regular haunt for many aspiring Right Bank winemakers. The tenets of lower yields, later picking (and therefore of higher sugar levels and alcohol), longer maceration and more new oak became widespread.

Parker and Rolland's detractors, numerous and vocal – not least the English press, piqued that it no longer held sway over opinion – complained that Bordeaux's wines were becoming too rich at the expense of freshness, terroir expression, typicity and drinkability. I would argue that it wasn't until the late nineties that styles became extreme, and I do not subscribe to the view that either Parker or Rolland's influence was detrimental to quality. On the contrary, go taste a few under-ripe and vegetal wines from preceding years. Even their most bitter detractors admit they inspired many to raise their game. Whereas previously producers could rely on the less scrupulous wine merchants to inveigle their customers into buying substandard wines, now there was an independent third-party assessor making Bordeaux less opaque. Whether you agreed with him or not, Parker gave you a straight-down-the-line appraisal that ignored history and reputation. What counted lay inside the bottle.

Parker's championing of Right Bank producers gave Saint-Émilion and Pomerol long overdue kudos, something he deserves more credit for. In 1978, Parker had a Damascene moment when served a 1961 Latour à Pomerol that, to quote the man himself, "recalibrated and redefined greatness". He also gave long-overdue coverage to upcoming satellite appellations such as Castillon and Fronsac, among others. Parker put every producer on a level playing field, enabling small and hitherto unknown estates to receive effusive reviews.

The powerful currency of scores based on the American 100-point system ignited demand and could potentially establish reputations overnight. The biggest beneficiary was probably Le Pin. Having debuted in 1979, Jacques Thienpont's initial releases struggled to find buyers. Thienpont once told me how he left a full case of Le Pin with a Bordeaux merchant and returned a few months later, only to spot the same case on the shelf, unopened and gathering dust. Parker's promulgation, particularly of the 1982 vintage, elevated Le Pin to one of the world's most coveted wines – and also one of the most unobtainable, since around 200 cases of the 1982 were produced. Even Thienpont has only one half-bottle of it left. The wine was priced at just £10 a bottle on release and he sold practically every last one because he needed the money. It has gone up in price since then.

This chapter in Bordeaux's history saw the introduction of the region's first new appellation since codification in 1935. After several years' negotiation, stalling, and the obligatory lawsuits, the I.N.A.O. ratified the creation of Pessac-Léognan. With the indefatigable André Lurton leading the charge, the goal was to distinguish the well-known estates clustered within the Bordeaux city limits and the northern Graves from lesser-known names in the south. This is exactly what it did, since Pessac-Léognan's 55 members contain practically all the famous names, while the rest continue to be labelled Graves. You can argue whether this cleaving has been detrimental to the appellation as a whole – undoubtedly benefiting the selected few but relegating the Graves to second-rate citizen status, unfair given the calibre of some wines.

After 1982 the region enjoyed a much more fecund run of growing seasons compared to the previous decade: 1983, 1985, 1986, 1988, 1989 and, by special derogation, 1990. These vintages are bejewelled with wines that continue to give pleasure to this day. This could not have come at a better moment because Bordeaux *had* to up its game in the aftermath of the Judgment of Paris. New competition, not just from California, but also from Australia and Chile, among others, was seeking to claim its own slice of the lucrative Cabernet/ Merlot pie. The eighties reaffirmed Bordeaux's eminence in the eyes and palates of wine-lovers. The throne was not for taking – not yet at least.

The 1980s witnessed the long overdue rise in the appreciation of Pomerol. Wine-makers such as the late Denis Duran-tou, pictured here, not long after taking over l'Eglise-Clinet, were instrumental in modernizing wineries. A future star in the making.

1980

Just like the fifties and sixties, the eighties stuttered at the beginning.

It remained cold throughout the first few weeks of 1980, all the way through to the end of March, which delayed vines' budding to around 2 April. Even then, the mercury stubbornly refused to rise, save for a couple of days, with most mornings seeing temperatures below zero and localised frost. As the weather finally began to warm in May, the risk of a damaging frost receded and vines began to grow. But it was a false dawn and the mercury fell again towards the end of the month. The season just refused to spring into action. Two days of 28°C (82°F) heat on 3 and 4 June at last coaxed more shoot growth and the first flowers were seen around 6 June. But this was followed by three days in which temperatures barely touched double figures and further rain meant flowering was irregular and with widespread coulure. In his diary entry on 1 July Daniel Lawton laments it is more like 1 November, articulating the frustration many winemakers must have felt during the chilly semester. The first 10 days of July saw heavy rain, though fortunately anti-rot sprays were now more widespread and inhibited the spread of disease. Summer-like conditions prevailed in the latter half of the month, though by now it was clear that millerandage had severely impacted the Merlot. August was warm but not particularly hot, with temperatures in the high twenties, and predicated a protracted *véraison* around 18 August.

September began well with more settled conditions and much-needed heat, interrupted by heavy storms on 20 September that saw 70 mm (2¾ in) of rain fall within a 24-hour period. "The rain wouldn't stop," recalled Jean Merlaut, proprietor of Gruaud Larose at one tasting. Warm weather at the end of September raised hopes, but the Merlot was now showing signs of rot. Cutting their losses, pickers entered vineyards at Haut-Brion and Montrose on 6 October, most others unsheathing secateurs two days later, but they had to put up with intermittent showers and cold conditions. The majority of harvests finished between 24 and 28 October with low sugar levels of around 11%, which duly obliged chaptalisation. It was yet another late harvest in Sauternes with pickers having to remove bunches affected by sour rot before the first passes from mid-October. Easterly winds concentrated the remaining fruit and rewarded those who had been patient. It was not easy to make a great Sauternes in 1980, but it was not impossible.

This vintage is one that I have tasted infrequently. Given its shortcomings, it would be easy to dismiss out of hand. Yet two wines miraculously transcend the growing season, one from the Left Bank and the other on the Right Bank. Firstly, a splendid 1980 Mouton Rothschild that I served blind at an off-line dinner around 2004. Our motley crew of tasters were gobsmacked by its vigour and purity and it was only later when visiting the estate that I discovered that Baron Philippe had expedited the harvest by recruiting 600 pickers in order to avoid the rain. It clearly worked. The other is a 1980 Le Pin. Having enjoyed a memorable Le Pin vertical in Los Angeles, this sophomore vintage was a glaring omission from my otherwise complete run of notes. Mentioning how difficult it was to carry on life without this note, a sympathetic Jacques Thienpont told me that he only had four bottles but would sacrifice one if I caught the train to Belgium to visit him. It was worth the trip. The Le Pin was absolutely delicious: silky smooth with ample fruit, though nowadays it is impossible to find. I have tasted others such as a rustic 1980 Pétrus and a bottle of 1980 Lafleur that suggested it had spent much of its life in a pigsty. Bottles of 1980 La Conseillante, La Mission Haut-Brion and Brane-Cantenac were all hollow. Much better were two bottles encountered in September 2021. First, a fragile but none too shabby 1980 Moulin de Carruades, Lafite Rothschild's second wine until it was rebranded Carruades, and second, a bottle of 1980 Siran recommended by proprietor Édouard Miailhe and served at a dinner to commemorate the late Steven Spurrier. My only two regrets were that it was not in magnum and that I was unable to share it with Steven himself. I have encountered few Sauternes, though I have worked my way through a few half-bottles of quite nutty 1980 Yquem over the years. It's better than the Climens, which felt a little past it.

Film
The Blues Brothers
– John Landis

Dan Ackroyd and John Belushi star as the besuited, sunglass-wearing paroled convicts, first seen in skits on *Saturday Night Live*, who set out on a mission from God to reunite their blues band and raise money to save the orphanage they grew up in. The plot plays second fiddle to the final chase scene around Chicago, which wrecked 103 cars, and the roll-call of famous singers who appear, including Aretha Franklin, James Brown, Cab Calloway and Ray Charles. Tragically, Belushi died from a drug overdose just two years later.

1980
(Continued)

Event
John Lennon is murdered
in New York

In March 1966, John Lennon
remarked that The Beatles
were more popular than Jesus.
Fourteen years later, this off-
the-cuff remark was bugging
25-year-old Mark Chapman.
On the morning of 8 December
1980, Chapman waited outside
Lennon's home in The Dakota
building in New York where
the star signed his copy of the
recently released *Double Fantasy*
album, his first after five years
out of the public eye bringing
up his son Sean. Returning at
10.50 p.m. to say good-night to
Sean, Lennon found Chapman
loitering outside his apartment.
This time, Chapman took out
a concealed revolver, fired five
shots, four of them hitting their
target, then sat down and read *The
Catcher in the Rye* until the police
arrived. Lennon was declared
dead at 11.15 p.m.

Music
Love Will Tear Us Apart
– Joy Division

Warsaw formed in 1976 after
guitarist Bernard Sumner
met bassist Peter Hook at the
legendary Sex Pistols' concert
at the Manchester Lesser Free
Trade Hall. Having changed
their name to Joy Division, they
signed to Factory Records, run
by impresario Tony Wilson. Their
seminal debut *Unknown Pleasures*
made songwriter and frontman
Ian Curtis a cult hero, renowned
for his personal and poetic lyrics
and magnetic stage presence.
Away from the spotlight, Curtis
suffered increasingly severe
epileptic seizures and bouts of
depression, much of it fuelled
by the extra-marital affair that
inspired the anthemic *Love Will
Tear Us Apart*. The song defined
the band, but by the time of its
release in June 1980, Curtis had
taken his own life.

The 1981 vintage was predestined to be overshadowed by 1982 but, like many, I have always had a soft spot for its wines.

It remained consistently cold, often below freezing throughout January and February, but conditions improved in March with 24°C (75°F) recorded on the 10th and 11th. It stayed unusually warm for the next couple of weeks, enticing the first leaves to unfurl from 26 March, much earlier than normal. In his book *Grands Vins* Clive Coates MW says the sortie was better for the Cabernet Sauvignon than the Merlot or Cabernet Franc. A drop in temperatures resulted in localised frost damage on 27 April plus severe hailstorms on 7 May that spared major châteaux. After that, the days warmed up, though nights were fresh, and by early June the mercury reached 25°C (77°F) as the first flowers were spotted. It remained clement and warm – perfect conditions for flowering, which was regular and not prolonged, just a couple of nippy days causing minor coulure. Examining the Tastet-Lawton archive, temperatures in July ranged from 24–34°C (75–93°F), though Coates contradicts this, stating the month was "cold, wet and sunless". Lawton says it was so dry that by the end of July, vines were exhibiting some water deficiency and grillure and estimates that around 5% of the crop had been lost. August began hot with the mercury reaching 35°C (95°F) accompanied by local storms, though bunches appeared to change from green to purple without hesitation. The month saw more days over 25°C (77°F) than any August since 1929 and only 27 mm (1 in) of rain.

September began with light showers that would have given the vines more energy, but the clement conditions began to break in the latter half of the month with intermittent storms. There was still sentiment that 1981 could be the best vintage since 1961 but it suffered one of the wettest ends to a season since 1945. Between 21 September and 15 October some 118 mm (4½ in) of rain drenched Bordeaux, mostly in the last 10 days of September, just prior to harvest. Pétrus dispatched pickers in the afternoons of 29 and 30 September. The 1 October was rainy in the morning, clearing up by the afternoon, and both 2 and 3 October, when most châteaux commenced their picking, were plagued by intermittent showers the whole day. It then cleared up for a short period and the patient team at Lafite Rothschild finally picked up their secateurs on 5 October, by which time Latour had finished. Unfortunately, it rained again between 9 and 15 October when the Lafite Rothschild secateurs were being put away. According to Clive Coates MW, Michel Delon of Léoville-Las Cases asked a lorry filled with grapes to raise its trailer without releasing the tail-flap, to allow water to drain out before the fruit was transferred into the vat. I suspect not all proprietors were as meticulous as Delon, but it also indicates just how fastidious harvests are today. Jean-Michel Cazes at Lynch-Bages also had problems in the winery. "Two-thirds of the crop had a stuck fermentation," he explained when we chatted in 2021. "Some of the vats were stuck with 15 or 18 g/l residual sugar.

I remember not sleeping at night, I was so worried. Professor Émile Peynaud came to help and he would always calm you down. He was a good technician but an even better psychologist. He said forget about fermenting, just add SO_2 and you'll get over it and we'll come back in May. Daniel Llose [Lynch-Bages' technical manager] didn't like the idea and so did not add too much sulphur. However, there was one vat, number 11, that *was* fermenting. So I drew off some wine from that vat in order to start the fermentation in the others. It didn't work. So we drained the vat and left some of the must inside, refilled it with must from another vat and after one or two weeks it started fermenting. Two-thirds of the harvest ended up going through vat 11 and the fermentation finished 31 December."

It was another challenging vintage in Sauternes. Late-September showers provoked some botrytis after a cool growing season and while the first passes yielded a small amount of botrytised fruit, it was difficult winnowing out berries with adequate concentration. Relief came in the form of an easterly wind that increased sugar levels in remaining bunches, making it possible for some to make a small quantity of good-quality Sauternes.

Under similar weather conditions, it can be argued that rigorous sorting and de-selection into Deuxième or Troisième Vins would have led to a superior vintage in 1981. But such practices were simply not widespread at the time. After a run of mediocre vintages, one can understand why proprietors sought quantity over quality. Although it is overshadowed by 1982 and does not rank among the best this decade, 1981 is a very "useful" vintage, a source of many overlooked and enjoyable wines. You just need to pick carefully. In the early days of my professional career, I regularly encountered the 1981 First Growths because they represented such good value. Lafite Rothschild and Mouton Rothschild are light and lack a bit of fruit, yet appeal to those who appreciate "classic claret" – though the 1981 Latour perhaps leaves you wanting more and I prefer the 1978. I also have positive notes for an excellent 1981 Pichon-Lalande, not embarrassed in the slightest when poured against the 1982 and 1983 at the château. Both Thomas Duroux and I were smitten by the 1981 Palmer at its vertical in March 2022, elegant and poised with just the right amount of leafiness. Saint-Julien also provides some lovely 1981s, not least Léoville-Las Cases and a very elegant Gruaud Larose, while Montrose has more to offer than Cos d'Estournel. There are others where I might have expected more, such as La Mission Haut-Brion, and some were treading water (that's you Pichon Baron).

The Right Bank is a mixed bag. The best I have ever tasted in Pomerol is the 1981 Le Pin, which like the previous vintage completely transcends the season's limitation, startling in terms of its freshness and concentration. Pity it's so rare. Both Pétrus and Lafleur are light and becoming frail, though the 1981 La Conseillante was an augury for the coming decade when the estate returned to Pomerol's top rank. In Saint-Émilion, the 1981 Cheval Blanc is another that is far better than you might imagine. It is so good that at one soirée, at The Ledbury in London if I recall, a guest forgot to bring his bottle and ordered a cab back to his apartment to chauffeur it to the restaurant. Others have come across as a little tired. I have drunk few 1981 Sauternes, though a diddy half-bottle of 1981 Yquem was impressive given the context of the growing season.

Film
Mad Max 2
– George Miller

Mad Max 2 shot Mel Gibson to international stardom as the titular ex-patrolman roaming the post-apocalyptic Australian wasteland on his super-charged Interceptor in search of food and gas – much like we all do driving up the M1. The laconic Max only has 16 lines of dialogue in the entire film, which is best known for its non-stop action sequences and stunts. Miller used more than 80 custom-made vehicles and managed to demolish more than half of them during its 12-week shoot. Released in Australia on Christmas Eve, the film was known as *The Road Warrior* in the US and is now considered a low-budget dystopian classic.

1981
(Continued)

Event
Lady Diana Spencer
marries Prince Charles

On 29 July 1981, as Lady Diana
Spencer walked down the aisle
of St. Paul's Cathedral to marry
the heir to the throne, the
population waved their Union
Jacks and tucked into their
jam sandwiches at countless
street parties. Speculation about
whom Prince Charles would
marry had been rife for years.
Inevitably, when he got engaged
to the pretty, demure, doe-eyed
19-year-old nursery assistant,
she instantly became one of the
world's most famous women.
Cracks in their relationship
appeared almost immediately
during a press interview in which
a reporter told the couple they
looked as if they were in love.
"Whatever love means," replies
Prince Charles awkwardly, Diana
only just managing to conceal
the awkwardness. According to
Diana's personal tapes, she had
only met her husband-to-be
13 times before the wedding
ceremony, so they must have
hardly known each other. But on
that hot summer's day it seemed
the entire world was swept up in
the pageantry and romance.

Music
Ghost Town
– The Specials

Few songs of the decade reflected
the state of a country at that exact
moment like *Ghost Town*. Written
by Jerry Dammers, founder of
the influential Two Tone record
label and the band's Hammond
keyboardist, its despairing
lyrics and eerie instrumentation
soundtracked a broken nation,
racked by inner-city riots and
spiralling unemployment.
Enhanced by a promo video
showing the band crammed into
a 1962 Vauxhall Cresta careening
through the Blackwall Tunnel, it
portrayed the multi-racial group
as a cohesive unit. In reality,
they were at each other's throats.
Dammers had exacerbated
tensions by forcing each member
to record *Ghost Town* separately
and matters came to a head as
they were about to perform on
British television. Neville Staple,
Lynval Golding and Terry Hall
announced they were leaving and
consequently *Ghost Town* was
their final release, a rare case of a
band acrimoniously disintegrating
with their defining hit.

The 1982 vintage is so gilded and loaded with import that you might easily assume the growing season was a doddle. But its success was no shoo-in.

A balmy 16°C (61°F) on 4 January augured the hot growing season and it remained relatively warm in February. Vineyard managers voiced concern that vines could not shut down, thus making pruning tricky. At the end of February there was a short cold spell, though temperatures did not fall below zero. All this meant the growth cycle got off to a flying start and the first leaves were seen around 16 March. Fears of frost were allayed by a warm April that was particularly dry, just 6 mm (¼ in) of rain, coupled with temperatures reaching 22°C (71.5°F). Unsurprisingly, vines maintained their rapid growth. Come the beginning of May and the prolonged dry spell was starting to worry winemakers. When temperatures dropped it was almost scripted that frost damage would ensue, this time hitting around Moulis and Listrac on 10 May. Unusually, Latour suffered some minor hail damage that affected its north-located parcels. The mercury shot up again, reaching 28°C (82°F) in mid-May, and some much-needed rain fell a week later. The first flowers were seen around 27 May with violent storms and heavy downpours on 31 May. Despite some rain at the beginning of June, flowering was early, quick and even, which all portended a bountiful crop. The rest of the month was warm with some occasional convectional rainfall, after which it really started to heat up, peaking at a sizzling 39°C (102°F) between 7 and 9 July, burning some of the berries. Despite sporadic showers and cooler temperatures, it remained hot and dry and heat stress was a constant worry. Contrary to what some people think, it was not particularly warm in August, with temperatures hovering around the mid-twenties and occasional rain. It was also quite overcast for that time of year. Nevertheless, winemakers still predicted an early picking – though summer was not over yet. After a sprinkling of rain at the beginning of the September, it became hot once again, averaging 30°C (86°F) between the 8th and 18th.

The Tastet-Lawton archives note that harvest began at Léoville-Las Cases on 13 September, the following day at Montrose and two days after at Latour, Ducru-Beaucaillou and Mouton Rothschild, the latter picking its entire crop within seven days. All châteaux were out in their vineyards by 17 September, though Saint-Émilion suffered heavy downpours on 19 September. Most of the picking was completed by 1 October though some took longer than usual because of the volume – 21 days instead of the normal 12 at Lynch-Bages, for example. After a remarkably clement year, conditions finally turned rainy at the end of the season – important for replenishing underground supplies of water for the next year. Must weights were 12.5–13% for the Merlots and 12–12.5% for the Cabernets, high compared to previous vintages and obviating any need for chaptalisation.

The challenge for many winemakers was the lingering warmth, which made it difficult controlling fermentation temperatures. As a consequence, success in 1982 was not only determined by what transpired out in the vineyard, but also the skill of winemaking teams coupled with their ability to regulate vat temperatures. According to a first-hand witness, Pichon-Lalande briefly considered discarding the entire vintage as it struggled with stuck fermentations, yeasts unaccustomed to working in such a high-alcohol environment. Given the success of the 1982, thank goodness it didn't. On top of this was the sheer volume. Château Margaux could barely cope with the quantity of fruit, convincing Corinne Mentzelopoulos of the need to expand their vat-room in time for the next vintage. "We had so much wine that we had to rent a truck to store the wine," Jean-Michel Cazes told me at Lynch-Bages. "We shortened the maceration time so that we could turn them over quickly to vinify the next lot, maybe two or three times." Over the years several winemakers have privately confided that actual yields were above their declarations at the time and occasionally exceeded 100 hl/ha. Yet for many these unprecedented volumes did not compromise quality. The vines' branches might have strained carrying so many bunches, but Mother Nature bequeathed sufficient sunshine and warmth to ripen them fully.

As the '82s bubbled away in the vats, Bordeaux was already talking about another '47. The wines were sumptuous from day one: relatively high in alcohol, rounded and voluptuous; approachable but against the predictions of some critics, born with longevity. The one weak spot in 1982 was the Sauternes. There was plenty of concentration in the bunches and the first passes from mid-September were beneficial. Then, five weeks of constant rain delayed many estates' harvests until around the last week of October. At Yquem, the team was restricted to a single pass through the vines from 25 October.

Early in my career I fantasised about what it would be like to taste a 1982 First Growth. The wines lay far beyond the stretch of my wallet after I accepted earning pittance for a job I had fallen in love with. But luckily over the last two decades I've managed to taste all the First Growths numerous times, several times altogether, as well as all the major Bordeaux châteaux. First and foremost, 1982 is not a uniform vintage. Its reputation is founded upon the outstanding quality of its elite 30-odd estates on the Left and Right Banks rather than the entire hierarchy. As mentioned, some estates lacked the means to efficiently control alcoholic fermentation. But what really underlied the disparity between success and failure was timing. The 1982 vintage broke the dismal run of vintages of the last 20 years, when small revenues stymied investment. Many wineries were still managed by old *maîtres de chai*, hidebound to outdated methods little-changed since the war. Often experienced, they were also sometimes supercilious and cocksure. For some now well-regarded estates such as Pichon Baron and Rauzan-

Ségla on the Left Bank, and Angélus and l'Église-Clinet on the Right, 1982 happened too early. As a result, as time has passed, a widening gap between the triumphs of the vintage and the also-rans has emerged.

On the Left Bank, the most consistent is the monumental 1982 Latour, unequivocally its finest since the '61. Both a magnum and a bottle in 2021 demonstrated that it has no intention of relinquishing its crown as finest Left Bank of the vintage. While Latour is an aristocrat, the 1982 Mouton Rothschild is a ravishing maximalist wine decorated with Christmas lights that might be less consistent bottle-to-bottle, but when it's on, you won't want to drink anything else. My most memorable of many encounters were double magnums poured when Mouton hosted the La Fête de la Fleur banquet in 2003. Sweating buckets in my hired polyester tuxedo, I filled my glass to the brim before shimmying onto the dance-floor to boogie with Placido Domingo and Catherine Deneuve. Provenance is key for this First Growth. But the 1982 that alerted me to the quality of the vintage was a bottle of fabulous 1982 Pichon-Lalande, brought by its grandiloquent former owner, May-Eliane de Lencquesaing, to a private dinner in Bordeaux around 1998. The wine was at its zenith and while numerous subsequent bottles have invariably been sensual and, like the Mouton, flamboyant, it has never quite flirted with perfection again. The 1982 Léoville-Las Cases was lauded by Parker though personally I always found it aloof, more impressive than delicious. Apparently, former proprietor Michel Delon preferred his 1986 and I am inclined to agree. I must namecheck the 1982 Montrose, not because it is a fantastic wine – on the contrary, it is one of the few outside the Margaux appellation that is surpassed by its '83 (ditto the slightly ossified '82 Palmer, which ought to be better) – but because it was my epiphany, the wine that explained why people become passionate about wine beyond its intoxicating properties. Without it, who knows, I might have pursued a different career.

On the Right Bank, the greatest wine hands-down is the leviathan 1982 Lafleur. My first of a dozen encounters came at Robert Parker's abode in Monkton. He promised to open a bottle if I joined his team and he kept his word, also uncorking the 1982 Trotanoy and l'Évangile for comparitive purposes. I faced a dilemma: guzzling this brilliant Pomerol and embarrassing myself in front of Parker or rationing my intake. I ended up on his payroll for over a decade, so I cannot have made too much of a fool of myself. (Or perhaps we were as inebriated as each other!) The 1982 Pétrus is excellent, though not quite as magical as the Lafleur, save for a magnum drunk one balmy evening overlooking Kowloon Bay in 2019. Tasted on two occasions, the 1982 Le Pin is cut from a similar cloth to the Mouton Rothschild, flamboyant, exotic and sexy, almost viscous in mouthfeel. Saint-Émilion does not possess the peaks of Pomerol. The 1982 Cheval Blanc went through a volatile phase but has since pulled through, and is sometimes

1982
(Continued)

oddly reminiscent of the 1982 Mouton. Some Saint-Émilions now look as if their best days are behind them, though a few continue to drink well such as L'Arrosée and Magdelaine (both defunct sadly). Sauternes suffered due to the lack of botrytis and the rain. Nevertheless, the few I have tasted have been enjoyable, including a wonderful 1982 Suduiraut Cuvée Madame and a sparkling 1982 Yquem proffered by Sauternes maven Bill Blatch that surprised everyone with its sparkling energy and precision, perhaps proving that a great wine can sometimes come from a single pass through the vines.

Event
The Falklands War between Britain and Argentina

On 2 April 1982, Argentina's army invaded the disputed Falkland Islands in the South Atlantic. Three days later, a British naval task force, including two aircraft carriers, was dispatched to recapture the territory. On 2 May, the Argentine vessel, ARA *General Belgrano* was sunk with 323 fatalities. Two days later, HMS *Sheffield* was sunk with the loss of 20 servicemen. A ceasefire was declared on 14 June after 74 days of conflict and 907 casualties. Despite the loss of life, the Falklands was recaptured and the accompanying swell of national pride rejuvenated Margaret Thatcher's waning popularity, laying the foundation for her re-election the following year.

Music
Rio
– Duran Duran

Towards the end of the iconic video for *Rio*, the body-painted model aboard the luxury yacht slicing through Antiguan waves under Captain Le Bon turns to camera and makes a knowing wink. I have always interpreted this as a signal to let us know that the expense lavished on the video's exotic location and pastel silk designer suits was ludicrous, but also that this was how things were going to be from now on. The Birmingham band later explained that *Rio* was their metaphor for America, the country that took the New Romantics to its heart after the constant rotation of their music on MTV. *Rio* was in marked contrast to the do-it-yourself ethos and edginess of the influential early synth groups. The watchword now was "excess".

Film
E.T. the Extra Terrestrial
– Steven Spielberg

E.T. is arguably the defining film of the early eighties. Spielberg coaxed wonderfully affecting performances from his mainly young cast, especially Henry Thomas and a scene-stealing seven-year-old Drew Barrymore. The director took a fantasy concept and ingeniously rooted it in reality, making the film as much about the struggles of single-parenting as a stranded alien. The movie unfolds from a child's perspective: many scenes are shot at hip-level and Spielberg filmed in chronological order to capture genuine reactions from his young cast, including their tears as *E.T* departs at the end. The film became the highest-grossing movie of all time and has lost none of its pathos or magic.

1983

This vintage joins a select club of years – along with 1948 and 1962 – which lie in the shadow of lauded growing seasons, but also have much to offer discerning oenophiles.

Following the eventual break in clement conditions that had sealed the success of the previous vintage, it rained consistently through the winter and into the first weeks of 1983. January and February were cold, March was little better, and the first shoots only began to appear around the 28th of that month. April dished up more of the same dreary weather and rationed springtime warmth. Only on 2 May do the Tastet-Lawton archives record a day without the need for umbrellas and damp conditions stymie growth until the end of the month. Things were looking a bit bleak. Then suddenly, as it has a propensity to do, the season turned on its heel. From 1 to 3 June the mercury rose to 26–30°C (79–86°F), then up to 32°C (90°F) in the following days. This clement hot spell was concurrent with flowering, with the first seen on 8 June and *pleine fleur* six days later. After an even and rapid flowering, merchants and châteaux predicted an even more abundant harvest than the previous year. July was punctured by violent storms on the 4th, but it was hot throughout the month with temperatures peaking at a sweltering 39°C (102°F) by the end. However, some coulure and millerandage affected the Merlot and thunderstorms on the night of 20 July had brought hail in Fronsac and Pomerol. August was also hot, though less so than in July, and 100 mm (4 in) of rain throughout the month dampened spirits. The wet was unevenly dispersed, with Sichel reporting that north Médoc received triple the amount of rain as the south. In bygone years, this would have predicated widespread black rot and mildew, but vineyard managers were becoming more adept at preventing cryptogamic diseases even if warm and humid nights obliged teams to be out in the vines and constantly spraying.

The first half of September saw a mini-heat wave before temperatures cooled off. Coates posits that at this stage, ripeness levels lagged behind those of 1981, but this devious season had one last trick up its sleeve. From 22 to 26 September the mercury shot back up to 30–34°C (86–93°F) before cooling to an optimal 26°C (79°F), preferable to the incessant heat of 12 months earlier. Pickers entered vineyards from 26 to 28 September and for the first time in years, picking was uninterrupted by rain. On 13 October, Tastet-Lawton notes that there was rain during the night, the first since 17 September. Except for the Margaux appellation, Bordeaux's volume of AC red was high at 3.2 million hl, though below the 3.5 million hl recorded in 1982. Alcohol degrees were a respectable 12.5%. By the time the weather broke in mid-October, the harvest was virtually over in the Médoc.

Sauternes enjoyed arguably its finest growing season between 1975 and 1989. After a benevolent few months the grapes had reached satisfying levels of concentration. Rain in August and early September ignited botrytis infection and the clement weather that stretched until 19 November allowed estates to make several passes through the vines at the right moment. Finally, there were smiles in Sauternes.

The '83s are fully mature and though they might lack the pizzazz and sensuality of the preceding vintage, they have a predilection to convey personality and charm. The appellation of Margaux boasts more successful wines than in 1982. My pick is the 1983 Palmer, even though my first bottle, which I opened for an old school friend, was so riddled with cork taint that I pretended to enjoy the taste of wet cardboard. Thankfully, subsequent bottles vouchsafe this as one of the legends of the decade, the last in September 2021 exquisite in balance, complete and utterly refined. The 1983 Château Margaux is constantly compared to the 1982 and whichever comes out on top depends on the circumstances at that moment. Perfumed with violets and iris on the nose, fine boned and harmonious on the palate, the 1982 maybe has a touch more density, yet the peacock's tail on the finish of the 1983 is fabulous. Rauzan-Ségla and Brane-Cantenac both produced superior wines to their respective '82s. Conversely, when I visited the Sichel family in 2021, I preferred the 1982 d'Angludet to their 1983.

On the Right Bank, the pick of the Pomerols is definitely the show-stopping 1983 Lafleur, overseen by Christian Moueix and Jean-Claude Berrouet after the Robin sisters' health began to wane, though ironically the 1983 Pétrus is rather lacklustre. It is rarely seen, but the 1983 Le Pin is a gem overshadowed by the 1982, though we only met once at renowned collector Bipin Desai's vertical in Los Angeles. Saint-Émilion can be up and down, though the 1983 Cheval Blanc is (a) excellent and (b) cheaper than the '82. Figeac is a little inconsistent, though the best bottles are a fine melange of Left and Right Bank.

This vintage provides a bevy of fantastic Sauternes, crowned by an exceptional 1983 Yquem: tangy and concentrated when re-tasted in February 2022. The 1983 Climens was firing on all pistons after almost four decades, while Doisy-Védrines, Raymond-Lafon and de Fargues are all worth seeking out. A couple of Sauternes such as Suduiraut had lost their mojo during this period and were unable to exploit the benevolent season, yet there are wines such as 1983 Rabaud-Promis that are delightful after three or four decades.

1983
(Continued)

1870

2020

1983
(Continued)

Event
Microsoft launches Word 1.0

The launch of Microsoft Word 1.0 in October 1983 is a significant landmark, given how much offices would eventually rely on it. Developed by Xerox programmers Charles Simonyi and Richard Brodie, who had been hired by Bill Gates and Paul Allen in 1981, the first version simply allowed people to create, save and print documents on MS-DOS and Xenix systems. Competition from WordPerfect meant that Word was no overnight success and it was only after it was packaged with other Microsoft applications following the 1990 launch of Windows 3.0 that it began to dominate the market. This paragraph was written on Word.

Film
Scarface
– Brian De Palma

Al Pacino, plus his "little friend", puts in a trademark bravura performance as Tony Montana. *Scarface* charts the ex-convict's ascent/descent from Florida refugee camp to deranged boss of a drug cartel. Scripted by Oliver Stone, De Palma's high-octane adaptation of the 1932 film contains a litany of memorable quotes and set-pieces, not least the almost comical mountain of cocaine (actually, powdered milk) in Montana's office as the film reaches its bloody conclusion. A machine-gun of profanities, violence and testosterone, *Scarface* is counterbalanced by its strong female characters, played by Michelle Pfeiffer and Mary Elizabeth Mastrantonio, even though both ultimately pay the price for being part of Montana's ambitions.

Music
This Charming Man – The Smiths

With his fifties quiff, hearing aid and flailing gladioli, Morrissey made the eighties tolerable for outsiders and misfits. Also featuring songwriter and guitarist Johnny Marr, who had pearl-like hooks and melodies on tap, his Manchester four-piece were the defining alternative band of the decade. The Smiths were a complete package who came with their own ideals and distinctive aesthetic. Written by Marr in a dazzlingly productive 20 minutes for a forthcoming John Peel session, *This Charming Man*'s audacious opening line about punctured bicycles and desolate hillsides sets the tone for Morrissey's enigmatic yet evocative lyrics, which embroider lines from the films *Sleuth* and *A Taste of Honey*. The band's debut on *Top of the Pops* was arguably as epochal as Bowie's in the seventies and inspired a future generation of musicians. (Incidentally, upon meeting Johnny Marr at a record signing, I enquired if he had a penchant for wine. He replied that though now teetotal, he has vague memories of enjoying Meursault and Pouilly-Fuissé.)

Nineteen eighty-four is the weak link in a run of excellent Bordeaux vintages that offers diminishing returns with passing time.

The growing season began cold and rainy. This inclemency continued into February and consequently the vines remained in stand-by mode. The chilly conditions continued to drag on so that barely a shoot was seen until 10 April. From then on, warm temperatures into the low twenties encouraged them to make up for lost time and by the end of the month the mercury had reached 28°C (82°F), a level not seen in April since 1893 or 1945, according to the Tastet-Lawton archives. May was cold and wet from start to finish, only improving from 8 June when the sap abruptly shot up. The first flowers appeared three days later and *pleine fleur* was on 17 June. Merchants talked optimistically of a decent crop. However, flowering was too rapid and by July it became clear that this had acutely affected the Merlot. Some Right Bank vineyards lost 60% to 70% of their crop, with losses only marginally lower on the Left Bank. Everything now relied on the Cabernets. July was hot with temperatures reaching 35°C (95°F) in the last 10 days and *véraison* began around 2 August. The month saw cooler temperatures, mainly in the mid to high-twenties with just one heat spike on 19 August.

September began well with the mercury reaching 35°C (95°F) but rain and cooler temperatures followed. The jury was out on whether 1984 could bestow a decent crop prior to picking, though there was hope after a warm and dry spell during the last five days of the month. The first pickers entered vineyards from 1 October, which unfortunately also marked the start of five rainy days. A lucky few had dispatched pickers earlier, including Château Margaux, which harvested on 29 and 30 September in much better conditions. A dry spell from 6 October signalled the majority to start the harvest and by now two things were clear: first, that the Merlot was around one-quarter of the average production and, second, must weights were low at around 10.5% for the Cabernets. At least the weather remained dry for the rest of the harvest, which finished around 15 October. In Sauternes, rain had prevented picking in September, so harvest was late, with Yquem only sending out pickers on 17 October. Harvesters were hampered by three weeks of rain and estates had to eke out a small amount of botrytised grapes that lacked real concentration.

Having infrequently tasted this vintage, I don't want to completely write it off. For example, a bottle of 1984 Château Margaux was splendid when opened at home in 2001, suggesting that the estate's decision to pick early and avoid the rain gave it the chance to make a successful wine. For years I badgered managing director Paul Pontallier to open another bottle and both of us kept forgetting… until sadly it was too late and he passed away. Eventually, his successor Philippe Bascaules obliged, bemused why I had requested such a derided

1984

1870

2020

1984
(Continued)

vintage, though he was pleasantly surprised when it showed just as well, albeit softer and more tertiary than two decades before. Some châteaux were so devastated by the coulure that they didn't add a single Merlot berry to their blends, including Lafite Rothschild, whose 1984 was rather surly in February 2019. In an odd way, the vintage provides an intriguing glimpse into how the estate's wines would taste without Merlot. My conclusion is that it's like playing a piano with one hand – you can listen to the tune but it doesn't sound complete. The 1984 La Mission Haut-Brion lacked vigour and felt chaptalised and the less said about Pichon Baron and Brane-Cantenac the better.

Nothing on the Right Bank has been of note. Two bottles of 1984 Le Pin were rustic and smudged; others such as Lafleur and La Conseillante offered a meatiness but, hey, you can get that with a Sunday roast. The only redeeming feature of this vintage is its overlooked dry whites, such as the 1984 Domaine de Chevalier Blanc, which was opened as part of a blind vertical by Olivier Bernard at Taillevent in Paris and elicited oohs and aahs from the mainly French journalists.

Event
Miners strike across the UK

After the National Coal Board announced the closure of 20 collieries in March 1984 with the loss of 20,000 jobs, miners began a series of strikes led by trade union firebrand Arthur Scargill. The following months saw an escalation in violence, with pitched clashes between miners and police that culminated in the so-called Battle of Orgreave on 18 June 1984. Policed charged on horseback wielding truncheons, resulting in bloody scenes sprawled across newspaper front pages the following day. Margaret Thatcher enflamed tensions by declaring it a "rule of the mob". With families to support and no income, miners returned to coalfaces almost a year after the strike had begun with the industry in terminal decline.

Music
When Doves Cry
– Prince and the Revolution

With multiple-platinum-selling album *Purple Rain* and box-office smash of the same name, Prince dominated 1984. *When Doves Cry* was the last song written for the semi-autobiographical film, recorded at Sunset Sound studios using his trusty Linn LM-1 drum machine. The Minneapolis polymath played all the instruments and after a discussion with singer Jill Jones, ingeniously stripped out the bass line to enhance its minimalism, telling his engineer: "There's nobody that's going to have the guts to do this" – a phrase applicable to Prince Roger Nelson's imperial reign throughout the decade.

Film
The Terminator
– James Cameron

He only uttered 14 lines in the entire movie but with his cache of automatic machine guns, Arnold Schwarzenegger needed few words to hunt down Sarah Connor. Thankfully, James Cameron rejected the production company's suggestion that Michael Biehn's character should travel back in time with a cyborg canine sidekick. During filming the crew created the movie's Tech Noir nightclub, where the Terminator first finds Connor, for real in the centre of L.A. and had to turn away would-be club-goers who assumed it was a genuine venue. Schwarzenegger also had trouble saying his famous catchphrase "I'll be back" and told Cameron it sounded strange enunciated in a German accent. Cameron refused his request to change it, but agreed to film multiple takes and choose the best. Made on a low budget, *The Terminator* initially met with mixed reviews but is now regarded as a sci-fi classic.

1985

Nineteen eight-five is the popular kid in class that nobody has a bad word to say against. Contentiously, that is something neither the more reputed 1982 or 1990 vintages can claim.

The year began with a severe cold snap, temperatures gradually falling to -16°C (3.2°F) in Bordeaux and -20°C (-4°F) out in rural areas, practically freezing the Garonne. The glacial period only ended in the final week of January and vineyard managers had to wait until vines had commenced growth to gauge how much damage had been sustained. Early February was much warmer and damp, though temperatures fell back below zero towards the end of the month. March remained chilly and rainy with spring-like weather finally deigning Bordeaux with its presence in April, when the mercury reached the low twenties and expedited leafing. The month was changeable but May saw rapid shoot-growth as temperatures reached 20°C (68°F). By this time, growers could see that the vines had escaped frost damage from January's freeze by a whisker, with only younger vines affected. Had it been a degree or two colder, there could have been a repeat of 1956. Cold weather at the beginning of May retarded growth and storms brought hail damage on 26 May in parts of Macau, Graves and Entre-Deux-Mers, with La Lagune losing around 30% of its crop. Sauternes and Barsac were also hit hard, especially the latter. June saw some relief with warmer and more benign conditions and the first flowers dotted the landscape on the 4th with flowering itself passing smoothly. July began very warm at 33°C (91°F) with two heat spikes of 36°C (97°F) and 35°C (95°F) on 13 and 24 July. August was less torrid with temperatures bobbing around in the higher twenties, interrupted by occasional rain.

September continued warm and it remained particularly dry, the driest since 1929, with just 22 mm (¾ in) of rain recorded in August and September. The dry whites were picked from 19 September and the reds were broached from around 25 September. It remained warm, with a balmy 30°C (86°F) at the end of the month. Only 1961 and 1964 had been hotter according to Sichel's records. It was an abundant crop that averaged around 60 hl/ha – more than in 1982 and unsurprisingly must weights were a healthy 12.5%. Rain finally returned on 4 October, though sunny and unseasonably warm conditions soon followed so that thermometers still read 25°C (77°F) when harvest ended around 15 October. Colours were deep, fruit was ripe, volumes were high and châteaux proprietors were smiling. The only weak spot, as in 1982, was down in Sauternes, where only one day of rain between 15 September and 1 November meant there was negligible botrytis formation. That did not stop the team at Yquem from conducting a rare December harvest.

The bottom line is that this growing season bestowed sensual wines with caressing textures and no hard edges – unlike 1986 – on both Left and Right Bank. This is embodied in the exquisite 1985 Léoville-Las

Cases. The formidable Saint-Julien has a proclivity to come across as a bit distant, like it doesn't want to get to know you, yet numerous bottles have left me completely smitten. The First Growths are drinking beautifully with the exception of the 1985 Latour, which inexplicably always lacks substance and chutzpah. I am a sucker for the 1985 Mouton Rothschild, partly because of the wine and partly because it sports one of my favourite artist labels, one by Paul Delvaux. Equal to those is the sublime 1985 Lynch-Bages, a textbook Pauillac that has entranced many times, most recently with Jean-Michel and Jean-Charles Cazes at the château during a (very) extended lunch. It shows no signs of losing its charm. Likewise, I was amazed by a 1985 Langoa Barton that I proffered for a La Paulée-style dinner in London: impressive concentration and fleshiness, perchance superior to Léoville Barton?

Over on the Right Bank, three bottles of the 1985 Le Pin have been gorgeous. The late John Avery MW once told me that he returned five cases erroneously sent to his Bristol cellar as he had never heard of this Pomerol cru. He could have kept them and exchanged them for a small terraced house. Jacques and Sylvie Guinaudeau opened their account at Lafleur with a sensational and almost stentorian wine, while Pétrus is curiously slight in stature, the estate dwelling in a rare off-period. In Saint-Émilion, the 1985 Cheval Blanc is lent mic-dropping complexity by its exquisite Cabernet Franc, though a few such as Ausone, Figeac and Canon did not reach full potential. Sauternes suffered a lack of botrytis and the wines are generally sound but uninteresting. If you are seeking a white Bordeaux, try to find the 1985 Haut-Brion Blanc, one of the greatest ever produced and still a crystalline beauty.

Film
My Beautiful Laundrette – Stephen Frears

In 1985, Daniel Day-Lewis starred in two films released on the same day (7 March) in New York: *My Beautiful Laundrette* and *A Room with a View*. They could not have been more different – in the former, Day-Lewis plays a working-class homosexual in love with a Pakistani businessman and, in the latter, an Edwardian snob – but both marked the introduction of a gifted and versatile actor. The screenplay for *My Beautiful Laundrette* was written by author Hanif Kureishi and the film was one of the first to directly attack Thatcherism. Shot on a £600,000 budget, it went on to become one of the most successful British independent movies.

1985
(Continued)

Event
Live Aid rocks the world

The next logical step after Band Aid was for Bob Geldof to organise the greatest charity concert in the world. The Boomtown Rat's hubris plus some well-intentioned coercion persuaded pop royalty to put egos and pay-packages aside for a 20-minute slot at either Wembley in London or John F. Kennedy Stadium in Philadelphia. At noon on 13 July 1985, Status Quo kicked off the live broadcast with an apt *Rocking All Over the World* and a cavalcade of acts followed. Over the next several hours, the concert signalled U2's imminent global stardom, introduced a four-letter expletive into children's lexicons after Geldof lost his rag in a live transmission, brought millions to tears as The Cars' *Drive* soundtracked images of starving children, saw Led Zeppelin's legacy jeopardised after a ramshackle performance, silenced Paul McCartney with a faulty microphone and confirmed a peerless Freddie Mercury as the frontman you'd least like to follow on-stage.

Music
Running Up That Hill
– Kate Bush

For her fifth album, Kate Bush retreated and built her own studio at East Wickham Farm where she could relax and take her time over the recording. Originally called "A Deal With God", the song started as a tribal drum pattern composed by then-partner Del Palmer, which she used to construct the melody with a cutting-edge Fairlight sampler. The track was renamed after Bush reluctantly acquiesced to the demands of nervous record execs, who feared it might alienate Catholic markets. *Running Up That Hill* reached a huge audience on Terry Wogan's midweek chat show on 5 August 1985, Bush's mesmerising performance at a lectern eerily prefiguring Donald Trump's mannerisms years later. It became her biggest hit since *Wuthering Heights*, though it took another 37 years to top the UK charts after it was discovered by a new generation of fans thanks to Netflix retro-drama *Stranger Things*.

This vintage definitely favoured the Left Bank and its Cabernet-based wines. The watchword here is patience.

The year began with a very cold winter, the growth cycle lagging a month behind by the end of April, though thankfully there were no frost episodes. May and June witnessed a turnaround, dry and hot conditions allowing vines to catch up. This meant that flowering was only slightly later than average, with mid-flowering on 20 June and finishing under ideal conditions. A long, dry and hot summer ensued, the driest for two decades, despite a welcome 60 mm (2½ in) of rain in August. *Mi-véraison* was around 19 August, which meant harvest would be around the beginning of October.

Dry conditions prevailed until mid-September, when storms compromised many of the earlier-picked dry white and Right Bank wines. On 14 and 15 September alone, many château were soaked with 40–60 mm (1½–2½ in) of rainfall, but it was a torrential downpour on 23 September that inflicted real damage, topping 100 mm (4 in) in a single day in the worst-affected areas such as the Graves, with flooding in Bordeaux city. These violent storms were localised, so other appellations were far less affected. The northern Médoc, for example, saw just 20 mm (¾ in) for the entire month, with Sichel comparing the violent weather to 1975 and 1983. The Right Bank witnessed exceptionally high yields with respect to the Merlot, which coupled with the rain led to widespread dilution. Those on the Left Bank could afford to wait for their later-ripening Cabernet Sauvignon and benefited from a remarkably dry spell when hardly a drop of rain fell over the first 10 days of October. In fact, there was rarely a moment when umbrellas were needed until 22 October. Yields on the Left Bank were not as high as on the Right and crop-thinning during the summer moderated volumes. Nevertheless, the Gironde produced 6.3 million hl of which 4.5 million hl constituted AC Bordeaux, the largest volume since 1934 and almost 30% higher than the abundant 1982 vintage. The protracted and dry growing season produced a crop of small, thick-skinned berries, which formed tannic, structured wines that were unapproachable in their youth. In fact, Jean-Michel Cazes recalled the barrel samples being so tannic that they could only taste 15 or 16 each session. On the Right Bank, the opposite was true and some properties tried to remedy their dilute wines by bleeding tanks to increase the skin-to-juice ratio and extract more density.

The September rains led to humidity and morning mists that provided ideal conditions for widespread botrytis in Sauternes, and there was even more in October after 40 mm (1½ in) of rain. Sunny conditions followed in November, though workers often had to work in the mists. Producers who picked earlier could have been affected by the rain, so it rewarded those who waited.

1986

This is a quasi-notorious vintage owing to a legion of Left Bank wines that tested wine lovers' patience to the limit and, for some, beyond the limit. It was definitely not a year for those seeking immediate gratification, who would be more attracted to the fleshier and sensual 1982s or 1985s. The structured, tannic '86s invite comparisons with the '75s, though whereas the latter tended to dry out with bottle age and at worst leave husks of austere and unappealing wines, the '86s were not resigned to a similar fate for two reasons. First, they possess superior balance and, second, they tend to contain more fruit. They are maturing on their own terms and reward those with the wherewithal to squirrel them away until the time is right for the wine and not for the wine lover. The 1986 Mouton Rothschild is a monumental First Growth endowed with stunning density and concentration, even if a bottle poured by former winemaker Philippe Dhalluin over lunch was so precocious that I mistook it for the 1982. I finished a couple of glasses and duly missed my return flight home, but some things are worth it. Paul Pontallier fashioned a 1986 Château Margaux with unerring symmetry, while a 1986 Haut-Brion was unbelievably youthful when poured blind after 35 years. Some previously backward wines that had "shop closed" signs dangling around their necks for years are now finally open for business, not least a stunning Léoville-Las Cases uncorked to celebrate the late great Steven Spurrier in October 2021. Again, the 1986 Latour fails to launch and I've upset many dinners by lamenting its so-so performance. I just cannot lie about a wine that ought to have knocked your socks off and, personally, I prefer the 1986 Pichon-Lalande (though not the Pichon Baron, whose renaissance still lay a couple of years ahead). Another oft-overlooked gem is the 1986 Talbot, a wonderful Saint-Julien that stood out at the château's vertical to celebrate a century's ownership by the Cordier family.

Unfortunately, the Right Bank is inconsistent. Even the titans of Pétrus and Lafleur are unable to muster their usual brilliance and Ausone and Cheval Blanc are rather austere. Few bottles from Pomerol or Saint-Émilion have left a positive impression – it was just not their year. One intriguing wine I've enjoyed several times is the mischievously titled 1986 Bâtard-Chevalier, the white Second Wine from Olivier Bernard's Domaine de Chevalier – at least until a letter from his friends in Burgundy, who failed to appreciate his tongue-in-cheek homage to their Grand Crus, forced him into a name change. I bought a few bottles for fun and even after 30 years it was fresh and delicious. Sauternes prospered in 1986 with several outstanding wines, though I find them less consistent than 1983. It is crowned by the 1986 Yquem and Climens, though Suduiraut was still "off the boil" in this era. I have also encountered wonderful bottles of Doisy-Védrines, an energetic Rieussec and a lush Château de Fargues that staggered under the weight of botrytis.

Event
Maradona's Hand of God

Never has a player turned from sinner to saint in such a short space of time. England were playing Argentina in the quarter-final of the World Cup at the Azteca Stadium in Mexico City. Tensions were rife as the teams were playing their first match since the Falklands War. Six minutes into the second half, Diego Maradona, the most gifted footballer of his generation, found himself competing for a high ball against goalkeeper Peter Shilton, some 20 cm (8 in) taller than the vertically challenged Argentinean, and it ended up bouncing in the goal. It was not completely obvious, but hadn't the ball come off Maradona's fist above his head? The ref would surely spot that… wouldn't he? Maradona pelted up the pitch in rapturous celebration. "I looked behind to see if the referee had taken the bait," Maradona confessed in an interview years later (to Gary Lineker, who scored England's consolation goal). Despite the remonstrating English players, the goal stood. Asked later whether it was a handball, Maradona replied that he had scored "A little with the head of Maradona, and a little with the hand of God". Fans would never have forgiven him, but then four minutes later he weaved his way through the England team with the ball glued to his boot to score arguably the greatest goal of all time.

Music
Walk This Way –
Run D.M.C.

Though the likes of The Sugarhill Gang, Grandmaster Flash and Run D.M.C. themselves had already laid the foundations of rap music, *Walk This Way* was the song that introduced many people to the genre. Apparently, when 22-year old Def Jam supremo Rick Rubin first telephoned to discuss the possibility of Aerosmith updating the 1975 hit, their manager replied: "What's rap?" That said, how many teenagers of the time would have known about Aerosmith, whose own career was in a tailspin? With the help of its memorable video – in which Steve Tyler smashes down the fake wall between the groups' rehearsal rooms to unite musicians and genres – *Walk This Way* became the first rap song to break the top 10 Stateside and provided a wake-up call to all those who had treated rap as a novelty. In the long-term, Aerosmith – uncredited on the sleeve – arguably benefited more from the team-up than Run D.M.C., becoming unit-shifting cross-generational elder statesmen of metal.

1986 *(Continued)*

Film
Ferris Bueller's Day Off
– John Hughes

Every teenager aspires to be as cool as Ferris Bueller in John Hughes's quintessential teen flick. He's the ultimate popular school kid: rebellious yet cherubic, with a beautiful girl on his arm, and utterly self-assured. Yet he's never smug or aloof because the audience is also part of his clique, in for the ride and hanging on to every word of sage advice. "Life moves pretty fast," he counsels. "If you don't stop and look around once in a while, you could miss it." Profound. Matthew Broderick inhabits the role to the extent that it's impossible to know where the actor ends and Bueller begins. We all like to imagine we have a bit of Bueller in all of us.

In a strong second half of the decade, the 1987 vintage is the only one that does not pass muster.

January was freezing cold, -18°C (0.5°F) in some places, making sure the sap was down to its lowest. Despite a brief cold snap, average temperatures for February were warmer, though it was a false dawn as it remained fresh throughout March, which stunted shoot growth. The weather turned volte face with a warm and clement April, temperatures hovering around the mid-twenties for the entire month and accelerating growth, particularly towards the end. May continued in the same vein and so châteaux were unconcerned about frost. But after the first flowers around 1 June, things turned for the worse on the afternoon of 7 June, when a fierce storm ripped through the region from the southeast. Fortunately, there was no vine damage but the rain disrupted flowering, and coulure was widespread across the region. That year, Prince Andrew and the Duchess of York attended the Fête de la Fleur at Beychevelle, though they picked the rainiest June since 1966 when 112 mm (4½ in) had drenched the area. July was hot with intermittent storms, the mercury peaking at 33°C (91°F) on 13 July but with fresh nights. The hot weather continued into August, 36°C (97°F) recorded on 20 August during one heat spike, cooling down a little towards the end of the month. According to Sichel's records, the average temperature from June to September was 20.3°C (68.5°F), equal to 1982. But the hot weather did not even out maturity as you would expect, so the Merlot and especially Cabernets began to show irregular sugar levels.

The Indian summer encouraged châteaux to wait. A high of 37°C (99°F) was recorded in one heat wave from 15 to 18 September and the final week of the month saw just 8mm of rain. The picking began on 1 October, but 50 mm (2 in) of rain deluged the region that first week and 67 mm (2½ in) the following. There was no time to waste and harvesters toiled through downpours. Lawton notes that this was the first time he had witnessed a washed-out harvest since 1974. Most of the picking was completed by 18 October, by which time most were suffering some dilution. In Sauternes, the combination of rain and tropical heat made picking a laborious, meticulous stop-start affair. It was difficult to make decent Sauternes, though not impossible.

So near, yet so far. The 1987 Bordeaux might have been another 1982, but rain washed away hopes of a great vintage at harvest. But they say it is better to pick dilute grapes than rotten ones and so the 1987s have never been regarded as an outright disaster. My introduction to the vintage was a 1987 Lafite Rothschild, light but balanced, not dissimilar to almost every wine I subsequently tasted from this growing season. The 1987 Latour, for example, tasted blind at the château in March 2022, was leafy and simple. It was perfectly drinkable but I had almost forgotten it by teatime. Several bottles of 1987 Mouton Rothschild

1987

were drinking well at around 15–20 years but are likely to have dried out since then. A 1987 Lagrange surpassed expectations at a vertical in 2019, though a 1987 Pichon Baron is more vegetal than a greengrocer, Pichon-Lalande far superior by comparison. On the Right Bank, I have fond memories of 1987 Le Pin, which could fool you into thinking there was stowaway Cabernet Franc in the blend. The 1987 Pétrus is fine-boned and leafy. Nothing sticks out as terrible, though nothing merits superlatives. The best wines are the dry whites picked before the rains: 1987 Domaine de Chevalier Blanc, Malartic-Lagravière Blanc and Haut-Brion Blanc, all delicious, slightly bitter, edgy and maturing beautifully. I have tasted few Sauternes and many, like Suduiraut, opted not to release any wine. The best is predictably Yquem.

Event
The great October hurricane

Music
Where the Streets Have No Name – U2

On the evening of 15 October 1987, BBC weatherman Michael Fish allayed viewers' fears of an impending storm. "Earlier on today, apparently, a woman rang the BBC and said she heard there was a hurricane on the way," he assured. "Well, if you're watching, don't worry, there isn't." A few hours later the worst storm since 1703 made landfall in Cornwall and tracked across southern England, wrecking everything in its path. Winds up to 115 mph (185 km/h) felled an estimated 15 million trees, ripped roofs off houses, capsized ferries and tragically killed 18 in the UK and 4 in France.

Where the Streets Have No Name is the opening track to the *The Joshua Tree* album, which catapulted U2 to the major league in 1987. It was co-produced by Brian Eno (with Daniel Lanois), who admitted in interviews that he laboured over the song's complex rhythm section. The accompanying video was an homage to The Beatles' 1969 rooftop performance. The group's impromptu show on the top of the Republic Liquor Shop in downtown Los Angeles on 27 March caused pandemonium. Cameras captured the ecstatic crowds and ensuing chaos until an increasingly frustrated L.A.P.D. closed everything down – though not before U2 had got through the song four times.

Film
Withnail and I
– Bruce Robinson

"We want the finest wines available to humanity! We want them here and we want them now!" Many reading this book will empathise with Withnail (Richard E. Grant) in Bruce Robinson's classic comedy. Making their big-screen debuts, Grant and Paul McGann play a pair of out-of-work actors-cum-dipsomaniacs who embark on the worst road trip ever to Uncle Monty's cottage in the damp, wet countryside. It surely inspired many to attempt rolling their own "Camberwell Carrot", which in the film consisted of herbal cigarettes.

1988

The 1988 vintage is the first and perhaps least revered of the triumvirate that finished the decade.

January and February were warm and ensured that vines were quick out of the blocks in terms of growth. April and May continued in similar fashion – 2°C (28.5°F) above normal but also very wet. Vineyard managers vexed about the sanitary state of the vines were constantly spraying to keep rot and insects at bay. Towards the end of May, the mercury plummeted and a late flowering was expected. But on 1 June, the wind suddenly swung to the south and warmer conditions brought things forward. Bill Blatch makes the important point that the warm weather leading up to flowering meant that, unlike in 1984, which saw similar conditions, the sap had risen in the vines, so flowering passed more smoothly than anticipated. Nevertheless, coulure and millerandage did affect some parcels of Merlot. After 12 June, the weather remained clement, yet a series of violent storms and hail followed, particularly on 29 June when the northern sectors of Margaux were hit. The Graves also suffered skirmishes. Yet again, vineyard teams had to be vigilant and pro-active in spraying against rot. Finally, from 4 July, the weather settled when a high-pressure system sashayed in from the Atlantic, bringing dryness that improved sanitary conditions. August was very dry with just 16 mm (½ in) of rain, though not particularly hot. Temperatures averaged 19.7°C (67.5°F) from July to September.

Despite a couple of storms in September, winemakers worried about drought and vine stress, particularly during a heat wave from the 4th to the 15th when the mercury reached 37°C (99°F). Fortunately, ample underground reserves of moisture alleviated stress and so vines continued to photosynthesise. It was not a completely trouble-free run-in. Cold northerlies between 15 and 19 September interrupted the cycle and some Cabernet Sauvignon vines on well-drained gravel soils suffered minor blockage. The week of 19 September saw dry conditions nudge ripeness levels on nicely, with one alcoholic degree added every four or five days, though sugar levels remained low and some of the smaller, less quality-driven growers cut their losses and picked before bunches had reached full ripeness. A storm crossed the region on 29 September, but this was followed by dry and warm conditions when much of the Merlot was picked. The Cabernets were still not quite ripe and rain on 12 October prompted some growers to pick early at low maturity levels, whereas those who sat it out and picked on or around 23 October reaped the rewards of waiting as weather conditions meliorated. It had been a case, as Sichel noted, of winemakers holding their nerve during changeable conditions. Those who waited made very good wines, those who didn't produced wines that were green and lacked fruit. Quality was concentrated at the top of the pyramid, where châteaux could perhaps afford to be more patient and sort the fruit more rigorously.

Sauternes enjoyed the first in an unprecedented golden trio of great vintages. Bill Blatch pointed out that they were considered extremely sweet for that time with residual sugar levels between 100 g/l and 125 g/l. By comparison the best Sauternes vintages between 1949 and 1976 were around 85 g/l to 95 g/l. Clement weather from July sealed in the concentration, though picking began late, after the September storms ignited botrytis infection. Harvest lasted from mid-October until the end of December and at Yquem required six passes through the vineyard.

Overall, the wines lacked the richness of the succeeding two vintages, but there was no rot and a clutch of châteaux produced excellent wines. Among the First Growths, the standout is 1988 Lafite Rothschild. Tasted blind in 2018 at an event to mark 150 years since Baron James de Rothschild acquired the First Growth, it showed the 1989 and 1990 a lesson or two – quintessential Lafite Rothschild, fine-boned, balanced and with effortless class. It just has the edge over a slightly savoury, almost meaty, but excellent Latour. I often find the Mouton Rothschild just a little hard-edged and prefer the 1988 Château Margaux, all cedar-tinged fruit and more pliant on the palate. An improving Rauzan-Ségla is also showing well after three decades. The 1988 La Mission Haut-Brion has lovely balance and welcome leafiness and can match Haut-Brion over the road. The 1988 Pichon Baron, tasted with Christian Seely, marked the beginning of the château's long-overdue comeback under new owners and new director Jean-Michel Cazes of Lynch-Bages, though has been eclipsed by the two succeeding vintages. I have fond memories of the 1988 Léoville Barton, which the late Anthony Barton brought to the Saint-Julien restaurant where I was interviewing him. The raconteur extraordinaire was midway through some ribald tale when his face contorted and he disappeared under the table. My God – was he having a heart attack? In fact, his false teeth had fallen out. "So sorry about that…" he said and just continued his story as if nothing had happened. Some Médoc wines such as Grand-Puy-Lacoste and Léoville-Las Cases can now taste a little hard, though others such as Haut-Bailly can still offer pleasure for those who like "trad claret".

The Right Bank is less consistent. I opened my own 1988 Le Pin to celebrate my recruitment to *The Wine Advocate* in 2006 and it offered grace and depth. The 1988 Lafleur with Baptiste and Julie Guinaudeau was endowed with a light liquorice tinge. The 1988 Pétrus lies in the shadow of the '89 and '90, though bestowed with what I described as a "discrete sense of breeding" amongst 30 other vintages at an epic vertical in 2019. The 1988s in Pomerol and Saint-Émilion can occasionally feel ponderous and rustic compared with recent vintages, though Cheval Blanc, Angélus and Figeac have leathery, tertiary noses that can be appealing. The 1988 Sauternes possess a revivifying piquancy, almost Aszú-like in style, a quite tangy bottle of 1988 Yquem almost stealing the show from a flight of Domaine Roumier '88s in 2021, several others such as Climens, Coutet and Doisy-Védrines continuing to drink splendidly.

1988

(Continued)

1870

2020

1988 *(Continued)*

Event
Moscow Summit between
Reagan and Gorbachev

The Cold War between the US
and the USSR had been thawing
in the lead-up to the Moscow
Summit between President
Ronald Reagan and Soviet leader
Mikhail Gorbachev. After the
previous year's Washington
meeting, the Moscow Summit
was held from 29 May to 3 June
1988 and saw the two statesmen
sign the Intermediate-Range
Nuclear Forces Treaty. The
spectre of nuclear war seemed
to be receding. On the 31 May,
Gorbachev took Reagan for a
tour of Red Square. Stopping
briefly, surrounded by reporters,
Reagan said that, "The one
thing that General Secretary
Gorbachev and I have in common
is that there must be friendship
between our two countries." Sadly,
little of that friendship can be
seen writing in 2022.

Music
Promised Land
– Joe Smooth

The so-called "Second Summer
of Love" saw illegal warehouse
parties spring up across the
English countryside, especially
around the M25. Sporting
bandanas and smiley t-shirts,
youths packed into sweaty
warehouses and unused fields
where sound-systems pumped
out the latest acid house or
Detroit techno. Anthems such
as Joe Smooth's *Promised Land*
fused gospel-like vocals and
optimism with a pounding techno
beat, paradoxically uplifting
yet somehow melancholic.
Though recorded in 1987 it only
breached the charts two years
later, yet was ubiquitous around
raves throughout 1988. Ask
any retired club-goer and they
still get misty-eyed at the mere
mention of *Promised Land* as they
momentarily relive those halcyon
days of what was arguably the last
genuine youthful rebellion.

Film
Die Hard – John McTiernan

A non-stop adrenaline rush, *Die Hard* is often described as "the
ultimate action movie". Bruce Willis stars as NYPD cop John McClane
single-handedly tackling a crack team of robbers in Nakatomi Plaza,
while Alan Rickman lifts the film above the norm with his sublime
turn as criminal mastermind Hans Gruber. The theatre actor, in his
first movie role, persuaded the writers to make Gruber intelligent
and urbane, and opted not to meet Willis until they performed their
first scene together in order to capture greater spontaneity on camera.
In fact, much of the whip-cracking, quotable script was improvised.
Debate continues over whether *Die Hard* is a Christmas movie or not.
Maybe unintentionally it is.

Nineteen eighty-nine received a mixed reception upon release. Too young to have tasted the vintage in its youth, I feel the wines have really come into their own with age.

The year began with mild temperatures and dry conditions relieved by deluges in late February. The end of March saw budding three weeks earlier than usual and there were whispers of a mid-August harvest (inconceivable at the time though half-expected in these days of climate change). The only downside was that the budding of white varieties was erratic, portending a small crop of dry whites. April was downright miserable, pouring for 24 out of 30 days. According to Bill Blatch's vintage report, temperatures languished between 4°C (39°F) and 8°C (46°F) for 21 of those days. Naturally, such inclement conditions slammed the brakes on the vines' growth cycle. May was the opposite of April: dry and around 5°C (41°F) warmer than usual with 50% more sunlight hours, predicating regular flowering from the end of May until around 12 June with minor coulure and millerandage. June was extremely hot with occasional heavy storms. Some hail damage on 6 July affected Sauternes – one-quarter of the crop was destroyed at Yquem – though it was just the first in a trilogy of hailstorms that continued on 7 and 16 August. Nevertheless, temperatures from June to September averaged 20.9°C (69.6°F), not dissimilar to 1947, and it was extraordinarily dry – just 195 mm (7½ in) of rain fell between May and September. As a consequence, winemakers faced a dilemma: go ahead and pick to avoid the risk of rain, or wait for the fruit to fully mature – even though some Merlot parcels were reaching 13% potential alcohol.

Most started the picking between 5 and 7 September, though one or two estates had sent their harvesters out to pick their young Merlot at the end of August. Rain on 10 September, heavy in the southern Médoc and Saint-Émilion, reduced some alcohol levels by an entire degree according to Bill Blatch's report, though it mainly served to revivify vines suffering blocked maturity. Overall the weather remained hot and dry, allowing châteaux to pick at leisure so that end-of-harvest celebrations could take place from 25 September. Yields were enormous, especially for the Merlot: a total of 4.9 million hl of red Bordeaux AC plus 1 million hl of white Bordeaux AC. However, some wines had troubled births, with some Merlot lacking acidity and the Cabernets excessively tannic.

Sauternes relished this vintage, despite unsettled weather earlier in the season and the July hailstorm. Thereafter, it became sunny and warm. The lack of rainfall meant that botrytis infection was drawn out from 18 September to around 4 November, but at least the clement conditions meant vineyard teams could wait and undertake several passes through the vines. Showers on 12 October finally got things going, and further rain five days later created more humidity, accelerating botrytis infection. Blatch describes seasons like this as "dry botrytis" years in which single berries instead of entire bunches are botrytised, as also happened in 1986.

1989

1989
(Continued)

Perhaps 1989 could be considered a late bloomer insofar as many wines required a couple of decades to show their mettle. Inevitably, the vintage is compared to 1990. Forced to choose one, I might well opt for 1989 since the wines possess a little more nerve, expressing the nuances of appellation, rather than the growing season's imprimatur with more clarity. The vintage is crowned by the monumental Haut-Brion, a wine that united critics in praise and is arguably winemaker Jean-Bernard Delmas's greatest achievement. My first encounter was a bottle from my own cellar. On a dreary Wednesday night with friends suffering my tuna pasta in my West Norwood flat, I made an impromptu decision to crack open my most expensive vinous possession to compensate for my lack of culinary flair. Would it live up to expectations? It left all of us speechless with its kaleidoscopic nose and multi-dimensional palate – and matched my pasta perfectly. Even though the 1989 Haut-Brion is magnificent, my feeling is that the 1989 La Mission Haut-Brion now not only equals the First Growth but can surpass it, a heavenly wine that stands alongside the legendary 1955. Tasting both side by side with Delmas's son and present winemaker Jean-Philippe, the La Mission had the edge, though it's a hair's width between them. Though the First Growths are excellent, particularly Château Margaux, the real sweet spot lies within lower tiers. Who am I talking about? Step forward Lynch-Bages, Pichon Baron and Palmer, three fabulous wines with the audacity to surpass some of the First Growths. Whoever said the 1855 Classification dictated quality? I have long preferred the brilliant 1989 Montrose to the mercurial 1990 and sure, if you can find a bottle of the latter not riddled with brettanomyces, it can give the 1989 a run for its money. Yet the finest bottles of 1989 Montrose show exceptional clarity and finesse.

The Right Bank is bejewelled with great wines. The 1989 Pétrus has breath-taking stature and when juxtaposed with the 1982 and 1990 Pétrus – not a daily occurrence I might add – the 1989 is the most complete. You cannot wish for anything more in a Pomerol. The 1989 La Conseillante is fleshy and beautifully balanced and more outgoing that the surly 1989 Lafleur, which can be bolshie, requiring a long decant – and even then you have to cross your fingers it will come out and play. The 1989 Le Pin is ravishingly gorgeous. A magnum brought to a lunch was untrammelled hedonism, though unfortunately my jet-lagged colleagues from Japan could barely finish their glasses. I assisted in the matter. In Saint-Émilion, I prefer the 1989 Cheval Blanc to Ausone, while the 1989 Tertre Rôteboeuf has a meaty sumptuousness and the 1989 Angélus is the first bona fide triumph under proprietor Hubert de Boüard. Sauternes tend to be less unctuous but more tensile than the 1990s, even though they initially contained less botrytis than their 1988 counterparts. They are crowned by a sensational 1989 Yquem that contains more frisson and complexity than vintages either side. There are also exceptional Sauternes from the likes of Climens, La Tour Blanche, Lafaurie-Peyraguey and a rejuvenated Suduiraut that continue to evolve magnificently in bottle.

Event
The fall of the Berlin Wall

Geopolitical tectonic plates seemed to be shifting in 1989: student protests in Tiananmen Square, Eastern Bloc regimes falling like dominos and then the tearing down of the Berlin Wall. The catalyst was a press conference on 9 November 1989 by Politbüro official and spokesman Günter Schabowski, who stumbled in front of a packed room of journalists when asked about the timing of new travel arrangements between East and West Berlin. Crowds began massing by the concrete barrier that had ruthlessly divided Berlin since 1961 and started chipping away pieces – the so-called *Mauerspechte* (Wallpeckers) demolition. Thankfully, they left enough to allow David Hasselhoff to perform on top of the wall that New Year's Eve.

Music
Fools Gold
– The Stone Roses

Alongside fellow Mancunians the Happy Mondays, The Stone Roses spearheaded the Manchester sound dubbed "baggy" that ushered indie music into the mainstream. *Fools Gold* was an infectious fusion of guitar and dance, featuring a looped sample of James Brown's ubiquitous *Funky Drummer*, John Squire's Byrds-influenced wah-wah guitar and a bass-line inspired by Young MC's *Know How*. Although it was initially released as a B-side on 13 November 1989, public demand soon persuaded the record company to market *Fool's Gold* as the A-side and a legendary performance on *Top of the Pops* inspired a whole generation of musicians.

Film
When Harry Met Sally... – Rob Reiner

When Harry Met Sally... virtually invented the romantic comedy and you could argue that it has never been bettered. Starring Billy Crystal and Meg Ryan as the couple trying and failing to get together, the movie is best known for its fake orgasm scene, filmed at Katz's Deli in New York. Ryan suggested that she enact the orgasm in a crowded deli while Crystal thought up the immortal "I'll have what she's having" line uttered by Estelle Reiner, the director's mother. It took Ryan 30 takes to get right. That's a lot of faking.

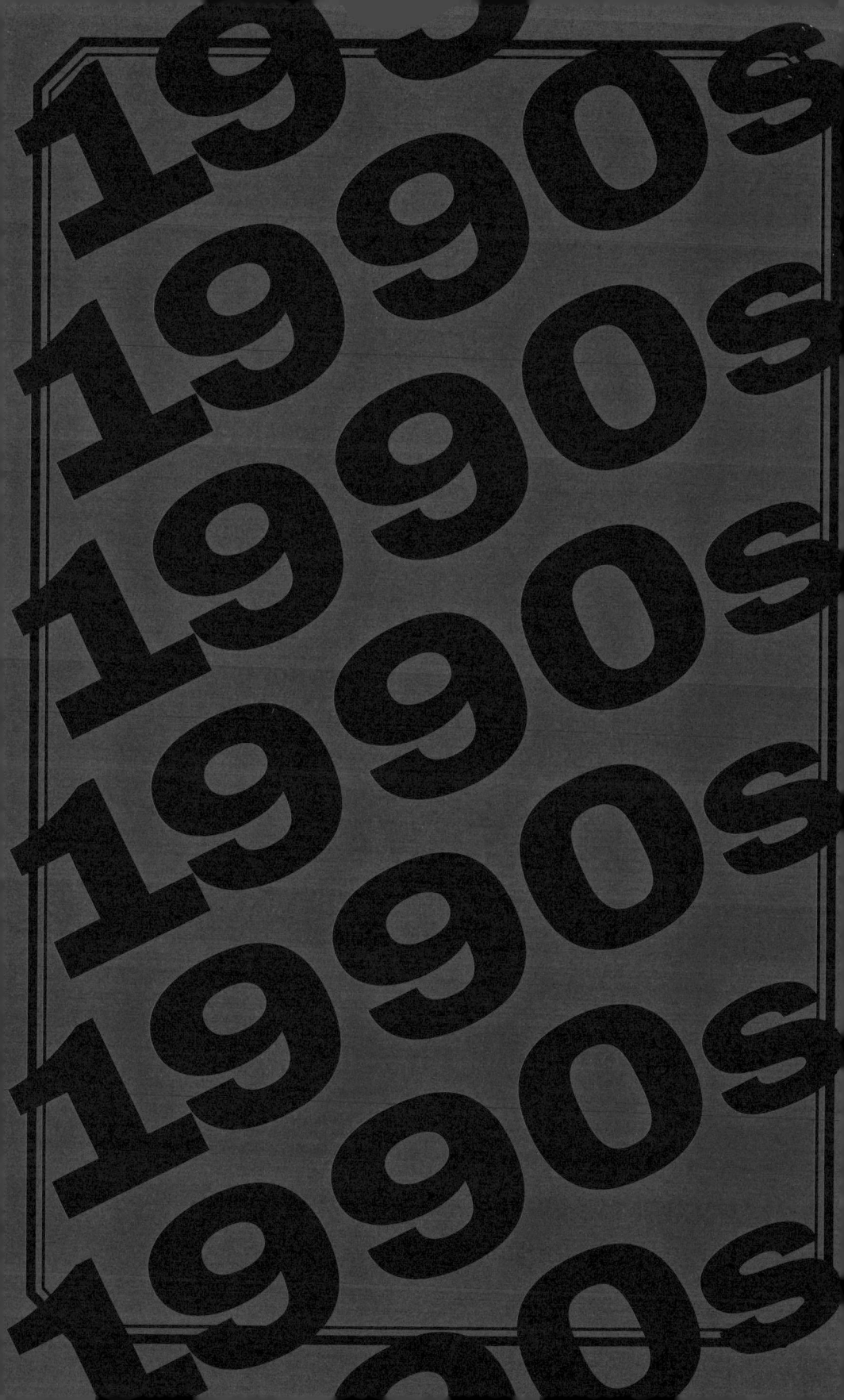

The nineties saw Bordeaux embrace technology, particularly inside wineries and, later, for communication. Alongside the concentrators that some estates had started using at the end of the eighties, many properties began dabbling with micro-oxygenation. This technical process imported from the Madiran region, where it was used to soften the stocky and somewhat obdurate Tannat grape, was employed to fix anthocyanins and tannins, render young wines more malleable and velvety, and to reduce the need for racking during barrel ageing. One of its main proponents was consultant Stéphane Derenoncourt, though he cautioned it had to be used carefully. Like the concentrators, it was a divisive technique and opponents such as John Kolasa, then at Rauzan-Ségla, Canon and Denis Dubourdieu argued that micro-oxygenated wines matured prematurely, traducing the practice as a shortcut to render samples more flattering at primeur.

Down in Sauternes, cryo-extraction was a means of removing excess water from botrytis-affected grapes by freezing bunches down to -7°C (19°F) and then pressing them. "We trialled cryo-extraction in 1986, then with a cold room in 1987, so that we could understand this technique," ex-Yquem winemaker Sandrine Garbay explained. "[It] was ultimately abandoned because it was contrary to the spirit of Yquem." Indeed, cryo-extraction quickly fell out of favour with most Sauternes estates, partly because of its prohibitive expense in a region where prices lagged behind their dry red counterparts. However, such techniques were used far more than admitted, though detractors argued that they homogenised wines and made appellations indistinguishable from each other.

The decade witnessed the rise of the so-called "*garagiste*" movement, which centred on Saint-Émilion. The catalyst was not Le Pin as some are wont to argue, rather the maiden release of Valandraud. "We had bought our first 0.6-hectare parcel in Fongaban near our current home," owner Jean-Luc Thunevin told me when I interviewed him in 2016. "In 1990 we had the land but no cellar or money to manage the vinification process. And maybe we had a bit of fear in not being able to do it right." He sold all the fruit that year, but encouraged by his friend Alain Vauthier at Ausone, decided to bottle the 1991. Thunevin subsequently augmented his original parcel with a second in Saint-Sulpice-de-Faleyrens. Established winemakers swiftly rebuked this outspoken *enfant terrible* whose vines occupied supposedly inferior sandy soil, but he cared little and established a loyal following over the decade, scotching the idea of a hierarchy based on quality of terroir. With a little help from Robert Parker, whose influence was at its peak, Thunevin led the way for both existing crus such as La Mondotte and entirely new entities such as Englishman Jonathan Maltus's

Le Dôme. Precepts of low yields, draconian green harvesting, late-picking and maturation entirely in new oak (200% for some over-zealous estates, which means the wine is transferred from one new oak barrel to a second new oak barrel during maturation) to create a kind of haute-couture wine rapidly gained popularity, especially in the US. It reached its zenith in the late nineties when it acted as an alternative hierarchy, riling those who pointed to the new producers' absence of a track record and cast doubt upon their wines' longevity. Such criticism was not unfounded. I found many failed to realise their potential, though there are exceptions, including both La Mondotte and Valandraud, which are now part Saint-Émilion's established order and producing better wines than ever. While it wasn't to everyone's taste, the movement forced consumers to rethink what makes great wine and encouraged growers to pull up their socks.

The market for Bordeaux changed throughout the 1990s. Traditional markets in Europe and the US were joined by growing demand from Asia, in particular Japan. The country always had an affinity with Bordeaux and interest and connoisseurship burgeoned among its extremely knowledgeable sommeliers, given a huge boost when Shinya Tasaki won the coveted Meilleur Sommelier du Monde title in 1995. At the same time many of the thousands of bars around Tokyo began exchanging bottles of Cognac and Armagnac for top-end Bordeaux.

As the new millennium approached, many hoped Bordeaux would bestow a vintage worthy of the numerical significance – at least once computers had been re-booted after Y2K had melted hard-drives. The nineties was the final decade in which the communication of wine relied on paper and ink, whether that meant a bimonthly copy of *The Wine Advocate* or a national newspaper column. Only a select number of journalists visited the region to report on the new vintage or were employed as full-time wine writers. Towards the end of the decade, the internet was still in its infancy, yet bulletin boards were already gaining popularity among oenophiles keen to use the new technology to share their passion. Jancis Robinson and Robert Parker were among the first to embrace the web, soon joined by others who realised they could create their own soapboxes from which to pontificate about wine.

In terms of growing seasons, whether you believe the decade began with a bang or a whimper depends on whether you define 1990 as the final year of the eighties or not. The 1991 vintage saw Bordeaux crash back down to Earth after a destructive late spring frost, providing a rude reminder that despite the progress châteaux had accomplished, Mother Nature was in charge, as mendacious

Jean-Luc Thunevin, pioneer
of the garagiste movement,
punching down an early vintage
of Valandraud.

as she is benevolent, as capricious as she can be predictable. The 1991 growing season commenced a succession of disappointing vintages: 1992, 1993 and to a lesser degree 1994, a quadruple whammy with echoes of the early thirties and seventies. However, the landscape was different. Technological progress and a growing number of quality-driven winemakers were raising the bar so that a difficult growing season – one that might have defeated producers in the past – could now bestow quite pleasurable and much more saleable wines.

It was not until 1995 that Bordeaux lovers had a crop to get excited about – arguably the last ripe vintage with modest alcohol levels, most clocking in at around 12.5% and 13%. That is partly because in the second half of the decade, more châteaux began fashioning wine designed to flatter critics, not least the omnipotent Robert Parker. Over subsequent years, a number of Bordeaux winemakers confessed feeling coerced into molding wines designed to achieve high scores rather than what suited their vineyard in that season, from proprietors some of whom rewarded and punished depending on how closely scores matched their ambitions. Of course, one must also consider climate change. Though not the headline issue that it is today, it is interesting, even disquieting, to read growing season reports from the likes of Bill Blatch and Sichel remarking on warmer temperatures. Was that coincidence or was there a pattern?

The second half of the decade includes the 1996 vintage, which was extremely well received, albeit only for the Left Bank. In 1998 the inverse occurred and the Right Bank flourished. In between, the 1997 primeur was the first in which I participated and I remember the English wine trade's howls of protest failing to coerce châteaux into reducing prices enough to stimulate demand. Nothing new there – the rhetoric had been the same in 1971. The decade finished with the 1999s, one of those in-between seasons that failed to finish the millennium in style, but offered generally decent wines with a few high spots. This is the year we perhaps started to see a challenge to the dogma of late pickings and extended macerations, with some winemakers adopting gentler pressing at lower temperatures more commensurate with the vintage, an approach that gathered momentum over the next two decades.

Last but not least, this is the first decade when Sauternes wines became hard to sell. The paucity of decent vintages between 1991 and 1994 did not help. A region relies on momentum and their absence took the wind out of its sails just as the taste for sweet wines waned. At the same time, there was a subtle stylistic change of tack. The three successful vintages of 1988, 1989 and 1990 began encouraging higher residual sugar levels and the trend continued with the success

of the 1995 vintage, partly in reaction to some critics awarding
higher scores to wines with more residual sugar. Some winemakers
believed fashioning wines that scored highly would be a bulwark
against declining demand, but it was arguably a short-term solution
as heavy sweetness was also one of the factors deterring sales.
Henceforth, many Sauternes would have to fight for demand and
respectable prices that enabled investment.

*Jacques Thienpont posing outside
the original, quaintly ramshackle
two-storey Le Pin in Pomerol.*

1990

Nineteen-ninety completes the unprecedented trio of vintages.

An unseasonably warm winter set the tone for the forthcoming season with temperatures reaching a balmy 26°C (79°F) at the end of February. Inevitably, budding was early, on 5 March, and ensuing settled conditions provoked rapid shoot growth. Word on the street was for an exceptionally early picking, but a northeasterly wind sent the mercury tumbling to -4°C (25°F) on 26 March and frost affected localised parts of Margaux and Graves, ditto areas of Sauternes. There was a second bout of frost on 3 April, this time affecting Graves and Entre-Deux-Mers. April saw temperatures rise and wetter conditions, especially towards the end of the month with minor hail damage in Pauillac and Barsac. The precipitation was welcome and a warm spell ensured flowering was 10 days earlier than the previous year. It coincided with erratic swings between hot and cold, which impacted the Cabernets more than the Merlot, producing irregular ripeness not only between vineyards but between bunches on the same vine. Talk was of a Right Bank vintage, but a cool and wetter June forced winemakers to revise their harvest diaries. A hot and humid start to July urged vineyard teams to crop thin in order to avoid potential rot and dilution since there were excessive bunches. From 11 July the most prolonged heat wave in living memory began as temperatures steadily climbed, reaching a sizzling 40°C (104°F) 10 days later, drying out the vineyards and shutting down sensitive vines unable to cope with the torrid heat. It only began to cool from mid-August, but the month remained some 3.5°C (38°F) above average and rainfall was 68% lower. You might presume this would have evened out the maturity of the Cabernets, but this never transpired.

Heavy rain (10 mm /⅓ in) on the night of 29 August kick-started the ripening process once more, benefiting some of the later-picked dry whites and coaxing a few intrepid pickers into vineyards from 9 September. It remained hot and dry throughout the main harvest, which got going on 14 September with just four spells of sporadic showers, though Pessac-Léognan suffered minor hail damage on 15 September. Most of the Merlot was picked by 26 September, though the irregular maturity of the Cabernets meant vineyard teams had to pick piecemeal, much like the top châteaux do nowadays, up until 24 October.

Sauternes marched to a slightly different beat in 1990. The drought conditions experienced elsewhere never transpired due to sporadic rainfall in the summer months. Bill Blatch points out in his original season report that whereas the Gironde suffered 68% lower rainfall in August, Sauternes had 24% more rain than average, allowing botrytis infection to develop easily, unlike in 1988 and 1989. Many estates undertook their first pass through the vines on 11 September and found concentrated, fully botrytised grapes loaded with 23–25% potential alcohol. Conditions remained dry throughout October and November, though unlike the previous seasons there was no insect damage. The challenge lay in the winery because indigenous yeast populations were unaccustomed to such high sugar levels and there were plenty of stuck fermentations. They just needed a bit of encouragement to get going.

Though both were well-regarded, around the turn of the millennium Bordeaux cognoscenti seemed to lean towards the 1990 vintage over the 1989. That was partly because, with the exception of Haut-Brion, none of the First Growths put in a show-stopping performance in 1989, which seemed to colour perceptions. But in recent years a revision of the 1989s, which have arguably matured better in bottle, has levelled things up. Stylistically, the 1990s tends to be more decadent and to articulate the vagaries of the growing season instead of individual terroirs. They often sport more conspicuous and advanced secondary aromas and flavours, notably traces of brettanomyces, which can bloom in higher alcohol wines. Still, given these caveats, there is no doubting that 1990 provides a raft of outstanding wines.

The 1990 Latour is one I have tasted a dozen or so times and you never know what to expect. It's like Russian roulette, without such dire consequences. Some have a crystalline purity that easily surpasses the 1989 and others feel muddled, knocked off course by brettanomyces. At Château Margaux, Paul Pontallier was firing on all cylinders and oversaw a brilliant 1990 that is silky smooth yet with fabulous depth and oodles of panache. The 1990 Haut-Brion and La Mission Haut-Brion are both severely underestimated – their only fault is that they had to follow their fêted 1989 counterparts. Comparing them side-by-side blind, one group of seasoned tasters was shocked to vote the 1990 better than the 1989. Do not underestimate this wine. The 1990 Lafite Rothschild has never really thrilled and I placed it between the 1989 and 1988 at the château's 150-year anniversary tasting. One infamous slipped catch is the 1990 Mouton Rothschild. Justifiably criticised by Robert Parker, it is a precursor to the bottles of the following decade, when quality became less consistent and the wines just lacked the breeding and complexity that Baron Philippe had found so easy to come by. Much better is the gargantuan yet profound 1990 Lynch-Bages. A double-magnum served in December 2019 was truly spectacular and needed more time in bottle, in contrast to a regular bottle in June 2021 with Jean-Charles Cazes that was much more approachable and exuded class. I also adore the 1990 Pichon Baron, which confirmed the château was back in the top league after the scintillating 1989, though the Pichon-Lalande was another curious misfire and lacks real complexity and vigour. The 1990 Montrose is not unlike Latour insofar as your pleasure will depend on the level of brettanomyces. You'll either find yourself marvelling at one of the greatest Saint-Estèphe wines ever made, or wondering if you've stumbled into a horses' stable long overdue a clean-out.

Right Bank winemakers tend to prefer their 1989 to their 1990 vintages. Several bottles of 1990 Pétrus tasted in London and Hong Kong (never in Bordeaux) were monumental in stature, yet juxtaposed against the '89, the '90 does not possess quite the same nobility in recent years. Jacques Guinaudeau cracked open a 1990 Lafleur at his home at Grand Village: a beast of Pomerol and yet compelling. Again, it is unpredictable and requires plenty of decanting. The 1990 Le Pin is a continuation of the 1989: sexy and Rubenesque. I drank numerous bottles of 1990 Cheval Blanc when a cigar-chomping regular held court at The Arches every Friday, sharing his bottle with anyone within ambit of his generosity. It was youthful and quite savoury when last tasted in 2018. The 1990 Beauséjour Duffau-Lagarrosse received an unexpected perfect score from Parker that increased demand and price to unprecedented levels. My only encounter revealed a deeply impressive Saint-Émilion with Left Bank tendencies, though you rarely see it nowadays. It's quite easy foraging for less expensive wines in this vintage, for example, a lovely Chasse-Spleen cracked open (again) at The Arches was velvety and beautifully balanced after nigh three decades. Then there's the 1990 La Dominique, served on my first trip to Bordeaux, and opening my eyes to the beauty of Saint-Émilion. It is still going strong after three decades.

The Sauternes are unctuous and decadent, though if forced to pick, I prefer the bite and tension of the 1989s. That said, the 1990 Yquem is almost overwhelming in precocity while the elusive 1990 Coutet Cuvée Madame, tasted with co-proprietor Aline Baly in a tacky cheap hotel next to Mérignac airport, managed to overcome its surroundings and flirted with perfection. Other highlights include the 1990 Gilette Crème de Tête, de Fargues, Doisy-Védrines and Climens.

Event
Tim Berners-Lee invents
the internet

CERN employee Tim Berners-Lee had heard that scientists at the particle physics laboratory were having difficulty sharing information, what with all those time-consuming multiple log-ins and different software programs on each computer. So in March 1989 he wrote a document titled "Information Management: A Proposal", which his boss dismissed as "vague but exciting". Still, he was allowed to work on the side-project and by October 1990 had written three principal technologies that became the foundation of the internet: HTML, URI and HTTP. The first web page appeared at the end of 1990. There are now over 50 billion. One can argue that Berners-Lee's invention has had a more profound effect on the human race than any other within the time span of this book.

Music
Vogue
– Madonna

The Queen of Pop had reached a creative peak with the previous year's *Like a Prayer* album and in 1990 maintained the momentum with *Vogue*, a paean to the dance-floor inspired by the titular dance craze in gay New York clubs. David Fincher, who would go on to direct the movies *Se7en* and *Fight Club*, shot the black-and-white video in which the singer pays homage to Hollywood stars of the golden era, name-checked in the song's bridge. That summer, Madonna set out on her *Blonde Ambition* tour, which together with the Rolling Stones' concurrent *Steel Wheels* tour introduced audiences to set design on an extravagant scale with spectacular choreography and theatre. Her gyrating on a bed in a Jean-Paul Gaultier-designed conical bra incensed Pope John Paul II, who urged citizens to boycott "one of the most satanic shows in the history of humanity". He had obviously never witnessed Throbbing Gristle.

Film
Cyrano de Bergerac – Jean-Paul Rappeneau

Seventeenth-century France is magnificently brought to life in this adaptation of Edmond Rostand's 1897 play based on a real-life tale. Gérard Depardieu was never better as the ungainly poet ashamed of his large nose whose unrequited love for his cousin Roxane leads to a tragic denouement. He won the best actor award at Cannes and an Academy Award nomination for his performance, though José Ferrer had gone one better by scooping the Oscar playing Cyrano in the inferior 1950 version.

1991

Bordeaux came down to earth with a bump after three great growing seasons. This was the year when winemakers shivered whenever the "f" word was mentioned.

The final weeks of 1990 were wet and 1991 began with extremely changeable conditions, warm one minute, cold the next. For the first time since the mid-eighties, there were freezing spells in January and February that shut down the vines. An uplift in temperatures between mid-February until the end of March provoked early budding and accelerated shoot growth across the entire region. This meant risk of frost damage was high and on 16 April a band of Arctic air descended from the north, sending daytime temperatures tumbling from 22°C (71.5°F) to 13°C (55°F) in the space of 24 hours, with some areas reporting 0°C (32°F) at night. Fortunately, a prevailing wind prevented frost, but on the evening of 20 April, the wind swung to the northwest before ominously dying away. The mercury duly dropped to -5°C (23°F) across the region, with some localised spots in Sauternes a bone-chilling -9°C (15°F). Practically all the buds were burned and only those next to the estuary in Pauillac and Saint-Estèphe, plus some parts of Pessac-Léognan near urban areas, escaped damage. Latour reports that the frost episode lasted 10 hours and damaged between 5% and 80% of its shoots depending on the location of each parcel (L'Enclos in the heart of the vineyard lost just 7%). The following morning temperatures shot back up to 17°C (62.5°F) before falling a little, insufficient to encourage secondary budding. In fact, the first three weeks in May were decidedly chilly so that only third or fourth buds were capable of producing fruit, leaving vines with a hotchpotch of surviving original and weaker later shoots. Storms at the end of May were followed by windy weather from 1 to 20 June, accompanied by cold and rain during the first 10 days before conditions settled. The first-generation fruit flowered well, but the later generation berries were protracted and uneven. July saw a couple of heat spikes before temperatures immediately retreated. Thankfully, August was hot and dry, reaching 36°C (97°F) on the 26th and evening out the irregular ripening. But violent storms on the 31st punctured the clement conditions, with thirsty vines sucking up the water and diluting fruit concentration, particularly on the Right Bank.

From 4 to 12 September, sticky and humid air exacerbated rot, punishing those who had failed to spray their vines. A dry period in mid-September provided a window when the dry whites and Sauternes were picked. The 25th marked the beginning of five days of persistent rain, after which the pickers went out from 1 October. Many Cabernets were picked directly after the Merlot as there was little benefit in waiting, so some of the fruit was under-ripe. Sorting was fundamental in determining quality, as was green harvesting earlier in the season. Further deluges arrived on 13 October by which time most of the harvest was completed, though some trudged on through the rain. Sauternes suffered outbreaks of rot after the storms at the end of August. Some of the first-generation bunches that had survived the frost yielded fruit with must weights of 17–20% with some botrytis, so it was not a complete write-off, though later passes through the vines hampered by showers meant final yields were pitifully small.

The result of this *annus horribilis* was a diminished crop of between one-third and two-thirds of average yields. Some winemakers were pleasantly surprised by the quality of the Merlot, which reached 12–13% alcohol, but the Cabernets were much more uneven, the fruit light and often green. The almost complete devastation of primary buds meant the Right Bank produced a tiny amount of 1991, if any at all, with illustrious names such as Pétrus, Lafleur and Cheval Blanc opting to sell off any fruit. The vintage is not completely devoid of quality, but you need to look to those vineyards near the Gironde such as Latour, whose 1991 is easily the finest Left Bank of the vintage. The 1991 Pichon-Lalande impressed winemaker Nicolas Glumineau when opened in September 2021, the highlight of an off-vintage-themed vertical. Likewise when Thomas Duroux included his 1991 Palmer in a vertical a few months later, both of us commended its showing. Another to look out for is the 1991 Montrose. Many Sauternes declined to release any wine. Little did they know that 1991 would be the first of a succession of appalling growing seasons that brought many estates to the brink. That said, I have several complimentary notes for the 1991 Doisy-Daëne, the last at the vertical in June 2021. It took more than a pesky frost to defeat Denis Dubourdieu.

Event
Operation Desert Storm frees occupied Kuwait

After the Iraqi army invaded Kuwait in August 1990, US-led forces responded with Operation Desert Storm. The military attack commenced with a naval and aerial bombardment on 17 January 1991, followed by a ground assault on 24 February. Kuwait's territorial rights aside, the West feared that Saddam Hussein's forces were within striking distance of Saudi Arabia and its oil fields. On 26 February, the Iraqi military began its retreat, setting oil wells on fire across the desert landscape. American casualties were low, but Hussein retained power. The first Gulf War was over. It would not be the last.

1991 *(Continued)*

Music
Smells Like Teen Spirit
– Nirvana

Released on 10 September 1991, the lead single from *Nevermind* sent reverberations across the music industry. Few artists as left-field and as artistically uncompromising as Kurt Cobain have had such an impact on mainstream culture, as evidenced by the number of teenagers that still wear Nirvana T-shirts. Inspired by a message that Bikini Kill singer Kathleen Hanna wrote on his apartment wall, *Smells Like Teen Spirit* chimed with a generation disenfranchised by disposable music and bands selling out for the highest dollar. It felt raw and visceral, instantly making everything else sound fake. Cobain dismissed the song as a rip-off of the Pixies and Boston's MOR anthem *More Than a Feeling* and eventually refused to play it live. Chronic health issues, heroin addiction and untold pressure piled up on the sensitive singer and reluctant spokesman for a generation. Alone in his house, Cobain killed himself with a shotgun on 5 April 1994.

Film
The Silence of the Lambs –
Jonathan Demme

"I ate his liver with some fava beans and a nice Chianti," goads the world's most intellectual cannibal to Agent Clarice Starling, considerably changing the wine from the "big Amarone" mentioned in Thomas Harris's novel to one she might recognise. Jodie Foster and Anthony Hopkins' outstanding performance as Starling and Dr. Hannibal Lecter are what distinguish Demme's gory edge-of-the-seat thriller. Hopkins based Lecter's voice on a cross between Katharine Hepburn and the computer HAL in *2001: A Space Odyssey* (page 298), though neither of those made that disquieting sucking noise. Several top actors turned down the roles as they felt the subject matter was too horrific, but the film went on to win five Academy Awards the following year. What it did for sales of Chianti is unknown.

After the traumatic 1991 growing season, the following year provided little relief.

Nineteen ninety-two began with an acute dry spell that extended from the previous November to virtually the end of March, a period in which rainfall figures bobbed between one-fifth and one-third of the average. As Bill Blatch notes in his annual report, cold weather allowed vineyard workers to take their time over pruning and choose the best wood to cut – crucial after the frost-affected 1991 season had left vines more sensitive than normal. From 22 March to 18 April conditions changed. A series of fronts dumped 155 mm (6 in) of rain over the region and by the end of April, the growth cycle was already running late. The lag was cut by a warm spell in which the mercury reached 30°C (86°F) so that flowering began eight days earlier than usual. Unfortunately heavy rainfall combined with cold temperatures disrupted and prolonged flowering, though somehow vines avoided serious coulure. The root of the season's problems came in June. After a hot spell from the 14th to the 18th, Bordeaux was drenched by 10 days of persistent rain between 20 and 30 June when precipitation was 50% more than usual. Even so, as Blatch points out, April–July rainfall was equivalent to that of 1988, so some were feeling upbeat. There is a bit of a contradiction over the following weeks. Blatch notes settled weather from 13 July to 30 August with the same number of days exceeding 30°C (86°F) as there had been in 1986. Conversely, Sichel talks of a "sad summer" with a wet August and the fewest sunshine hours since 1980. Certainly, Blatch refers to a humid heat this year, unlike the dry heat of 1989 and 1990, which meant rot remained a constant risk. Many châteaux thinned their bunches to enhance air circulation and ripening and to remedy any irregular grape maturity. The humid heat was exacerbated by intermittent thunderstorms, one on 8 August bringing hail to the northern Médoc, Sauternes and the appellation of Margaux, where the communes of Arsac and Cantenac suffered up to 95% damage.

Heavy rain at the end of August had little effect since the atmosphere had been humid throughout the season. In any case, a warm spell from 7 to 20 September helped to increase sugar levels that tempted some Right Bank estates to conduct a few early "exploratory" pickings. Pickers began on the Merlot after a storm had swept through on 20 September and with bad weather forecasted they set about their task with gusto. Temperatures started to fall at the end of the month, encouraging many to plough on and pick their Cabernets. But this coincided with patchy rain at the beginning of October, compromising quality and dampening harvesters' spirits. Yields were high and unlike in 1991, estates were motivated to discard unsatisfactory bunches to meet authorised yields. There was also widespread *saignée*, bleeding of the vats, in order to increase density and concentrate the must. In Sauternes, after such a difficult growing season, many were surprised

1992
(Continued)

when the last week of August saw some botrytis formation not dissimilar to the fruit picked in 1988. The first passes through the vineyard at the end of September were promising, but matters worsened and rain washed away hopes for a good Sauternes vintage.

I used to buy and consume many bottles of the 1992 Bordeaux because they were such bargains. Even First Growths didn't cost an arm or a leg. To be frank, few amounted to much and most are rather hollow, hardly any predestined to age much more than a decade. The best I encountered has been 1992 Latour, though that was back in 2004 and the 1991 has much more to offer in terms of concentration and freshness. The 1992 Lafite Rothschild is reasonable and can err towards Saint-Julien in character, although you do not see it often. On the Right Bank, the best I have drunk were certainly two or three bottles of 1992 Pétrus. This was the vintage that Christian Moueix covered his vines both here and at Trotanoy with black plastic sheeting to prevent rain drenching the soil. Authorities slapped his wrist for trying to make a better wine. The 1992 Ausone showed better than expected at a vertical in early 2018 while Denis Durantou eked out a half-decent l'Église-Clinet. Some 1992s are barely drinkable – a couple that I shall not name opened out of curiosity when I visited châteaux in 2022 risked long-term damage to my palate. Sauternes was essentially a write-off with many electing not to release a Grand Vin. Much better to seek out some of the excellent dry whites, such as Haut-Brion Blanc and Domaine de Chevalier Blanc. Apart from these, 1992 is a vintage with little going for it. Sauternes suffered another forgettable growing season.

Event
The signing of the Maastricht Treaty

After several years of discussion, the Treaty on European Union was signed in Maastricht on 7 February 1992. It laid the foundations of the EU, the euro currency and the European Central Bank, while allowing citizens to move freely between member states. Prime Minister John Major negotiated an opt-out for the UK that was also granted to Denmark and though seen as a triumph at the time, it created a schism both within the Conservative Party and between the UK and Europe that ultimately led to the Brexit referendum in 2016.

Music
Everybody Hurts
– R.E.M.

R.E.M.'s rise from cult college band to one of the biggest-selling acts of the early nineties is one of rock 'n' roll's unlikeliest success stories. Drummer Bill Berry composed the lion's share of *Everybody Hurts*, even though he ended up being replaced by a drum machine, while John Paul Jones, Led Zeppelin's bassist, arranged the strings. The poignant video was filmed in San Antonio, Texas by Jake Scott, son of the director of this book's entry for 1979 (page 338), and featured the band stuck in a traffic jam with Michael Stipe walking over cars. The track was a highlight of the multi-platinum-selling *Automatic for the People* released in 1992 and was deemed worthy of a single release the following year.

Film
Reservoir Dogs
– Quentin Tarantino

Such was the impact of Tarantino's debut that his name became adjectival: a whip-cracking script, bloody violence, a non-linear plot line and a Hollywood star overdue a comeback all became tropes of a Tarantino-esque movie. *Reservoir Dogs* has you hooked even before the opening titles as you eavesdrop on the criminals' inane dissection of Madonna's *Like a Virgin* and the whys and wherefores of tipping. Shot over 35 days on such a minuscule budget that actors used their own wardrobe and Harvey Keitel paid for the casting sessions, it's a heist movie *sans* heist since there wasn't any money to film one. But leaving the audience to imagine the botched jewellery robbery only adds to the mystique. The infamous torture scene soundtracked by *Stuck in the Middle with You* took three takes, with Michael Madsen improvising his dance before severing the cop's ear, though the squeamish actor was apparently repulsed by the whole sequence.

1993

The 1993 vintage was a slight improvement on the previous two years, though that might be damning with faint praise.

After a benign January, February continued in a similar vein with a cold snap from 20 February that forced down the sap. It was dry for the time of year and when mid-March temperatures leapt to 25°C (77°F), some growers began to worry about the lack of water. April finally saw some much-needed rainfall, then May was warm and clement so that the first flowers were seen around 25 May, after which the mercury reached the low thirties. According to Lawton, Paul Pontallier at Château Margaux had never witnessed such rapid flowering, portending a decent-sized crop. June continued in a warm vein and July saw daytime temperatures between 28–32°C (82–90°F). Apart from a heat wave between 16 – 21 August when it reached 34°C (93°F), August was moderate in terms of heat and *véraison* was excellent, the fruit turning deep red by 18 August. Bunches tended to be quite small though well spread out, and a few vineyard managers lopped off anything excessive. Everyone was excited about the 1993 vintage, even though May to September witnessed the lowest average temperature since 1985, the most rain in 30 years (apart from 1992) and 6% less sunshine that usual.

It was a wet September, on the eve of harvest, that ruined hopes. Sichel makes an important point when he talks about taking care with statistics because although the weather station in Mérignac recorded 248 mm (9¾ in), Pauillac recorded 152 mm (6 in) that month. Even so, that is still twice as much rain as usual. The downpours began from 6 September with 80 mm (3 in) falling between 12 and 14 September. An ensuing dry spell was short-lived as further rain fell from 20 to 22 September, coinciding with the picking of the reds. At least the cool temperatures, some 3°C (37°F) below normal, plus the berries' thick skins inhibited the spread of rot in these soggy conditions. Essentially, vineyard teams had to do their best and skirt around rain showers. Some estates such as Haut-Brion finished their harvest by the end of the month, with the last buckets of grapes entering reception areas by around 8 October. Tannin levels were similar to those in 1989 and 1990, but it was clear the rain had diluted some of the musts. As a consequence, quality was governed by how rigorously châteaux de-selected vats, how gently fruit was macerated and how judiciously they used pressed wine, which could easily render wines excessively tannic. Some opted for a technological fix and used reverse osmosis to extract water. In Sauternes, a thunderstorm on 10 August triggered botrytis, but was premature – grapes are never going to have sufficient concentration by then. The aforementioned showers from 6 September led to rapid botrytis infection and a second pass through the vines after a dry period at the end of the month, followed by a third in the second week of October, provided concentrated berries that just lacked some acidity.

To be frank, I never found much pleasure in the 1993 Bordeaux wines, which too often came across as tannic, dry and rather hard. They provide glimpses of what might have been had it not rained at precisely the wrong time. Perusing my notes on both the Left and Right Banks, none of the First Growths merited superlatives, though like the 1994s they represented good value vis-à-vis other vintages for a period of time. The only exception was a magnificent magnum of 1993 Palmer, poured blind at a vertical at Pierre Gagnaire's restaurant in London, where I had to double-check I hadn't misread the vintage. The 1993 La Mission Haut-Brion is decent enough, though I pithily described it as "no frills". The bell pepper-scented Pétrus just about passes muster, though I find the 1993 Lafleur better, even if I last drank it to drown my sorrows after bidding farewell to my pet cat. Sauternes was nixed by those autumn rains that produced the wrong kind of rot.

Event
The Waco religious cult siege

Music
Nuthin' but a "G" Thang – Dr. Dre featuring Snoop Doggy Dog

The events of the Waco siege might be viewed as comical were it not for the fatalities. On 28 February 1993, federal agents attempted to raid the headquarters of the Branch Davidian religious cult led by David Koresh to investigate allegations of an illegal arms cache. A gunfight broke out and during the ensuing 51-day siege, the FBI tried to negotiate with Koresh and spur cult members into ending their standoff by playing noises at deafening volume to deprive them of sleep, including the sound of dying cats, chanting Tibetan monks, ringing telephones and Nancy Sinatra's *These Boots Are Made for Walkin'*. Finally, on 19 April, the authorities raided the compound, but fires that engulfed the site during the assault cost the lives of 76 Branch Davidian members.

Having revolutionised hip-hop with the incendiary N.W.A., Compton-born Andre Romelle Young, better known as producer Dr. Dre, dissolved the rap collective and went solo with epochal album *The Chronic*. First single *Nuthin' but a "G" Thang* gave a new twist to gangsta rap: the groove, sampled from Leon Haywood's *I Want'a Do Something Freaky to You*, introduced a more laid-back and funk-influenced sound, as well as the mellow flow of protégé Snoop Doggy Dog to the masses, reaching number two in the American charts in March 1993. Dre and Snoop defined the sound of that year, paving the way for rappers such as Tupac Shakur and The Notorious B.I.G.

1993
(Continued)

Film
The Remains of the Day
– James Ivory

The Merchant Ivory production
company specialised in period
dramas and its adaptation of
Kazuo Ishiguro's 1989 Booker
Prize-winning novel remains one
of its most lauded. Harold Pinter
owned the original rights and
some of his script survives in the
final film, though the playwright
requested that his name be
removed from the credits.
Anthony Hopkins channels the
detachment he used for Hannibal
Lecter to play butler James
Stevens and many scenes are
full of Pinteresque pauses, with
unspoken dialogue an integral
part of the film. It was another
acting masterclass by Hopkins,
whose character's unrequited
love for Ms. Kenton, a sublime
turn by Emma Thompson, leads
to a devastating denouement as
her bus disappears into the rainy
night, both of them imagining
what might have been.

This vintage was a stepping stone back in the right direction, a forerunner to the 1995 growing season.

January saw the continuation of above-average rainfall that had begun as the '93s were fermenting, though temperatures were higher than normal. Come early March and a high-pressure system encouraged vines to awake from their light winter slumber. One of the earliest recorded bud breaks ever heightened the risk of frost, though concerns were allayed in the last few days of March as temperatures reached 20°C (68°F) and shoots responded with rapid growth. April saw lower temperatures and heavy rainfall, 110 mm (4 in) in 10 days at its peak, while an easterly wind on 14 April was followed by frost in the southern Graves, Margaux and Barsac with some vineyards totally destroyed. Unlike three years earlier, the mercury rapidly rose into early May, allowing secondary buds to grow rapidly on affected vines. Flowering commenced early on 23 May, with *mi-fleuraison* around 4 June, the earliest since 1952. In that year's annual report Bill Blatch notes that despite wild swings in temperature throughout this process, there was little coulure and no millerandage, though a spun-out Cabernet placed it on a different cycle from the Merlot. June was hot, with 30°C (86°F) recorded on three days, and July was textbook: 24 days over 25°C (77°F), but cloud cover helped avoid heat spikes. A smattering of violent storms were beneficial, though some areas of the Médoc began to suffer hydric stress, not least those on well-drained gravel soils. July witnessed a very early *véraison* and storms on 8 and 9 August helped berries to change colour promptly. It was drier and hotter than normal and sugar levels began to surpass those seen in 1982 by August's end.

In early September, potential alcohol levels were relatively high albeit with low acidities. Though the month began fine and warm, a front brought rain on the 7th that became heavier, with forecasters predicting worse to come. Winemakers had to gamble and decide whether to cross their fingers and wait, or to fire the harvest starting gun. Some picked on 12 September and took a chance harvesting unripe grapes. Most just crossed their fingers and prayed that conditions would improve. Instead, the following week saw three days of continuous downpours. Most of the Merlots were picked from Monday 19 September under dry conditions, yet the Cabernets lagged far behind since they were on a slower growth cycle as a result of the disturbed flowering. With the threat of frost lurking, some winemakers picked from 24 September and over the weekend under fine conditions. Those who planned to start on Monday 27 September pulled back their curtains to see more rain. Some of them thought there was no point in waiting any further, but those who held their pickers back were rewarded with a generally dry spell through to 18 October, though by this time some fruit had become diluted. The combination of better vineyard sanitary conditions compared to 1993, lower overall rainfall figures and drier weather during the Cabernet harvest meant the wines were generally

1994
(Continued)

better than those of the previous three years: tannic, high in acidity and broad-shouldered, though more pliant in Saint-Émilion where there had been more rain. Alcoholic fermentations were slower and this potentially enhanced complexity. In Sauternes, some high-quality Sauvignon Blanc was picked after rain on 13 September. Thereafter, conditions slowly deteriorated and some picked their Sémillon before it was fully ripe. But those who waited were able to pick much ripe Sémillon in the first half of October.

This is a vintage that I drank regularly in the salad days of my professional career simply because it offered an unbeatable quality-to-price ratio. The wines might have lacked flair, but they aged better than the '93s. The First Growths are solid and dependable, my favourite perhaps the 1994 Lafite Rothschild, almost entirely Cabernet Sauvignon, or the 1994 Latour. Jean-Hubert Delon produced a fine and sturdy Léoville-Las Cases, while the 1994 Pichon Baron is certainly one of its better offerings in a patchy period. But some Left Bank wines, even my favourites such as Pichon-Lalande and Lynch-Bages, began to dry out after around 15 years. On the Right Bank, I drank numerous bottles of 1994 Angélus when it was on the list at Andrew Edmunds' restaurant for thruppence. In Pomerol, one over-achiever is 1994 Le Pin, an underrated gem if you can find a bottle. When I suggested to Jacques Thienpont that it surpasses his 1995, he was inclined to agree. Some famous names did not quite deliver: Lafleur is a little under-ripe in terms of its Cabernet Franc and Pétrus is just a little dowdy. Some of the dry whites are well worth hunting down, not least the tensile 1994 Laville Haut-Brion, which offered gorgeous Japanese yuzu scents when cracked open at an all-too-rare dry white Bordeaux dinner at Portland restaurant. The Sauternes are inconsistent, but "useful" examples can be found among those that skirted around the showers to pick the ripe Sémillon. I have tasted only a handful and to be frank, none were worth writing home about.

Event
The Channel Tunnel links England and France

For the first time since Britain separated from continental Europe 450,000 years ago, the two land masses were reconnected via the 50-km (31-mile) Channel Tunnel. Construction had begun six years earlier, with teams boring though the chalk marl stratum from both coastlines until they met in October 1990. The tunnel was opened by Queen Elizabeth II and President François Mitterand on 6 May 1994 and Britain was technically an island no more. Despite Brexit, the tunnel remains open.

Music
Girls and Boys
– Blur

Girls and Boys heralded a heady couple of years when Britpop invaded the mainstream. Vocalist Damon Albarn was inspired to write the song while holidaying in Magaluf, surrounded by hordes of youths basically drinking and shagging on Club 18–30 holidays. It neither condones nor criticises, instead suggesting that you can go to bed with whomever you like, just as long as it's "someone you really love". Bassist Alex James described it as a mix of disco drums, nasty guitars and Duran Duran bass, a combination that not only appealed to Blur's indie fanbase, but also to mainstream audiences who took it into the UK top five. Blur would mature as a band and pen a stream of classics, though *Girls and Boys* would always be their catchiest anthem.

Film
The Shawshank Redemption –
Frank Darabont

Many people have no idea when *The Shawshank Redemption* hit cinema screens because few went to see it. Its initial gross failed to cover production costs and it only became a commercial success via word-of-mouth from video rentals. Based on a Stephen King novella, the film takes inspiration from Martin Scorsese's *Goodfellas* in its use of voiceover to narrate the story of Andy Dufresne, imprisoned for a murder in a jail rife with corruption. Some scenes make harrowing viewing, yet Morgan Freeman's mellifluous voice makes it sound like he's reading a bedtime story. Featuring one of the best twists and most satisfying comeuppances in movie history, it bears repeated viewing. In case you were wondering, the film was released on 23 September 1994 in the US.

1995

Bordeaux was finally blessed with a vintage to get pulses racing and merchants' phones ringing.

December and January were unseasonably warm, then from 21 February, sub-zero temperatures finally allowed the vines to rest after the previous year's exertions. Temperatures ticked up in March, spurring vines to bud by the end of the month, though a northerly brought cold temperatures and frost in Saint-Émilion and Graves before the calendar flipped. April began warm and settled before the mercury fell again, leading to a second bout of local frost damage. After a wet and warm May that saw temperatures exceed 30°C (86°F), flowering began early on 21 May with *mi-fleuraison* on 4 June, a day ahead of 1982. Temperatures swung wildly during this critical period, though winemakers escaped with just a little coulure. June saw around one-third of the usual rainfall while July was hotter than average with just 44 mm (1¾ in). Bill Blatch notes that clear skies helped provide a generous 812 hours of sunshine, with no berry skins burnt. The drought continued with just 22 mm (¾ in) of rain in August and temperatures 3.2°C (37.8°F) above normal. Conditions were not dissimilar to those in 1976 but with underground water reserves replenished only fledgling vines and those on free-draining gravel soils suffered much stress. The clayey soils gave vines in Saint-Estèphe an advantage, underlying their eventual higher yields.

Intermittent storms and heavy rain between 6 and 12 September nudged vines towards phenolic ripeness, though they diluted some of the Merlot and conversely refuelled the later-ripening Cabernets. The first Merlot grapes were picked from 14 to 19 September, which coincided with six days of heavy rain. Those picked later, between 20 and 24 September, were harvested in drier conditions, though they now had a degree less potential alcohol. Fortunately, dry weather from 20 September prevented widespread rot and the Cabernets were picked from 25 September, earlier than planned since winemakers feared swelling might break the berries' skins. Berry sizes were "no bigger than peas", according to Bill Blatch's annual report – fortunately, they did not taste like them. Picking conditions were ideal and most had finished their harvest by 3 October. Yields were high on the Left Bank, approaching the 65 hl/ha set by the I.N.A.O., but lower in Saint-Julien, Margaux and Graves, sometimes down to 40 hl/ha. The fruit was tannic but not hard and most winemakers opted for an extended maceration of between 21 and 25 days. In Sauternes, the 110 mm (4 in) of rain in September triggered widespread botrytis. There was also ample concentration, to the point that some estates had to be careful not to pick excessively ripe bunches.

The 1995 vintage was the first that I tasted just after the wines had been bottled. Initially, I preferred the 1996s as they featured more "snow-capped peaks" – attention-grabbing wines that add sparkle to vintage reputations. Over the years, my appreciation for the 1995 vintage has risen a little, though having re-examined my notes and re-tasted wines, I have not found any of them transcendental. Among the First Growths, the 1995 Haut-Brion tasted, for want of a better word, confident, completely at ease with itself when served blind at 26 years of age, while Paul Pontallier conjured a regal Château Margaux unfairly eclipsed by the 1996. At around a decade old, several bottles of 1995 Lafite Rothschild were decent enough but lacked a bit of horsepower, as did the 1995 Latour. Likewise, the 1995 Mouton Rothschild comes from a period where I feel the estate took its eye off the ball and was playing catch-up with the others. In the Médoc, standouts include the 1995 Ducru-Beaucaillou. Last poured with Bruno Borie at the château's epic Saturday-morning vertical, it is unquestionably a strong return to form after a troubled period. The late Mme. Gasqueton oversaw a rustic yet charming Calon Ségur. This redoubtable lady always expected visitors to arrive punctually, tapping her watch if they showed up late. She often served the 1995 at lunches, when together my Japanese colleagues I tried to persuade her to sell thousands of cases to star-crossed Japanese oenophiles who viewed the heart symbol on the label as the ultimate romantic gesture. The 1995 Pichon-Lalande combines ripeness with a judicious herbaceous element and the 1995 Grand-Puy-Lacoste is the quintessential Pauillac with its nose in front of the 1995 Pichon Baron, then charting a path to greatness. The 1995 Brane-Cantenac is Henri Lurton's first great wine since taking over at the beginning of the decade, while fellow Margaux resident Rauzan-Ségla possesses wonderful structure.

The vintage excels more on the Right Bank. Both the 1995 Pétrus and Lafleur are splendid expressions of the growing season, though curiously I have always found the 1995 Le Pin a little short. There have been several sterling Pomerols over the years, including La Conseillante, l'Église-Clinet and a l'Évangile that seemed to take aeons to reach maturity. Over in Saint-Émilion, the 1995s from Cheval Blanc and Ausone continue to motor on nicely, if without the fireworks of their respective '98s, though the 1995 Angélus maybe just misses the purity and precocity of later vintages. Sauternes are also worth seeking out, not least a sumptuous 1995 Yquem served by Pierre Lurton during my first ever visit to the estate in 1999. Several sightings since then suggest that it is blossoming into one of its finest performances of the decade. Also, keep a lookout for a fine Lafaurie-Peyraguey and Coutet, though Suduiraut felt one-dimensional when tasted at a vertical at the château. Generally, the Sauternes show strongly in 1995 with just one of two afflicted by grey rot.

Event
Sarin nerve gas attack in Tokyo

Walking to the Tokyo English school where I was teaching on 20 March 1995, a stream of police cars sped past me and towards the local metro station. Unbeknownst to me, the city had just suffered a co-ordinated domestic terrorist attack by Aum Shinrikyo, a cult led by Shoko Asahara. Five operatives leaked the highly toxic sarin nerve agent in crowded trains during rush hour, killing 14 and injuring hundreds more. The domestic terrorist act was shocking in a country accustomed to low crime levels. The perpetrators were eventually found and their leader was executed.

Music
Common People
– Pulp

Pulp released its anthem on 22 May 1995, 17 years after Jarvis Cocker had formed the band in his Sheffield hometown. As its memorable opening line explains, the song was inspired by a crass comment made by a fellow student of Cocker's studying sculpture at Saint Martins College about moving to Hackney to slum it with the common people. Several years later, Cocker wrote the basics of the song on a second-hand Casiotone MT-500 keyboard. Its triumphant sound and breathless delivery almost diverts attention away from its withering attack on what the singer termed "class tourism". *Common People* became an instant era-defining Britpop classic and Pulp's performance at the Glastonbury Festival – after being called in at the last minute to replace The Stone Roses – turned Cocker into a polyester-suited national treasure.

Film
Toy Story – John Lasseter

The story of Woody the cowboy doll heralded an era of computer animation. At that time, digital animators struggled to achieve advanced 3-D effects such as realistic explosions and long hair, which is why rocket fire in the film takes place off-screen and every character's hair is either short or tied-back. *Toy Story* became the first animation to earn an Oscar nomination for its screenplay and went on to become the highest-grossing film of the year. It also launched Pixar Animation Studios, which went on to produce classics such as *WALL-E*, *Up* and three critically acclaimed *Toy Story* sequels.

I joined the wine trade in June 1996, so this is the first vintage I remember tasting in Bordeaux during en primeur the following spring. For many, 1996 is the high point of the decade.

The winter was relatively mild and wet, the rain welcome insofar as it replenished reserves after the previous year's drought. The conditions predicated an early budding, with Lawton noting that the first buds swelled from 23 March when the mercury reached the mid-twenties. A cold snap from 3 to 5 April caused minor damage and it remained dry for the rest of the month, encouraging shoot growth. Bill Blatch observes that the embryonic bunches were longer than in 1995, a sign that the berries might be large in size. May was cool up until the final week when temperatures reached 31°C (88°F) in the final three days. The first flowers could be seen on 29 May. A dip in temperature was followed by a heat wave on 6 and 7 June that reached 34°C (93°F) and the mercury remained in the low thirties until around 22 June. Winemakers believed that fruit set had gone without a hitch and rapid flowering augured even ripeness, but by the end of the month it was clear that the Merlot had suffered extensive millerandage. July was warm, with Sichel noting it was 1°C (34°F) above normal, though 2°C (35°F) cooler than the previous year with average rainfall concentrated in the first 10 days. August began warm and thermometers gradually rose. "Glorious week-end," writes Lawton in the archives on 15 August when it reached 33°C (91°F). But the weather grew more unstable from 19 August, becoming much cooler and wetter. Precipitation varied between appellations: Médoc received a regular 60–70 mm (2½–2¾ in) while other areas experienced just 30–40 mm (1–1½ in), but Saint-Émilion had 115 mm (4½ in) on less free-draining clayey soils and Sauternes got 150 mm (6 in). This resulted in a spun-out *véraison* and, as a result, uneven ripeness, while cold nights locked in higher levels of malic acid. The rain-affected vineyards were now populated by bloated berries and fears were another storm would nix the vintage.

September saved the day. From 1 September there was a daily average of eight hours of sunshine and it was remarkably dry and cool. The conditions re-concentrated dilute berries, increased sugar levels and essentially turned winemakers' frowns upside down. The weather deteriorated from 17 to 22 September and, with forecasts of downpours, pickers began to harvest the Merlot from 23 September. After two bands of rain, the Cabernet Sauvignon was harvested from around 5 October under settled conditions. Much of the picking was completed a week later, though others took advantage of the sunshine, finishing around 19 October. The Cabernet had resisted the rainfall and showed impressive colour and sugar levels, so from the start, it was patently a Left Bank vintage. In terms of vinification, there was less *saignée* than the previous year, while thick tannins coerced gentler macerations. In Sauternes, after a difficult season, many estates had to clean up their vineyards to eliminate grey rot in early September.

1996

1870

2020

Thereafter, picking was delayed. According to Bill Blatch, producers had picked only one-quarter of the crop by 4 October – Yquem hadn't collected even a single berry. Drizzle on 17 October finally led to botrytis and this final, for many fourth, pass through the vines provided the heart of their Sauternes.

The wines were well received on release, not least thanks to Robert Parker's ecstatic reception for the top Left Bank bottles, though quality is unevenly spread. Among the First Growths, the 1996 Château Margaux is the high point of the decade, so pure and fragrant on the violet-scented nose, while the 1996 Lafite Rothschild, served blind in Bordeaux at the end of 2021, was so youthful that I guessed it was a vintage 10 years younger. The 1996 Haut-Brion has come into its own in recent years and shows more backbone than La Mission Haut-Brion. The dense and grippy 1996 Mouton Rothschild is its best for several years, even though it does not quite scale the heights that head winemaker Philippe Dhalluin would achieve the following decade. The 1996 Latour is the one First Growth that I feel does not reach its full potential in context of the growing season, not least when compared with its peers. There are a clutch of wonderful wines from vineyards on deep gravel soils, particularly Pichon Baron, Pontet-Canet and Léoville-Las Cases, not to mention a stunning atypically Cabernet Sauvignon-driven 1996 Pichon-Lalande. There are a few misfires, such as an inexplicably disjointed Léoville Poyferré, but generally the 1996 Left Banks have much to offer. The Right Bank is a different matter. There are a couple of decent wines such as 1996 La Conseillante and Ausone, but even Pétrus and Lafleur were compromised by a season that never favoured even the best Pomerol or Saint-Émilion estates. Many of the Sauternes were quite fat and rich, maybe less refined than the '95s. About the 1996 Yquem I once wrote: "As harmonious as a Verdi and as pretty as a Mozart sonata". Perusing my notes, it stands head and shoulders above everything else. Generally, I find the sweet wines of Bordeaux more decadent than the 1995s but less noble than the 1997s.

Event
Google begins searching

Ever heard of BackRub? Thankfully, Stanford PhD students Larry Page and Sergey Brin decided to rename their web-based search engine to a play on the mathematical expression for the number 1 followed by 100 zeros. The original computer storage assembly cabinet that held the disc drives was constructed out of Mega Blok plastic bricks. The search engine used the duo's PageRank algorithm, which was based on links instead of the number of times a term is mentioned on a webpage, and began searching the web in March 1996. The first version of Google on the Stanford website was released the following August and the URL google.com was registered in September 1997. It is probably no exaggeration to say that it changed not just the internet, but modern life itself.

Music
Wannabe
– Spice Girls

Sporty. Ginger. Posh. Baby. Scary. As "Cool Britannia" reached its zenith, the Spice Girls unleashed their debut single *Wannabe*. There is no subtle build-up. Instead it dives straight into the piano riff inspired by Grease's *You're the One That I Want* and the clarion call-and-reply between Mel B and Geri Halliwell asking each other what they really really want. Which, it turns out, is to "zigazig-ah". Does it make any sense? Not really. Nobody cared. It rocketed to the top of the charts in 37 countries and unlike the legion of predominantly male Britpop bands, the Spice Girls broke the US. Moreover, the group provided a battle cry for a generation of girls forced to swallow the toxic lad environment that besmirched the mid-nineties. They could have been a one-hit wonder, but *Wannabe* kick-started a hugely successful career and made them household names.

Film
Trainspotting – Danny Boyle

Eye-catching black-and-white posters around the London Underground gave notice that something different was about to hit cinemas. *Trainspotting*? That was an odd title. How could you make a film about that hobby? From its opening sequence influenced by Spike Jonze's video for Beastie Boys' *Sabotage*, *Trainspotting* is a roller-coaster ride through drug addition, gritty inner-city squalor, pop culture, Python-esque surrealism, spontaneous violence and a polemic about why Scots hate the English. Perhaps its most memorable image is Ewan McGregor's dive into a disgustingly filthy toilet, which in fact smelled quite sweet as it was shot using chocolate. Choose this film.

1997

This vintage is the first I tasted from barrel, but it is generally regarded as the weakest of the late-nineties.

It was another relatively warm winter, though a cold snap at the beginning of the year at least permitted the vines to rest and killed off bugs. After a rainy February, they were raring to go and although budding was a fortnight earlier than usual, it was spun-out. A warm March encouraged rapid vine growth and winemakers became concerned about frost given the early budding. But apart from a skirmish in Pessac-Léognan where temperatures fell to -2°C (28.5°F), vines escaped any real damage. The problem was more one of dryness, though showers at the end of April and beginning of May relieved parched throats. A combination of showers, cold nights and sudden heat disrupted flowering and resulted in widespread coulure and millerandage. The irregularity was not just between vineyards but within bunches, so unless an extremely warm and clement summer followed, uneven ripeness was going to be a major problem. Vines were some three weeks ahead of their usual growth cycle and despite a warm June, bunches stubbornly refused to ripen, which Bill Blatch suggests may have been due to the dry conditions in April. June was cool and showery – cold towards the end of the month – and oidium remained a constant threat, with any split berries attracting insects. Vineyard teams had to constantly spray vines and snip away infected bunches. July was humid and cooler, though from the 25th a high-pressure system squatted over the region for a month, raising temperatures to 3.5°C (38°F) warmer than average. This was just what was needed, except that vines concentrated the energy into growing foliage rather than ripening bunches, which obliged crop-thinning. *Véraison* was early but the berries were gorged with water and measured a third larger than average, though at least sugar levels were high and perfect conditions until harvest might still rescue the vintage.

The dry whites were picked very early, with some estates out in the vines on 18 August, the earliest since 1893. The reds were reaching decent must weights, but rain at the end of the month dashed hopes of another 1989 or 1990 and downpours at the beginning of September persuaded some to pick early. Others decided to wait it out and were rewarded with barely a drop of rain and warm temperatures almost 3°C (37°F) above average throughout September and into October. The Merlot was picked from around 8 September while the Cabernets were harvested up to 16 October, energised by light showers after the dry period. Sauternes had suffered frosts and acid rot during the summer and winemakers were pessimistic as late as September. But that month gave them a window to clear out undesirable bunches and, unlike the previous year, it remained mostly dry and sunny, with sporadic light showers nudging botrytis infection along and cool easterly winds concentrating the berries. Teams had to be meticulous in picking the right parcel: Yquem required seven passes through the vineyard over 32 days of picking, though that comes naturally in Sauternes and the result was a low yield of concentrated sweet wines.

Nineteen ninety-seven was the first vintage I tasted en primeur in Bordeaux and also marked the first time I got to taste all the First Growths together. This was not because I was a wine writer, but because I was working for a wine importer that purchased vast quantities of this unloved vintage for restaurants in Japan. Châteaux had been criticised for not lowering their release prices at en primeur and so were passed over by many merchants. After two or three years, even the First Growths were relatively cheap and absolute bargains. Though it was not a great vintage by any means, improvements in viticulture ensured that quality was higher than it might have been a decade earlier. The 1997 Lafite Rothschild retains some of its charm, but is not particularly exciting and after two decades, none of the First Growths will improve. Scanning dozens of notes over the years, nothing particularly stands out on either Left or Right Bank, but I will namecheck one over-performer, the delightful 1997 Poujeaux. I was smitten by this Moulis-en-Médoc after drinking it during my en primeur trip to taste the 2000 vintage. Re-tasting it again in 2019, it had lost none of its charm. The vintage was touted as one for Sauternes, though curiously perusing my notes over the years, I cannot muster a huge amount of enthusiasm, not even for the 1997 Yquem. That said, I found pleasure in Coutet (especially its brilliant but elusive Cuvée Madame) and Lafaurie-Peyraguey, while d'Arche lacks a little pizzazz on the nose and Suduiraut is prone to a bit of oxidation.

Event
Princess Diana killed in a car crash

The death of Princess Diana on the night of 31 August 1997 stunned the world. Even the most stoic newsreaders found their disbelief impossible to hide. The fairy tale was not supposed to end in a Parisian underpass being chased by the paparazzi in her chauffeured car. Compounding the sense of grief was a feeling that she finally seemed to be finding a sense of contentment, happiness and liberation, a role in post-royal life. As a tide of bouquets swamped the iron gates of Buckingham Palace, the Queen had to be cajoled into greeting her mourning subjects. The tragedy seemed to evaporate English reserve as the country cried publicly. Days later, her grieving sons walked behind her coffin under the unrelenting glare of publicity. The future of the monarchy would rest on their shoulders.

Music
Paranoid Android
– Radiohead

The lead single from Radiohead's highly anticipated album *OK Computer* is a fusion of three separate songs in different keys, each written by a different member of the band. Inspired by The Beatles' *Happiness Is a Warm Gun*, the original version was 14 minutes long including an organ outro. Lyrically themed around capitalism, violence and madness, the line "squealing Gucci little piggy" refers to a woman who singer Thom Yorke saw have a hissy fit in an L.A. bar when drink was accidentally spilled on her dress. Edited down to six-and-a-half minutes, the final version sealed the Oxford quintet's reputation as a ground-breaking band, one of the few to enjoy both critical and commercial success.

Film
Boogie Nights
– Paul Thomas Anderson

Anderson established himself as one of cinema's leading directors with his critically acclaimed account of the rise and fall of porn star Dirk Diggler (Mark Wahlberg) in the pre-AIDS heyday of the sex film industry. Sex is a sideshow to the main themes of family, the desire to belong and fame. Burt Reynolds had a fractious relationship with the director and reportedly the two almost came to blows on set. After seeing a rough cut, Reynolds distanced himself from the film despite winning a Golden Globe for his performance. Wahlberg apparently kept one of his prosthetic phalluses as a souvenir, though it has sadly begun to degrade.

Like 1964, this is a vintage that favours one Bank over the other.

The end of 1997 and beginning of 1998 saw generally warm and very wet conditions. But a series of intermittent frosty nights kept the sap low and delayed bud burst despite a balmy late February. A gradual appearance of buds at the end of March gathered pace when a blast of warm air hit the region. An unsettled April saw twice as much rain as normal (170 mm/6¾ in) and retarded shoot growth. Muddy vineyards made it difficult to drive the heavy tractors and obliged workers to strap on their backpacks and spray manually. Fortunately, calm and warm conditions in May allowed vines' growth cycle to catch up by the end of the month. Flowers speckled the landscape from 25 May with *mi-floraison* on 4 June. Unsettled rainy and cold weather threatened to disturb flowering and yet coulure did not really materialise. June saw a heat wave as the mercury touched 36°C (97°F), and enjoyed 515 hours of sunshine compared with 410 hours the previous year, yet July was cooler and overcast with nights uncharacteristically nippy for the time of year. (Indeed, I vividly recall having to wear a thick coat while walking around Pavie, which was undergoing reconstruction under new owner Gérard Perse.) It remained dry with Pauillac receiving just 18 mm (¾ in) of rain, which fell as brief deluges and water ran off into gullies instead of soaking the soil. Hail in Pomerol also caused some damage, though many regarded it as Nature providing a green harvest. Normal service was resumed in August with a majority of the month over 30°C (86°F), peaking at almost 39°C (102°F) on 9 August, which caused vine stress and shrivelled bunches, particularly on gravel soils that reflect heat. *Véraison* passed quickly over a fortnight although despite this and the recent warmth, the cool July meant sugar levels remained low, with crisp nights maintaining high acidity levels.

In September, as winemakers began to make preparations for the harvest, Bill Blatch remarks in his annual report that predictions of poor weather from 7 September, which perhaps encouraged some to bring their picking forward, never materialised. Warm and mainly dry weather in the first few days helped increase sugar levels and reduced acidity, while the second half of the month saw ideal conditions – an Indian summer with cool nights that ripened the Merlot. The Right Bank and Pessac-Léognan prospered. But then on 27 September, 30 mm (1 in) of rain fell across the region and rain storms interrupted the harvesting of later-ripening Cabernets, forcing châteaux to pick during dry windows rather than when they wanted. There was some dilution of the Cabernets, whereas the Merlot was high in sugar with thick skins. Sauternes enjoyed a benevolent season since there was less rain and less intense heat during August, allowing berries to accrete sugar to the same levels as in 1989. September showers ignited botrytis, so it was an early picking for some, especially in Barsac. After early October rain, those who had decided to wait were rewarded with sunny, misty mornings to complete the harvest, which they did by the end of the month with their fourth and fifth passes through the vineyard.

The 1998 vintage is the archetypal "Right Bank" vintage. Simply put, the Merlot could be picked at optimal ripeness before the rain and the later-ripening Cabernets could not. There are a couple of caveats. Merlot imposes a shorter picking window and so harvest teams had to be on their toes to snip bunches at the right moment, Cabernet affording a wider timeframe. But having tasted this vintage regularly over the years, the best wines unequivocally lie on the Right Bank, with Pomerol a notable epicentre of quality. The 1998 Pétrus could lay claim to the title of greatest Bordeaux of the entire decade, a monumental Pomerol with a half-century lifespan. Several bottles, the last in Hong Kong, have reaffirmed its pedigree but it will need time. The 1998 Lafleur took longer to loosen up, as usual, but is worth waiting for, while I must confess I have found the 1998 Le Pin veering a little too close stylistically to Napa than I would like. I vividly recollect tasting the 1998 l'Église-Clinet from barrel with the late Denis Durantou – a benchmark wine that you intuitively knew was destined to become a legend and elevate Durantou's profile. My most recent encounter in October 2021 justifies the praise heaped upon it. Some wines, such as the 1998 Clinet, do suffer from a bit of over-extraction as it was in vogue at that time. The same goes for Saint-Émilion; the 1998 Pavie has aged well, but not as well as, say, Cheval Blanc or a resurgent Ausone.

The Left Bank is less consistent and some wines can feel obdurate, missing a sense of *joie-de-vivre*, though there are exceptions such as the 1998 Lafite Rothschild, which has its nose in front of Mouton Rothschild and Latour. The real focus of quality is in Pessac-Léognan. Both the 1998 Haut-Brion and La Mission Haut-Brion, which have higher Merlot contents compared to the Médocs, produced exceptional wines that were initially undervalued but are now receiving due respect. I once cracked open a 1998 Haut-Brion for a couple of old Essex friends who declared it one of the most beautiful wines they had ever drunk. They might have had little experience, but their delight proved it had been uncorked for the right people. The 1998 Haut-Bailly and Domaine de Chevalier also deliver the goods, perhaps more so than Pape Clément, which like Clinet was being pushed a bit hard in the winery in this era. The 1998 Sauternes can be excellent and perhaps remain a little overlooked. Look out for the likes of Climens, Doisy-Daëne and especially Coutet.

Event
The Good Friday Agreement

Music
Doo Wop (That Thing)
– Lauryn Hill

On Good Friday, 10 April 1998, the British and Irish governments reached an agreement on the future running of Northern Ireland that would see unionists and nationalists sharing power in a government devolved from London to Belfast. The agreement was ratified in two referendums held in both parts of Ireland on 22 May. It was hoped that what became known as the Good Friday Agreement would bring an end to the Troubles between republicans and loyalists that had begun in the twenties. The first election to the Northern Ireland Assembly was held on 8 June and the leaders of the two main political parties, David Trimble and John Hume, were awarded the Nobel Peace Prize later that year.

Singer and rapper Lauryn Hill had become an international star as the focal point of The Fugees, who had split the previous year to pursue solo projects. *Doo Wop (That Thing)* was the lead single from her debut album, a sublime hip-hop/R&B number that showcased her impeccable vocals and rapping flow. Both the single and its album, *The Miseducation of Lauryn Hill*, received unanimous praise. But the fame and attention proved overwhelming and Hill became a recluse, facing financial problems and spending time in prison for tax evasion. None of that takes away from the brilliance of her music at this time. Before Beyoncé ascended the throne, Hill was queen.

Film
The Big Lebowski – Joel and Ethan Coen

Jeff "The Dude" Lebowski, copious amounts of marijuana and a rug are the stars of the ultimate slacker movie, made by the Coen brothers. Jeff Bridges admitted that his character was essentially a parody of himself in the seventies, though he hesitated before accepting the role as he feared it would set a bad example for his daughters. According to the Internet Movie Database, the Dude says "man" a total of 147 times in the film. Such is the cult around *The Big Lebowski* that it has spawned a religious movement named The Church of the Latter-Day Dude.

1999

The most dramatic event of the 1999 vintage occurred just before the year began.

On 26 and 27 December two Atlantic depressions deepened and France fell victim to some of the most violent storms it had seen in a century, bringing widespread destruction and loss of life. The second, the slightly weaker weather system, had Bordeaux in its crosshairs. Gusts of 89 mph (144 km/h) slammed into the city, with even stronger winds in the more exposed Médoc. Though few vines were damaged, I remember driving through the region just a week later and seeing felled trees, including some of the willows that line the main road outside Lafite Rothschild, and several roofless buildings. A cold snap in late November 1998 had allowed vineyards to be pruned back and in the aftermath of the storms, January began unseasonably warm. February was cooler and a warm spell in mid-March provoked the first buds of Merlot around the 15th. As Bill Blatch notes in his report, the vines felt the urge to reproduce and yield fruit right from the start, spurring some vineyard teams to cut away nascent buds to avoid overproduction. May was quite humid and hot with rain in the second half that threatened serious mildew and obliged spraying in the vineyard. Hot and dry conditions between 23 May and 1 June led to flowering, just over a week earlier than normal, portending a September picking. But inclement weather between 4 and 8 June disturbed the flowering of the Cabernets and vines suffered coulure – though in a high-volume year that was not necessarily unwelcome. June and July were warm, with few rainy spells or heat spikes, allowing an accretion of tannins. From 3 August, the settled conditions began to break down and heavy storms dumped 50–75 mm (2–3 in) of rain on the region, followed by cooler temperatures in the low twenties. Mildew, rot and oidium were now constant threats and the season began to differentiate between those who were prepared to spend hours tending their vines and those who were not. *Véraison* was around 5 August but the bad weather prolonged the change of colour for the Cabernets. Just as hopes were drifting away, a period of clement settled weather from 21 August brought relief as temperatures topped 30°C (86°F), allowing large and dilute grapes to concentrate and accumulate sugar. A storm on 26 August affected the Right Bank more than the Médoc, while Saint-Émilion was devastated by hail on 5 September that acutely affected châteaux located on the slopes (I vividly recall seeing the sorry-looking state of Trotte Vieille just a couple of days afterwards). As it was just 10 days before the harvest, all vineyard hands could do was manually pick any bunches that had survived before the rest turned rotten. Fortunately, the hail was localised and only affected 10% of the appellation, so many were unscathed. The Left Bank had enjoyed just over three weeks of perfect weather.

With practically everyone ready to pick the first Merlot on Monday 20 September, predictions of heavy rain came true on the preceding Friday. There was some picking over the weekend, but most started as scheduled in the pouring rain, which gradually cleared up as the week progressed. The Cabernets were harvested straight after the Merlot as there was no point in waiting, so that by the time heavy rain returned in early October, most of the vines had been picked. To rub salt into winemakers' wounds, the rest of the month was dry and ideal for picking – but, alas, you can't glue bunches back on to vines. Fermentations were quick and, with high must levels of around the 14.5% for the most precocious Merlots, did not mandate a lot of extraction, in some ways prefiguring the trend towards gentler maceration in the following decades.

Sauternes enjoyed a decent but not spectacular season. A storm on 26 August prompted the first wave of botrytis, though berries were not concentrated and most of the affected fruit was discarded. After a dry September, the second wave of botrytis at the end of the month lasted several days until 5 October. According to Bill Blatch, fruit from this picking comprised around two-thirds of blends, supplemented by small passes during a cold but fine October.

Nineteen ninety-nine is sandwiched between two headline-grabbing vintages and as such is overlooked. Yet it had its dramatic moments with the winter storm and last-minute hail in Saint-Émilion, and upon re-examination reveals itself as a potentially very fine vintage knocked off course by rain at the wrong time, just as the harvest was about to begin. The season punished estates that failed to tend their vines throughout the year, but despite irregularity, the wines have much to offer. On the Left Bank, the Margaux appellation excelled and the 1999 Château Margaux is the pick of the First Growths, a magnificent magnum served at 20 years of age at a pre-Christmas bacchanal suggesting it remains a few years away from a lofty plateau. The 1999s from Lafite Rothschild and Latour are both what you might call "solid performers", while 1999 Palmer transcends the vintage and might even show the 2000 a thing or two. Rauzan-Ségla, Brane-Cantenac and d'Issan are not bad, but were predestined to produce better in the following years. Across the Médoc, there are very commendable wines from Cos d'Estournel, Léoville-Las Cases, Domaine de Chevalier and Pontet-Canet, though my most favourable encounters tend to come from the Right Bank, not least delightful 1999s from Ausone, Le Pin and Pétrus. La Conseillante and Vieux Château Certan are also well worth attention, even if they are no longer the bargains they once were. Sauternes had a good rather than a great vintage – dependable you might say – with fine contributions from Yquem and Suduiraut in particular.

1999

(Continued)

1870

2020

1999
(Continued)

Event
Harry Potter and the Prisoner of Azkaban is published

The third instalment of the *Harry Potter* saga marks the tipping point that the famous wizard waved his magic wand and became an unprecedented global phenomenon. The draft of J.K. Rowling's first Potter book, typed on a manual typewriter, was rejected by 12 publishers before it was picked up by Bloomsbury, which printed 1,000 now ultra-collectable copies – around half going to libraries. *Harry Potter and the Prisoner of Azkaban* hit bookshops on 8 July 1999 and sold 68,000 copies in its first three days. Soon adults were hooked by *Harry Potter* as much as their children.

Music
...Baby One More Time – Britney Spears

Technically, Britney Spears's debut should be included in the previous year since it was released in October 1998, but its slow ascent meant it topped the charts in 22 countries in early 1999. Written by Swedish producer Max Martin, it was first offered to R&B group TLC, who disapproved of its abusive lyrical connotations, so it was passed on to the 16-year-old former star of *The Mickey Mouse Club*. Shot in Venice High School (where *Grease* was also filmed), the video was criticised for Spears's schoolgirl attire, even though it had been the singer's own suggestion to wear the Kmart uniform. A perfect earworm, the song went on to sell 10 million copies and influence a slew of female pop stars.

Film
The Blair Witch Project – Daniel Myrick and Eduardo Sánchez

In many ways, this horror film changed the rules of cinema. Its principal photography cost just $35,000 but its use of amateur hand-held camerawork inspired a raft of films featuring shaky images. Most of all, the way it accrued an audience through word-of-mouth and viral guerrilla marketing tactics on the nascent internet – essentially creating what is nowadays termed an "expanded universe" – set a new template for how films could be promoted. At its heart, *The Blair Witch Project* is a well-acted, unsettling horror flick that has stood the test of time and presaged 21st century cinema.

The

2

0

0

0

s

Some decades can be split into before and after watershed vintages. The growing seasons of 1878, 1945 and 1982 spring to mind. In the opening decade of the new millennium, the game-changing vintage was 2005. It was not just a watershed for Bordeaux, but for how all fine wine was conceived. Until then, wine connoisseurship was a niche interest, the preserve of the middle and upper classes, those with disposable income. Directly involved in the wine trade at the time, I noticed how 2005 lit the touchpaper for interest to grow beyond a core of oenophiles who bought year after year. In retrospect it was the start of an expansion that has gathered momentum.

There are a number of inter-related reasons that explain this phenomenon. First, widening wealth inequality led to greater numbers of people with disposable income to spend. Despite inflation, fine wine is a relatively accessible luxury compared with, say, the mind-boggling sums spent on fine art. One person's exorbitant price tag is another's inexpensive entry point. Second, Robert Parker's enthusiasm fired up the 2005 primeur campaign. Nothing new there, but this time his blessing ignited secondary market prices and highlighted Bordeaux's investment potential. Profiteering has always been part and parcel of Bordeaux but now it was also apparent to those who had hitherto overlooked fine wine. Higher market prices were no longer just a neat way to finance further wine purchases – they could be enough to pay off you mortgage. Third, as Bordeaux entered the bailiwick of affluent people, it created a desire to buy into the attendant lifestyle: the glamour and hedonism, the schmoozing with proprietors at glitzy dinners, the satisfaction of knowledge, the historical prestige and the sharing of a common interest/passion. Apologies to any numismatists out there, but fine wine seems a lot more fun than collecting coins.

The 2005 vintage spawned increasing numbers of investment companies promising enticing capital tax-free returns on their wine portfolios, setting in motion spiralling demand. The speculative element of claret became a more important – sometimes the sole – motivating factor when choosing which wine to buy. The only difference between such investments and buying stocks is that wine tastes better and can induce mild intoxication. Two-thousand and five was a precursor to what transpired at the end of the decade, a literal and figurative taste of things to come. Bordeaux was turning from a mortal beverage into an aspirational luxury brand – one not just confined to traditional Western markets.

In 2007 Hong Kong halved its 80% import duty levied on wines and the following year abolished it altogether. I was visiting a London-based merchant on the morning of the announcement and recall the frenzied atmosphere as its implications were digested. Virtually overnight, the Far East market became much more potent and London-based merchants wasted little time establishing outposts, mainly in Hong Kong, creating a new hub of Bordeaux trade. Hong Kong served as a conduit into mainland China, which seemed to have limitless demand for Bordeaux (though whether that will continue amid current political changes remains to be seen).

Fine wine was perceived as the ideal gift for Chinese businessmen to give to each other, especially if it was the apogee of Bordeaux, which according to the tablet of stone written in 1855 is Lafite Rothschild. The First Growth stoked demand further by engraving the Chinese symbol for the number eight on its bottle, a lucky number in China supposed to bring good fortune. Market prices duly skyrocketed to eye-watering levels. When the 2009 Bordeaux vintage was released just a few months later with its small armada of perfect Parker scores, the primeur campaign witnessed demand never seen before or since. To give you an example, I remember sitting next to one young collector at a dinner in Hong Kong – someone passionate about wine but no expert – who cool as a cucumber divulged to me that he had bought 600 cases of 2009 Cos d'Estournel. This was an individual, not a company acquisition.

In the coming months, flights to Hong Kong, Beijing and Shanghai were packed with château proprietors tutoring masterclasses in luxury hotels. In the opposite direction, budding young Far Eastern oenophiles descended upon Bordeaux châteaux, often received by owners not entirely unsure whether they were important distributors or merely tourists trying their luck. Best to roll out the red carpet just in case. Estates stationed brand ambassadors in mainland China and translated their brochures into Mandarin and Cantonese. The ever-mercantile Bordelais rubbed their hands as requests for allocations and blank cheques arrived from aspirational and presumably naive consumers. By the end of the decade many châteaux acted like the cats who had got the cream, eyeing fortunes to be made. There was only one unanswered question... How long would this bubble last? They would soon find out.

Back in the vineyard, technology took an increasingly prominent role. When I visited Bordeaux during the 2009 primeur campaign I found proprietors eager to show me their brand new "toy" – optical sorting machines. The first were released on to the market in 2008 by Bucher Vaslin and Pellenc. By automatically detecting chlorophyll levels and removing unripe berries, leaves and grass, these did the same job as workers who manually picked out unwanted berries on the sorting line using eyes and nimble fingers. Neither the 2009 vintage nor the 2010 were the kind of damp growing seasons that might have necessitated such expensive gadgetry, but châteaux such as Haut-Brion and Pavie rented them for a couple of years before deciding whether they would become a permanent fixture, which they did at the latter but not at the former.

At the same time organic and biodynamic viticulture was becoming more widely accepted and applied. More estates had begun to eschew chemical fertilisers, herbicides and insecticides during the nineties and the trend accelerated in the first decade of the new millennium. As the mantra of Bordeaux's top estates changed from quantity to quality, organic practices became a core tenet. The next logical step was biodynamics. This alternative approach to viticulture and winemaking stems from a series of 1924 lectures by Austrian scholar Rudolf Steiner and involves the use of prescribed natural products instead of chemicals that can destroy biodiversity, following the lunar and astrological calendars, and viewing the vineyard as a holistic organism. Bordeaux was much more reluctant to adopt biodynamics than the likes of the Loire or Burgundy, where practitioners such as Nicolas Joly and Lalou-Bize Leroy pioneered its use. The Bordelais initially saw biodynamics as a fad, as hokum, and not least a significant risk, given that it potentially leaves vineyard exposed to rot.

Though estates such as Pavie Macquin, Fonroque and Gombaude-Guillot were also early adopters of organic/biodynamics, the highest-profile and most influential adherent was undoubtedly Pontet-Canet in Pauillac. In the mid-nineties proprietor Alfred Tesseron, together with former wingman Jean-Michel Comme, began converting their not inconsiderable 800,000 vines to organic viticulture, eschewing weedkillers and fertilisers before trialling biodynamics on 14 hectares of vine in 2004. This was unheard of at Grand Cru Classé level. At a lunch, one of the duo's esteemed Pauillac cohabitants scoffed at their efforts to apply biodynamics and traduced it as a mere fad. In 2007, Tesseron was forced to use chemical sprays when rot threatened to wipe out a significant percentage of his crop, thus forfeiting the certification he had been due after converting to biodynamics three years before. It was a decision he immediately regretted and from 2008 onwards, with even greater zeal, reverted to biodynamics, ultimately proving that it was viable on a large scale. That said, the practice does require total, dare I say, almost monomaniacal dedication, as well as a preparedness to lose a substantial part of your harvest in an inclement season, even if climate change has reduced that risk. Inspired by Tesseron, others followed in the next decade.

2000

Numerical significance conspired with a favourable growing season to fuel the hype leading up to the millennial Bordeaux primeur campaign. Winemakers, merchants and consumers hankered for a vintage they could bang their drums about and 2000 delivered. But it was not a growing season without challenges.

The year started difficultly as Bordeaux recovered from a destructive storm on 26 December that had felled around 400,000 trees and taken lives. In its aftermath, January was normal and February was warmer but wet. Vines awoke from their dormancy around 14 March and temperatures continued to rise steadily throughout the following weeks, reaching 30°C (86°F) in mid-May. But it was certainly wet, with some 252 mm (10 in) falling in April and May compared with a 30-year average of 140 mm (5½ in) and vineyard managers had to be vigilant and spray at the right time, especially as many were trying to reduce the number of treatments. Flowers began to speckle the landscape on 1 June with full flowering a week later. A fortnight of settled dry weather meant it was even, though the combination of showers and warm temperatures provoked mildew, as well as coulure and millerandage that mostly affected the Cabernets. The first two weeks in July were humid and hot, encouraging foliage growth, and there were storms on 3 and 24 July that cast doubts on exactly where the growing season was heading. That was answered on 29 July when a large high-pressure system moved over the region. August was wall-to-wall sunshine with temperatures peaking around 35°C (95°F) and then falling after showers on the 25th and 26th, which alleviated some of the stress suffered by younger vines on gravel soils. Despite brief outbreaks of rain in early September, temperatures remained high – up to 33°C (91°F) in some places.

Haut-Brion began picking its reds on 13 September, with Cheval Blanc marching in the next day, and the Merlot harvest kicked off in earnest under perfect conditions on 21 September. The media began to get excited. The *Sud Ouest* newspaper's headline on 27 September read "*Le millésime 2000 s'annonce grandiose*" ("The 2000 vintage promises to be spectacular"), before much of the Cabernet had even been picked. But it isn't over until the fat lady sings. A forecasted storm swept across the region from the evening of 28 September, prompting some winemakers to expedite their harvest and others to wait it out. Estates started on the Cabernet Franc and Cabernet Sauvignon from 2 October under cooler and more autumnal conditions in the first week of that month and consequently the optimal picking window was shorter than in other years. The door slammed shut on 10 October when the weather deteriorated considerably and it remained inclement through November. In Sauternes, the *pourriture noble* unfortunately failed to develop due to thick skins that had developed in August, not to mention a lack of humidity and then rain. A little fruit was picked out after 20 mm (¾ in) of rain on 19 September, so there is a tiny amount of rather simple, but at least clean Sauternes.

The 2000 vintage came after a rather fallow decade of indubitably great growing seasons. Consequently there was pent-up enthusiasm from most sectors of the industry, including critics. One cannot write about 2000 without mentioning the praise lavished by Robert Parker, who at primeur called it the best vintage since 1990, ratcheting up demand to fever pitch. Merchants reported the best sales en primeur ever, at least until 2009 trundled along. In subsequent years more and more have joined those who claim 2000 is not all it was cracked up to be. As the trend for lighter and more terroir-driven wines gathered pace, enthusiastic winemakers began to downplay their own 2000s. The commonly heard phrase was: "My 2001 is the style that I want to make." Both the 2000 and 2001 Bordeaux vintages have much to offer, but their stylistic differences have bifurcated as time has passed, their evolutionary paths going in different directions, dramatically so in some cases. Occasionally, temporal proximity seems to be the only thing they have in common.

I aver that the 2000 vintage looks back in time, whereas 2001 looks forward. While you can draw a line connecting 2000 with previous vintages, 2001 contains a stylistic consanguinity with future growing seasons. Some 2000s have not aged in a distinguished manner and have a scintilla of underlying greenness that you could contentiously argue many wine lovers miss. They often have an undeniably higher level of brettanomyces, which can be abided in small measures, but occasionally comes at the cost of freshness and precision, certainly to a far greater degree than in 2001.

I find the First Growths firing on all cylinders at over 20 years of age, living up to the hype that surrounded their birth. On the top of the podium is the imperious 2000 Latour, with the 2000 Château Margaux and Haut-Brion in joint silver position, and Lafite Rothschild only a small step behind. I have never been taken by the 2000 Mouton Rothschild, which comes in an eye-catching embossed gold bottle, and numerous tastings, sighted and blind, have validated my original dismissive review. On the last occasion, tasted blind in Hong Kong, it was surpassed by its Californian sibling Opus One. Jean-Hubert Delon crafted a spellbinding Léoville-Las Cases, while the 2000 Pichon Baron was a realisation of all the improvements the estate had made over the last decade. Grand-Puy-Lacoste, Rauzan-Ségla and Palmer all excel while Calon Ségur trumped a rather demonstrative Cos d'Estournel.

On the Right Bank, the 2000 Lafleur is a stag with sky-scraping antlers, the Guinaudeaus' best since the '82, albeit maturing at glacial pace. My last bottle poured in Christie's boardroom with Baptiste Guinaudeau drew gasps from around the room, but was still years from its drinking window. Pétrus is magnificent, though the 2000 Le Pin is easily trounced by its far superior follow-up – Jacques Thienpont

2000
(Continued)

was almost disparaging when he served a bottle in December 2021. In Saint-Émilion, Ausone, Pavie, Cheval Blanc, Tertre Rôteboeuf, Beauséjour Duffau-Lagarrosse and Angélus are wonderful. As you move away from the most revered estates on both Banks, you find more inconsistency, especially in terms of brettanomyces, though there are hidden gems such as the 2000 Branaire-Ducru. Unfortunately, it was a forgettable year for Sauternes with some estates choosing to skip the vintage, though predictably Yquem and Lafaurie-Peyraguey are not bad. Their time to shine would come 12 months later.

Event
Tiger Woods wins the Career Grand Slam

Golfer Tiger Woods was a breath of fresh air in the world of professional golf. Having won his first major three years earlier, by 2000 he was unquestionably the best player in the world. At 24 years of age, he became the youngest golfer to win a Career Grand Slam, triumphing in nine PGA tour events and recording the lowest average score in history. Troubles in his personal life upended his startling career, but nothing should take away what he achieved in his unbeatable prime.

Music
Yellow
– Coldplay

Coldplay formed in 1997 when the four members were studying at University College London. *Yellow* was composed in 1999 after co-producer Ken Nelson had invited the band to come outside and look at the stars during recording for their debut album at Rockfield studios. The title came into singer Chris Martin's head as it simply sounded right. "The tempo of that song became such a huge issue," drummer and oenophile Will Champion told me. "Minuscule tweaks that would probably be inaudible to any sane person became the difference between failure and success. There was so much riding on that song and we only had one chance to get it right. Sometimes I still wonder if it is too slow." Well, the tempo must have been right because *Yellow* broke the band on both sides of the Atlantic.

1870

Film
In the Mood for Love
– Wong Kar-Wai

Early-sixties Hong Kong is
brought to life in Wong Kar-
Wai's masterpiece thanks to its
meticulous attention to period
detail and Christopher Doyle's
exquisite cinematography, which
contrasts dark shadows with vivid
colours. Maggie Cheung and
Tony Leung play the neighbours
drawn together when they realise
their spouses, neither of whom are
shown on screen, are embroiled in
an affair. Along crowded corridors
and through windows, the camera
voyeuristically captures their
smouldering, unrequited ardour
and festering guilt, hurt and
sadness as each opportunity for
happiness slips from their grasp.
Cheung wore 46 figure-hugging
cheongsam dresses during
filming that are works of art in
themselves.

2020

2001

Initially overshadowed by the millennial vintage, the reputation of 2001 has steadily grown over time.

A high-pressure system lodged itself over Bordeaux between November and January, which led to a very wet and warm winter that saw only three spring frosts. This delayed pruning as the sap would not retract sufficiently, but everything changed on 15 January when temperatures finally dropped and vines shut down. Warmth returned in March and budding began on 19 March with regular leaf burst. April was cool, which retarded vine growth and led to frost alerts, though a westerly wind managed to blow most of the cold air on, apart from lingering pockets that affected Léognan on 20 April. May saw the mercury rise and conditions were perfect during flowering in early June – 20–25°C (68–77°F) with a light breeze. Flowering was around five days later than in the previous two years, though June was hot, with seven days in excess of 30°C (86°F) during which many vineyard managers thinned their crop and de-leafed canopies. July witnessed a fortnight of cold and rainy weather, which dampened spirits since rain was surplus to requirements after the wet winter. Some areas received as much as 91% more precipitation than usual. From 21 July to 1 August the pendulum swung back the other way with a heat wave but the weather then refused to settle and fruit was reluctant to concentrate. "Chaotic" with "jabs of heat" is how Bill Blatch described things in his annual growing season summary. The conditions led to a delayed and spun-out *véraison* and more gradual and irregular ripening than in 2000, spurring vineyard managers to lop off bunches.

September was not as hot as the previous year, though very constant with daytime temperatures of 20–25°C (68–77°F), which allowed skins to thicken, anthocyanins to build and sugar to accumulate, albeit slowly. Thankfully it was very dry, helping avoid any swelling of grapes, which still had access to ample underground water reserves – a crucial factor. The dry whites were picked from 10 September and the Médoc reds from 1 October after a forecast of heavy rain that never really materialised. There were downpours on 3 October but a southerly wind soon dried the vineyards and most of the Cabernets were picked in the middle of the month when temperatures reached 25°C (77°F). Ferments were quite prolonged, partly because night-time temperatures were low and partly because winemakers were aiming for finer wines with more fruit and less structure than the previous year, meaning soft extractions were commonplace. Many winemakers expected a shorter maceration time, but when they saw the balance of the 2001s they were encouraged to extend the duration of skin contact, up to 30 days in some cases. It was a perfect season down in Sauternes, compensating for the previous year. After early passes through the vineyard following showers at the end of August, September's coolness inhibited further botrytis infection. Occasional showers in the first week of October coupled with warm temperatures around 25°C (77°F) led to perfect picking conditions between 12 and 17 October and the collected grapes constituted around three-quarters of the final blends. Some picked later into November, but the results were inferior in quality.

I have praised this vintage since I began writing about Bordeaux. Even when received wisdom was that 2000 was superior, I stuck my neck out and praised the 2001s' freshness and vitality, how the wines articulated their respective terroirs with more clarity, and their greater focus and tension. Juxtaposing the two vintages over a month of tastings in 2020, I found that most of the 2001s had evolved with real class. It's not a total victory. There are plenty of cases in which the 2000 is better, not least among the First Growths where few 2001s match the previous vintage. But extending the purview across the top estates on both Left and Right Bank, the 2001 vintage has much to offer. Pomerol is bejewelled with exceptional wines. Baptiste Guinaudeau's 2001 Lafleur, cracked open at his favourite bistro in the town of Branne in June 2021, was a beacon of loveliness despite needing a few years in bottle. The 2001 Le Pin is one of Jacques Thienpont's crowning achievements, a magnum just scintillating with laser-like precision at 20 years old and embarrassing his 2000. Jean-Claude Berrouet spent years proselytising the 2001 Pétrus and it continues to shine, elegance and grace from tip to toe. In Saint-Émilion, the 2001 Cheval Blanc is sensual yet with insistent grip, while the Figeac is fully mature and a precocious Pavie magically gains complexity in the glass. François Mitjavile conjured a gorgeous Tertre Rôteboeuf that is irresistible.

On the Left Bank, the 2001 Lafite Rothschild is vivid and typically blue-blooded, exuding class when tasted with winemaker Eric Kohler. The 2001 Latour is quintessential Pauillac, though if push comes to shove, I might prefer the 2002. There are some absolute gems in the Médoc: Calon Ségur, Langoa Barton (even better than Léoville Barton) and Giscours.

The 2001 Sauternes are magnificent, crowned by the rapturously received Yquem, surely wine of the vintage. Some 20-odd encounters from in barrel to 2022 all attest to a magnificent Yquem that will last a century. Re-tasting Sauternes after two decades, I advise seeking out mellifluous offerings from La Tour Blanche, Suduiraut and Raymond-Lafon. Not wishing to pour cold water on the wines, I am perhaps less eulogistic about the vintage than others and I wager that the 2009s will ultimately surpass the 2001s.

2001

Event
9/11

8.45 a.m., 11 September 2001 – the moment when the first Boeing 767 crashed into the Twin Towers and terrorism arrived in the heart of the West. The co-ordinated attack unfolded in real time across global media. Viewers gazed in horror and disbelief as workers threw themselves from burning skyscrapers, heart-breaking final farewells to loved ones surfacing in the following days. The buildings collapsed and we dreaded to think how many were inside. As the deadly plume of debris and smoke engulfed Manhattan, news of concurrent terrorist attacks on the Pentagon and Flight 93 unfolded, the magnitude of events almost surreal and impossible to digest. Nineteen members of Al-Qaeda put history on a different and darker timeline. Everything changed on 9/11.

Music
Can't Get You Out of My Head – Kylie Minogue

Kylie Minogue's reinvention as a sassy, sexy pop star reached its zenith with the impeccable and aptly titled *Can't Get You Out of My Head*. Written by nineties pop star Cathy Dennis and Rob Davis, founder of glam rockers Mud, it was built up from a drum loop created on Cubase software. Both S Club 7 manager Simon Fuller and Sophie Ellis-Bextor turned it down before it was handed to one of Minogue's representatives. The singer apparently only had to listen to 20 seconds of the demo before agreeing to put her sultry vocals over the pulsing New Order-like beat. Released on 8 September 2001, it topped the charts in practically every European country, sold over a million copies in the UK and entered the US top 10, her first Stateside hit since 1987.

Film
Amélie – Jean-Pierre Jeunet

Jeunet had struggled to find the actress to play the titular shy waitress whose entire *raison d'être* is to make others' lives better. The director had Emily Watson in mind, but she declined as she could not speak French. Then he spotted a poster for romantic comedy *Venus Beauty* starring Audrey Tautou. Today you couldn't imagine anyone else as Amélie. Similarly to *In the Mood for Love* (page 425), colour plays a crucial role, helping bring the film's Montmartre café to life with vivid greens, yellows and reds. The president of the Cannes Film Festival rejected the movie, but its feel-good factor was cinematic balm at a turbulent time and *Amélie* went on to become a huge critical and commercial success.

The 2002 vintage is one of those neither here nor there seasons whose wines rarely set the pulse racing.

The winter of 2001/2002 was exceptionally dry. This meant unseasonal warm weather in early February did not encourage early budding because, unlike in previous years, the vines did not have access to water reserves. March was cold and dry with just 28 mm (1 in) of rain, but a warmer second half of the month saw the Merlot bud from around the 18th. The Cabernets were retarded by a cold spell. There was no frost damage this year despite a skirmish around mid-April. May began with overcast and drizzly conditions that slowed shoot growth but then the mercury rocketed to 31°C (88°F) on 16 May. The first flowers appeared five days later before temperatures dropped and showers plagued the region. As a result flowering was spun out over four weeks, laying the foundation for irregular ripening cycles, especially for the Merlot. Up to 75% of the potential Merlot crop was lost due to coulure and millerandage. Although most estates practised a green harvest in the summer, the loss of so many bunches discouraged some and, as Bill Blatch observes, the same châteaux tended not to de-leaf. July and August were fairly dry with a modest 29 mm (1 in) and 79 mm (3 in) of precipitation respectively, but just like four years earlier, it remained dull and overcast despite the warmth, with a 20% shortfall in sunlight hours, according to Sichel's report. Showers in the latter half of August diluted some berries and precipitated grey rot that was exacerbated by warmish nights. This also made *véraison* very protracted, increasing irregularity between vineyards.

The beginning of September was showery and rot was beginning to get a grip in the vines, prompting the most pessimistic winemakers to give up on the vintage. Then, just like in the last two seasons, rescue came in the form of a high-pressure system that settled over Bordeaux from 10 September, remaining there for the entire harvest. There was just 32 mm (1¼ in) of rain in the entire month. Cool nights curtailed the spread of rot and the prevailing warmth allowed berries in well-tended vineyards to achieve phenolic maturity. In contrast, those who had allowed rot to fester throughout the season were unable to take advantage. Merlots reached a reasonable 12–12.5% potential alcohol. There was some hail damage in the northern Médoc, Fronsac and parts of Moulis while areas of Pessac-Léognan were hit by rain. But many in Bordeaux began getting excited by the later-ripening Cabernets and Petit Verdot, which estates were able to pick at leisure until around 9 October when the weather finally broke. The fruit was generally healthy, with good acidity levels thanks to the cool summer nights and high tannin levels, meaning winemakers had to be prudent with vinification. After the euphoria that had surrounded the 2001 harvest, the following year was a bit of a comedown in Sauternes. Simply put, September was just too dry and botrytis failed to form. Third and fourth passes after rain on 9 October at least provided pockets of noble rot, but overall

2002
(Continued)

it was a spun-out affair and quality was patchy, subject to the degree châteaux were prepared to undertake a laboriously precise picking.

The 2002 vintage produced a mixed bunch of wines with an absence of superstars to get excited about. One of the high points are the Left Bank's Cabernet Sauvignon-based wines and, predictably, top of the pile is an outstanding Latour, easily the best of the First Growths. A blind tasting of the last 20 vintages in magnum highlighted its calibre, despite the Arctic temperatures in Latour's cellar that evening. The other Firsts are decent but lack fireworks and have never really evolved with the same élan. Elsewhere, I have a penchant for the 2002 Léoville Barton but otherwise, these are wines that do the job with no frills and a minimum of fuss. Generally you have no regrets drinking them but they will not stick in your head like the best 2001s. The Right Bank also boasts few fine wines of note. In Pomerol, the 2002 Lafleur has a sense of density and grip perhaps lacking in others, while a magnum of 2002 Pétrus was balanced if just missing a little flair. Even the l'Église-Clinet is capable but rather dour on the finish. Alexandre Thienpont oversaw a commendable Vieux Château Certan though it lacks fireworks. In Saint-Émilion, Alain Vauthier crafted an exceptional Ausone that probably pips the Cheval Blanc, otherwise just like in Pomerol, they are not wines to get the pulse racing – more content to pedal gently along than perform wheelies.

Event
Serena Williams wins her first Wimbledon title

Having made her professional debut in 1995 at the tender age of 14, Serena Williams took her first Wimbledon Ladies' Singles title this year, defeating her sister Venus 7-6, 6-3 and stealing her top ranking. It was Williams' second tournament victory on her way to a Grand Slam, proving unbeatable at the French, US and Australian Opens. She went on to win Wimbledon seven times, introducing a more powerful style of play and higher athleticism, and dominating the game longer than almost any other player.

Music
Lose Yourself
– Eminem

Marshall Bruce Mathers III, a.k.a. Eminem/Slim Shady, had shot to stardom three years earlier as a gifted protégé of Dr. Dre. Provocative and brilliant in equal measure, he had reached a level of fame where he was given the chance to star in *8 Mile*, a film loosely based upon his life growing up in Detroit and the challenges he faced as a white rapper. *Lose Yourself* was written between takes in his trailer and the sheet on which he wrote the words appears in one of the scenes. Unveiling a more guitar-driven and denser sound, the song won critical acclaim and became the first rap song to triumph at the Oscars. Rumours circulated that Eminem refused to perform at the ceremony because the Academy insisted on censoring his lyrics, but he has since explained that he just assumed he wouldn't win and instead spent the night at home with his daughter.

Film
Spirited Away
– Hayao Miyazaki

Miyazaki entranced audiences for years with a succession of acclaimed animated features for Studio Ghibli. The maestro had alarmed his vast fanbase after 1997's *Princess Mononoke* by intimating his retirement, but fortunately his boundless imagination had other ideas. *Spirited Away* is his masterpiece, introducing another fantastical world burgeoning with creatures and spirits, many inspired by Japanese folklore. Feisty 10-year-old Chihiro must navigate her way back to the normal world and rescue her parents, who have been inconveniently turned into swine. Much of the action takes place in a labyrinthine bathhouse inspired by one in Miyazaki's hometown and every cell dazzles with detail, the furthest corners constantly alive with movement. Released in Japan on 20 July 2001, *Spirited Away* become the country's highest-ever grossing film before enjoying a hugely successful global release in summer 2002. It won Best Animated Feature at the following year's Oscars, though Miyazaki refused to attend the ceremony in protest over America's involvement in the Iraq war.

2002 *(Continued)*

1870

2020

431

2003

Who could have predicted the growing season that lay ahead on 1 January 2003?

The winter did not augur anything out of the ordinary with regular rainfall replenishing underground reserves. Three of four freezing spells forced the sap to retreat and Bill Blatch reported that there were 22 days of frost. But temperatures began increasing towards the end of February as the wind swung from the south and March was the warmest since 1945. The vines duly responded, sprinting into action and by April were a fortnight ahead of normal growth. Blatch notes that this was a crucial feature of the season because it encouraged roots to tunnel deep into the soil and seek moisture, though the dry conditions meant few bunches. Prospects for a large harvest were nipped in the bud from the outset. A colder April retarded the vines' growth and fortunately there were only minor skirmishes with frost when temperatures hovered just below zero. May was dry, but flowering was interrupted by cold mornings and then a storm on the 19 May. The Merlot suffered more than the Cabernets as further heat spikes towards the end of the month caused coulure and millerandage.

Then, from 29 May until 28 August, the region and indeed much of Europe, witnessed an unprecedented and unrelenting heat wave. June saw 10 days over 30°C (86°F) and July 11 days, but that was just the warm-up. In August a host of records were shattered as average daytime temperatures tipped 32°C (90°F) and a sweltering 40.7°C (105.3°F) was recorded during an intense heat wave from the 3rd to the 13th. I remember the unbearable heat myself, though my suffering was trifling as an estimated 15,000 people died from heat exhaustion across France. Touring châteaux that summer, I noticed few signs of stress among the vines in the Médoc. Where were the curling and browning leaves? Indeed, light Atlantic breezes brought some moisture to relieve the Left Bank, while the winter's underground reserves provided just enough water to prevent most vines from shutting down. Blatch also makes the valid point that the heat only *gradually* built up towards the August peak, allowing vines to acclimatise to the conditions – more sudden bursts of heat can shock vines into shutting down in fear of their own survival. There were also two tremendous thunderstorms on 24 June and 15 July. The first I vividly recall during the Vinexpo wine fair – day suddenly turned to night, squalls wrought havoc at a banquet in Saint-Émilion, and gusts toppled rows of vines. There was also localised hail in Graves, Entre-Deux-Mers and parts of Saint-Émilion. Vine stress started to impact the Right Bank from mid-August, particularly in Pomerol and parts of Saint-Émilion on freer-draining soils and on younger vines, punishing those who had de-leafed earlier in the season. Indeed, the growing season prompted many to reconsider the practice, which has become less common in light of climate change (2021 excepting).

As expected given the summer, the dry whites were picked extraordinarily early – on 13 and 14 August at Haut-Brion, though later pickers benefited from welcome showers a few days later. The Merlot picking took place from 3 September to around 14 September under clement sunny conditions, some châteaux expediting the harvest as showers led to sporadic grey rot, but also gave berries a little pep after the taxing year. Otherwise, it stayed remarkably dry and this staved off any widespread rot infection. The Cabernets were mostly picked from 22 September under sunny conditions and as temperatures finally began cooling off.

The harvest was virtually finished by 3 October when the weather deteriorated. Because bunches were being picked at around 35°C (95°F), keeping them cool as they were transferred to winery receptions was vital. Technological advances made over the last decade such as cold rooms and air-conditioning units meant this was much less problematic than it had been during previous Indian summers in 1947 or 1982. Rich musts meant maceration had to be prudent and light to avoid volatility and oxidation. Acidity levels were low prior to malolactic fermentation and winemakers I visited during primeur assured me that acidity had been leeched from skins that had lower pH levels than originally thought.

Sauternes producers had a tricky start to the harvest after receiving twice as much rainfall as the rest of Bordeaux at the start of the month. Heat and dryness had prevented noble rot formation until the second week when pickers finally swarmed into the vines to harvest the botrytised fruit. There was a second onrush of botrytis on 17 September with some sugar levels reaching 28% due to the heat. Then, unusually for Sauternes, it was all over by 26 September – just 10 days of picking instead of several weeks. Even Yquem had picked everything in a single pass.

The result was a crop of wines very different to those of recent years. In many ways they prefigure those of hot growing seasons such as 2018 and 2019, even though winemaking techniques have since progressed and manifested purer and fresher styles under similar conditions. When the 2003s were released, the headlines were fixated on the spat that erupted between Robert Parker and Jancis Robinson, who likened the 2003 Pavie to Amarone. I will not enter the debate here as it has been discussed ad nauseam, but it does illustrate how opinions of the vintage diverged depending on people's penchant for very ripe, some might say "turbocharged", Bordeaux.

It is not my favourite vintage. The 2003s are decadent, powerful and rich with tendencies towards the Southern Rhône (not Amarone) at times. Many wines lack the freshness and tension that underlie great claret. Whilst endowed with less volatility than they would have had in eras gone by, they tend to be overtly sweet and occasionally cloying. It was

2003
(Continued)

clear from the outset that the best come from the northern Médoc. Both Saint-Estèphe and Pauillac benefited from greater exposure to the temperature-moderating effects of the yawning estuary, while the former also had the advantage of its clay soils. Both 2003 Montrose and Cos d'Estournel excel and can fool you into believing they were born in cooler growing seasons (as they did me after I tasted both blind at a private dinner in Bordeaux in 2020). Also seek out the 2003 Sociando-Mallet and Lafon-Rochet, the latter tasted at a vertical with Basile Tesseron just before his family sold the estate. Pauillac also fared well, notably the 2003 Latour, which is better than the Lafite Rothschild or Mouton Rothschild as a result of its proximity to the estuary. Lynch-Bages, Pichon-Lalande and Pichon Baron have aged with aplomb. It is in Saint-Julien where inconsistency creeps in. While 2003 Léoville-Las Cases and Ducru-Beaucaillou acquitted themselves admirably, some vineyards located further inland come across as one-dimensional by comparison and matured less well. In the Margaux appellation, the summer heat makes a deeper impression, though Paul Pontallier fashioned a very respectable Château Margaux, more successful than Palmer this year. Pessac-Léognan is a mixed bunch and I feel Haut-Brion trails the other First Growths this season, perhaps due to its urban microclimate.

The Right Bank is even more inconsistent. Many Pomerols feel cloying and occasionally stewed, though some located on the gravel plateau aged reasonably well, notably Pétrus and l'Église-Clinet. Saint-Émilion is likewise a mixed bag. Some winemakers dogmatically produced intensely powerful wines in a season when you needed to put your foot on the brakes, not the accelerator. A number have since fallen apart, some affected by brettanomyces.

Sauternes are generally successful in terms of offering rich, botrytis-laden wines. This was an era when châteaux were gunning for higher residual sugar levels, which seemed to seduce influential critics, so some produced unctuous Sauternes loaded with up to 190 g/l of residual sugar in 2003 – excessive in my opinion, as many lack the tension that gives the '05s their edge or the best '02s their elegance. Aside from Yquem, the 2003 La Tour Blanche, Sigalas Rabaud and Rabaud-Promis evolved well in bottle, though others come across as just a bit ponderous, especially after two or three sips.

Event
American-led troops enter Iraq

On 20 March 2003, just under 180,000 American-led ground troops entered Iraq. Their primary goal was to capture President Saddam Hussein, who was allegedly stockpiling weapons of mass destruction. Some countries opposed the invasion, seeking a diplomatic resolution and in the event, after the regime was toppled several weeks later, no such weapons were found. Though coalition forces occupied Iraq, Hussein's whereabouts remained unknown. He was finally discovered hiding in a hole the following December and hanged on 30 December 2006.

Music
Seven Nation Army
– The White Stripes

That bass line is already in your head. Upon first hearing *Seven Nation Army*, it was hard to fathom how nobody had ever come up with that simple infectious riff before. The song took on a life of its own and before long was echoing around football stadiums and being chanted at political rallies. According to an interview in *The Independent* newspaper, singer Jack White stumbled upon the riff while warming up his hollow-body guitar and used a pitch-shift pedal to shift it down an octave to resemble a distorted bass. Its title was inspired by his childhood mishearing of "Salvation Army", a holding name that just stuck. The track became The White Stripes' defining anthem and bagged them a Grammy the following year.

Film
Lost in Translation – Sofia Coppola

A 17-year-old Scarlett Johansson and comedy-genius Bill Murray share one of the most absorbing platonic relationships portrayed on the silver screen. The movie was shot in just under four weeks in Tokyo, with some scenes having to be filmed guerrilla-style since Coppola could not obtain permission from authorities. The genius of *Lost in Translation* is that although little happens, it draws you in to the growing bond between a past-his-prime actor and a young girl both adrift in a foreign metropolis. There has been much speculation about what Murray whispers into Johansson's ear in the final scene. Despite efforts to enhance the audio, no one will ever know, apart from the actors and the director.

2003

(Continued)

1870

2020

2004

After the previous season's unprecedented growing season, winemakers wondered what 2004 would have in store. As it turned out, it was rather benign.

The previous October's frost pushed the sap straight down after the torrid heat of the summer. Thereafter winter was comparatively warm but dry, with a quarter less rainfall than normal, most of it falling in January. Cold northerly winds in the first half of March delayed budding until the end of the month, which was protracted, auguring a late picking. Shoot growth also lagged and vineyard hands used the time to remove some of the excess buds and counter-buds. The lead-up to flowering was textbook, with showers at the end of May followed by a heat wave. A clement and hot June saw temperatures of 2.9°C (37.2°F) above average and raised hopes of a great vintage. The setback was a lack of water and as the calendar flipped over to July, vines began to show symptoms of stress, laden with bountiful bunches struggling to ripen. Not helping matters were overcast skies, though a streak of nine hot days at the end July brought some relief. August was humid and warm, encouraging vines to invest their energy into foliage instead of fruit and heightening grey rot pressure, while an unexpected swelling of berries meant those who had already thinned the fruit-laden vines in July were obliged to repeat the exercise in August. *Véraison* was also irregular due to inclement weather, with the Cabernets particularly uneven in colour.

Not for the first time, September saved the vintage. The sun shone throughout the entire month with three days in excess of 30°C (86°F). When I visited Smith Haut Lafitte that month, co-proprietor Florence Cathiard was ecstatic about the conditions. According to Bill Blatch's report, the average September temperature was 19.3°C (66.7°F) compared with an average of 18.1°C (64.6°F), with just 51 mm (2 in) of rain. The heat evaporated some of the excess water inside the berries and enhanced concentration. The Merlots were picked from 27 September with some châteaux holding off a couple of days to obtain more ripeness. The harvesting of the Cabernet Franc began from 4 October and that of the Cabernet Sauvignon around four days later, finishing mid-October before the rain. The fruit needed careful sorting due to the irregular ripeness not just between bunches but within bunches, green berries hidden inside purple outer ones. Some of the skins had not reached phenolic ripeness and could impart unwanted bitterness if pressed too hard or over-macerated. But at least temperatures were much lower than the previous year and newly installed gravity-fed wineries allowed gentler handling of the fruit. In Sauternes, the combination of August's tropical conditions and the abundance of bunches meant vineyards first had to be cleaned up to eradicate grey rot and damaged berries. Thunderstorms on 9 and 10 September led to sporadic botrytis formation and a first pass through the vines. Ensuing dry weather delayed further formation until the end of the month when second or third passes took place. Downpours from 11 October curtailed further picking by all but a few stragglers, who managed to collect some concentrated fruit at the beginning of November.

The 2004 vintage is often overlooked. It does not possess the infamy of 2003 and it lies in the shadow of the lauded 2005. Not unlike the season two years earlier, it lacks superstar wines that transcend the growing season. Alcohol levels tend to be on the high side, albeit lower than nowadays, but what the wines miss are seductive aromatics and a bit of mid-weight ballast. Among the First Growths, my pick is probably the 2004 Château Margaux, closely followed by the 2004 Lafite Rothschild and Latour, with Mouton Rothschild and Haut-Brion just a step behind. But to be honest, there is little between them. Léoville-Las Cases and Pichon Baron show well, whereas many others just lack fireworks.

Overall, the vintage leans towards the Right Bank, especially those properties that could benefit from the outstanding quality of the Cabernet Franc. These include Lafleur, l'Église-Clinet and Vieux Château Certan, the first vintage in which I believe Alexandre Thienpont took his Pomerol to a higher level. Cheval Blanc and Ausone in Saint-Émilion also show why they are within the top rank. The Sauternes are overlooked – nothing new there. It was a similar harvest to 1997, though the botrytis-affected grapes could be picked a little earlier, at the start of October. Yquem is predictably excellent, but look out for 2004 Château de Fargues and Raymond-Lafon.

Event
Mark Zuckerberg launches Facebook

In 2003, Harvard computer science undergraduate Mark Zuckerberg wrote software for a website called FaceMash that allowed visitors to view students' photos and rate them "hot" or "not". (Political correctness was obviously in shorter supply back then.) Having seen it taken down after two days for violating copyright and breach of security, Zuckerberg launched a new website on 4 February: TheFacebook, where Harvard students could post photos and add personal information. By June that year some 250,000 people had signed up. Today that number is approaching 3 billion and Facebook is by far the world's largest social networking site.

2004
(Continued)

Music
Dry Your Eyes
– The Streets

Dry Your Eyes hit the top of the UK charts on 25 July 2004 out of the blue. Mike Skinner had already proven you didn't need a faux American accent to rap, but what took listeners aback were the candid, heartfelt, almost lachrymose lyrics that detail the anguish in breaking up with a girl. Who anticipated those heart-tugging violins in the background? The original version featured Chris Martin singing the chorus, but the Coldplay frontman didn't like the sound of his voice and it was never released. If you were suffering a broken heart in 2004, then you sobbed to *Dry Your Eyes* and remembered there were always plenty more fish in the sea.

Film
Sideways
– Alexander Payne

Wine and film never made a finer blend than in Alexander Payne's *Sideways*. Paul Giamatti stars as Miles, the oenophile whom I suspect many of us recognise/sympathise with, although the actor later confessed he had little vinous knowledge. Fortunately for him, they used mostly non-alcoholic wine on set. The film includes the classic exchange between Miles and Maya about why he's waiting to drink his prized bottle of 1961 Cheval Blanc. Miles replies that he is holding on for a special occasion with the right person to which Maya rejoinders: "The day you open a '61 Cheval Blanc, that's the special occasion." Exactly. He ends up drinking it from a Styrofoam cup in a fast-food restaurant.

Finally, Bordeaux winemakers were blessed with a textbook growing season.

The 2004–2005 winter set the pattern for the next few months: very dry with long spells of frost that ensured vines firmly shut down, not least in late February when the mercury plunged to -8°C (17.5°F). Spring burst into life mid-March and the end of the month saw unseasonal warm temperatures that touched 27°C (80°F), though vines were reluctant to awake due to the dryness. When they did finally bud, it was around a fortnight later than usual. A cool and damp April slowed down the growth cycle, though the final days were summer-like and at last the vines reacted, just a bit late out of the blocks. May was warm and dry and the first flowers speckled the landscape from around the 23rd, after which the thermometer shot up to 33°C (91°F). Together with April's rainfall, this prompted a rapid flowering, though it was clear afterwards that the Merlot had suffered some coulure. June was the warmest since 2003, though vines did not suffer since the preceding dry weather had forced roots deep into the soil to eke out moisture. Essentially, vines had "toughened up" to the warmer conditions. June saw 20% more sunshine hours than average and 10 days over 30°C (86°F). A similar July of intense heat might have pushed vines over the limit. Fortunately, it remained sunny and temperatures were slightly cooler, nevertheless Saint-Émilion still suffered hail damage on 4 July and lost around 10% of potential crop. The storm provided around 25 mm (1 in) of much-needed rain for the Right Bank and Graves, though the Médoc had to wait until 25 August to enjoy light showers. *Véraison* was rapid and despite the lack of rainfall the vines showed little stress, not least because temperatures were only marginally above normal.

The dry whites were picked around the final week in August. Sporadic showers between 8 and 13 September were out of the way once the picking of the Merlot began from around the 7th at Pétrus and l'Église-Clinet. Pavie did not commence picking until an entire month later, indicative of differences in winemaking ideology at the time. Continuing sunny and clement conditions meant harvest could be carried out at a leisurely pace, which was important as dry conditions had differentiated ripeness levels between soil types, with gravel soils requiring longer than clay. Most of the Merlot was safely in the vat by the end of September. The Cabernets were picked from around 26 September to 12 October, though Cos d'Estournel did not dispatch its harvesters until 10 October. Musts were high in sugar with easily extractable tannins. Some châteaux were now easing away from the high-octane wines of the previous decade and many conducted early *remontage* or *délestages*, very few *saignées*, and applied moderate heat during alcoholic fermentation. The Sauternes were picked through October, benefiting from cool nights followed by fog, which created ideal conditions for botrytis formation. Many estates were able to conduct four or five passes through the vineyard.

2005

Anticipation was palpable leading up to the first look at the 2005s from barrel, with château owners aware that wines of serious pedigree were gestating in their cellars. Some could barely disguise their elation. The wines were met with thunderous applause from most quarters, including yours truly, though a few wrung their hands at the high alcohol levels, which sometimes reached 14.5% – a portent of things to come. Greeted as almost infallible, the apotheosis of Bordeaux, the wines are highly touted even if subsequent vintages, not least 2009, went on to eclipse them. In fact, it became almost hip to chip away at the '05s' reputation, with even the winemakers who had eulogised them at primeur joining in. The common phrase was: "If we had made the 2005 today, we would have done it differently and the wines would have been better." Perhaps. That might be hindsight talking. The 2005s tend to be dense and powerful, almost dramatic, sometimes leviathan wines made of iron girders that can seem brutish compared to contemporary Bordeaux. Tannin management was not the byword it is now and many winemakers' measure of quality was power and depth rather than elegance and poise.

The 2005 vintage could be viewed as one of the last that required wine lovers' patience as they matured at their own steady, at times almost begrudging pace. Nevertheless, it was a consistent vintage that has much to offer at every rung of the ladder as many 'minnows' had pulled their socks up since previous lauded growing seasons. Reviewing the wines en primeur, I complimented their intellect with the caveat that the dry tannins could mar some extraordinary wines with clipped finishes, writing: "as if someone pruned a rose-bush too severely and prevented flowers from blooming". Reassessing the top wines blind at the annual 10-year-on tasting, I found they "lived up to the billing" and that the First Growths were "astonishing" even if many were some distance from their respective drinking windows. Highlights on the Left Bank include a stentorian 2005 Latour and a classically styled Grand-Puy-Lacoste, though the 2005 Pichon-Lalande has begun falling short of its peers. The Right Bank is crowned by a 2005 Lafleur that takes no prisoners with its cathedral-like structure. You will have to wait aeons but they will be worth it. Cheval Blanc, Ausone, Trotanoy, l'Église-Clinet and Pétrus are all maturing with grace and will likely reach their drinking plateaus sooner. Do not overlook Sauternes because though it was a late harvest, the botrytis was very pure and in many cases I find them better than their lauded 2001 counterparts. Yquem and Rieussec lead the charge with de Fargues not far behind and La Tour Blanche perhaps the insider's choice.

Event
London bombings
kill 52

At 8.49 a.m. on 7 July 2005,
Islamic terrorists carried out
co-ordinated attacks on the
Circle and Piccadilly lines on
the London Underground
using improvised home-made
devices hidden in backpacks.
All exploded within a minute of
each other. A fourth bomb on a
double-decker bus in Tavistock
Square detonated one hour later.
Fifty-two people were killed and
hundreds injured in one of the
worst attacks in the UK since the
Second World War.

Film
Brokeback Mountain
– Ang Lee

Heath Ledger and Jake
Gyllenhaal play the two Wyoming
cowboys unable to repress "the
love that dare not speak its name".
The film is based on a short story
set in the summer of 1963 by
Annie Proulx. The author felt
that Ledger, who accepted the
role of Ennis as soon as he read
the script, completely subsumed
himself into the role of the laconic
gay man hiding his feelings by
striking up a romantic liaison
with co-star Michelle Williams.
The film helped break the stigma
of portraying homosexuality in
mainstream cinema and, according
to the Internet Movie Database
(IMDb), encouraged two
members of Lee's crew to come
out during filming.

Music
*I Bet You Look Good on the
Dancefloor* – Arctic Monkeys

Rock 'n' roll was dead, wasn't it?
Not according to the Sheffield
four-piece who hit the ground
running with their whip-cracking
debut featuring a lightning strike
of a guitar riff, Alex Turner's
clever wordplay and a breakneck
guitar solo that took three
attempts to nail in the studio.
Arctic Monkeys were one of the
first bands to use file-sharing and
MySpace to build a fan base. In
so doing, they guaranteed that
when the single was released on
17 October 2005, it shot straight
to number one. Their debut album
went on to sell a record-breaking
360,000 copies in the first week
and they have since enjoyed
a commercially and critically
successful career.

2006

Two thousand and six would have had to have knocked the ball out of the park not to be eclipsed by the previous vintage. In the event, it hit the ball but didn't make a home run.

The 2005–2006 winter was freezing cold, particularly in December, which was 3°C (37°F) below average, meaning the sap retreated and pruning could be carried out as and when. It also continued the pattern of dry winters, particularly during an arid February, and so water reserves were not replenished. March provided rain but budding was delayed and prolonged by nippy night-time temperatures the following month. On 11 April, the Right Bank and parts of the Graves suffered localised frost damage, which combined with the paucity of embryonic bunches predicated a smaller-than-average crop. May saw regular showers and the mercury rise. Flowering began around 26 May and settled conditions ensured it was completed by 15 June, just minor coulure affecting some of the Merlot. The second half of June was very dry, interrupted by a handful of convectional storms. The dryness continued into July, combined with high temperatures – 4.4°C (39.9°F) above average and the hottest since the infamous August three years earlier. Bordeaux simmered for a long time with the mercury almost reaching 38°C (100°F) towards the end of the month. August was cooler as minor fronts swept in from the Atlantic bringing changeable, often drizzly weather. Bill Blatch points out that overcast skies in summer can make it feel cooler than it actually is and in fact, the month was only 1.6°C (34.9°F) below average. Berries became gorged with moisture and *véraison* was spun out, which led to some under-ripe bunches. Vineyard managers tried to remedy the situation by green harvesting and removing leaf cover to give bunches more exposure.

Riding to the rescue (yet again) was an early September heat wave that turned out to be the hottest since 1921. Much of the excellent dry white was picked during this period. The early-ripening Merlot began to be harvested from 11 September just as the settled weather deteriorated. The Médoc saw over 100 mm (4 in) of rain, with 150 mm (6 in) on the Right Bank and in Sauternes. Some châteaux panicked and ended up with Merlot that had failed to reach phenolic ripeness, whereas those who waited until the end of September were rewarded with drier, sunny conditions. Those wishing to avoid the risk of rot began picking their Cabernets from the final week in September, but the more patient were rewarded with warm and dry weather – one night of heavy rainfall aside – in the first week of October. Although many estates picked one or two parcels that did not quite reach phenolic ripeness, alcohol was generally high at over 13%. Sentiment favoured the Cabernet over the Merlot due to the heat in early September. Sauternes' vines had required a lot of *nettoyage* – cleaning out the vineyard to get rid of rotten or under-ripe bunches – with the best fruit picked at the end of September in the second pass.

In my primeur report published the following year I wrote: "If Bordeaux 2005 was equivalent to *Sgt. Pepper's Lonely Hearts Club Band* then 2006 is *The White Album* insofar as for every *Dear Prudence* or *Blackbird*, there is an *Ob-La-Di, Ob-La-Da* or at worse, a *Revolution 9*." That's my obtuse way of saying that quality is up and down, not just between appellations but between châteaux. Reassessing the 2006s after 10 years, I found them linear and strait-laced, though what they lack in fruit intensity is compensated with freshness. They express their respective terroirs yet generally fall short of true excellence. A tasting at the Savoy Hotel of the top 30 châteaux in October 2021 revealed wines that remain a little austere and conservative with the occasional unexpected surprise. Among the First Growths, the 2006 Mouton Rothschild benefits from winemaker Philippe Dhalluin's magic touch, while the 2006 Château Margaux and Haut-Brion has the edge over Lafite Rothschild and Latour. Alfred Tesseron oversaw an excellent Pontet-Canet as he converted his vineyard to biodynamics, while Ducru-Beaucaillou and Léoville-Las Cases stand shoulder-to-shoulder with the First Growths. Palmer is floral and precise, though there are disappointments such as Montrose and Gruaud Larose, Saint-Julien uncharacteristically inconsistent.

Though I initially favoured the Left Bank, this tasting revealed commendable wines from Angélus and Ausone in Saint-Émilion and l'Église-Clinet and La Conseillante in Pomerol, though I felt that l'Évangile and Figeac lacked some panache. Generally, the 2006s are fine if you choose carefully and do not expect sensory thrills. Sauternes is up and down, though both Suduiraut and Lafaurie-Peyraguey are worth looking out for.

Film
Pan's Labyrinth – Guillermo del Toro

Set in post-Civil War Spain in 1944, Guillermo del Toro's fable deftly interweaves the real and the mythical, a leitmotif in several of his films. Ivana Baquero is perfect as young Ofelia, confronted with the brutal violence of Franco's army, not least the despicable Captain Vidal. While tending her ailing mother, she completes the tasks set by a mysterious Faun who inhabits an overgrown labyrinth alongside other fantastical creatures. The film received a 22-minute ovation when it premiered at Cannes, establishing the Mexican director as a maestro of dark fantasy.

2006 *(Continued)*

1870

2020

2006
(Continued)

Event
Pluto loses its planetary status

Like most kids, I grew up memorising the nine planets of our Solar System in order of distance from the sun. Thanks to astronomical pedantry, there were now eight. Pluto had been discovered in 1930 by Clyde Tombaugh, but in recent years similarly sized objects in the Kuiper Belt in the outer Solar System had cast doubt on its planetary credentials. After intense debate in Prague on 24 August, the International Astronomical Union announced that Pluto had failed to meet one of the three criteria required for it to be considered a planet and was unceremoniously stripped of its status. Debate rages on among astronomers. When the *New Horizons* spacecraft sent back astonishing images of the dwarf planet in 2015, I like to think those who had demoted poor Pluto came to regret their decision.

Music
Rehab
– Amy Winehouse

Amy Winehouse's second album is a modern masterpiece. Born with the finest voice of her generation to the extent that it overshadows her song-writing skills, she used the production nous of Salaam Remi and Mark Ronson, plus the consummate musicianship of The Dap-Kings, to create songs that ingeniously update the sounds of early sixties girl groups, Motown and her favourite singer, Etta James. Autobiographical lead single *Rehab* recounts the singer's refusal to attend an alcohol rehabilitation centre, the chorus's words lifted from an exchange between Winehouse and Ronson. On release, it sounded tongue-in-cheek, yet the fragile singer's demons overcame her and she tragically died in her Camden flat five years later, robbing the world of a uniquely talented artist.

The 2007 growing season is regarded as the weakest in the second half of the decade, though is not without its charms.

The 2006–2007 winter was mild with fewer days of frost than recent vintages, duping vines into thinking it was spring. If only they had eyes. Or a calendar. As a consequence, bud break was early, taking place around mid-March, but then cooler conditions not only retarded growth but also bifurcated the ripeness of the Merlot and the Cabernets, laying the foundation for an irregular growing season. Continuing warm conditions in April encouraged rapid growth while May was rainy and, again, warm. Flowering began a fortnight ahead of normal in mid-May, but temperatures swung wildly and caused widespread coulure, which particularly affected the Cabernets. Bill Blatch reports that vineyard teams were also confronted with oidium and an outbreak of snails, which like nothing better than to munch on young juicy shoots. Mildew was also endemic and affected not just the leaves, but also bunches. As a result those estates with the means and wherewithal to spray had an advantage, but if you were practising biodynamics, you faced an almost unenviable situation – as Pontet-Canet did (page 421). July was cool, overcast and damp, then August was plagued by half-a-dozen torrential showers in the second half of the month that saw around 110 mm (4 in) of rain dumped on the region. The month also had 15% fewer sunlight hours than normal. As you might expect given the inclemency, *véraison* was spun out and vineyard teams traipsed through the vines snipping off under-ripe bunches in a quest to even everything out. With rot beginning to take a grip from the end of August, châteaux proprietors became pessimistic.

Then, on 30 August, the weather settled and the sun miraculously seemed to vanquish the rot, allowing vines to recoup some of the shortfall in sunlight. The dry whites were picked in ideal conditions from early September and the red wine producers decided to hedge their bets and delayed picking. They were rewarded with a dry spell from 21 September to 10 October, enabling vineyard teams to undertake stop-start picking to mitigate irregular ripeness levels. It transpired to be the driest September since 1985. A majority of the Cabernets were picked around the week of 8 October as the mercury began rising again, albeit with cooler nights (Bill Blatch compares it with 1986 in terms of the drying effect on the vineyard). Several châteaux experienced hang times in excess of 140 days – compared with an average of just 110 – the longer duration and slower evolution between flowering and harvest enhancing complexity The must tended to have regular alcohol levels, slightly lower than in recent years and the best-quality fruit appeared to be among the later-ripening Merlot and Cabernet Franc on the Right Bank and the best gravel sites in the Médoc. But Didier Cuvelier at Léoville Poyferré told me at the time that the Merlot suffered dilution from the August rains.

2007

1870

2020

2007
(Continued)

The aforementioned October showers benefited Sauternes, whose wines were perhaps the highlight of the season, though success did not come easy. September saw two or three passes through the vineyard that yielded only a small amount of botrytised berries. That changed at the end of the month after rain, a rise in temperatures and an easterly wind nudged the grapes from the *pourri rôti* stage to full botrytis. Not unlike in 2001, two-thirds to three-quarters of the Sauternes were picked in mid-October with some estates conducting small sixth or seventh passes through the vines up to mid-November.

There are no real standouts that truly transcend the limitations of a challenging growing season. But vineyard techniques had improved in recent years, as had approaches to vinification, and with more quality-driven winemakers, many estates provided what I term "useful" wines. They are lighter than the 2006s but more harmonious and pliant, mainly early-drinkers ideal for the bar and restaurant trade, which cannot afford more expensive vintages. The First Growths hover around the same level, the 2007 Lafite Rothschild perhaps a step ahead of the rest. I also have fond memories of Léoville-Las Cases, Rauzan-Ségla and La Lagune on the Left Bank and La Conseillante and Pétrus on the Right Bank. If you must head anywhere in 2007, it should be to Sauternes. This was the first of its vintages that I officially reviewed for *The Wine Advocate* and it enjoyed a fecund growing season, with nearly all the top estates overseeing excellent wines thanks to those northeasterly winds that engendered freshness and tension. They are generally not rich in style, yet brim with energy, purity and exuberance. The 2007 Yquem was surprisingly deep in colour when tasted in February 2022 with winemaker Sandrine Garbay and displayed refreshing piquancy, while Château de Fargues and Rayne Vigneau are also well worth seeking out.

Event
Steve Jobs unveils the iPhone

The world had become accustomed to Apple co-founder Steve Jobs, casually attired in jeans and trademark black roll-neck, unveiling new products that changed how we lived. But few envisaged the impact of the iPhone when it was unveiled at the Macworld conference on 9 January 2007. It was not the first mobile device equipped with a touchscreen, but it deftly tied hitherto disparate elements of technology into one irresistible package designed by Sir Jonathan Ive. "We're gonna make some history together today," Jobs began his sermon. For once, that was no exaggeration. This paragraph was written on my iPhone 12 Pro.

Music
Umbrella
– Rihanna ft. Jay-Z

"Ella… Ella… Ella…" Barbadian R&B singer Rihanna became a superstar with one of the hooks of the decade. Composed by The-Dream, Christopher Stewart, Kuk Harrell and Jay-Z, who contributed the rap verse, *Umbrella* was turned down by Britney Spears' label before Spears even heard it. Listening now, what makes *Umbrella* stand the test of time is Rihanna's almost icy detachment, which marries perfectly with the brutal looped drumbeat and layers of just-as-icy synth. It hit number one in numerous countries – including the UK, just as it was enduring the rainiest summer for years. Shame she hadn't called it "Suntan Lotion".

Film
The Bourne Ultimatum – Paul Greengrass

Adapted from Robert Ludlum's books, the Jason Bourne films are essentially one edge-of-the-seat spectacular chase after another, given gravitas by Matt Damon's committed performance as a secret agent trying to work out who the hell he is. Someone could have tapped him on the shoulder and informed him that he was the fugitive spy giving 007 notice that he needed to reboot or die (which he did, thanks to Daniel Craig). This third outing was filmed in multiple locations, from the rooftops of Tangier to the concourse at Waterloo Station. The director's trademark "shaky camerawork" and long takes prompted complaints from audiences who said they made them feel dizzy. It's a good job they weren't doing Bourne's job.

2008

In some ways, 2008 was a rerun of the previous growing season, another year when the meteorological pattern was influenced by the cooler equatorial Pacific waters of La Niña.

January and February were slightly warmer than usual with average rainfall. Bud burst was around mid-March, but irregular, setting in motion out-of-sync Cabernet and Merlot ripening cycles. A cold snap on 6 April caused some blackened buds in Sauternes, parts of the Graves and Listrac, and whereas a damp and warm May should have accelerated growth, the vines showed signs of inertia and, later, mildew. Localised hail on 28 May saw Palmer lose 60% of its crop and retarded the vegetative cycle for a fortnight. Flowering began around 27 May, but was again spun out over the following month, which experienced changeable weather. This inevitably led to coulure and millerandage, which reduced the crop further, particularly white varieties and Right Bank Merlot. It was going to be an extremely late picking. June was warm and sunny, with 25% more sunlight hours than normal, and July was dry, receiving just 20 mm (¾ in) of rainfall, and enjoying 20 days over 25°C (77°F) with no heat waves. August, however, was rainy – 82 mm (3¼ in) fell in mostly four bursts – and skies remained grey. The mercury only breached 30°C (86°F) on four days. As a result, *véraison*, just like flowering, was irregular and prolonged, widening the disparity between ripening cycles. Workers were obliged to enter vineyards to snip away green bunches and reduce foliage to give vines maximise exposure to the sun. September began with inclement weather – a spot of rain every other day that the vines began to suck up, swelling berries. Then, from 13 September, everything turned on its heel as dry and warm weather settled over the region until mid-October. There was sudden improvement in the sanitary conditions in the vineyard, which Blatch attributes to the build-up of tannins in July that strengthened their resistance to rot and locked in acidity enhanced by September's cool nights.

Picking on the Right Bank and in Pessac-Léognan began towards the end of the month. After a short burst of rain that conveniently fell at night, a crucial 10-day stretch followed in mid-October that saw temperatures rise to 5°C (41°F) above average and concentrate berries. A majority of growers picked in the second half of October, with a few in Saint-Émilion chancing their luck and harvesting in early November, despite conditions turning autumnal. Sorting was fundamental if you wanted a decent 2008. Christian Moueix at Ets. Jean-Pierre Moueix wheeled out four sorting tables per estate to make sure no substandard fruit entered the vat. With bunches hanging on the vine for between 130 and 150 days, berries could attain high degrees of complexity while the lack of heat spikes avoided over maturity. Fruit was mostly healthy with thick skins and extraction tended to be easier than it had been in the previous two vintages. Meanwhile, Sauternes had a tough time of it, having been impacted by the 7 April frost harder than any other appellation. Although a fine summer and plenty of early botrytis raised hopes, further botrytis infection failed to take hold. Picking attempts were made up to 20 November, but later passes lacked a little concentration.

I tasted the vintage from barrel, after bottling and then after 10 years. After bottling the wines were quite hard, most tasting like "classic" Bordeaux but without too much astringency. While the 2008s lag below the quality of the 2009s and 2010s, I find them better than the 2007s and 2011s because the extended hang time imparted complexity and freshness. On the Left Bank, the First Growths are generally excellent, except for 2008 Lafite Rothschild, which I have found curiously underwhelming despite the supposedly lucky Chinese number eight symbol engraved on it that year. Overall, I would not say there is an enormous gap between the First Growths and the best Grands Crus Classés unless you are more interested in speculation. For drinking, go no further than the outstanding 2008 Pichon Baron, which is intense and terroir-driven. Jean-Hubert Delon crafted a typically structured but balanced Léoville-Las Cases that should be more approachable than either the 2009 or 2010 vintages. That said, its neighbour Léoville Poyferré might offer better value, its trademark opulence kept on a leash by the vagaries of the growing season. On the Right Bank, Ausone and Cheval Blanc are excellent, although I have always been smitten by the 2008 Beauséjour Duffau-Lagarrosse. Clos l'Église and Canon-la-Gaffelière are two others to look out for, while François Mitjavile oversaw a gorgeous and typically lush Tertre Rôteboeuf. The 1998 Sauternes lie in the shadow of the previous vintage. Despite losing almost half the crop, the 2008 Château de Fargues is splendid, likewise Clos Haut-Peyraguey, de Malle and La Tour Blanche, which was cropped at a measly 2 hl/ha.

Event
The subprime crisis sparks the global economic crash

The ramifications of the subprime crisis extended far beyond the immediate economic fallout. American homeowners began defaulting on mortgages and losing their homes. Before long, banks were staring into a financial abyss, with Lehman Brothers the most high-profile casualty. Taking a wider view, the financial crisis sowed the seeds of distrust between ordinary people and those who wielded power, whether it was bankers, politicians or business leaders, ultimately giving rise to the populist movements underlying Brexit and the election of Donald Trump.

2008
(Continued)

1870

2020

2008 *(Continued)*

Music
Single Ladies (Put a Ring on It)
– Beyoncé

Post-Destiny's Child, Beyoncé Knowles had made her intentions of world domination clear with the all-conquering *Crazy in Love*. Five years later she released the peerless *Single Ladies*. As its title suggests, the song is Queen Bey's advice to women to give their boyfriends the old heave-ho if they have no intentions of walking down that aisle. The singer herself had no worries in that respect since hubby Jay-Z had just put what I assume must have been an obscenely expensive ring on her finger at their nuptials in April that year. The song's harsh electronic beat is not far removed from that of *Umbrella* (page 447) – no surprise given it was co-written with the same production team. Topped with Beyoncé's powerful, soulful vocals, all the package required was Jake Nava's breathless monochrome video and soon everyone was trying (and failing) to copy the dance moves as they mulled giving their partner their ultimatum.

Film
Iron Man
– Jon Favreau

Iron Man kicked off the phenomenally successful Marvel Cinematic Universe that continues to dominate cinema screens with its myriad sequels, prequels and spin-offs. The development of *Iron Man* stretches back to 1990, with the rights passing from one studio to another until eventually Marvel decided to make the film itself. Robert Downey Jr. plays industrialist/playboy Tony Stark, donning five different Iron Man suits in the film. Stan Lee, who created the character and makes a cameo in the movie, said he based Stark on media mogul Howard Hughes. Since the script was incomplete when shooting began, some scenes were ad-libbed, lending the dialogue a bit of snap and crackle.

Two thousand and nine was canonised from the outset. It is a great vintage, and one that in retrospect might be seen as the last of its kind in terms of its hedonistic style. Even so, it can divide opinion.

The 2008–2009 winter was colder compared with recent years, with 22 frosty mornings recorded from January to March. January in particular was bitter with the mercury plunging to -6°C (21°F). It was also fairly dry, though deluges the previous November had ensured underground reserves were replenished, a factor that underlies the success of the vintage. March saw spring-like temperatures up into the low twenties, but the vines seemed reluctant to awaken, the first signs of budding not visible until the end of the month. From the start there were disparities between cold and warmer soils and between Right Bank and Left. April was typically showery with a warm spell in the latter half allaying any fear of frost. May was warm, some 1.9°C (35.4°F) above average, with more sunshine hours than normal. This was a perfect backdrop for the vines to put all their energy into shoot growth and compensate for the late budding. But a hailstorm on 11 May severely damaged Côtes de Bourg and Blaye and localised parts of Margaux, with a second hailstorm the following morning devastating Entre-Deux-Mers and parts of Saint-Émilion. Bill Blatch remarks in his annual report that it was the most devastating hailstorm since 1935 and that a total of 18,000 hectares suffered damaged vines. Compounding the situation, it was all slightly too late for secondary buds to develop.

Flowering passed evenly and quickly thanks to warm and settled weather from 27 May until 4 June. The Cabernets were slightly spun out by a few showers, but overall flowering finished ahead of schedule on around 14 June. It portended a large crop – unless you were one of the victims of hail. June was blissfully warm, with temperatures 2°C (35°F) above average and ample sunshine. The next two months continued in similar fashion as thermometers gradually rose. Expectations for a great vintage began to grow. There were no real heat spikes, with 13 days over 30°C (86°F), far fewer than in 2003. Also, like in 1982, the vines' throats were quenched by occasional showers. All this, coupled with more sunlight hours – 532 over the two months compared with an average of 484 – meant sugar levels accreted. So, everything was perfect? Not quite. Towards the end of August temperatures topped 36°C (97°F) and finally some of the younger vines began to show stress as showers petered out completely in the Médoc. Unlike in 2003 when de-leafing had been de rigueur, vineyard teams carried out a very prudent leaf removal in order to maintain shade, while at the same time removing under-ripe bunches caused by the protracted *véraison* where necessary.

The dry whites were picked in early September under perfect conditions, the weather fronts that normally plague Bordeaux never materialising. Some rain in the middle of the month prompted a few

Right Bank growers to pick before they arrived since sugar levels were already high. Most decided to wait and they were rewarded by unusually dry and sunny weather all the way through to the cutting of the last bunches. It was unseasonably warm, with Blatch noting that the average temperature over the last 10 days of September was 25.8°C (78.4°F) and only marginally lower in the first 10 days in October, which concentrated bunches. Most Merlot was picked at the end of September with the Cabernets harvested from 1 October to around 12 October. Many winemakers were mindful to pick not just according to sugar level but also to phenolic ripeness because, as Blatch notes, they wanted to ensure their 2009s were more like 1982s than 1975s. The headline was the alcohol levels. Many properties reported up to 14% alcohol on the Left Bank, and between 14–15.5% on the Right Bank. By 16 October, it was all over and wineries were busy turning grapes into wine. Unlike in 1947, modern technology and knowhow meant châteaux made sure no sugar remained after the alcoholic fermentation. The fruit had high levels of tannins so macerations needed to be gentle.

In Sauternes, after a dry summer that Yquem's technical-manager Francis Mayeur tagged a "crescendo of heat", showers from 2 to 4 September and then temperatures of 30°C (86°F) revitalised the vines and set them up nicely for the impending harvest. By mid-September berries were touching 14% potential alcohol and more showers from 18 to 20 September provoked botrytis, even if cool nights put the brakes on and held bunches at the *pourri rôti* stage. By September 28 harvesters were flooding into the vineyards to stay on top of the onrush of botrytis and sugar levels threatened to shoot through the roof. The week of October 5 saw intense picking, to the degree that some had no time to sort the berries between various stages of infection.

When he unveiled his report, Robert Parker loaded his 100-point blunderbuss and unleashed an unprecedented number of perfect scores, some with asterisks denoting best-ever releases. Inevitably, this poured fuel on already strong demand that no one had seen before or since, turbo-charged by the Hong Kong government's abolition of import taxes the previous year and gifting the ever-opportunistic Bordelais what to all intents and purposes seemed like an insatiable Chinese market. It lent the vintage an irreproachable aura. It was almost sacrosanct to say a bad word against 2009. Yet it should be remembered that some châteaux picked earlier than optimal to avoid the effects of mid-September rain, while late-picking remained a dogma to others and accusations of over-ripeness surfaced as time passed. Between these extremes, there undeniably exists a bounty of sensual, ripe, flamboyant, rich and perhaps lascivious 2009s.

I have drunk this vintage numerous times since en primeur when I remember the Cheshire cat grins on winemakers' faces. I tasted them comprehensively after bottling (sighted and blind) and most recently at 10 years in bottle (again blind). Yes, the vintage boasts a smorgasbord of gorgeous wines and many fulfil the promise heaped upon them at birth. Generally, the style is fleshy and powerful, rich and sumptuous, a veritable hedonist's playground, especially on the Right Bank. After 10 years, I found them more evolved in terms of secondary aromas and flavours, some with attractive tertiary and savoury characteristics that occasionally tip over into animally, almost feral notes. But sometimes they lack precision on the finish. Great claret ends on a cliffhanger – you have to take another sip to find out what happens next and sometimes that suspense is missing. I have also found some bottle variation over the years, which is compounded by the fact that the quality of the cork used was inferior to that used nowadays.

Putting these caveats aside, the 2009 vintage remains one I always look forward to tasting and as they lose those layers of baby fat, I expect more of their terroir to show through and accentuate their individualities. Do not assume they have all followed the same evolutionary path in bottle. Some 2009s firmed up, shed their velvety veneers and became more structured and slightly more austere than you might presuppose. As a parsimonious scorer, I would only entertain the idea of the 2009 Latour achieving notional perfection and even then will it ultimately match the 2000 or 2010? Time will tell. There are a number of other wines that come within touching distance of perfection, including Château Margaux and Montrose on the Left Bank, and Cheval Blanc, Lafleur and Pétrus on the Right. Nearly all the major names deliver fabulous wines – too many to list. And don't forget over-achievers such as Saint-Pierre and Le Gay that might represent better value for money. I absolutely adore the 2009s in Sauternes and rue the fact that in a vintage that boasts so much success, Bordeaux's sweet wines are denied their share of attention. It might be a contentious view but I have long suspected that the 2009 Sauternes might surpass the 2001s and that includes the perfectly formed Yquem. Essentially, pick a 2009 Sauternes and you are in for a treat. They are wines destined to last many years.

2009
(Continued)

1870

2020

453

2009
(Continued)

Event
Obama becomes the first
African-American US President

On Tuesday 20 January 2009,
the US's first African-American
citizen was sworn in as president
in front of an ecstatic crowd. Born
in Honolulu, Hawaii, Obama
had graduated from Harvard
Law School and become a civil
rights attorney before moving
into politics. He caught the wider
public's attention with a well-
received keynote speech at the
Democratic convention in 2004.
Having defeated Hillary Clinton
in a closely fought primary, he
then beat Republican nominee
John McCain to become the 44th
president of the United States.
He was re-elected four years later
after defeating Mitt Romney.

Music
Poker Face
– Lady Gaga

Poker Face shot Lady Gaga to
international stardom. The song
had been released the previous
September, but only topped the
charts in March and April 2009
in the UK and US respectively.
Stefani Joanne Angelina
Germanotta does not quite trip
off the tongue as well as her
adopted pseudonym inspired by
Queen's hit *Radio Ga Ga*. *Poker
Face* was an in-your-face slice of
perfectly executed electro-pop
stuffed with sexual innuendo that
became the world's biggest-selling
single of 2009 as it reached sales
of 10 million. As well as enjoying
further chart success, Gaga has
gone on to become one of the few
pop stars to embark on a credible
acting career.

Film
District 9
– Neill Blomkamp

Such was his faith in rookie director Neill Blomkamp that Peter Jackson, fresh from his *Lord of the Rings* success, offered him $30 million to make any film he wanted after the film adaptation of the *Halo* videogame Blomkamp was working on collapsed. Blomkamp's film about an extra-terrestrial spaceship marooned above Johannesburg was a clever, thought-provoking allegory of South African apartheid and post-apartheid ghettoisation. Shooting the film in Soweto and interpolating found-footage scenes lent *District 9* a sense of realism that makes it stand out from many of the decade's sci-fi movies.

the

20
10

s

This decade witnessed a dichotomous trend both towards and away from technology. Bordeaux winemakers are misleadingly portrayed as conservative and hidebound to traditional techniques, but many have been willing to embrace innovation. Some see it as a badge of honour. Top estates are not short of money and many can afford to experiment with new techniques or road-test equipment that at worst can be written off as tax deductions. Moreover, their comparatively large vineyards afford them room to undertake trials without risking their entire crop.

Optical sorting machines proved their worth during the 2011 growing season, which obliged more sorting of fruit than the previous two relatively dry seasons. Opinion was divided over their effectiveness, however. While some proprietors proudly displayed their machines in their forecourts, all set to analyse every single berry in the vineyard, other winemakers were dismissive and remained loyal to beady eyes and nimble fingers, opining that a few unripe berries or MOG (matter other than grapes) enhanced their wines. It is a view with which I concur – beauty comes with imperfections. In 2017, optical sorting machines began to be superseded by densimetric machines, which measure berries' sugar content by passing them through a pool of sugar, allowing winemakers to guide potential alcohol levels. The denser ripe berries sink to the bottom while lighter unripe berries and undesirable MOGs rise to the surface and are removed.

Organic and biodynamic viticulture became more prevalent across Bordeaux this decade, particularly among the Classed Growths. The importance of Alfred Tesseron and Jean-Michel Comme's work at Pontet-Canet in Pauillac cannot be overstated. Other châteaux were intrigued, but had demurred, only taking the plunge once they had seen success in terms of better-quality wines and the way organic/biodynamic methods chimed with a more ecologically aware society. High-profile estates such as Château Palmer converted to biodynamics and on a couple of occasions I have spotted sheep being shepherded through their vines to act as natural lawn mowers and fertilisers as part of the more holistic approach. Bordeaux is now more environmentally conscious than ever, with winemakers willing to accept that forgoing the protective veil of chemical sprays means inclement vintages might imperil their entire production – exactly what transpired in 2018.

The 2014 Bordeaux en primeur was significant as it was the first vintage not reviewed by the most powerful critic in the world since he founded *The Wine Advocate* in 1978. Robert Parker bowed out with the 2013s, a valedictory vintage unbefitting of his illustrious career. While Bordeaux was indebted to his services and hard work, tastes were changing and his absence liberated winemakers who wished to pursue styles that diverged from the so-called Parker palate. I had the honour of taking over coverage and, unsurprisingly, his exit accelerated changes already afoot. Thanks to the internet, wine criticism no longer had one dominant voice and by the end of the decade a flurry of scores, tabulated and analysed, was coming out each primeur. However, none of them, including my own, will ever approach the sway that Parker's had at the height of his powers.

The latter-half of the decade witnessed a tangible shift towards more restraint: lower alcohol levels, greater freshness and terroir expression, most notably in the appellation most swayed/straightjacketed by Parker's opinion – Saint-Émilion. This wasn't so much a sea change in winemaking approaches, since some wine lovers retain a predilection for a richer style of Bordeaux and there is nothing wrong with that. It was more a diversification of winemaking approaches in order to appease consumers' diverse tastes – surely a positive development. In the winery, pressings became far gentler with shorter durations and cooler temperatures, so-called "infusion" techniques. Climate change means winemakers no longer need to press hard on the accelerator in the winery – quite the opposite. This change in outlook coincided with the rise of new consultants, notably Thomas Duclos on the Right Bank and Éric Boissenot on the Left. Like his late father Jacques, Boissenot prefers to stay out of the limelight, but his counsel is sought by numerous Médoc châteaux, including First Growths. The decade also witnessed what Bill Blatch aptly describes as a back-pedalling on residual sugar levels in Sauternes, which risked becoming excessive in the noughties. Many winemakers lowered residual sugar to an average 120–150 g/l as they sought balance rather than obvious sweetness. Sauternes wines can quickly become cloying at higher levels, so essentially they became more drinkable.

The decade saw a number of lauded growing seasons, not least in the second half courtesy of 2015, 2016, 2018 and 2019, the last two forming a triumvirate with 2020. Bordeaux winemakers almost became embarrassed wheeling out the superlatives, with every incipient en primeur campaign presaged by "best-ever" proclamations. What differed this time was that many attributed this unprecedented run of vintages to climate change: milder winters, earlier growth cycles, hotter and especially drier summers and earlier harvests, which all resulted in higher sugar and alcohol levels. Any remaining winemakers sceptical about climate change finally accepted that these changes were too frequent to be random events. These kind of growing seasons were now the new normal – at least until 2021 came along to remind them that nothing could be taken for granted.

In response, many châteaux adopted long-term strategies of cultivating later-ripening varieties. Over the last 20 years, the Right Bank has seen Cabernet Franc usurp rows of Merlot and later, since the end of the decade, estates such as l'Evangile and La Conseillante have begun planting Cabernet Sauvignon. In the past, the standard of clones had dissuaded many from cultivating Cabernet Franc, with winemakers such as Baptiste Guinaudeau at Lafleur preferring to propagate their own cuttings obtained through massal selection. But towards the end of the decade, the rising quality of nursery Cabernet Franc clones encouraged more to plant it – a positive development. There was a significant change in 2019 when the I.N.A.O. legitimised the limited addition of four red grape varieties (Marselan, Touriga Nacional, Castets and Arinarnoa) and three white varieties (Alvarinho, Petit Manseng and Liliorila) within Bordeaux AC and Bordeaux Supérieur categories. Depending on whom you spoke to, this was either a much-needed step towards adapting to climate change or the start of a slippery slope to a future of anything goes. I welcomed the decision, not least if it enables better wines to be made.

———————

Jean-Charles Cazes oversees fruit being received at the cavernous new reception area at Château Lynch-Bages in 2021. Apart from eagle-eyed, nimble-fingered sorters that inspect incoming bunches, technology analyses berries at lightning-speed to ensure they cannot enter the vat.

2010

Predestined to be compared with 2009, the 2010 vintage was similarly fêted on release, yet is cut from a very different cloth.

You need to look back at the previous year to explain how 2010 would shape up. Crucially, the beginning of November 2009 saw plenty of rain that replenished water reserves, with precipitation around average over the following two months. From December to February prevailing easterly winds fostered colder-than-average temperatures, ensuring that vines shut down, the sap retreated and vineyard hands could undertake pruning. March was unusually cold with frosty mornings that discouraged vines from waking, even when it became warmer and wetter. As a consequence, bud break was tardy and spun out. Pendulum-like weather in April and May also influenced vines' stuttering development, in marked contrast to the steady growth of a year earlier. Otherwise, there were no incidences of frost and negligible disease pressure as May was so dry. Flowering continued in the stop-start vein due to the changeable conditions, resulting in coulure and millerandage, the latter acute among the older Merlot vines. Some 91 mm (3½ in) of much-needed rain in mid-June revivified vines, though they had to make the most of it as dry conditions prevailed thereafter. Stationary high pressure brought temperatures up to 28°C (82°F) for the final 10 days of June. Only 11 days in July and August saw rain, with just 32 mm (1¼ in) falling compared with an average of 114 mm (1½ in), and it was certainly sunny – 534 sun hours in total, two more than in 2009. Unlike in 2005, no thunderstorms materialised to provide relief but fortunately there were no heat spikes either, with 17 days over 30°C (86°F) and just three days over 35°C (95°F).

One difference from 2009 is that August was slightly cooler, which meant sugar accumulation took place earlier in the ripening cycle, while colder night-time temperatures – occasionally 10–11°C (50–52°F) – locked in acidity. Berries lost almost one-third of their weight through dehydration and this intensified aromatics and hardened tannins, two leitmotifs of the 2010 vintage. September began with a few occasional showers and the dry whites were picked from 31 August under dry and warm conditions, cool nights continuing to preserve acidity. The drought-like conditions continued with September seeing barely 24 mm (1 in) of rain, which delayed the picking of the reds. Pomerol commenced from 22 to 24 September, then rain on 4 and 10 October gave the vines more energy as an unexpected prevailing easterly concentrated the Cabernets. The Left Bank completed picking by 23 October.

In Sauternes, the long, dry summer concentrated berries, but the dry September stymied botrytisation, filling vineyards with golden berries that had thick skins but little botrytis. A spike in temperatures around mid-September caused some patchy shrivel and infection and the first pass yielded tiny quantities of berries with high acidity. Then 30 mm (1 in) of rain on 4 October and warmer temperatures finally provoked widespread botrytis, but frustratingly berries failed to concentrate – until the arrival of an easterly wind on 12 October. This was the signal for pickers to enter vineyards en masse and 80% of the crop was picked during the second half of October.

The 2010s were never inclined to flatter in the same way as the 2009s, which gleefully doled out precocious fruit. Maybe it is some kind of synaesthesia, but I picture 2009 as spherical and 2010 as cuboid. It is certainly not an infallible vintage and as the wines evolve, minor deficiencies become more apparent. They lack the silky veneer of the 2016s, which benefited from subsequent improvements in tannin management; gentler pressings at lower temperatures, more care in selection and blending of the pressed wine. Time has exposed their big-boned tannins, which put off some oenophiles – as did their high alcohol levels with some touching a whopping 16%. Prices on release were as high, if not higher, than the 2009s, though there wasn't quite as much enthusiasm from Parker and demand from the Far East was already waning. They had a less rapturous reception in some quarters. Putting all that aside, we're left with a vintage that produced monumental, concentrated, powerful wines that many château owners held up as a paradigm of what they wanted to make every year.

Having tasted all the major châteaux numerous times, the standout on the Left Bank is the monumental 2010 Latour, which ranks alongside legends such as the '61 and '82. Mouton Rothschild and Lafite Rothschild are just a step behind, while there are several astonishing wines that would surpass the First Growths in another vintage. Blind, I just have a slight preference for the La Mission Haut-Brion over the Haut-Brion. There are numerous outstanding wines on the Left Bank, too many to mention individually, though I will namecheck Grand-Puy-Lacoste, Saint-Pierre, Brane-Cantenac and Smith Haut Lafitte. Again, on the Right Bank, it is difficult to go wrong; the 2010 Pétrus is utterly profound, the Lafleur is bestowed with enormous grip and arching structure, and the 2010 Angélus is typically audacious. Do not overlook the Sauternes, even if they lie in the shadow of their dry red counterparts and perhaps of the previous year's sweet wines. Tasting them after bottling and again after 10 years, such is the consistency that there is not a huge gap between Yquem and top-performers such as Rieussec, Suduiraut and Coutet.

2010 *(Continued)*

Event
Eyjafjallajökull causes chaos in the air

Eyjafjallajökull. No, not an expletive, though airport terminals probably heard quite a few when on 14 April 2010, after weeks of seismic activity, Iceland's Eyjafjallajökull volcano began spewing an estimated 250 million cubic metres (9 billion cubic feet) of ash and hard volcanic debris 10,000 m (33,000 ft) into the air, directly obstructing the transatlantic flight path. Flights around the world were cancelled and a month of chaos ensued. It was not until around the end of May that air travel started getting back to normal and it wasn't until October that the eruption was officially declared over. For the record, I have no clue how to pronounce Eyjafjallajökull.

Music
Runaway
– Kanye West ft. Pusha T

Easily the most controversial, gifted, egotistical or frustrating artist in recent years, depending on your point of view, Kanye West undeniably pushed hip hop forward and took musical risks few of his contemporaries would dare. Taken from his critically lauded album *My Beautiful Dark Twisted Fantasy*, *Runaway* embraced previous controversies, not least his stage invasion at the previous year's MTV Video Music Awards during Taylor Swift's acceptance speech, and his own fallibilities as one of the "douchebags". It was another highpoint in a fascinating career for the artist now known as Ye.

Film
Inception – Christopher Nolan

Starring Leonardo DiCaprio as mind-hacker Dom Cobb, Christopher Nolan's mind-bending dream-within-a-dream thriller is a visual and cerebral treat. According to the IMDb, such is the complexity of its matryoshka doll-like plot that Japanese broadcasters insert a number into the top corner of the screen to help viewers keep track of which dream level they are watching. Cillian Murphy's character was named Robert Fischer after the chess champion (I did work that one out), while together the first letter of each of the main characters' names spells "dreams pay" (thanks IMDb). The final scene in which Cobb spins his miniature spinning top leaves it open-ended as to whether or not he's still inside his dream. Nolan has given his own opinion, but I won't repeat that here so as not to ruin this breathtaking piece of cinema for those yet to see it.

Two thousand and eleven was a fairly challenging growing season – one might say "topsy-turvy" insofar as summer was more like spring and vice versa.

Such was the springtime warmth that bud break was just over a week earlier than usual and flowering was even earlier than in 2003 – 15 days ahead of schedule at Lafite Rothschild. Summer was unseasonably cool, except for a blistering heat wave towards the end of June. Dry conditions caused hydric stress, particularly among the Cabernets on free-draining gravel soils and among those who had chosen to leaf-thin to compensate for the lack of warmth, who now risked grilled and shrivelled berries. These were small and thick-skinned with average weights of 1 g per berry instead of 1.5 g. August was wet and cold, the rain encouraging vines to increase foliage rather than pump energy into their fruit and grey rot was a constant risk. Given that risk and with berries fully ripe, the picking of the dry whites commenced extremely early, on 17 August.

Come September and châteaux faced a dilemma: avoid risk and pick potentially unripe fruit or hold firm and hope conditions improved. Forecasts of unsettled conditions encouraged some to dispatch pickers early and the Merlot was picked from around 5 September. Harvest teams had to endure a major storm that slammed into the Médoc on 10 September, but those who had waited were then rewarded with a fortnight's warm and dry weather that stretched into October. Such was the extent of this Indian summer that it skewed average temperature figures enough to suggest it was one of the warmest years on record. In truth, it simply delayed ripening. Because autumn ripening is less effective than summer ripening in terms of sugar accumulation, the heat perhaps averted a poor vintage rather than guaranteed a great one. This was a year when châteaux had to sort carefully, advantaging those with optical sorting machines and/or numerous eyes and hands to discard under-ripe or rotten bunches before they entered the vat. Mouton Rothschild parsed out 8% of its crop that in previous years might have ended up in the final blend. Alcoholic fermentations were surprisingly quick, so winemakers had to be careful to control must temperatures or else risk over-extracting during the rest of the *cuvaison* period. Some châteaux also deselected some of the Merlot from their Grand Vins as they felt it detracted from the final quality.

Sauternes had a minor skirmish with frost on 25 April and then the summer saw far less rain than in the Médoc. Rain in July and August provoked some sour rot that needed eradicating. Three storms affected the region in late August/early September, though the second missed Barsac, meaning botrytisation occurred a week or so earlier there than in the rest of Sauternes. The first passes were made in mid-September and then an easterly concentrated the rest of the crop so that harvest was done and dusted by the end of the month. Yields were generally low – nothing new there.

2011
(Continued)

The 2011 Bordeaux vintage was a return to reality after the highs of 2009 and 2010. Having tasted the wines from barrel, then after bottling and most recently at 10 years, they would appeal to those seeking "classic claret". Don't queue up here for fruit-driven or flamboyant wines on either bank. They can be a little green around the edges, with no frills or thrill-a-minute rides towards sensory nirvana. Yet improvements in vineyard management and stricter selection yielded plenty of decent wines that drink well after a decade, even if they lack the density and backbone to encourage long-term cellaring. Re-tasting the vintage after 10 years in bottle, I found it lacks a bit of charm – easy to like but difficult to love. What the wines miss on both Left Bank and the Right Bank is aromatic complexity and mid-palate depth. They can feel a little conservative and brusque compared to other vintages. On the other hand, improvements in technical knowhow mean there are still plenty of fine 2011s. At the Southwold blind tasting in October 2011, the 2011 Latour (the last vintage to be offered en primeur) and La Mission Haut-Brion took top honours, while Château Margaux, Pichon Baron, Haut-Brion and Léoville Barton show well on the Left Bank; Figeac, Le Pin and Lafleur on the Right Bank. Both the dry whites and the Sauternes are well worth seeking out, with Climens, Coutet and Yquem all showing beautifully during blind tastings in 2021.

Event
A tsunami devastates
coastal Japan

On 11 March at 2.46 p.m., a
9.1 magnitude earthquake struck
around 81 miles (130 km) east of
the city of Sendai in the Tōhoku
region of Japan. Lasting six
minutes, it was one of the largest
seismic tremors ever recorded.
But the disaster was only just
beginning to unfold. Residents
had 10 to 20 minutes before
tsunamis up to 40 m (130 ft)
high breached coastal defences,
sweeping away entire towns and
causing the meltdown of three
reactors at the Fukushima Daiichi
nuclear power station. The natural
disaster was one of the first in
which terrified victims relayed
mobile-phone images of the
carnage to news channels. Almost
20,000 people lost their lives and
around 2,500 went missing.

Music
Someone Like You
– Adele

The Brit Awards was accustomed
to spectacular, highly
choreographed live performances,
but at the 2011 event a nervous
22-year-old Adele took to a
darkened stage accompanied by
just a grand piano to sing her
tear-jerking ballad about her
rejection by the man she thought
was the love of her life. The
silenced audience was cast under
the spell of her powerful yet
vulnerable voice and its sincerity.
Voice cracking towards the end,
she bites her lip and turns her
back to the audience almost in
embarrassment as she tries to
hold back the tears. It was the
moment Adele became a global
superstar. Remarkably, according
to Billboard, it was the first
piano-and-vocal-only song to top
the Hot 100 in the US since the
charts began in 1958.

Film
Bridesmaids – Paul Feig

Kristen Wiig stars as hapless maid-of-honour Annie, whose life
unravels spectacularly as she struggles to organise her best friend's
hen party and nuptials. Fans of producer Judd Apatow's gross-out
humour were satiated by the notorious vomit and diarrhoea gags, but
Bridesmaids is a cut-above thanks to its sharp and witty script, the
emotional engagement that Wiig gives to Annie, and top performances
from its female ensemble cast, particularly the indefatigable Melissa
McCarthy. Some described *Bridesmaids* as a breakthrough for feminism
in Hollywood. Well, it can't have done it any harm. What is certain is
that it was the funniest movie of 2011.

2012

Often compared to 2011, the 2012 vintage had both shortcomings and virtues, though some of its best wines only flourished once in bottle.

The previous winter was remarkably dry and mild, dissuading vines from shutting down and delaying pruning, at least until a spell of freezing weather in late February. Between October 2011 and March 2012, 336 mm (13½ in) of rain fell compared with a 10-year average of 457 mm (18 in). Budding was late, retarded by the inclement weather, the flip-reverse of the previous year when it took place three weeks earlier. April was a wash-out with 194 mm (7½ in) of rain and this, combined with cooler temperatures averaging around 10°C (50°F), led to stunted shoot growth. May saw average amounts of precipitation, but there were further downpours between 2 and 20 June that totalled around 80 mm (3 in) of rain. Combined with a cold second week of June, flowering was 10 days later than average and very uneven. Wet conditions meant vineyard managers faced acute mildew pressure, particularly with the Merlot, Cabernet Franc and Sauvignon Blanc. What they needed was a spell of dry weather and July began sunny, though not particularly warm and interrupted by occasional showers. Finally, hot weather settled from the 15th and hopes raised, even though an average temperature of 19.4°C (66.9°F) was below the 30-year norm. Consequently, when *véraison* began in early August, it was spun out over three weeks, with green berries hidden inside uneven bunches despite more sunlight hours from June to August than in the previous year. August saw the mercury tip 30°C (86°F) for 12 days and rainfall was just 20 mm (¾ in) compared with 90 mm (3½ in) in 2011, which meant younger vines and those on more porous limestone soils began to show symptoms of stress. Badly affected vines shut down and stalled ripening.

By early September, the lack of rain was becoming a major concern. The dry whites were picked under excellent dry conditions in the first two weeks of September, the cooler nights locking in acidity. Rainclouds gathered on 25 September, ensuring picking dates would be crucial to success as teams dodged the showers, while grey rot became a constant threat. Most of the Cabernet was picked between 8 and 18 October. The Merlot berries were healthy and displayed similar sugar levels to 2009, while the Cabernet Sauvignon had slightly high malic acid levels and often under-ripe herbaceous traits. This was the first vintage in which optical sorting machines played a crucial role and improved the quality of the wines beyond the limitations of the growing season.

The decision of Yquem, Suduiraut and Rieussec not to declare any 2012 on the eve of en primeur prejudiced opinion against Sauternes, with many writing the wines off on the basis of what was not produced instead of what was. Rain during harvest prevented grapes from progressing from *pourri plein* to the crucial *pourri rôti* stage and finding any *pourriture noble* was extremely difficult, though not impossible. Heavy rain at the end of October was enough to make the aforementioned and a few others throw in the towel.

The 2012 vintage was an eventful and challenging growing season that presented winemakers with as many pitfalls as opportunities. The vintage is often compared with 2011. Both came out of the blocks at a similar pace but the 2012s seemed to "kick on" in bottle, not least on the Right Bank. So for the first decade at least, my preference was for 2012 over 2011. Reassessing the top 150-odd Bordeaux at the annual blind 10-year-on tasting, I felt there had been some shift. First, the Saint-Émilions had not matured as well as expected, as if they had blossomed in their flush of youth and then suddenly remembered they were not for the long course. Many of the wines felt evolved, particularly those evincing a rather passé style of winemaking that pursued power over finesse. Thankfully these were the twilight days of that dogma. It is only at the very top end of the Right Bank that you find wines that continue to evolve, with those containing healthy proportions of Cabernet Franc showing best: Cheval Blanc, Figeac, Vieux Château Certan, l'Église-Clinet and Lafleur. Certan de May and Clos l'Église likewise repay cellaring.

Over on the Left Bank, the wines are generally good but devoid of standouts to get excited about. Even the ever-reliable Saint-Julien appellation fails to entice with the exception of a splendid Léoville Barton. The Margaux wines appeal in the sense that they show personality and *typicité*, even if there are no real humdingers. The First Growths show their class, though frankly there is not a huge gap in quality, Haut-Brion perhaps the pick of the bunch. Sauternes is certainly not the write-off that the non-appearance by some of its most famous names infers, but re-examined after a decade – and with the exceptions of Climens and Rayne Vigneau – the wines are enjoyable yet rather one-dimensional and unlikely to evolve further with bottle age.

Event

The attempted murder of Malala Yousafzai

In October 2012, 14-year-old Pakistani schoolgirl Malala Yousafzai was shot in the head. The bullet entered just above her left eye and ran along her jawline. Her crime? Campaigning for the right of girls to go to school, which was forbidden under strict Pakistani Taliban rule. Miraculously she survived and after being flown to Birmingham in the UK, woke up in hospital 10 days later. Not only did Malala make a full recovery, but she also graduated from Oxford University, became a symbol of defiance against oppressive Islamist rule, and won the Nobel Peace Prize in 2014. The shot had missed its target.

2012
(Continued)

Music
We Are Never Ever Getting Back Together – Taylor Swift

We Are Never Ever Getting Back Together was a major step in Taylor Swift's transition from successful Nashville-based country star to global pop phenomenon. Based on a looped acoustic guitar, it contained traces of her country background, but co-writers Max Martin and Shellback introduced a more synth-based sound and clipped syncopation, giving notice that Swift was heading in a pop direction. Allegedly written in 25 minutes, it contains all the tropes of a Taylor Swift song, including an insanely catchy chorus and clever put-down lyrics, and was the first of many US number ones for the singer. The accompanying promo video is worth watching. Filmed in a single take, it necessitated some swift costume changes.

Film
The Hunt
– Thomas Vinterberg

Danish drama *The Hunt* stars Mads Mikkelsen as a kindergarten teacher who becomes the target of hysteria in a close-knit village when a young girl fabricates a story that he exposed himself to her. Mikkelsen brilliantly conveys the teacher's anguish and confusion as he desperately tries to convince his sceptical friends and family of his innocence and even when the evidence is clear, he is never out of the woods (literally, if you watch the tense final scene). Mikkelsen's performance deservedly won him the Best Actor Award at that year's Cannes Film Festival.

If Bordeaux winemakers knew what lay ahead in this growing season, I wonder whether they would have opted to stay in bed for the year? Welcome to the *annus horribilis* of the modern era. So what happened?

Winter was extremely damp, October to March seeing 70 mm (2¾ in) more rain than the 30-year average and 91 days when umbrellas were required – 28 more than in 2008. Okay, no problem – the water tables are nicely replenished for the ensuing months of dry weather. But dry conditions did not materialise until much later. March was unusually cool and wet, with 71 mm (2¾ in) of rain compared with 31 mm (1¼ in) in 2012, and it rained on and off through to July. The soils and subsoil became cold and vines forgot what warmth felt like, sapped of the energy needed to fuel their growth cycle. Unsurprisingly, bud break was delayed and flowering did not begin until the second week of June, two weeks later than the previous year. After a storm crossed the region on 8 June, coulure and millerandage became endemic with the Merlot and older vines, acutely affected – which is why the likes of Pichon-Lalande and Lafite Rothschild produced '13s that were almost entirely composed of Cabernet Sauvignon. June was cold, some 7°C (44°F) under the 30-year average, and the rain just would not cease – the month saw 132 mm (5 in) instead of an average 64 mm (2½ in). (I remember visiting Gruaud Larose that month, fighting off the clammy cold in my winter coat, and standing atop its tower in more drizzle as its winemaker tried to keep a happy face.) Rot was running wild, with some seasoned winemakers claiming they had never seen it so widespread, despite preventive sprays. But it is important to dispel the idea that it was inclement the entire year. July was particularly sunny with temperatures 3°C (37°F) above average and 330 sunlight hours instead of 262 in 2009. However, a violent hailstorm swept across the region on the night of 25 July, severely impacting Pessac-Léognan, and more hail on 2 August decimated 10,000 hectares of Entre-Deux-Mers, with some estates losing 80% of their crop. Gavin Quinney, proprietor of Château Bauduc, lost half his crop in 10 minutes. *Véraison* was drawn out, but a two-month spell of hot weather in August and September saved the vintage by burning away the pyrazine notes. It did not last.

On 20 September, the weather became unstable, cool and drizzly, increasing the pressure for rot, though hopes lifted in the final week when a warm and sunny window allowed the dry whites and some Sauternes to be picked. That was Mother Nature just fooling around. The final weekend in September saw downpours return, followed by warm and humid days to encourage yet more rot, compounded by further deluges on 4 October. Everyone had had just about enough and sent pickers into the vines from late September aware that many parcels of Cabernet Sauvignon still lacked full ripeness. It called for precise management of the troops, directing pickers to plots at most risk of rot – sandier soils were less resistant than clay and limestone. The one exception was Saint-Estèphe where just 25 mm (1 in) of rain fell between 1 and 25 October – one-third of the level in other appellations. Berries were small with lower sugar and higher acidity levels compared with the previous two vintages, though anthocyanin levels were similar. Sorting the fruit was essential if you wanted to make a half-decent wine and vibrating/optical sorting tables were wheeled out to varying degrees of success. Some hailed optical sorting tables as saviours. Ducru-Beaucaillou, for example, parsed away around 5% of the crop using this technology. But others, such as Jean-Philippe Delmas at Haut-Brion, claimed they were redundant as the thin skins caused berries to split, making them difficult for sensors to analyse.

Sauternes was also affected by the growing season, and by September grapes were green, bunches irregular and the spectre of grey rot lurked round the corner. Then fortunes turned around when three days of rain from 28–30 September and a hot spell in the first week of October led to perfect conditions for botrytis infection. The inevitable rush of picking was halted on 4 October by a violent storm and subsequent passes through the vines were staggered and fruit lacked a little complexity. Some discarded these later pickings.

In 2013, some Bordeaux château took the bold decision not to release any wine, including Hosanna and Providence from Ets. Jean-Pierre Moueix and Le Pin, which I did actually taste with Jacques Thienpont before he decided to declassify it. When he asked my opinion, my reply was not exactly complimentary. The en primeur campaign the following spring was a rare instance when even the most euphemistic château owners were not inclined to reel out superlatives. The commonly heard phrases were a resigned: "It's not as bad as we thought" or "It's a Burgundy vintage" – rather derogatory to that region's hard-working winemakers. The press had a field day hammering the Bordeaux to the chagrin of some owners, who felt their wines should at least be tasted before being traduced. Fair enough.

So, what's the truth? It is not a great vintage. It is not even a good one, the weakest that I have tasted in my career. Blame cannot be aimed at winemakers who I witnessed first-hand gritting their teeth and toiling away with the odds stacked against them. Though I might be damning with faint praise, the resulting wines are not as execrable as those from 1965 or 1977 due to the strides that had been made in viticulture, especially in terms of rigorous selection at reception areas.

The wines are generally light and simplistic. They feel hollow but rarely vegetal thanks to the sunny and warm July and August. Pessac-Léognan produced a handful of worthy wines despite hail damage: Pape Clément and Haut-Bailly for starters, notwithstanding contributions from Saint-Estèphe (such as Cos d'Estournel) and Saint-Julien (such as Léoville-Las Cases) that should not be dismissed out of hand. Warmer soils in the Margaux appellation gave it some advantage

– Rauzan-Ségla and Palmer were both pleasant as recently as 2021. The Right Bank faired best for estates with a good proportion of Cabernet Franc, such as Cheval Blanc, Ausone and Lafleur. The bright spot is a clutch of excellent dry whites from the likes of Smith Haut Lafitte, Malartic-Lagravière and Domaine de Chevalier. So what is best from this bad crop? Definitely Sauternes, with a clutch of lovely sweet wines from Yquem, Climens, Lafaurie-Peyraguey and Suduiraut. They are no match for the 2009s or maybe the 2011s, but are more pleasurable than the dry reds.

Event
The death of Nelson Mandela

Nelson Mandela had become a defiant symbol for the anti-apartheid cause after he was imprisoned on Robben Island for 27 years. Released in February 1990, the former ANC leader was elected president of South Africa four years later. While his record is not unimpeachable, he worked tirelessly to unite the multicultural "Rainbow Nation", address wealth inequality, and provide a symbol of hope for a brighter future. Despite ailing health, he remained a God-like figure for many South Africans after his retirement and when he passed away on 5 December 2013 from a lung infection, probably caused by his long incarceration, a nation mourned.

Music
Get Lucky
– Daft Punk

Guy-Manuel de Homem-Christo and Thomas Bangalter got lucky when they teamed up with Pharrell Williams and Nile Rodgers for this ubiquitous disco-funk floor-filler. The song had an 18-month gestation period before it was revealed in two 15-second advertisements during *Saturday Night Live*. A seamless blend of Rodgers' infectious signature guitar licks – perfected during his time in disco giants Chic – Williams' pure falsetto and the Parisian duo's vocoder-effects and meticulous production, *Get Lucky* was a ray of sunshine that topped the charts after its release in April 2013.

2013
(Continued)

Film
12 Years a Slave
– Steve McQueen

Based on Solomon Northup's
1853 memoirs, McQueen's
acclaimed biopic tells the true
story of how this free black man
in antebellum New York was
abducted, sold into slavery and
fought for 12 years to reclaim
his stolen liberty. McQueen
does not flinch from depicting
the cruelty meted out to slaves,
not least when Patsey, played
by newcomer Lupita Nyong'o,
is chained and whipped in an
explicit five-minute scene. One
would like to think racism is in
the past and McQueen becoming
the first black British film-maker
to win an Oscar is a sign of long
overdue progress. On the other
hand, posters advertising the film
in Italy only showed two white
actors because they were "better
known" than lead Chiwetel
Ejiofor. There's a long way to go.

Robert Parker retired and handed over responsibility for Bordeaux to some guy from Essex – something nobody would have predicted a few years earlier, least of all me. It coincided with a shift in style that would soon gather pace.

The year began with the warmest winter for some 24 years, temperatures rarely dipping below freezing, but it was also wet. March continued in the same vein and would have prompted early budding had vines not been dissuaded by cold night-time temperatures. Buds finally broke around mid-March, approximately a fortnight earlier than average, and a warm and dry April prevented frost, unlike three years later. Inclement weather towards the end of April saw some white varieties affected by *filage en vrille* – when the vine expends energy on producing tendrils instead of bunches. May was cool and damp, which caused coulure and millerandage, and also diluted mineral uptake. Fortunately flowering passed evenly and quickly over a week in early June, 10 days earlier than in 2013. Two heat spikes on 21 June and 17 July caused some burnt berry skins, especially towards the eastern flank of Saint-Émilion. This aside, June was relatively benign and raised hopes for a growing season worth getting excited about. Alas, July and August were cooler than expected insofar as temperatures only exceeded 30°C (86°F) on three occasions in July and not once in August. Denis Dubourdieu's report notes that temperatures were 5.8°C (42°F) below the 1981–2010 average in July and 2.2°C (36°F) below average in August, coupled with 12% fewer sunlight hours. Thus for a second year vines got their priorities wrong and refocused their energy upon foliage to increase photosynthesis instead of on bunches, which led to a protracted *véraison*. Bunches began pigmenting in mid-July in some localities, but in other spots cool temperatures, lack of diurnal temperature variation, and high moisture levels meant pigmenting did not take place until the end of August. Uneven ripeness levels obliged constant vigilance and work in the vineyard to thin out green bunches. It's important to note that Saint-Émilion and Margaux suffered more rainfall than either Saint-Julien or Saint-Estèphe. To add to woes, there was the constant lurking threat of oidium, as well as an outbreak of cicadellidae (leafhoppers), which made vineyard work uncomfortable. By the end of August hopes of a great vintage had been snuffed out. I recall one winemaker confessing at the time that 2014 would end up even worse than 2013.

Fortunately, his predictions did not transpire. An Indian summer saved the day as a high-pressure system squatted over Europe and warded off the low depressions from the Atlantic. Temperatures in September were 27.8°C (82°F) above average and despite shorter days, there were 27% more sunlight hours than in August. Thunderstorms over Saint-Émilion aside, it was a perfect month that verged on excessive as high temperatures caused some berries to shrivel. These had to be discarded before entering the vat, although at least the heat compensated for the lack of concentration earlier that summer.

2014

2014
(Continued)

The harvest kicked off around 3 September with the dry whites under dry conditions. The Merlot started coming in around 22 September after potential alcohol levels rocketed by almost a degree per week. The clement conditions enabled vineyard managers to drag out the growing season, with most of the Cabernets picked in a warmer-than-usual October that only saw 20 mm (¾ in) of rain. Berries were small and concentrated. Maceration periods were a little shorter and *remontage* less frequent compared with other vintages as many feared over-extracting. In Sauternes, the Indian summer was a mixed blessing since it precluded the onset of botrytis, at least until an outbreak of rain on 9 October caused an explosion of it that necessitated block-by-block picking instead of ritual piecemeal *tries* through the vineyard. Pickers had to be careful since some vineyard managers had noticed *bouïroc*, or sour rot, in a small number of bunches. Finally, though, they were able to harvest high-quality fruit, which had to be kept cool prior to fermentation due to the warm temperatures. Most Sauternes châteaux had completed their final pass by the end of the month.

As described in my decade summary, 2014 saw some winemakers re-evaluate their practices. Several continued in a similar vein, while others chose a different approach. Châteaux were less coerced to follow a singular path, not least on the Right Bank and in Saint-Émilion. The appellation saw the resurgence of two Saint-Émilion stalwarts: Canon and Figeac under estate managers Nicolas Audebert and Frédéric Faye, respectively, while even Pavie, which had enjoyed so much success with what many referred to as a "Parker style", began reeling back alcohol levels and introducing more Cabernet into the blend. The Pomerols are very fine, although I am not convinced that either Pétrus, Le Pin or Clinet fulfilled their full potential. Both l'Église-Clinet and Vieux Château Certan show better.

All three Pauillac First Growths produced excellent wines, the 2014 Mouton Rothschild perhaps with its nose out in front in the first furlongs, though their supremacy is challenged by the likes of Grand-Puy-Lacoste, Pichon Baron and Pichon-Lalande. Both Cos d'Estournel and Montrose tussle it out to the benefit of Saint-Estèphe lovers, with Meyney the "dark horse" for those whose wallets don't open as wide. The appellation of Saint-Julien is consistent (as usual), with a rejuvenated Saint-Pierre its over-achiever. Despite fine performances from Rauzan-Ségla and Marquis d'Alesme, the Margaux appellation never quite clicked in 2014 and I prefer Pessac-Léognan, notably La Mission Haut-Brion, which has the edge of Haut-Brion. Elsewhere, I admire the 2014s from Haut-Bailly, Domaine de Chevalier and Smith Haut Lafitte.

Sauternes benefited from a rush of botrytis caused by mid-October rain after a long dry spell, and are not as tensile as recent vintages. But at the top level, those who picked carefully produced gorgeous wines, such as Yquem, Climens, Doisy-Daëne, Doisy-Védrines and Coutet.

Event
Islamic State caliphate declared in Iraq and Syria

In June 2014, a group of hard-line jihadists, ISIS, overran a large swathe of Syria and Iraq. Its leader, Abu Bakr al-Baghdadi, announced the formation of a caliphate to be known as Islamic State. The brutal regime exploited social media to spread its repressive ideology and the following weeks saw filmed beheadings of prisoners and the enslavement of the Yazidi minority among countless heinous crimes. A US-led coalition responded by bombarding IS-held territory from 8 August, which ultimately led to the crumbling of Islamic State and the death of Baghdadi.

Music
Uptown Funk
– Mark Ronson ft. Bruno Mars

Uptown Funk was weaponised with more hooks than the rest of that year's songs assembled. Both Ronson and Mars spent several months piecing the song together, obliging dozens of takes that apparently drove Ronson to the point of exhaustion. The final version was essentially an homage to eighties slap-bass funk, though similarities to The Gap Band's *Oops Up Side Your Head* resulted in a copyright claim and eventually co-writing credits. Released in November 2014, it ended up topping the Billboard chart for a record 14 weeks from January to April the following year.

Film
Boyhood – Richard Linklater

Boyhood is another in a long line of coming-of-age movies, but its USP is that Linklater filmed it over 11 years using the same cast. The boy, played by Ellar Coltrane, was seven years old when shooting began in 2002 and 19 when it finished in 2013. Each year of his family's lives are depicted in approximately 14-minute segments of the 165-minute screen-time. In real life during this period, his on-screen parents, played by Ethan Hawke and Patricia Arquette, went through their own separations and re-marriages. The time frame is never disclosed, though years can be deduced by cultural references such as DVDs in the background and technology on screen. Its working title of "12 Years" was altered when McQueen's *12 Years a Slave* was released and the film went on to win numerous awards.

2015

Though 2015 is now regarded as the best vintage since 2010, the growing season was complicated.

January and February were wet and served to replenish the depleted water table and March was the warmest since 1880. Bud burst was retarded by low night-time temperatures and vines accumulated pent-up energy, the landscape finally bursting into green at the beginning of April with some shoots growing up to 13 cm (5 in) in a day. Dry conditions put the brakes on growth, with rainfall 70% and 60% below average in April and May, respectively. Warm temperatures reached 24°C (75°F) and led to a quick and even flowering, before a period of strong heat and record sunlight hours that saw 11 consecutive days above 30°C (86°F). Vines began to stress before the season turned volte-face with two violent storms on 22 and 24 July. Temperatures remained high in August but welcome rain fell over three or four deluges, evening out *véraison* and redirecting energy towards bunches instead of foliage. Come harvest, and dry conditions meant there was little risk of rot.

The dry whites were picked between 28 August and 11 September, with cool nights benefiting the Sauvignon Blanc. But on 12 September the remnants of Tropical Storm Henri unleashed a 48-hour deluge and several days of rain. Fortunately, a warm southerly breeze descending from the leeward side of the Alps, known as a föhn wind, warded the storm away from Bordeaux and limited rain in many appellations to 40 mm (1½ in). Alas, its protective reach did not quite stretch as far as Saint-Estèphe, which saw 100 mm (4 in) of rain and consequently a shorter picking window. Many properties delayed picking instead of expediting as they had done in 1999, allowing time for berries to recover from the damp spell, avoiding swelling and potential dilution. The lion's share of the Merlot was harvested between 20 September and 1 October during sunny days and cold nights, with most picked on the final four days of the month. The Cabernet Franc on the Right Bank and the Cabernet Sauvignon were picked almost simultaneously from October 8 under blue skies and a cooling northerly breeze, and the harvest was more or less complete by October 22.

Sauternes enjoyed a rather benign season. The catalyst for botrytis was a storm on August 31 that brought 9 mm (⅓ in) of rain followed by warm sunny conditions: perfect for noble rot formation with cool nights capturing acidity. Botrytis was so regular and even that vineyard managers could almost saunter into the vines and pick exactly how they wanted. Often, four passes through the vines was sufficient to get everything, with many reaching 20–22% potential alcohol and reasonable yields at 15 hl/ha.

The Bordelais cranked up the hype machine when the 2015s came on to market, noting the numerical sequence of fêted vintages ending in five, such as 1945 and 1995 (nobody was supposed to mention 1965). Then 2016 trotted along and rather eclipsed it, partly because Saint-Estèphe, Pauillac and Pomerol were just a shade off their best. Tasting the wines blind in bottle in 2019, the Margaux appellation stood out for me with wonderful wines from not only usual suspects such as Palmer and Rauzan-Ségla, but also Boyd-Cantenac, Cantenac Brown, Dauzac, Labégorce and Pouget. The 2015 Château Margaux comes in a commemorative bottle to honour the untimely passing of winemaker Paul Pontallier and its contents are commensurate of the man instrumental in the First Growth's resurgence. The Saint-Juliens are like Sir Ian McKellen in that they never put in a bad performance and that is especially applicable this season. The 2015 Léoville-Las Cases is sophisticated and Léoville Poyferré voluptuous. In Pauillac, I feel the wines don't quite reach their respective apotheosis – the First Growths are all impressive with Latour's nose out in front, Haut-Bages Libéral is the "dark horse", and both Pichons are nipping at the heels of the Firsts. Saint-Estèphe's brush with the remnants of Tropical Storm Henri meant that, despite protestations from Saint-Estèphe proprietors, its wines are a couple of steps behind other appellations, but watch out for Calon Ségur and Meyney. The dry whites are generally very fine this year. Pessac-Léognan's reds are solid even though one or two might baulk at the almost 15% alcohol in La Mission and Haut-Brion. Some of the Saint-Émilions continue to show signs of late picking and yet Ausone and Cheval Blanc are marvels, Clos Fourtet punches above its weight and Beauséjour Duffau-Lagarrosse is fabulous. Pomerol has a clutch of magnificent wines but, like those of Saint-Estèphe, they do not quite match their 2016 counterparts. The finest Sauternes congregate in the top tier, not least in Barsac, courtesy of Doisy-Daëne, Coutet and Climens, while de Fargues is a perfect alternative if Yquem is too expensive.

Event
Massacre at the Bataclan

Flying over Paris from Lyon on a clear night on 13 November 2015, looking down on Europe's prettiest, most romantic capital, I could not imagine the bloodshed and terror unfolding among the lattice of twinkling lights below. A co-ordinated series of bombings and shootings by Islamic terrorists, first outside the Stade de France, then in cafés in the 10th arrondissement and a siege and massacre during a concert at the Bataclan theatre, resulted in 130 fatalities and hundreds of injuries in one of Europe's deadliest, most horrific attacks.

2015

Music
Alright
– Kendrick Lamar

Compton-born Kendrick Lamar's mellifluous flowing style and hard-hitting semi-autobiographical lyrics had already made him the kingpin of rap. In 2015, he reached a new artistic height with the era-defining *To Pimp a Butterfly* album that melded jazz, neo-soul and rap with contemporaneous political issues. Pharrell Williams had created the beat for its best-known cut, *Alright*, some months before Lamar found the right lyrics, purportedly inspired by witnessing the poverty in South Africa. An uncredited Williams sings the "We gon' be alright" refrain that was seen as a message of hope after it was adopted by the Black Lives Matter movement. It became an instant modern-day anthem.

Film
The Revenant
– Alejandro G. Iñárritu

The Revenant was adapted on Michael Punke's 2002 novel about frontiersman and fur trapper Hugh Glass, played by Leonardo DiCaprio. Loosely based on real events of 1823, it tells how Glass's party is attacked by Native Americans and then, separated from his party and practically mauled to death by a grizzly bear, Glass makes the tortuous journey home to take revenge upon the duplicitous John Fitzgerald (Tom Hardy). Emmanuel Lubezki's cinematography uses natural light to translate the panoramic snowy wilderness on to the silver screen. DiCaprio, who carries the entire film, faced a demanding shoot, diving into freezing rivers and eating raw bison – not easy when you're a committed vegetarian. The star took two years off before accepting another role, but his Herculean efforts were rewarded with his first Oscar win.

The 2016 Bordeaux is a benchmark vintage that may ultimately be regarded as a pivotal turning point for the region.

It was a game of two halves, the first wet and the second dry. Torrential rains delayed pruning and bud burst. April and May were inclement with fluctuating temperatures and persistent wet conditions. Difficult as it is to believe now, this prompted fears of another 2013 washout. The Bordelais enjoyed their first stroke of luck between 3 and 11 June when the weather remained fine and daytime temperatures hovered between 21–28°C (70–82°F), allowing flowering to take place evenly and quickly. But between January and June over 700 mm (27½ in) of rain fell and vineyards were sodden. On 20 June the rain stopped and the sun returned although hot temperatures did not arrive until mid-July and drought-like conditions followed. Between 20 June and 13 September there was just 25 mm (1 in) of rainfall and in Saint-Estèphe just 5.5 mm (¼ in) was recorded. Fortunately, the occasional nighttime shower plus plentiful underground water reserves were enough to prevent vines from shutting down. August was crucial in terms of sunlight hours. Although the thermometer only exceeded 30°C (86°F) on four days, there were 26% more sunlight hours than normal. *Véraison* was uniform thanks to two small showers on 30 July and 4 August that recharged vines' batteries to ensure the berries changed colour.

The picking of the whites began on 1 September. On 13 September summer declared it had had enough and passed the baton to autumn and rainfall shimmied up from the Basque region. Temperatures fell by around 10°C (50°F) to 15°C (59°F) and 20–25 mm (¾–1 in) of rainfall revivified the vines at the end of September, nudging physiological ripeness towards full maturity. Most of the Merlot was harvested between 3 – 7 October and the picking of the Cabernet Sauvignon commenced on 5 – 6 October. It was a comparatively relaxed picking, which was conducted in piecemeal fashion until around 20 October. In Sauternes, summer had been dry, so light showers on 13 September benefited botrytis infection, especially in Barsac. Rain and humidity at the end of the month really got the vintage going with an even spread of botrytis, which meant between 70% and 95% of picking was undertaken in late October and early November.

Having tasted all the major wines out of barrel and in bottle, there is no doubt that 2016 is a sensational vintage across Bordeaux, with the Left Bank perhaps boasting more genuine superstars. The wines are praised for their unerring purity and finesse, with tannin profiles far finer than just a few years before, textures silky and seductive. They are generally more approachable than the 2009s and 2010s, though the best will clearly last for many years. Two thousand and sixteen is the yardstick by which subsequent growing seasons will be measured.

2016

1870

2020

479

2016
(Continued)

Tasting the vintage blind after bottling, I found the wines to be sublime and, at times, entrancing from the top to the bottom of the Bordeaux hierarchy – the true litmus test of a great growing season. There is a case to be made that the Right Bank and Margaux are slightly stronger in 2015 – the former due to the triumphant Cabernet Franc – but certainly Saint-Estèphe and Saint-Julien are better in 2016. The wines showcase how Bordeaux's top estates now manage tannins, and texturally feel different to the 2009s and 2010s. It is a bit like upgrading your bicycle to a titanium frame – lighter and yet just as strong – and comes as the result of greater precision in the vineyard, draconian fruit selection at winery receptions, and, most significantly, gentler pressing and more selection of the pressed wine so that only the best is used. Another facet of the 2016s is their aromatics. They are remarkably, seductively perfumed – often quite floral in style, as if a little bit of Margaux had been distributed around the appellations. The peaks are scattered across Bordeaux but I would point to Latour, Mouton Rothschild, Cos d'Estournel, Figeac and Vieux Château Certan as flirting with perfection, then Haut-Brion, La Mission Haut-Brion, Léoville-Las Cases, Pétrus and Cheval Blanc as incontrovertibly brilliant. Many of these 2016s will drink well after five or six years, though personally I would be broaching my 2012s and 2014s before delving into the 2015s and 2016s. Several estates produced wines that stand as benchmarks including a sensational Malescot Saint-Exupéry, a multi-dimensional Ducru-Beaucaillou, plus brilliant wines from Beychevelle, Clos Fourtet, Clos l'Église, Canon, Valandraud, Meyney, Beauséjour Héritiers Duffau-Lagarrosse, de Fieuzal and Gazin. The list goes on and on. The Sauternes have to fight for attention in this fecund season, but they are certainly worth hunting down. Apart from the well-known names, seek out the likes of Château de Myrat and Rabaud-Promis.

Event
Donald J. Trump becomes the 45th US President

In a year full of upsets, nothing approached the shock result of outside candidate, former reality TV star and business mogul Donald J. Trump triumphing over Democrat candidate Hillary Clinton in the US presidential election. So-called "Teflon Don" defied every poll to defeat 15 politically experienced Republican hopefuls in the primaries, then swatted away scandals during a divisive and vitriolic campaign to win at the ballot box, signifying an era of populist votes. Press conferences at the White House subsequently became somewhat livelier, though Trump would only serve one term in office.

Music
Cranes in the Sky
– Solange

Cranes in the Sky was evidence that musical DNA was shared among the Knowles family. Solange, sister of Beyoncé, had written the song several years earlier when mourning a break-up with her childhood sweetheart and father to her son, and the lyrics express the difficulty of exorcising the sadness and the self-doubt that followed. Producer Raphael Saadiq gave *Cranes in the Sky* a sublime neo-soul, jazzy vibe that perfectly matches Solange's sultry vocals, giving notice that her album *A Seat at the Table* would be one of the most-lauded releases that year.

Film
La La Land – Damien Chazelle

At the end of what had been a traumatising year for many after a run of celebrity deaths and unexpected votes, this throwback musical provided much-needed escapism. Ryan Gosling stars as Sebastian Wilder, the struggling jazz pianist who falls for struggling actress Mia Dolan, an exquisite turn by Emma Stone. Their relationship is played out through a series of brilliantly choreographed musical numbers, not least the opening scene filmed on the L.A. freeway ramp. Gosling learned to play piano for the role, obviating the need for a hand double, while Stone sang the moving *Audition (The Fools Who Dream)* live without any pre-recorded track. Then there's the ending: *La La Land* might be a film about dreams, but its final scene is pure reality.

2017

Two thousand and seventeen is perceived as the weakest vintage in the latter half of the decade, but some might see its wines as antidotes to the extravagance of the 2018s.

The winter of 2016–17 was relatively warm as a high-pressure system wedged itself over France, with December average temperatures 2.2°C (36°F) above normal. After an arid January, February and March saw temperatures 2.5–2.9°C (36.5–37.2°F) above average. Bud burst should theoretically have been in early March, but the previous season's drought meant leaves did not unfurl until the end of that month. Producers speculated about an early harvest and some touted 2014-2015-2016 as a modern-day 1988-1989-1990, to which I impertinently quipped that that would make 2017 the new 1991 and they should expect to be frosted over. What were the odds? Quite high, as it turned out.

While wary of frost, some younger winemakers had no first-hand recollection of 1991. Perhaps the uninterrupted succession of frost-free seasons had deceived some into believing that extensive frost damage was either a thing of the past or only happened in other regions, such as Volnay or Pommard. By mid-April, warm weather meant shoots were already 30 cm (12 in) long with six to eight leaves, so any frost would be certain to exact a lot of damage. Sure enough, from 20 April a first wave of frost devastated several French wine regions, though Bordeaux escaped relatively unscathed thanks to the dry conditions, with just some vineyards in Saint-Émilion reporting a 10% loss. That changed on 24 and 25 April after a spell of rain drifted up from Spain. On the night of 26 April, the wind and temperatures dropped in tandem, plunging to -2°C (28.5°F) and as low as -6°C (21°F) in the worst-affected areas. Frost attacked on three consecutive nights, inflicting the most damage on the second and third. The following day, the verdant canopy discoloured into ugly brown and blacks. Unlike in 1991, frost damage was ubiquitous but the Grands Crus Classés, whose vines are located near the Gironde, were spared. On the Right Bank, the Pomerol gravel plateau, Saint-Émilion limestone plateau and the côtes also got away unscathed, but lower-lying areas on the plain were often severely impacted. Even so, some famous names were hit, not least Cheval Blanc, which lost two-thirds of its crop. Some properties suffered a total loss as the frost destroyed counter-buds, while others were only partially affected, retaining a mix of surviving first-generation growth and counter-buds that could produce second-generation fruit. A few lucky ones got away scot-free.

May was hot and warm with heat spikes over 30°C (86°F). *Mi-fleuraison* was on 30 May, around two weeks earlier than normal and flowering was spread over 10 days in almost perfect conditions. Eric Kohler at Lafite Rothschild described it as the best he had ever seen. It was rubbing salt in the wounds of those who faced the prospect of a minuscule harvest, or none at all. June was baking hot with temperatures 5.5°C (41.9°F) above average, the third hottest since 1959 and not far from

2003. If the conditions prevailed, the second-generation fruit might catch up, as it had in 1961. But after 100 mm (4 in) of rain at the end of June, July was relatively cool despite a couple of heat spikes. There were fewer sunshine hours and it was dry, with just 28 mm (1 in) of rain, causing young vines to suffer heat stress. All this meant those affected by frost suffered irregular ripening, hampering their prospects of being able to supplement the shortfall in first-generation fruit. Another setback was water stress, which arrived after *véraison* and deprived some of the wines of the flesh and sweetness of the 2015s and 2016s. August was also dry with just 30 mm (1 in) of rain, compensated for by more sunshine hours. But temperatures languished in the low twenties until 21 August. This cool August is the defining factor that influenced the 2017s, inhibiting high sugar and polyphenol levels. It laid the foundation for more austere, drier wine, albeit with good acidity and freshness levels.

Alas, a balmy September did not come to the rescue. The first fortnight was drizzly and overcast, with up to 120 mm (4¾ in) of rain on the Left Bank, down to 30 mm (1 in) on the Right Bank. By this time, the picking of the whites had already started – as early as 21 August at Haut-Brion – and some of the dry whites that avoided these early September rains are excellent. Harvesting of the Merlot began around 11 September, much of it diluted by the rain, prompting some to reduce its contribution to the blend. Much of the Cabernet Sauvignon was picked from 22 or 23 September under fine and warm conditions, but the return of drizzle at the end of September forced expedited picking and most were finished by 29 September. Some properties such as Canon-la-Gaffelière did resort to using secondary fruit, though this was more prevalent lower down the Bordeaux hierarchy. Top estates weeded out secondary fruit in the vineyard or at reception using all the technology at their disposal, while extractions were soft and gentle. Output was 40% down due to the frost.

Re-tasting the top 250 blind at the annual Southwold tasting in October 2021, the 2017s had their virtues, with the best displaying attractive, delineated and classic aromatics – leitmotifs of tobacco and graphite, and plenty of freshness on the palate. But they lack fruit and flesh, and are also sometimes hard in texture. Among the First Growths, the 2017 Mouton Rothschild had its nose in front, though the 2017 La Mission Haut-Brion is outstanding. These are both challenged by fine offerings from Lynch-Bages, Léoville Poyferré and Grand-Puy-Lacoste. On the Right Bank, the standouts include Trotanoy, Vieux Château Certan, Bélair-Monange, Ausone and, perhaps best of all, l'Église-Clinet. I never quite took to the 2017 Cheval Blanc because I missed the contribution of the Merlot, which was missing in action due to the season's frost. The dry whites are quite impressive, especially the 2017 Malartic-Lagravière Blanc and Haut-Brion Blanc, while the Sauternes are certainly worth delving into. Yquem finally came out on top after being slow out of the blocks, while Rieussec, Coutet and de Fargues all have much to offer.

2017
(Continued)

Event
#MeToo

Movie mogul Harvey Weinstein produced many modern classics, including *Reservoir Dogs*. In October 2017, sexual harassment allegations against him dating back years began surfacing on social media, prompting actress Alyssa Milano to suggest victims use the hashtag "Me too" to highlight the scale of male misconduct beyond Weinstein (the phrase had first been used by civil rights activist Tarana Burke in 2006). The hashtag went viral and was used 19 million times within 12 months as women around the world came forward with personal tales of abuse. Weinstein was convicted of rape and sexual assault in February 2020 and sentenced to 23 years in prison.

Music
Big for Your Boots
– Stormzy

By 2017, grime had burst out of inner-city council estates and into the mainstream. Leading the charge was Croydon-born Michael Ebenezer Kwadjo Omari Owuo Jr., better known as Stormzy. Produced by Sir Spyro and Adele-collaborator Fraser T. Smith, *Big for Your Boots* was his biggest hit to date, slightly more commercial in sound yet still with Stormzy's frenetic and tightly coiled flow. The accompanying video kept it real with the rapper performing in a chicken shop. When Croydon M.P. Sarah Jones quoted the song in the House of Commons it became immortalised in the *Hansard* historical record.

Film
Lady Bird – Greta Gerwig

Saoirse Ronan stars as a 17-year-old Catholic high-school senior in Gerwig's wistful, semi-autobiographical coming-of-age movie set in Sacramento circa 2002. Her character's nickname has nothing to do with Lyndon B. Johnson's wife, but instead relates to the nursery rhyme "Lady bird, lady bird, fly away home", which apparently became lodged in Gerwig's subconscious. Lady Bird herself is a churn of emotions brought on by her spiky relationship with her mother, fumbling the loss of her virginity, the ups and downs of adolescent friendship, and that liminal moment in life when you're impatiently tapping on the table, waiting for everything to burst into action.

The 2018 vintage can be split into two halves. If you want to distil the growing season down to three words, it would be "rainy then sunny".

The winter had plenty of rain, not least in December and January, when around 155 mm (6 in) drenched the region. Come spring, someone forgot to turn off the tap. March saw 126 mm (5 in), compared with a 64 mm (2½ in) average over the previous decade, and temperatures a degree lower than normal (9°C/48°F), which delayed bud break. The following months experienced average amounts of precipitation, but of course, it was falling on saturated ground. Such humid conditions led to intense mildew pressure from mid-April onwards, with approximately one-third of the vineyards affected and few dry windows in which to spray and protect vines. Mildew affected not just leaves but bunches, which are more difficult to treat. The average June temperature was higher than normal at 20.3°C (68.5°F) and, combined with rain, the warm conditions compounded mildew pressure, especially in organic and biodynamic vineyards such as Palmer and Pontet-Canet's. Both estates suffered large depletions in crop, but to their credit refused to throw in the towel and revert to chemical sprays. Flowering in late May went well, though a storm moved northwards from the northern Graves on 26 May, passing though the southern Haut-Médoc and then into Côtes de Bourg and Blaye, unleashing localised hailstorms. The rainclouds persisted through June. I vividly recall being caught up in a downpour in Pomerol and almost abandoning my car near Clinet as I unsuccessfully attempted to traverse a flooded road.

Everything changed from 4 July. Mother Nature just flicked a switch. Clouds dispersed and vineyards enjoyed a blissfully hot and dry summer, one of the hottest for half a century. The mercury averaged 22.5°C (72.5°F) in July, though a vicious hailstorm on Sunday 15 July – imprinted on many winemakers' memories since it was the same day France won the World Cup – ripped through Sauternes and the Haut-Médoc, and battered the Côtes de Bourg a second time. This was really the only trauma of the summer. Temperatures were 22.1°C (71.8°F) in August, which saw five days in excess of 35°C (95°F), and 19.2°C (66.6°F) in September, both above the 10-year averages. It was the second-hottest high season since 1947, after the notorious 2003 vintage. These temperatures, especially the short heat wave in August, led to hydric stress, exacerbated by winds just prior to harvest. Saint-Émilion enjoyed around 34 mm (1⅓ in) of rain on 5 and 6 September that reinvigorated vines, though the precipitation was localised, so that Margaux, for example, only received 1 mm (¹⁄₃₂ in) of rain. The picking was generally prolonged as clement conditions prevailed, permitting teams to pick when and where they wished in accordance to optimal ripeness. The harvest had kicked off early on 21 August with the dry white Pessac-Léognan wines, while the Merlots were picked from mid-September. In Sauternes it was a vexing growing season even without the aforementioned hailstorm on 15 July, since the dry September inhibited the formation of botrytis until 30 mm (1 in) of rain fell at the end of the month. The noble rot developed in a sudden rush from around 20 October – a last-minute victory for some Sauternes winemakers, who managed to get to the end of the season unscathed. Volumes, though, were minuscule.

Away from the elite names blessed with the finest terroirs, the 2018 vintage exaggerates the differences between the haves and the have-nots – between those who practise meticulous vineyard husbandry and those who cut corners; between those prepared to pick at the optimal moment and those who play safe and pick at the earliest opportunity; and between those with modern wineries and those with only rudimentary tools at their disposal. All these factors widened the gap in quality, yet the most important difference was between those blessed with great terroir and those who get by with what they have. Dry conditions amplified inter-terroir differences. While the top châteaux could take the 2018 growing season in their stride to the point where they had to resist intervention, those on less propitious terroirs were sometimes compelled to use winemaking techniques to buff up their wine. As a result, winemakers' competence and experience could determine final quality. Some minor châteaux conjured splendid wines. Others, to put it bluntly, made a pig's ear of it. In 2018 you do not have to step too far away from the best terroirs to find more inconsistencies than in other vintages.

Two thousand and eighteen is a vintage I have re-assessed comprehensively twice since bottling, most recently at the annual Southwold blind tasting in January 2022. The vintage launched an armada of powerful wines marked by bold tannins and comparatively high alcohol levels. The overall style is unashamedly concentrated and ripe, bold and brassy. It's not an elegant vintage and lacks the nuances that distinguish the 2016s or nascent 2019s. You can make comparisons to 2009, yet the 2018s possess more polished tannins. While not a perfect growing season by any means, the wines dole out tremendous hedonistic pleasure.

Quality is equally dispersed across both the Left Bank and Right Bank. The appellations of Saint-Estèphe, Pauillac and Saint-Julien are particularly strong as the Cabernet Sauvignon coped ably with the hot summer temperatures. Margaux is a little more sensitive and slightly less consistent, though it still bestowed the audacious, extraordinary 2018 Palmer, which was eked out from a minuscule yield of 11 hl/ha after most vines succumbed to mildew. It is undeniably atypical for Palmer, yet I am convinced it is destined to become a legend for those prepared to wait. Among the First Growths, the as-yet unreleased 2018 Latour is magnificent as usual with Mouton Rothschild close on its tails. At least in the blind tasting, the 2018 Lafite Rothschild lagged a little behind, though that is not unusual in such beauty contests when its nuances can be lost, as I think they were here. Jean-Philippe Delmas crafted a wonderful Haut-Brion and La Mission Haut-Brion in 2018, the former with its nose in front when the two are compared side-by-side. There are plenty of strong performers across the Médoc, attuned to those with a predilection for intense fruit and general "big wines", even if a few appear to be closing up. Highlights include fabulous wines from Montrose, Calon Ségur, Lynch-Bages, Haut-Batailley, Grand-Puy Lacoste, Saint-Pierre, Brane-Cantenac, Batailley and a fantastic Ormes de Pez that has meliorated since bottling.

Over on the Right Bank, stars include l'Église-Clinet, Lafleur, Le Pin, La Fleur-Pétrus, the resurgent Figeac, Ausone and Pavie Macquin. Saint-Émilion clearly shows more restraint in terms of winemaking than there would have been a decade earlier, when I would have anticipated a flotilla of turbo-charged wines. The dry whites can be worth seeking out, though there was clearly a large gap between good and great terroirs. The same goes for Sauternes, where the finest include Yquem, La Tour Blanche, Doisy-Daëne and Rieussec. Some like Guiraud were only able to eke out a dry white due to the hail.

Event
Wildfires devastate California

Music
Love It If We Made It
– The 1975

The global climate was becoming increasingly wild and unpredictable, resulting in disasters such as the 2018 California wildfires. Dry and hot conditions coupled with previous years of drought had turned the California countryside into a tinderbox, leading to the deadliest wildfire season on record with over 8,527 incidents that incinerated some 1,975,086 acres. A national disaster was declared on 4 August as strong winds fanned the flames in the north of the state. Almost 25,000 homes and buildings were destroyed and 103 people tragically lost their lives.

Few songs in recent years have captured the moment with the clarity and directness of *Love It If We Made It*. The tracks's entire *raison d'être* is to distil 2018 into a four-minute electro-pop song that almost pummels you with images. Lead singer Matty Healy's lyrics broach everything from Trump to Kanye West, to the Salisbury spy poisoning to drowned toddlers washing up on beaches as Europe's migrant crisis worsened. The result is to effortlessly portray the disorientating volatility of events that made it feel like the world had gone into hyperdrive. Healy makes sure there's some positive sentiment in the title – even though it *does* contain the crucial word "if". Fingers crossed.

2018

Film
Roma
– Alfonso Cuarón

Cuarón's depiction of domestic
worker Cleo in the service of
a wealthy family in seventies
Mexico City is based on the
director's real-life nanny, to
whom the film is dedicated.
Exquisitely shot in black and
white, each frame is a work of
art. *Roma* wields emotional heft
thanks to the natural performance
of Yalitza Aparicio, who was
waiting to become a teacher
when Cuarón plucked her out
from 100 others. Aparicio only
attended the audition because
her sister had requested she
come with her. Critics hailed it a
masterpiece and *Roma* went on to
win three Oscars. The film caused
controversy when it was released
directly on to streaming network
Netflix, though in some ways,
it was a prescient move. Within
months, all cinemas would be
forced to close.

The 2019 vintage has similarities to the 2018 growing season in that it was also hot. But there are major differences that moulded a slightly different style of wine.

It was yet another mild and short winter. February saw temperatures reach a balmy 28°C (82°F) but cooler weather retarded vine development and bud break was normal for the time of year. April was overcast and cool, especially during the night, which led to minor frost damage on 12 April and heterogeneity between plots. On 15 April, warmer weather encouraged shoot growth, though the last week of the month saw more precipitation, which hindered growth. May was among the coolest of the last 30 years and despite a series of thunderstorms saw average monthly rainfall. After a brief spell of warm weather at the end of May, the first three weeks of June were inclement, with Entre-Deux-Mers experiencing its coolest June day since 1978 at 14.2°C (57.6°F). Rainfall was around 37% above normal – 85 mm (3⅓ in) compared to a 30-year average of 62 mm (2½ in). These cool and humid conditions coincided with flowering (*mi-floraison* was on 4 June – one day later than the previous year) and capped potential yields. The Left Bank escaped serious episodes of millerandage and coulure, although the Right Bank was not so lucky – the vineyards of Ets. Jean-Pierre Moueix lost 20% of their potential crop. On 23 June, warm air from Africa settled over the region and soon temperatures topped 35°C (95°F), accelerating cluster formation. Localised storms on 16 and 26 July replenished water reserves, although the amount varied between regions: 40 mm (1½ in) in Pessac-Léognan, 45 mm (1¾ in) at Lafite Rothschild and 32 mm (1¼ in) at Pichon-Lalande, while Sauternes saw a deluge of around 100 mm (4 in) that, unlike on the Left Bank, was unwelcome since it provoked outbreaks of acid rot. July was the sunniest in 30 years, with 319 sunlight hours compared with a 30-year average of 249. Apart from a brief spell of cooler weather on the 10th and 11th, August was mainly hot and dry except for a crucial spell of 20–30 mm (¾–1 in) of rain at the start of the month that evened out *véraison* and allowed the Cabernet Sauvignon to continue ripening. Many claimed that 2019 was devoid of heat spikes, but I recall sweltering in 39°C (102°F) heat on 23/24 August in Bordeaux. All the heat and intense sunshine punished anyone who had de-leafed their vines, though vineyard managers now practise this far less in light of climate change, knowing they are likely to need that shade.

September began relatively cool, though a benign warm and settled period lasted from September 11 to 20, during which the red grapes attained colour and tannins. Monthly rainfall was 20% below average but, at 69 mm (2¾ in), was higher than in 2014 or 2018. Precipitation became more widespread and persistent during the last 10 days of the month, which limited stress on the more free-draining, gravelly soils.

One interesting aspect of the 2019 vintage is yield. Pierre-Olivier Clouet at Cheval Blanc argues that vines absorbed a tremendous amount of energy and rapidly accumulated sugar. Therefore, a higher yield was preferable since it dispersed all that energy across a greater number of bunches, limiting sugar and potential alcohol levels. (At Cheval Blanc, they picked at around 41 hl/ha.) It is a complete reversal of the 1990s mantra of lower yields. Far fewer vineyard teams now carry out green harvesting compared with a decade ago. That practice has been replaced by canopy management – careful de-leafing to protect bunches from the sun and potentially manage photosynthesis. Nevertheless, drinkers should steel themselves for high alcohol levels that often clock in between 14.5% and 15.0%, particularly on the Right Bank. I would describe the best 2019s as opulent rather than blockbuster wines, partly because the growing season – rather than the now-outdated premeditated push toward richness – corralled them toward higher alcohol levels. The 2019s are, broadly, manifestations of nature, not man.

Sauternes received significantly higher rainfall in the summer, around 100 mm (4 in) compared with 30–40 mm (1–1½ in) on the Left Bank, thanks to a storm that deluged the region in August and weakened berries' skins. This caused some acid rot in early September, while berries located on vines planted in free-draining arid soils began to shrivel. As a result, growers were forced to undertake a labour-intensive *nettoyage* to eradicate any affected berries/bunches before *pourriture noble* developed. Mid-September rains sparked minor outbreaks of botrytis formation, but the next fortnight until the start of October was too dry to accelerate it further and tended to concentrate the berries. After a damper spell, much of the harvest was conducted from 10 October, many estates finishing before 14 October when heavy rain was forecasted. A second window of picking opened up from 18 to 23 October but producers were unable to use any fruit for their Grand Vin after this. Hence yields for 2019 in Sauternes are extremely low. *Plus ça change.*

At time of writing, the 2019 Bordeaux are bottled but still in their cribs. When I judged the 2019s from barrel, I was unequivocal in my praise and felt the vintage deserved a place among the top tier of growing seasons. The best 2019s demonstrate more control and freshness than their 2018 counterparts, less subjugated by the warmth of the season. I cautioned that it was not a consistent vintage – the variegated terroirs ensured that the prolonged dry conditions impacted châteaux to different degrees, compromising quality of fruit on younger vines with shallower root systems that struggled to eke moisture from the ground. The weather disadvantaged those without the technology or manpower to handle its challenges, making 2019 another growing season that jemmied open the gap between the haves and have-nots. Nobody ever said winemaking was fair.

Tasting the 2019s in bottle in December 2021, this time in Bordeaux instead of in the UK, where I had been sent samples during the Covid lockdown, they continue to display more detail and delineation than the 2018s. They just have a little more verve and panache. If they're going to face a challenge, it may well come from the '20s. Re-tasting some of the '20s in barrel, I found them evolving beautifully and, who knows, they may snatch the gold medal from 2019. It will be fun finding out. Does 2019 surpass that modern-day benchmark, the 2016 vintage? I am not convinced, and suggest it's only the case in a few instances, notwithstanding the fact that 2019 is less consistent at lower levels of the hierarchy. Some wines are compromised by over-maturity due to late picking; others by under-maturity in cases where dry conditions forced vines to shut down and halt photosynthesis, not to mention the inevitable array of misjudgements in the winery. That said, casting the net wide, I have been able to find many excellent wines that are less well known and affordably priced, including Pouget, Féret-Lambert, Bolaire and Doyac, to name but a few – you just have to pick and choose.

Event
Anti-government protests in
Hong Kong

Civil unrest was widespread in 2019 as protestors took to the streets everywhere from Sudan to Moscow. In Hong Kong thousands swarmed among the skyscrapers to protest about the extradition bill that they claimed violated the one country/two systems policy agreed between China and the UK when the colony was handed over in 1997. Demonstrations gathered momentum throughout the year and turned violent as police fired tear gas, protestors using umbrellas to protect themselves as they had done during protests five years earlier. The rallies subsided as the Covid-19 pandemic began to spread in early 2020.

Music
Bad Guy
– Billy Eilish

Co-written with brother and producer Finneas O'Connell, *Bad Guy* sounded different to anything else when it was released. It wasn't just the jolting tempo change in the last 10 bars that made it sound so fresh and new; it was also the minimalist production, echoing Prince's *When Doves Cry* (page 362) – the way it eschews any chorus, and its almost indecipherable, whispered, half-spoken lyrics. It made the 18-year-old Eilish a global pop star, especially among teenagers looking to connect with their darker side. Within months, she was the first artist born post-2000 to top the Hot 100 and recorded the title song for the next Bond movie.

2019
(Continued)

Film
Parasite
– Bong Joon-ho

Korean music and film culture
had rapidly gained critical and
commercial success in the West
throughout the decade and
Bong Joon-ho's Oscar-winner,
a brilliant portrayal of wealth
inequality and class differences
in Seoul, was the culmination.
Alfred Hitchcock is a major
influence in terms of the film's
twisting plot line, its staircase
motif – used to represent the
social divides – and the way it
shoots through windows to create
a sense of voyeurism. Elevated
by outstanding performances
from the whole cast, it deservedly
became the first non-English-
language film to win Best Picture
at the Academy Awards.

The 2020 growing season is the third in a series of well-received vintages marked by summer heat waves.

It began with an unseasonably warm winter that saw the highest temperatures for a century and one-third of the average frost. This was now becoming the norm. After the previous dry summer, vineyard managers welcomed the high rainfall, which was twice the average in November, December and March. Some châteaux reported they saw a year's worth of rain fall in just six months. A series of storm-laden low-pressure systems swept across the region during January and February. Warm temperatures that peaked at 23.1°C (73.6°F) in Mérignac and rainfall 58% above average kick-started the growth cycle three weeks earlier than normal. An uneven bud break largely took place in the middle of March before the end of the month saw temperatures dive to -12°C (10.5°F) in some localities and the rare sight of snow on the 30th. Thankfully, frost damage was minimal and limited to prone spots. April warmed up nicely – the third warmest in half a century, after 2007 and 2011 – and with mid-month rain storms resulting in 34% more precipitation than average, rapid shoot growth ensued. The heaviest rain fell in Saint-Émilion, which saw some 31 mm (1¼ in) on the 17th, along with some localised hail that also affected parts of Castillon. May was more like summer with hot spells at the beginning and end of the month: 16 days above 25°C (77°F) made it the fourth hottest May in 75 years. The combination of wet and warmth provided perfect conditions for mildew, so vineyard managers had to be vigilant and reactive, seizing every dry window to spray and protect vines. Below-average temperatures from 10 to 15 May coincided with another rainy spell, with over 100 mm (4 in) falling in Listrac. The conditions led to continued precocious growth and predicated early flowering, which took place in mid to late-May rather than early June, with little coulure. *Mi-fleuraison* was on 26 May compared with 3 and 4 June in 2018 and 2019. By now, winemakers knew they were heading toward an early harvest. June began cool and overcast – the month saw 148 fewer sunshine hours than normal – which put the brakes on vine growth. Persistent rain increased mildew pressure, provoking painful memories of 2018, and some estates suffered considerable losses due to millerandage. Consequently, the late Prof. Denis Dubourdieu's second condition for an ideal red wine vintage – the absence of rainfall after fruit set – was not entirely fulfilled.

The final week of June saw the weather change again with two months of warm and extremely dry conditions. Overall, the Gironde received an average of just 10 mm (⅓ in) of rain in July, with some estates recording less than 5 mm (¼ in) and several claiming they did not get a drop during the 54-day dry period. Hydric stress was initially contained by the preceding months' rain, with only young vines located on free-draining gravel and sandy soils slightly affected. The moisture-retaining capacity of the clayey soils in Saint-Estèphe and on the Right Bank was beneficial. The water deficit still led to an uneven *véraison* that slowed down in the most stressed plots, even if *mi-véraison* on 1 August was six days earlier than average. Winemakers became anxious as vines began to suffer during a heat wave in the second week of August when night temperatures remained above 20°C (68°F), giving them no time to rest. This heat triggered convectional storms between August 9 and 14, which were crucial in alleviating hydric stress, but the compacted, sometimes concrete-hard clay soils meant the rain often washed straight off the vineyard. The amount of rainfall varied per appellation, with the northern Médoc receiving the most – Saint-Estèphe saw 110 mm (4 in) or more – going down to 20–30 mm (¾–1 in) on the Right Bank. This exaggerated the vintage's unevenness between appellations and terroirs depending on grape varieties and vine age. The Merlot and Petit Verdot berries swelled more than the Cabernet Sauvignon, which predicated a greater proportion of the latter going into some blends. Once the storm clouds had dispersed, clement warm and dry conditions prevailed through to harvest, concentrating the berries and sugar levels. In fact, temperatures were slightly lower than average and the cool nights, 12–14°C (54 –57°F), enabled berries to retain acidity that ultimately imparted freshness in the wines. The first two weeks of September were warm and sunny, which accelerated sugar accumulation.

Estates had to navigate their way around restrictions due to the Covid-19 pandemic, though at least picking takes place out in the open air, so there were few cases of viral transmission. Harvesting of the dry whites began from 14 August with the earliest-ripening Sauvignon Blanc and was completed over the final 10 days of the month, now the norm. The Merlot was picked from around 10 September under warm and dry conditions, with the fruit quite precocious on the Right Bank. Some châteaux picked in the morning to avoid daytime heat and keep their workers cool and a few used increasingly necessary cool rooms. Afterwards several estates continued straight on with the Cabernets, since they had already reached phenolic ripeness, which proved crucial. The weather turned inclement around mid-September, with sporadic light rain showers and here the true quality of the 2020 growing season becomes a little opaque. Many winemakers brushed the rainfall off as "inconsequential", claiming it was too light to dilute the grapes and merely warded off shrivelling, nudging berries toward full ripeness. But the conditions worsened courtesy of Storm Alex, panicking some winemakers who hadn't already done so into harvesting the later-ripening Cabernet Sauvignon. Most harvests were done and dusted by the end of September or early October.

The capricious weather during harvest made things terribly complicated in Sauternes, offering brief windows of sufficient botrytis formation together with dry and warm conditions. Essentially, picking crews had to be on their toes, ready to unsheathe their secateurs at short notice. Botrytis formation began slightly earlier in Barsac because of higher rainfall in August. Hot and dry conditions in the first half of September allowed berries to continue accumulating sugar levels, though there was insufficient moisture for botrytis. This coincided with perfect conditions to commence the first *tries* through the vineyard, which mainly collected aromatic *passerillé* berries and the odd botrytised grape. Picking stopped during a rainy spell from 18 to 26 September and then from 30 September to 6 October, a month's worth of rain fell within a week, prompting some estates to just pick whatever they could. Most top-performing winemakers elected to wait and used a dry spell from 7 October accompanied by drying northerly winds to bring home a second *trie* that formed the main part of many estates' 2020. Most harvests were completed by 20 October. For the reasons stated earlier, yields in Sauternes were minuscule, often 3–6 hl/ha, and only slightly higher in Barsac where they occasionally reach double figures.

The 2020s are on the cusp of being bottled at time of writing, though based on my tastings from barrel, conducted at home instead of in Bordeaux, it is clear that the vintage forms a triumvirate of very successful growing seasons. My intuition is that 2020 will surpass 2018 in terms of lower alcohol levels and more backbone, though the '19 vintage will provide a stiff challenge. We will see. For sure it is a small vintage – Saint-Julien produced 82% of the 10-year average.

Event
Covid-19

Who in January 2020 could have predicted that within weeks the entire world would grind to a halt due to a virus spreading, allegedly, from a live animal market in Wuhan to every corner of the planet? An invisible enemy upturned our lives like nothing else had since the Second World War and its full ramifications will not be fully comprehended for many years. Science stepped in and, against predictions, mass-produced vaccines within months instead of years, gifting the world an exit strategy.

2020

(Continued)

1870

2020

Film
Portrait of a Lady on Fire
– Céline Sciamma

Since the industry was ostensibly mothballed during the Covid-19 pandemic, many of 2020's most popular films were made the previous year. Noémie Merlant and Adèle Haenel star in Sciamma's exquisitely shot *Portrait de la Jeune Fille en Feu*, to give it its original French title. Marianne, an art teacher, is commissioned to paint a wedding portrait of a countess's daughter, Héloïse. Against the backdrop of windswept Brittany beaches, erotic tension simmers between the two young women as Sciamma's film portrays the transformative effects of a love doomed from the beginning. If you want to see a masterful example of acting without uttering a single word, just watch the final scene.

Music
WAP
– Cardi B ft. Megan Thee Stallion

Somebody reading this has their head in their hands, aghast that culture has slid from *Ride of the Valkyries* to this shameless paean to sex in all its gynaecological glory. The main sample comes from 1993's *Whores in this House* by Frank Ski, a song with which I am sure most regular attendees of Bayreuth are unfamiliar. *WAP* is essentially a shopping list of coital demands by two of the best female rappers in the business and despite inevitably provoking criticism, it is simply an in-your-face hip hop track that gleefully flips gender stereotypes, declaring women's desires in the bedroom without euphemism. If your angelic child asks what the title means, just pretend you didn't hear.

Final Thought

"A vintage is more than a slice of time. It is the unscripted act of a never-ending play. Drama and upheaval, tragedy and triumph unfold in every vineyard, every year."

When my daughter read the sentence with which I open this book on a recent trip to Bordeaux, she laughed and told me it was "a bit dramatic". Hours later, after an idyllic clement spell of weather, parts of the region were subjected to a violent hailstorm that left some vineyards looking like war zones and the following month vineyards in the commune of Landiras were threatened by wildfires during a record heatwave. Such are the vicissitudes of fortune. No, I don't believe that statement *is* an exaggeration. Indeed, over the years I have seen two or three winemakers wipe away a tear as they recount similar devastating events. I have also seen the ecstasy when Mother Nature rides to the rescue, providing that desperately needed shower or rot-busting clement spell.

The growing cycle might follow a predictable course through winter, spring, summer and autumn, but its kaleidoscope of permutations and myriad of terroirs ensures that no two wines are ever exactly the same, however much appellation laws might corral them into a recognisable style. Most fine wine fails miserably as a standardised product and for that we must rejoice. It all stems from the imprimatur of the growing season, which bestows an intellectual aspect upon a beverage as mundane as fermented grape juice, elevating it to a spiritual level among converts.

This book has reinforced how life is unpredictable, crazy, stupid, bewildering, frightening and thrilling. Thank goodness there's always a bottle of wine at the end of the day and friends to share it with.

Glossary

Botrytis – the process whereby white grapes are infected by a particular fungus, *botrytis cinerea*, known as *pourriture noble* or "noble rot", that shrivels the berry and concentrates the sugar inside to create sweet wine such as Sauternes

Chaptalisation – the addition of sugar to the must in order to increase the alcohol level

Chef de culture – vineyard manager

Coulure – when vines' flowers fail to set and become grapes due to inclement weather during *fleuraison*

Cuvaison – the period when the wine is in vat

Cuverie – the vat-room where wines are fermented

Débourrement – bud break

Délestage – the process of draining the wine from the fermentation vat, then pumping it back in over the cap of grape solids to enhance colour and flavour. Often referred to as "rack and return", it is frequently used in weaker growing seasons

Éclaircissage – the removal of buds early in the growing season to thin the crop and lower yields

Égrappage – de-stalking. Practically all of Bordeaux's wines have their stalks removed by a de-stemmer, or *égrappoir*, in contrast to Burgundy where the stems are often left on

Eudemis botrana – more commonly known as the grape berry moth (*Lobesia botrana*), it tends to invade vineyards in June. The first generation feeds on the leaves while the second bores into berries to munch away the pulp. It seemed to beset Cheval Blanc and doubtless many other estates in the first decade of the 20th century, as recounted in the diaries of proprietor Albert Fourcaud-Laussac

Fleuraison – or flowering of the vine, which usually occurs around the end of May or beginning of June. A good flowering gives the potential for a larger crop and vice versa. *Mi-fleuraison* is the midway point, often used as a timing indicator to compare with other growing seasons

Green harvest – the removal of bunches during the growing season to reduce yields. Known as *vendange en vert* in France

Grêle – French for hail

I.N.A.O. – Institut National des Appellation d'Origine (renamed the Institut National de l'Origine et de la Qualité in 2007), the French government's legislative body that sets the rules of viticulture and winemaking

Maceration – the practice of leaving red wine in contact with the skins, stalks and seeds after the must has fermented in order to extract colour, flavour and tannic structure. This is done by pumping-over (*remontage*) or pressing-down (*pigeage*), which increase the level of contact to whatever degree the winemaker desires. The skins, stalks and seeds are then removed and pressed, with some added back into the must

Maitre de chai – cellar-master

Mildew/downy mildew – cryptogamic or fungal diseases that can flourish in wet conditions and are remedied by spraying copper sulphate

Millerandage – when poor fertilisation during flowering creates berries that differ in ripeness and size within the same bunch, making picking more difficult

Must – the unfermented grape juice after crushing and pressing

Must weight – the level of sugar (mainly fructose and glucose) in grape juice; the higher the sugar, the higher the potential degree of alcohol

Négociant – basically a wine merchant

Nettoyage – readying the vines for harvest, perhaps by removing excess leaves or obviously unripe bunches, to help make picking efficient

Oidium – otherwise known as powdery mildew, this cryptogamic/ fungal disease is remedied by the application of sulphur

Passerillé – bunches that are left on the vine to dry and shrivel, increasing sugar concentration

Phylloxera – a parasitic disease that came close to wiping out winemaking in Bordeaux and indeed, around the world. The only solution is re-grafting the vine onto American rootstock that was found to be phylloxera-resistant. Nearly every vine in Bordeaux is on this rootstock

Primeur (en) – the sale of the most recent vintage by *négociants* to merchants the spring after harvest, sometimes known as "futures". The wines are unfinished, though by the time they are tasted by merchants and critics, the final blend has usually been done

Racking – the transfer of wine from one vessel to another. It often refers to moving maturing wine from one barrel to another in order to remove the gross lees that fall to the bottom and expose the wine to oxygen. This is traditionally done by pump, though many wineries are now designed so it can be done via gravity alone, which disturbs the wine less

Reductive winemaking – limiting the exposure of grapes, pre-fermented juice and maturing wine to oxygen via the use of inert gas and sulphur dioxide in order to preserve fruit

Remontage – see *Maceration*

Rendement – French for the yield of a vineyard

Reverse osmosis – a technique for reducing alcohol by passing the wine through a semi-permeable membrane. Often shortened to R.O.

Rootstock – known in France as a *porte-greffe*, this is the base of the vine, which now always comes from American plants to protect from phylloxera. The upper part is grafted on top

Smudge pots – oil-burners placed in vineyards at night to increase ground temperatures when there is a high risk of frost

Sorting table – a table installed at the winery reception during harvest where eagle-eyed and nimble-fingered workers (often women, it must be said) extract damaged or unripe berries, leaves, or simply anything undesirable in the vat. Optical sorting tables use technology to carry out the same process and were introduced in the early 2000s

Tannin – essentially tannins are the skeleton of the wine, providing the backbone and grip and lending the wine weight. These will polymerise with bottle age, so that an initially hard wine softens over time

Vendange – French term for harvest

Vendangeur – a harvester

Véraison – the changing of berry colour from green to red, which usually occurs around early August

Vin de presse – the pressed wine. The grape skins and pips are pressed and the free-run juice, often high in tannins, may be added to the blend to impart more colour and structure

Volatile acidity – excessive acidity that can be caused by an uncontrolled alcoholic fermentation. In small doses it can be pleasant, but often causes malodorous vinegary smells

Bibliography

Bordeaux Legends – Jane Anson (2012)

Inside Bordeaux – Jane Anson (2020)

Château Haut-Bailly: An Exceptional Terroir – Jane Anson (2021)

In Search of Wine – Charles Walter Berry (1935)

Grands Vins – Clive Coates MW (1995)

Bordeaux: Une Histoire de Cépages – Jean-Baptiste Duquesne (2022)

Carnet de Culture (1896-1913) – Albert Fourcaud-Laussac

Mozipedia – The Encyclopaedia of Morrissey and The Smiths
  – Simon Goddard (2012)

"Walk This Way: how Run-D.M.C. and Aerosmith changed pop"
  – *The Guardian* 4 July 2016

Château Pichon Longueville Comtesse de Lalande – David Haziot (2007)

Stay Me with Flagons – Maurice Healy (1940)

Château Latour: The History of a Great Vineyard – Ed. Charles
  Higounet (Trans. Edmund Penning-Rowsell) (1993 – original
  work published 1974)

Wine & War – Don & Petie Kladstrup (2001)

Encyclopaedia of Wines & Spirits – Alexis Lichine (1967)

Pomerol – Neal Martin (2012)

"Looking the Part: Pichon Baron 1953-2015" – Vinous.com
  – Neal Martin (2019)

"How To Run a Château: Lynch-Bages" – Wine-Journal website
  – Neal Martin (2009)

"The Reality of Dreams: Chateau Pontet-Canet" – Wine-Journal
  website – Neal Martin (2006)

"Timely Incisions I-IV, Gruaud Larose 1831-2003" – Wine-Journal
  website – Neal Martin (2010–2014)

"Last Man Standing: Château Bel Air-Marquis d'Aligre" – Vinous.com
  – Neal Martin (2018)

"The Margaux Paragon: Château Rauzan-Ségla" – Vinous.com (2019)

Yquem – Richard Olnay (2008)

The Wines of Bordeaux – Edmund Penning-Rowsell (1969 and 1973)

Bordeaux – David Peppercorn (1982 and 2004)

My Life – Édith Piaf/Jean Noli (1990)

Gruaud Larose – René Pijassou (1997)

*Château Rauzan-Ségla – La Naissance d'un Grand Cru Class*é – René
  Pijassou (2004)
Château Montrose – privately printed (1984)
La Conseillante: A Family Passion for 150 Years – (2021)
Vignobles et Vignerons du Bordelais (1850-1980) – Philippe Roudié (1994)
Notes on a Cellar-Book – George Saintsbury (1920)
Vintage-wise – André L. Simon (1945)
Steven Spurrier: A Life In Wine – Steven Spurrier (2020)
Tastet & Lawton: De l'air du temps 1900-1944 and *1945-2000* – (2005)
Yeah, Yeah, Yeah: The Story of Modern Pop – Bob Stanley (2013)
Let's Do It: The Birth of Pop – Bob Stanley (2022)
Under the Ivy – The Life & Music of Kate Bush – Graeme Thomson (2010)
Chronicle of the Cinema – Various (1995)
On Bordeaux – Various (2020)

Picture Credits

p. 61   With kind permission from the author
p. 75   With kind permission from Château Lafite-Rothschild
p. 97   © J. Roumazeille Editions
p. 123   With kind permission from Château La Conseillante
p. 147   © Domaine Clarence Dillon
p. 179   With kind permission from Château Grand-Puy-Lacoste –
         Domaines F-Xavier Borie
p. 207 and 209 With kind permission from Château Malescot
         St-Exupéry
p. 239   © Baron Philippe de Rothschild SA
p. 271   With kind permission from Château-Figeac
p. 305   With kind permission from Château Talbot
p. 345   With kind permission from Vignobles Denis Durantou
p. 383   With kind permission from Jean-Luc Thunevin
p. 385   With kind permission from Jacques Thienpont
p. 459   With kind permission from the author

Index

Note: page numbers in **bold** refer to information contained in captions.

Acknowledgements

There are too many people who have generously opened bottles over the years. I would be remiss not to mention the vital role played by Linden Wilkie and Jordi Oriols-Gil in the numerous events that both have organised over many years. Also to Michael Vollmerich who introduced me to the tasting group in Hong Kong that has organised some incredible line-ups.

Of course, I am always grateful for the châteaux prepared to raid their own cellars to conduct vertical tastings, some of which were specifically organised for this book. A special thanks also to Bill Blatch, whose insight into Bordeaux is unparalleled and whose vintage reports are the gold standard for reporting a growing season. I must also thank the following who cracked a few bottles of Bordeaux over the years: Mark Andrew, Nicolas Audebert, Claire Bailey, Aline Baly, Lilian Barton-Sartorius, Juliette Bécot, Johan Berglund, Olivier Bernard, Jean-Claude and Olivier Berrouet, Gareth Birchley, Philippe Blanc, Jean-Jacques and Séverine Bonnie, Mathieu Bordes, Bruno Borie, Emeline and François-Xavier Borie, Hubert and Stéphanie de Boüard, Jean-Baptist Bourotte, Brinda Brouhis, Stephen Browett, Lord Bruce, Frédéric and Philippe Castéja, Pierre Antoine Castéja, Marielle Cazaux, Jean-Michel and Jean-Charles Cazes, Dr. Kevin Chan, Chris Chan, Joost Clarjis, Emmanuel Cruse, Didier Cuvelier, Mathieu Cuvelier, Sara Lecompte Cuvelier, Paul Day, Jean-Philippe Delmas, Jean-Hubert Delon, Philippe Dhalluin, Thomas Duroux, Frédéric Engerer, Frédéric Faye, Hélène and Patrice Garçin-Lévêque, Aymeric Gironde, Sam Gleave, Nicolas Glumineau, Baptiste Guinaudeau, Lindsay Hamilton, Matthew Hemming MW, Alex Hunt MW for casting an erudite eye upon the classical selections, Herwig Janssen, Dan Keeling, John Kolasa, Ken Lamb, Ronan Laborde, Jean-Michel Laporte, Bérénice Lurton, Henri Lurton, Pierre Lurton, Lili Ma, Marie-France Manoncourt, François-Xavier Maroteaux, Jean Merlaut, Édouard Miailhe, François Mitjavile, Christian and Édouard Moueix, the NHS for the life extension, Jean-Antoine Nony and "Mrs. Mango", Gérard Perse, Michel Reybier, Roy Richards, Saskia de Rothschild, Véronique Sanders, Christian Seely, all the "Sexy Muscles" gang in Hong Kong, Daisy Sichel, esteemed members of the "Southwold" group, José Sanfins, Oliver Slocock, Sam Tan and the CEC posse, Alfred Tesseron, Basile Tesseron, Alexandre Thienpont, Jacques and Fiona Thienpont, Jean-Luc "Bad Boy" Thunevin, Alexander van Beek, David Wainwright, Katharina and Konstantin Wolf and anyone else I have forgotten to mention. Also, I would like to thank all those that allowed me to reproduce some of the marvellous, evocative photographs for this book. Finally, never to forget those no longer with us: John Avery MW, Anthony Barton, Michael Broadbent MW, Prof. Denis Dubourdieu, Denis Durantou, Harry Gill, Thierry Manoncourt, Paul Pontallier and Steven Spurrier.

Last but not least, thanks to my oldest friends in Leigh-on-Sea for keeping it real and, of course, my family, Tomoko, Lily, Daisy and Popo, the Japanese-speaking budgerigar.

About the author

Neal Martin's career in wine began in 1996 as a wine buyer for Japan Airlines where he specialised in Bordeaux and Burgundy. In 2006 Neal was asked by the most influential wine critic in the world, Robert Parker, to join his team at The Wine Advocate where he was the first non-American to hold a position. In December 2012 Neal self-published a 600-page book, *Pomerol*, that became the standard text for the region, winning the inaugural André Simon John Avery Award and the Louis Roederer Chairman's Award in 2013. He took over coverage of Bordeaux when Parker retired in 2014. In 2018 Neal accepted a position at Vinous where he covers Bordeaux and Burgundy to the present day. His reviews and scores are quoted by merchants around the world and over 25 years he has amassed considerable first-hand knowledge of mature vintages.